Sarasota,
Sanibel Island
& Naples

A Great Destination

Sarasota, Sanibel Island & Naples

A Great Destination

Chelle Koster Walton

with photographs by the author

The Countryman Press ✳ Woodstock, Vermont

FIFTH EDITION

Fifth Edition

Sarasota, Sanibel Island & Naples

ISBN 978-0-88150-119-6

All interior photos by the author unless otherwise noted
Book design by Bodenweber Design
Page composition by PerfecType, Nashville, TN
Maps by Erin Greb Cartography
© The Countryman Press

Published by The Countryman Press, P.O. Box 748, Woodstock, Vermont 05091

Distributed by W. W. Norton & Company, Inc., 500 Fifth Avenue, New York, NY 10110

Printed in the United States of America

10 9 8 7 6 5 4 3 2 1

To my husband, Rob, with whom I first discovered many
of Southwest Florida's treasures and pleasures.

EXPLORE WITH US!

Here's how this book works: The area bounded on the north by the Manatee River and on the south by Ten Thousand Islands is often lumped under the heading Southwest Florida. Sometimes the Bradenton-Sarasota area is omitted from the region this heading defines and otherwise grouped with Tampa as Central West Florida. For the purpose of this guide, the Bradenton-Sarasota area is included in the coverage. The book often refers to the region covered as Gulf Coast Florida or West Coast Florida, although, of course, it does not cover the entire coast. It does cover in depth the cities, towns, and communities from Bradenton–Sarasota in the north to Naples–Marco Island and the Everglades in the south.

I have sliced this delectable pie into four regional chapters, north to south: Sarasota Bay Coast, Charlotte Harbor Coast, Island Coast, and South Coast. Within these chapters I scan under separate headings each region's lodging, dining, culture, recreation, and shopping.

Other sections deal with the coastline's history as a whole, transportation, and nitty-gritty information.

A series of indexes at the back of the book provides easy access to information. The first, a standard index, lists entries and subjects in alphabetical order. Next, hotels, inns, and resorts are categorized by price. Restaurants are organized in two separate indexes: one by price, one by type of cuisine.

HIGH FIVES

In the *Information* chapter, I have rated listings within a number of fun—and sometimes quirky—categories, from Splurge Accommodations and Martini Meccas to Kid Cool and Paddle Happy. They begin under the Chelle's High Fives heading on page 309.

Within the chapters, listings that have earned a High Five get a ✪ next to their names.

WHAT'S WHERE

In the beginning of the book you'll find an alphabetical listing of special highlights and important information that you may want to reference quickly. There you'll find everything from where to spot alligators to finding the best beaches.

LODGING

I've selected lodging places for mention in this book based on their merit alone; we do not charge innkeepers to be listed. The author always checks every property personally.

PRICES

Rather than give specific prices, this guide rates dining and lodging options within a range.

Lodging prices are normally based on per person/double occupancy for hotel rooms and per unit for efficiencies, apartments, cottages, suites, and villas. Price ranges reflect the difference in the off-season and high season (usually Christmas through Easter).

Generally, the colder the weather up north, the higher the cost of accommodations here. Rates can double during the course of a year. Many resorts offer off-season packages at special rates. Pricing does not include the 6 percent Florida sales tax. Furthermore, many large resorts add gratuities or housekeeping charges, and most counties also impose a tourist tax, proceeds from which are applied to beach and environmental maintenance.

If rates seem high for rooms on the Gulf Coast, it's partially because many resorts cater to families by providing kitchen facilities. Take into consideration what this could save you on dining bills. Dining cost categories are based on the range of dinner entrée prices or, if dinner is not served, on lunch entrées. Restaurants at some large resorts add gratuities to the tab. This is also customary for large parties at most restaurants, so check your bill carefully before leaving a tip. Satisfied diners are expected to tip between 15 and 20 percent.

Heavy state taxes on liquor served in-house can boost a drinking tab quickly. Paying as you drink is a wise way to prevent sticker shock.

Price Codes

	Lodging	*Dining*
Inexpensive	Up to $100	Up to $15
Moderate	$100 to $200	$15 to $25
Expensive	$200 to $300	$25 to $35
Very Expensive	$300 and up	$35 or more

(An asterisk after the pricing designation indicates that the rate includes at least a continental breakfast in the cost of lodging and possibly more extensive meal service as noted in the listing.)

KEY TO SYMBOLS

⚬ **Weddings**. The wedding-ring symbol appears next to lodging venues that specialize in weddings.

✾ **Special value**. The blue-ribbon symbol appears next to selected lodging and restaurants that combine quality and moderate prices.

🐾 **Pets**. The dog-paw symbol appears next to venues that accept pets.

✎ **Child-friendly**. The crayon symbol appears next to lodging, restaurants, activities, and shops of special interest or appeal to youngsters.

♿ **Handicapped access**. The wheelchair symbol appears next to lodging, restaurants, and attractions that are partially or completely handicapped accessible.

(((ų))) **Wireless Internet**. The wireless symbol appears next to lodging, restaurants, and attractions that offer wireless Internet access.

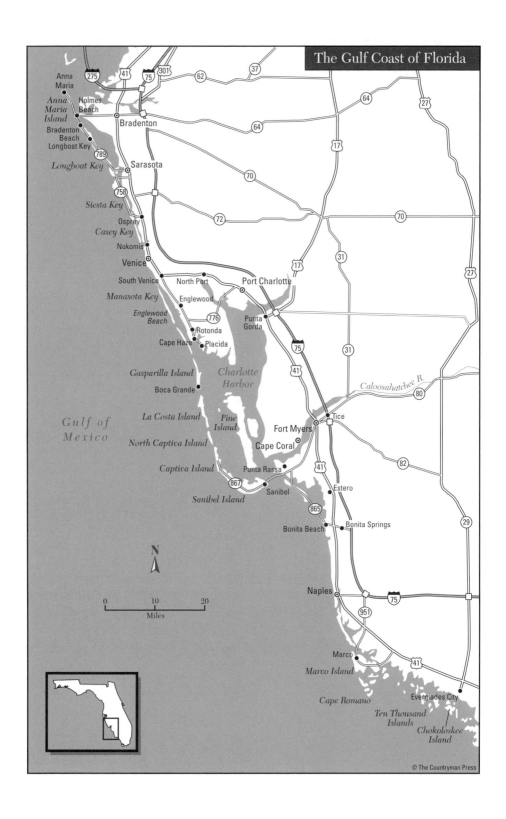

The Gulf Coast of Florida

Anna Maria
Anna Maria Island
Holmes Beach
Bradenton
Bradenton Beach
Longboat Key
Longboat Key
Sarasota
Siesta Key
Osprey
Casey Key
Nokomis
Venice
South Venice
North Port
Port Charlotte
Manasota Key
Englewood
Englewood Beach
Rotonda
Punta Gorda
Cape Haze
Placida
Gasparilla Island
Charlotte Harbor
Boca Grande
La Costa Island
Pine Island
North Captiva Island
Fort Myers
Captiva Island
Cape Coral
Punta Rassa
Sanibel
Tice
Caloosahatchee R.
Gulf of Mexico
Sanibel Island
Estero
Bonita Springs
Bonita Beach
Naples
Marco
Marco Island
Cape Romano
Everglades City
Ten Thousand Islands
Chokoloskee Island

N

0   10   20
Miles

© The Countryman Press

CONTENTS

MAPS

INTRODUCTION

Morning dawns like a boater's dream. The sky is clear except for a trace of last night's moon: wispy, like a wadded-up cloud. The water stretches like cellophane pulled taut between Sanibel and Pine Islands. It is a morning to wonder why one ever does anything else on days off but return to the sea. On cue, a family of three dolphins pierces the surface with their fins and their smiles. The show has begun.

In the course of our leisurely, two-hour cruise between Sanibel Island and Boca Grande, we are entertained by leaping stingrays, a school of mackerel, and the usual dive-bombing squadron of brown pelicans.

At lights-out call—after lunch in a marinaside fish house, beach time on an unbridged island, and a duck-the-afternoon-rains cocktail at a historic island inn—nature's revue reaches its spectacular finale. In the moonless dark, the wake behind our boat sparkles like a watery fireworks display. The gulf has thrown an electric breaker switch. Liquid lightning strikes all around us as our 21-foot Mako powerboat parts the seas. Whitecaps puff like nuclear popcorn.

Scientists call the phenomena dinoflagellates. Lay folks call the glowing organisms phosphorescence. Jamaicans call them sea-blinkies. The Ancient Mariner called them death-fires. I call their unpredictable visits to our summer waters magic, imparting a topsy-turvy, ethereal feeling that someone—without warning—has transformed the sea into a starry sky.

Such a perfect day isn't required to fully appreciate this inimitable slice of Gulf Coast Florida, but such days do help to remind me why I moved here from long-johns land 20-some years ago. Like so many who constitute our hodgepodge population, I escaped, I loved, I dug in. I stayed for the exotic, warm quality of tropical nature. I remain because of the miracles I discover—and watched my young son discover—every day.

I can't list all the people on whose patience and understanding I counted to see me through this project. First dibs on my gratitude must go to my husband, Rob, for not divorcing me, and my son, Aaron, who helped particularly with my beach and "kids' stuff" research.

Special thanks to Prudy Taylor Board, who checked up on my historical facts and who will no doubt cringe at the pirate legends I couldn't bring myself to omit. Big thanks to Mindy Koster, who spent hours on the phone doing the nitty-gritty final fact-checking.

Nancy Hamilton at the Lee County Visitor & Convention Bureau, Jennifer

Huber with Charlotte Harbor & the Gulf Island Visitor's Bureau, Jonell Modys representing Collier County, and Erin Duggan at the Sarasota Convention & Visitors Bureau have been particularly helpful.

—Chelle Koster Walton, Sanibel Island, Florida

WHAT'S WHERE IN SARASOTA, SANIBEL ISLAND & NAPLES

ALLIGATORS Southwest Florida has a love-hate relationship with this prehistoric survivor. The reptiles prefer freshwater and so congregate most heavily in the Everglades' River of Grass, largely removed from human habitation. Sometimes, however, they show up unannounced in someone's yard. They may steal a pet from time to time, and that's where the hate comes in. They prey on humans infrequently, usually under circumstances where the gator has been fed by them. Sanibel Island figures importantly in the complex relationship locals have with these beasts, because it is one of Florida's few islands with freshwater and one of the state's most conservation-minded cities. With its groundbreaking laws against feeding, it helped bring back alligators from endangerment. However, after two beloved citizens were taken down by gators a few years back, the city cracked down on nuisance gator removal, effecting a solid decrease in their population on the refuge island as gator trappers were allowed to take more than just the nuisance gator when they showed up. The best place to see alligators remains the Everglades, especially (and most safely) at the Oasis Visitor Center in Big Cypress National Preserve (239-695-1201; www .nps.gov/bicy).

AREA CODE The 941 area code applies to the Sarasota Bay Coast and Charlotte Harbor Coast; the Island Coast and South Coast regions use 239. Numbers prefixed with 800, 888, 866, and 877 are toll free.

ARTS, PERFORMANCE Sarasota claims a lively theater scene downtown and at the **John & Mable Ringling Museum of Art** (941-355-5101; www .ringling.org) complex. Performance art ranges from the **Sarasota Ballet** (941-351-8000 or 800-361-8388; www .sarasotaballet.org) and the **Sarasota**

Opera House (941-366-8450; www
.sarasotaopera.org) to Broadway shows
at **Van Wezel Performing Arts Hall**
(941-953-3368 or 800-826-9303; www
.vanwezel.org) and the circus, an art
form deeply embedded in Sarasota's
genes. Fort Myers and Naples have
their performing arts halls and professional and community acting troupes,
too. In Fort Myers, **Florida Repertory Theatre** (239-332-4488 or 877-
787-8053; www.floridarep.org) professionals stage dramas and comedies in a
historic theater downtown. For musical
theater, try **Broadway Palm Theatre**
(239-278-4422; www.broadwaypalm
.com) in **Fort Myers and Herb
Strauss Schoolhouse Theater** (239-
472-6862; www.theschoolhousetheater
.com) on Sanibel Island. **Sugden
Community Theatre's** (239-263-
7990) **Naples Players** perform in
downtown Naples.

ARTS, VISUAL Sarasota has always
been the region's headquarters for the
arts, a reputation established early on
by circus master and avid art collector
John Ringling. That still holds true
with the **John & Mable Ringling
Museum of Art** (941-355-5101; www
.ringling.org) complex, the Ringling
School of Art, and the town's multitude
of galleries. Naples, however, is catching up with its lively gallery scene and
highly respectable **Naples Museum
of Art** (239-597-1900 or 800-597-
1900; www.thephil.org). More recently,
Fort Myers received an important
boost in the eyes of the art world when
it saw the opening of **Art of the
Olympians Museum** (239-335-5055;
www.artoftheolympians.com) downtown. Fort Myers's year-round monthly
ArtWalk is one of several such events
you'll find throughout the area.

BARRIER ISLANDS Islands line the
shores of the Southwest Florida coast-

line, buffeting it from waves and
weather, and providing it its famed
beachfront. The chain of islands starts
in the north with **Anna Maria Island**
and runs continuously to **Marco
Island** and some of the **Ten Thousand Islands** in Everglades territory.
The islands are constantly in flux as
they roll with the forces of nature and
man—erosion, mangrove-building on
their leeward sides, and seawalls and
other structures that change the flow
of things. The **Intracoastal Waterway** runs between the islands and the
mainland on the islands' east side.

BEACHES Boasting some of the best
beaches in the world, Southwest Florida can also claim great variety and
superiority in its coastal makeup. **Siesta Key** in Sarasota, for instance, wins
accolades for having some of the
whitest sand in the world, made up of
ground quartz that originates in the
Appalachian Mountains. **Venice
Beach**, on the other hand, is known
for its dark flecks and shark teeth fos-

and preserves along the coast are part of the **Great Florida Birding Trail** (www.floridabirdingtrail.com).

DOG BEACHES South Brohard Park (941-316-1172) in Venice and **Dog Beach** (239-229-0649; www.leeparks.org) on Lovers Key south of Fort Myers Beach are the only area beaches where dogs can run leash-free. Dogs must have all the proper tags. **Sanibel Island** allows dogs on the beach when leashed. Most other beach parks do not allow dogs at all. Throughout this book, lodgings and selected other places that accept pets are indicated with the dog-paw symbol 🐾. It's a good idea to call ahead when traveling with your pet.

EVERGLADES The Everglades refers to the dominant type of environment in southern Florida. It actually begins in Central Florida with the flow of the Kissimmee River. A large portion of the habitat is protected by Everglades National Park, Big Cypress National Preserve, Florida Panther and Ten Thousand Islands National Wildlife Refuges, and other state parks. Its ecological composition ranges from slow-moving river and saltwater marshes to mangrove forest and barrier islands. Vital to the region's water supply and the survival of hundreds of species of animals, many threatened or endangered, it is undergoing a multimillion-dollar restoration.

sils, while **Sanibel Island** has a world-renowned reputation for seashell picking.

BIRDS Much of Southwest Florida lies along a major "flyway" for migrating birds. This means superb birding, particularly late fall through the spring months. White pelicans, bald eagles, ospreys, and pileated woodpeckers are among the most spectacular migrating species. Brown pelicans, roseate spoonbills (in the southern latitudes), great blue and green herons, great white and snowy egrets, white ibis, gulls, terns, sandpipers, oystercatchers, mangrove cuckoos, and more than a hundred other species inhabit the region year-round. Dozens of parks

FISHING Recreational fishing brings much of the region's tourism. **Boca Grande Pass** has a big reputation for tarpon fishing and holds annual tournaments in the late spring-early summer. Other prized catches include snook, redfish, shark, snapper, ladyfish, mackerel, and sheepsheads. Any number of fishing charters and head boats can take you to the fish, or you can

cast from land or fishing piers through-out the area. You'll need a fishing license if you're not covered by a boat's or pier's licensing.

FRUIT Citrus and tropical fruit thrives in the sunny climes of South-west Florida. Besides grapefruit, oranges, key limes, and tangerines, local residents and commercial farmers grow mangoes, guava, sapodilla, papaya, coconuts, jackfruit, mameys, and avocados (different from Califor-nia avocados in size, sweetness, and lower oil content). **Pine Island** is par-ticularly known for its fruit farms and **MangoMania** festival every July.

GARDENS Everything grows like crazy in this part of the world, so it's only natural that public gardens play an important role in the landscape. Many gardens are part of a greater attraction, such as **Sarasota Jungle Gardens** (941-355-5305 or 877-861-6547; www.sarasotajunglegardens .com), **Ringling Museums** (941-355-5101; www.ringling.org) in Sarasota, **Lakes Regional Park** (239-432-2034; www.leeparks.org) in Fort Myers, **Edi-son & Ford Winter Estates** (239-334-7419; www.efwefla.org) in Fort Myers, the **Naples Zoo** (239-262-5409; www.napleszoo.com), and **Palm**

Cottage (239-261-8164; www.naples historicalsociety.org) in Naples. The **Naples Botanical Garden** (239-643-7275 or 877-433-1874; www.naples garden.org) is the area's one such attraction devoted entirely to the appreciation of plants.

GROUPER Grouper sandwich—crisp fried filet of a local white, meaty fish—is the most signature dish of the coast. The mild flavor of the large fish lends itself to multiple preparations, howev-er, and most menus list more than one. Its popularity, unfortunately, has meant its overfishing, and now groupe fishing season is closed for a few months dur-ing the winter.

HANDICAPPED ACCESS
Within this book, handicapped-accessi-ble lodging, restaurants, and attrac-tions are marked with a wheelchair symbol &.

INSECTS Among the rich wildlife one finds in Southwest Florida is an abundance of bugs, spiders, and but-terflies. Of course the last is the most appreciated, and you can find butterfly

houses at several nature centers such as **Calusa Nature Center** (239-275-3435; www.calusanature.org) in Fort Myers, which devotes an entire room—its Insectarium—to bugs. In Fort Myers, the **Butterfly Estates** (239-690-2359 or 877-690-2359; http://thebutterflyestates.com) immerses curious visitors in a winged experience. In the great wide open and quite possibly even on your doorstep, you will see (or feel) a wide variety of less desirable insects, including palmetto bugs (our euphemism for flying cockroaches), biting mosquitoes and no-see-ums (sand flies), huge lubber grasshoppers, golden orb spiders, ants in assorted variety (avoid the red, biting fire ant), and the occasional scorpion.

KEY LIMES Yellow and pingpong ball–sized, these cousins of the more common green Persian lime are typically juicier and more flavorful. They are the ONLY fruit that should go into a key lime pie. If you see a green key lime pie, it's either not the real thing or it's been colored—a travesty to key lime pie lovers. Hardly a coastal restaurant neglects the ubiquitous dessert on its menu. The best I've tasted in the region? Those renditions at **Gramma Dot's** (239-472-8138) on Sanibel Island and **Randy's Paradise Shrimp** (239-949-6001 or 866-949-6005; www.paradiseshrimpcompany.com) in Bonita Springs.

KIDS' STUFF Southwest Florida prides itself as a family destination that is the flip side of the Orlando scene. You will find children's museums in every geographical chapter of this book, but what lies outdoors is what kids love most. No nature-deficit disorders here—between the beaches, the seas, and the nature parks, there's no end to what families can explore. Many of the parks, preserves, and nature

centers offer special programs just for families. Some nature tours are geared toward teaching kids about the environment using seining nets, touch tanks, games, and other tools. Throughout this book, attractions that are of special interest to children are indicated by the crayon symbol ✐.

LATE-NIGHT FOOD & FUEL Certain categories of Florida liquor licensing require bars to serve food, which provides a good source for late-night eating. Many chain restaurants located along major thoroughfares—such as Denny's and Perkins—stay open late or all night. Chain convenience stores, gas stations, and fuel/food marts also are open around the clock. These include 7-Eleven, Mobil Mart, and Circle K.

MANATEES One of Florida's most well-loved and docile creatures, this prehistoric marine mammal teeters on the brink of survival. Cold spells, red tide, and boat propellers threaten their existence in our fresh waterways. Boat tours in Fort Myers and Naples take you into their habitat to see them. In winter, you can see them at **Manatee Park** (239-533-7440 or 239-533-7275; www.leeparks.org), where they come to bask in the warm runoff waters from the local electric company. For a close-up educational experience, visit them

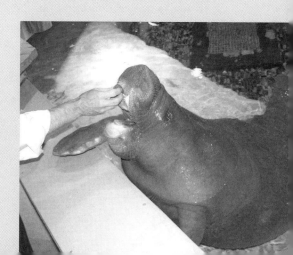

at the **South Florida Museum** (941-746-4131; www.southfloridamuseum.org) in Bradenton or **Mote Marine Aquarium** (941-388-4441 or 800-691-MOTE, ext. 536; www.mote.org) in Sarasota.

PARKS & PRESERVES Southwest Florida's rare ecology deserves keeping, and a number of government entities—from city to county to federal— take up the cause. Federal parks and preserves include **De Soto National Memorial** (941-792-0458; www.nps.gov/deso) in Bradenton, **J.N. "Ding" Darling National Wildlife Refuge** (239-472-1100, www.fws.gov/dingdarling) on Sanibel Island, and in the Everglades area **Florida Panther National Wildlife Refuge, Ten Thousand Islands National Wildlife Refuge, Everglades National Park** (239-695-2591 or 866-628-2591; www.nps.gov/ever), **Big Cypress National Preserve** (239-695-1201; www.nps.gov/bicy), and **Rookery Bay National Estuarine Research Reserve** (239-417-6310; www.rookerybay.org). You'll find state parks and wildlife management areas in every section of this book. Private organizations—such as **Corkscrew Swamp Sanctuary** (239-348-9151; www.corkscrew.audubon.org) near Naples, the **Conservancy of Southwest Florida** (239-262-0304; www.conservancy.org) in Naples, and the **Sanibel-Captiva Conservation Foundation** (239-472-2329; www.sccf.org)—have stepped up to preserve vast tracts of delicate land and water.

SEAFOOD Besides the grouper and stone crab I cover individually here, local fishermen and chefs bring to the table a vast selection of fin and shellfish. Snapper comes in mangrove and red varieties locally. Pompano, redfish, and cobia sometimes show up on menus, but any other fish is imported.

Yellowtail snapper, mahimahi, Florida lobster, and Apalachicola oysters come from other parts of Florida. If you're lucky enough to catch a snook, rejoice! As a game fish, it can't be sold in fish markets and restaurants, but it is one of the region's most highly prized food fish. Shrimp fleets bring pink shrimp into port at Fort Myers Beach's working waterfront. (Make sure to ask if they're wild shrimp; otherwise, they're probably imported and possibly shot up with antibiotics and other unknowns.) Blue crab is also caught locally (again, ask if they're local). Best place to relish it is **Peace River Seafood & Crab Shack** (941-505-8440) in Punta Gorda.

SEASHELLS BY THE SEASHORE **Sanibel Island** is the recognized leading shell-collecting beach in the region, perhaps in the whole country. The offshore island of **Cayo Costa** also attracts rabid shellers. **Bonita Springs** too can boast its shellacious treasures. Shelling is a favorite pastime throughout the region, and the variety is infinite. Prize shells include the junonia, lion's paw, and wentletrap. Shell shops throughout the region sell perfect specimens that cost anywhere from 20 cents to four figures.

SHRIMP Gulf shrimp are graded by size and assigned all sorts of vague measurements: jumbo, large, medium-sized, boat grade, etc. The surest way to know what size shrimp you are ordering is to ask for the count-per-pound designation. This will be something like "21–25s," meaning there are 21 to 25 shrimp per pound. "Boat grade" normally designates a mixture of sizes, usually on the small side.

STONE CRAB Possibly Florida's most exquisite dining pleasure, stone crab are harvested from local waters

SURFING Most surfers equate Florida's east coast with the best wave action. Storms and fronts, however, do reward the west coast with breakers of surfable quality. Best spots are at the jetties on **Venice Beach** and at **Turner Beach** on Sanibel Island. Both, however, have dangerous undercurrents, so are not for beginners or weak swimmers. The latest craze, standup surfing—where surfers use long paddles to maneuver into waves—has strongly hit Southwest Florida.

TIDES Unlike some coastal areas, the Gulf Coast area usually only experiences one low and one high tide every day, meaning its tides are diurnal. Several Web sites give times for high and low tides, which are important mostly to fishermen, boaters, and shellers. Bait shops and local newspapers can also provide this information.

WEDDINGS Within the book, properties that specialize in weddings are noted with the ring symbol ♂.

VISITOR INFORMATION Local visitors bureaus, tourism development councils, and chambers of commerce are adept at the dissemination of materials and information about their area. These are listed in chapter 5, *Information*. For information on the entire region and other parts of Florida, contact Visit Florida, 888-7FLA-USA; www.flausa.com; 661 E. Jefferson St., Suite 300, Tallahassee, FL 32301.

between October 15 and May 15. Named for their tough-to-crack shells, they are cherished for their sweet, meaty flesh, usually eaten chilled and dipped in tangy mustard sauce. **Everglades City** and **Marco Island** are the major home ports for the sensational shellfish, but you'll find them fresh up and down the coast.

HISTORY

T he essence of Gulf Coast Florida seems to be a balance of polar extremes: the ultimate in both natural wilderness and social civility. To understand the region and the richness of its heritage, culture, and environment, one must understand its roots, learn the names, and revel in the legends of its past—a past steeped in romance, adventure, and power.

The story begins with a single mangrove tree and evolves around humanity's need to conquer that tree's primeval world. Enter the characters: Ambition, Wealth, and Social Grace. How does the story end? Happily, we can hope, with the modern rediscovery of the coast's unique natural and historical heritage.

NATURAL HISTORY
FROM GRAINS OF SAND

Each wave helps build a ridge of accumulating sand and shell that runs roughly parallel to the beach. Over a period of hundreds or thousands of years, a ridge may become a barrier island.

—Lynn Stone, Voyageurs Series, Sanibel Island, 1991

On the floor is a straw mat. Under the mat is a layer of sand that has been tracked into the cottage and has sifted through the straw. I have thought some of taking the mat up and sweeping the sand into a pile and removing it, but have decided against it. This is the way keys form, apparently, and I have no particular reason to interfere.

—E. B. White, "On a Florida Key," 1941

Billions of years ago, the Florida peninsula existed only as a scattering of volcanic keys, akin to the Caribbean islands. The passing years, silt, and the sea's power eventually buried all evidence of these volcanic origins. What is now Florida remained submerged until some 20 million years ago, when matter buildup brought land to the surface in the form of new islands.

Ice Age sea fluctuations molded Florida into solid land, and islands continued to grow along its fringes. From a single grain of sand or a lone mangrove sprout they stabilized into masses of sand and forests composed of leggy roots and finger shoots. As shells and marine encrustations accumulated, islands fell into formation along the Gulf Coast, protecting it from the battering of a storm-driven sea. In the gaps between the islands, the gulf's waters scoured the shore to forge inlets, estuaries, bayous, creeks, and rivers. The sea chiseled a mottled, labyrinthine shoreline that kept the southern Gulf Coast a secret while the rest of the state was being tamed.

During its infancy, the region hosted a slow parade of ever-changing creatures. In prehistoric graveyards modern archaeologists have found mummified remains of rhinoceroses, crocodiles, llamas, camels, pygmy horses, saber-toothed tigers, mastodons, and great woolly mammoths—Florida's first winter visitors at the advent of the Ice Age. Another era brought giant armadillos, tapirs, and other South American creatures. Fauna and flora from these ancient eras survive today: cabbage palms (the state tree), saw palmettos, garfish, seahorses, horseshoe crabs, alligators, manatees, armadillos, and loggerhead sea turtles.

AN EARLY PICTURE

> *In the bay of Juan Ponce De León, in the west side of the land, we meet with innumerable small islands, and several fresh streams: the land in general is drowned mangrove swamp. . . From this place Cape Romano, latitude 25:43 to latitude 26:30 are many inconsiderable inlets, all carefully laid down in the chart, here is Carlos Bay, and the Coloosa Hatchee, or Coloosa river, with the island San Ybell, where we find the southern entrance of Charlotte harbour.*
>
> —*Bernard Romans, 1775*

One of the earliest recorders of Florida native life and topography, Bernard Romans is credited with naming Charlotte Harbor after the queen of his adopted homeland, England, and Cape Romano in Ten Thousand Islands after himself. Native Americans and earlier Spanish explorers are responsible for other regional place names.

The harbor was already the center of west-coast life when the first explorers discovered it. Its deep waters and barrier-island protection created a pocket of unusually mild climate, attracting early aborigines and their descendants.

Romans and his contemporaries found the Gulf Coast alive with wild turkeys, black bears, deer, golden panthers, bobcats, possums, raccoons, alligators, river otters, lizards, and snakes. Wild boars and scrub cattle roamed freely, descendants of stock brought by Spanish missionaries. Land birds and waterfowl of all varieties—some permanent, some migratory—filled the skies and back bays. Majestic ospreys and bald eagles swooped; kites soared effortlessly; sandhill cranes dotted the countryside; wood storks nested; pelicans came in brown and white; gulls, terns, and sandpipers patrolled seashores; cormorants, ducks, anhingas, ibises, egrets, roseate spoonbills, and herons fed among the mangroves.

Marine life flourished. Manatees cleared waterways, dolphins frolicked in the waves, and mullet burst from bay waters like cannon shot. Tarpon, rays, snapper, snook, flounder, ladyfish, and mackerel churned the otherwise calm backwaters. Grouper, tripletail, tuna, and shark lurked in deep waters offshore.

On land, a wide variety of indigenous vegetation abounded. Sea grapes, sea oats, nickerbeans, and railroad vines anchored sandy coasts. Thick, impenetrable jungles clogged inland areas. Cabbage palms and gumbo-limbo trees stood tall. Papayas flourished along with flowering shrubs. In mixed-wood forests pines climbed skyward and live oaks fluttered their eerie veils of Spanish moss. Cedars fringed islands along the Sarasota Bay coast. Ferns and grasses carpeted the marshes. Swamplands were home to great cypress trees with bony knees and branches full of parasitic mistletoe and epiphytic orchids and bromeliads.

Primeval and teeming, Florida held an exotic and mysterious aura. The swamp and the estuary nurtured all of life, from the Everglades upward along the lowlands of the Gulf Coast. It was a perfect ecosystem, designed by nature to withstand all forces—except humankind.

FACE-LIFTS AND IMPLANTS With the arrival of the first settlers, the natural balance that existed along the Gulf Coast began to tilt. The Spanish brought citrus seedlings and livestock. Naturalists and growers introduced specimens from the north and south: mangoes, avocados, bougainvillea, hibiscus, frangipani, coconut palms, pineapples, sapodillas, tomatoes, and legumes. For the most part these exotics proved harmless to the fragile environment.

Three nonnative plants brought to the area in the past century, however, have harmed the ecosystem and changed the profile of the land. The prolific melaleuca tree (or cajeput), casuarina (Australian pine), and Brazilian pepper choke out the native vegetation that wildlife feeds on and harm both man and property. Many communities are attempting to eradicate these noxious plants, particularly the pepper tree.

The complexion of the west coast was changed further by dredging and plowing. In times when swampland was equated with slimy monsters and slick real estate agents, developers and governments thought nothing of filling it in to create more buildable land. This, too, threw the ecosystem off balance. Fortunately, such mistakes were recognized before their effects became irreversible. Today government strives to preserve, even restore, the delicate balance of the wetlands, most notably through the massive, $8 billion, 30-year Everglades restoration project.

SOCIAL HISTORY

TIME LINE: GULF COAST FLORIDA The modern settlement of Florida's southwest coast can be traced like a time line that begins on the shores of Sarasota

THE MIRACLE OF THE MANGROVE

The mangrove forest is both a fertile incubator and a marine graveyard, the home of an island construction crew and a vegetative ballet troupe. It is a self-sustaining world marked by vivid contrasts. The Mangrove Coast (as one local historian terms it) is riddled with red, black, and white species of the tree. Red mangroves strut along mainland coastlines, canals, and the leeward sides of islands on graceful prop roots—or at least they look graceful until low tide reveals the oysters, barnacles, and tiny marine metropolises that weigh them down and keep them connected to the sea.

Farther inland, black-and-white mangroves create thick, impenetrable forests that buffer waves, filter pollutants, sent out shoots, and always busi-ly build. Encrustations of shellfish grab algae, silt, and sand, creating rich soil out of decaying material. Fish, crabs, and mollusks skitter among the roots, nibbling dinner, depositing eggs, and tending to their young. Birds rest and nest in the mangroves' scraggly branches, ready to dive for the fish on which they feed. Mother trees send their tubular offspring bobbing upon sea currents to find a foothold elsewhere and perhaps begin a new island.

The cycle is ancient and ongoing, threatened only by the chainsaws of developers. A few decades ago these natural builders, the mangroves, were leveled in favor of cement seawalls. Today, strict regulations prohibit man-grove destruction. The crucial role of the mangrove in the survival of Flori-da's sea life finally has been realize—and cherished.

Bay in 1841 and ends at Naples in 1887. At first glance this time frame makes the region look young, without the gracious patina of age and the wrinkles of an inter-esting past. Common is the belief, in fact, that the Gulf Coast has no history because it lacks Williamsburg's colonial homes or Philadelphia's monuments.

True, the Gulf Coast's early pioneers left no standing architecture. Termites, flimsy building styles, erosion, and tropical storms saw to that. But earlier settlers did leave other proof of their existence—artifacts that date as far back as 10,000 years. If that isn't history, what is?

CALUSA KINGDOM Archaeologists of this century have discovered remnants of early architecture and lifeways in the shell mounds of the Calusa and Timucua tribes, who settled the coastlines more than 2,500 years ago. The Timucua inhabit-ed the Sarasota Bay coast for many years and then migrated northward and to the east; the Calusa later moved into the Sarasota area and were centered around Charlotte Harbor.

Evidence of still earlier civilizations has been found, placing Florida's first immigrants, possibly from Asia, in the upper coast regions around 8200 B.C. Little is known about these early arrivals except that they used pointed spears.

Archaeological excavations and the writings of Spanish explorers give us a more complete picture of the Calusa and other tribes, who built shell mounds to bury

A TYPICAL TIMUCUA INDIAN VILLAGE HAS BEEN RE-CREATED AT DE SOTO NATIONAL MEMORIAL PARK IN BRADENTON.

their dead and debris. Learned consensus brings the Calusa and the Timucua to southern Florida from Caribbean islands—evidence of similar lifestyles and sustained contact suggests a connection to the peaceful Arawak Indians of the West Indies. Similarities have also been found between the Calusa and South American tribes, and, given indications of the Florida's tribes' great engineering skills, some historians consider them wayward relatives of the Mayans or Aztecs. (Others say they are connected to the Mayans and Aztecs by trade rather than origin.)

The name Calusa, or Caloosa, was used first by Spanish conquerors who understood the name of the tribe's chief to be Calos. They were said to be tall people with hip-length hair that men wore in a topknot. When clothed, men dressed in breeches of deerskin or woven palmetto fiber, and women fashioned garments out of Spanish moss. They cultivated corn, pumpkins, squash, and tobacco; fished for mullet and mackerel with harpoons and palmetto-fiber nets; hunted for turkey, deer, and bear with bow and arrow, deer-bone dirks, and Aztec-style weapons; and harvested wild sea grapes, fruit, yams, swamp cabbage (hearts of palm), and the coontie root, out of which they pounded flour for bread. Conch and whelk shells were crafted into tools for building and cooking. The natives spent their leisure time wrestling, celebrating the corn harvest, and worshiping the sun god. Great seafarers, the Calusa built canoes and traveled in them to Caribbean islands and the Yucatán. A different style of pirogue took them along rivers and bay waters to visit villages of their own tribe and those of other nations.

Much of our information about the Calusa comes from the son of a Spanish official stationed in Cartagena, in what is now Colombia. The youngster, Hernando de Escalante Fontaneda, was shipwrecked along Calusa shores en route to Spain. He lived among the tribe for 17 years, learned its language, and, upon returning to Spain in 1574, recorded its customs. In 1895 Frank Hamilton Cushing explored Charlotte Harbor's Amerindian heritage. He surmised that the Calusa's religious structures and palmetto-piling homes had perched on shell mounds along riverbanks and coastlines. Terraces and steps bit into the towering mounds where gardens and courts had been built. Man-made canals up to 30 feet wide connected neighboring villages. Pine Island, Mound Key, Manasota Key, and Marco Island were important religious and governmental centers for the Calusa.

Excavations along the Gulf Coast continually provide new information about the region's native inhabitants and their symbiotic relationship with nature. The University of Florida funds a research center on Pine Island for the sole purpose of excavating mounds to discover more truth about the vanished civilization.

SPANISH IMPOSITION Greed and religious fervor eventually warped this idyllic picture, and the Calusa showed themselves to be vicious warriors when it came to preserving the life they knew. Juan Ponce de León first crashed the party in 1513. It's possible that early slavers from the Caribbean were responsible for the Calusa hostility he encountered, or perhaps the Amerindians' early hatred of the conquistadores was gained secondhand, from trading with island natives. Whatever the reason, Ponce was "blacklisted" by the Calusa shortly after he began his search, according to legend, for Bimini, a storied land of treasure and youth.

Ponce de León first landed on Florida's east coast at Eastertime without strife, and the conqueror named the land after the Spanish name for the holiday, *Pascua Florida*. However, on his second landing, days later, he was met by shell-tipped spears and bows and arrows. His three wounded sailors were the first Europeans known to shed blood in Florida. Ponce de León's ship continued to the west coast, where it stopped in the vicinity of Marco Island. Here one native astounded him by speaking to him in Spanish—learned, perhaps, from West Indies contacts. Impressed, Ponce de León allowed his party to be tricked by a marauding native army in canoes, but escaped with the loss of only one man's life.

After several trips to Florida and the Gulf Coast, Ponce de León returned to Puerto Rico—still treasureless and now middle-aged—to plot a new scheme. In 1521 he set out to establish a Gulf Coast colony as a base for treasure explorations. This time the party he crashed had been forewarned, possibly by smoke signals. Calusa arrows pierced the heavy armor of the Spaniards, killing and wounding many, including the great seeker of youth himself. After returning to Havana for medical attention, Ponce de León died there at the age of 60.

Lust for gold overcame common sense as more explorers and invaders followed in Ponce de León's tragic footsteps. In 1539 Hernando de Soto sailed from Havana and headed up the Gulf Coast, seeking, it would seem, a way to confuse future historians. Three different crewmen described the expedition three different ways. The Smithsonian Institution has published a report some locals still dispute, which

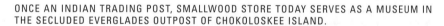

ONCE AN INDIAN TRADING POST, SMALLWOOD STORE TODAY SERVES AS A MUSEUM IN THE SECLUDED EVERGLADES OUTPOST OF CHOKOLOSKEE ISLAND.

claims that de Soto landed first on Longboat Key and then, looking for fresh water, headed toward Tampa Bay. According to the Smithsonian, de Soto set up his first mainland camp at an abandoned native village at the mouth of the Manatee River, near modern-day Bradenton. Others are convinced that his first landfall was at Fort Myers Beach. Regardless of where the landing took place, we know that de Soto scoured the coast for gold, all the while torturing and killing Native Americans who would not, could not, lead him to it.

Sarasota and its environs embrace the Smithsonian study's findings. Some say the name of the town itself, initially written as "Sara Sota," comes from the conqueror. Others prefer a more romantic legend regarding his fictional daughter, Sara. Sarasota's first hotel, in any case, took its name from de Soto. Near Bradenton, a small national park marks the alleged spot of his first landing.

In 1565 Pedro Menéndez de Avilés came to the Gulf Coast, searching for a son lost to shipwreck and a group of Spaniards being held captive by the Calusa. With the aid of one of Chief Calos's Spanish captives, Menéndez befriended Calos with flattery and gifts, then built a fort and a mission at a spot called San Anton, believed to have been on Pine Island. But Menéndez insulted the great chieftain by rejecting his sister as a wife and allying himself with enemy tribes. Sensing Calos's anger, Menéndez tricked the leader into captivity and had him beheaded. When Menéndez later executed Calos's son and heir to the throne, along with 11 of his subchiefs, tribesmen burned their own villages, forcing the settlers to bail out in search of food.

The century that followed is considered the Golden Age of the Calusa. It was marked by freedom from European intrusion and great cultural advances, heightened by the contribution of Spanish captives who had refused to be saved by

IN PALMETTO, VISITORS CAN CLIMB TO THE TOP OF AN ANCIENT INDIAN MOUND AT EMERSON POINT PRESERVE.

Menéndez's rescue party and by others who found Calusa ways preferable to "civilization."

Eventually, peaceful trading softened the hostility between Spanish settlers and the Calusa. Cuban immigrants began building a fishing industry around Charlotte Harbor. Although the Calusa had won the war against Spanish invaders, they were defenseless against the diseases the Europeans brought with them. By the turn of the 19th century, smallpox and other diseases had killed off most Calusa; the remainder were absorbed by intermarrying with the Cubans and newly arriving tribes. The most prominent of the latter were the Seminole—a name meaning "wanderer"—a mixture of Georgian Creek, African, and Spanish bloodlines.

THE VARMINT ERA "A haunt of the picaroons of all nations," explorer James Grant Forbes wrote in 1772, referring to Charlotte Harbor—layover, if not home, for every scoundrel who sailed its island-clotted waters. The Gulf Coast's maze of forbidding bayous and barely navigable waterways made it a favorite hideout for escaped criminals, bootleggers, government refugees, smugglers, and—that most popular of all local folk characters—buccaneers.

Pirate legends color the pages of regional history books in shades of blood red and doubloon gold. Besides willing to residents a certain cavalier spirit, these pirates have left—if one believes the tales—millions of dollars in buried treasure. "After researching the subject in 1950 . . . then state Attorney General Ralph E. Odum estimated that some $165 million is still buried beneath Florida's sands and waters," reported a 1978 issue of *The Miami Herald's Florida Almanac*, "$30 million of it originally the property of Jose Gaspar."

Besides the mostly mythical Gaspar, other picaresque names resound along the Gulf Coast: Jean Lafitte, of New Orleans fame; Bru Baker, Gaspar's Pine Island cohort; and a dark soul named Black Caesar. Henry Castor supposedly buried treasure on Egmont Key in the mid-1700s. Local legend places the notorious Calico Jack Rackham and his pirate lover, Anne Bonny, on the shores of Fort Myers Beach for a playful honeymoon. Black Augustus lived and died a hermit on Mound Key, to the south. On Panther Key, John Gomez, Gaspar's self-proclaimed cabin boy, lived to be 122 and sold maps purportedly leading to Gasparillan gold to many a gullible treasure hunter.

According to more reliable historical records, island pirate havens were replaced by or coexisted with crude Spanish fishing ranchos, which cropped up as early as the 1600s. The camps—which provided Cuban traders with salted mullet and roe to eat—consisted of thatched shacks, some built on pilings in shallow waters. Here families lived, according to customs inspector Henry B. Crews, "in a state

THE FOUNTAIN FROM THE OLD HOTEL CHARLOTTE HARBOR NOW GRACES THE GROUNDS OF PUNTA GORDA HISTORY PARK.

of Savage Barbarism with no associate but the Seminole Indians and the lowest class of refugee Spaniards who from crime have most generally been compelled to abandon the haunts of civilized life."

Ice-making and railroads changed the direction of fish exportation from southern points to northern destinations. Punta Gorda, with the area's first railroad station, became the center for the transshipment of fresh fish. Major fish-shipping companies built stilt houses for the more than 200 men who harvested their mullet crops. These structures straddled shallows from Charlotte Harbor to Ten Thousand Islands, providing homes for the fishermen and their families until the late 1930s, when modern roads and the burning of Punta Gorda's Long Dock brought the era to a close. Fewer than a dozen of the historic fish shacks have survived hurricanes, erosion, and the state's determination to tear them down as a public nuisance. They strut along the shallows of Charlotte Harbor, in greatest concentration offshore of North Captiva Island.

"It is highly important that no person should be permitted to settle on the Islands forming 'Charlotte Harbor' . . . which are of no value for the purpose of agriculture, being in general formed of sand and shells," advised Assistant Adjutant General Captain Lorenzo Thomas in 1844. Nonetheless, out of this era of varmints sprouted a tradition of farming. Plucky pioneers raised coconuts, citrus, tomatoes, and other crops, despite hardship and heartbreak, as they trickled in to coax their livelihood from a hostile environment.

YEARS OF DISCONTENT The bloody years of the Wars of Indian Removal began in 1821, when Andrew Jackson—then governor of the territory—decided to claim northern Florida from the Seminole tribes that were wreaking havoc on

KINGDOM OF GASPARILLA

Of all the rum-chugging and throat-slashing visitors to have set foot upon Southwest Florida's tolerant shores, José Gaspar (known by the more properly pirate-sounding name "Gasparilla") is the one remembered most fondly. Gaspar set up headquarters, it is said, on Gasparilla Island, where Boca Grande now sits. In his time it was called High Town. He built a palmetto palace there and furnished it with the finest booty. Low Town he placed on a separate island so as to distance himself from the crude lifestyles of his rowdy shipmates. Gasparilla's fort stood on Cayo Costa.

Legends say Gasparilla got his start as a pirate after some nasty business with the wife of a crown prince. He gave up his cushy position as admiral of the Spanish navy for the hardships of life at sea and in the jungles of late 18th-century Florida.

His address might have changed, but his love of beautiful women did not. He kidnapped the fairest and wealthiest of them from captured ships and whisked them off to another Gulf Coast island named for its inhabitants—Captiva—until ransom money arrived. Gasparilla took the most

American settlers. By 1837 fighting had spread to the southern reaches of the peninsula, and two forts were built upriver from present-day Fort Myers. The following year the government reached an agreement with the Seminoles, restricting them to mainland areas along the Charlotte Harbor coast, the Caloosahatchee River, and southward.

News of imminent peace prompted Josiah Gates to build a hotel on the banks of the Manatee River, near modern-day Bradenton, in anticipation of the influx of settlers from Fort Brooke (Tampa) that the treaty would bring. A modest community rose up around this precursor of southwest Florida resorts. Families of soldiers and wealthy Southern planters settled in the area. The latter brought their slaves and built sugarcane plantations on vast expanses of land that they bought for $1.25 an acre.

Sarasota got its first permanent settler in 1842 when William Whitaker, a fisherman, built his home on Yellow Bluff, overlooking Sarasota Bay. He and his new

THE STORY OF THE CALUSA AND SEMINOLE PEOPLES, INCLUDING SEMINOLE CHIEF BILLY BOWLEGS, FINDS AN AUDIENCE ALONG VENICE'S MAIN THOROUGHFARE.

beautiful of his captives to High Town to woo them with fine wines, jewels, and Spanish poetry. One object of his affection, a Mexican princess named Joséfa, would have nothing to do with such a barbarian. Finally, driven to madness by her insults, Gasparilla beheaded his beloved. He carried her body to another key in his island fiefdom, where he buried her with remorse and sand. He named the island Joséfa, which, through the years and the twistings of rum-swollen tongues, has been perverted to Useppa. And so the exclusive island is called today.

Nearby Sanibel Island, according to one legend, got its name from the abandoned lover of Gaspar's gunner. However, variations abound and improve with each telling. The legend began with the ramblings of old "Panther Key John" Gomez and was perpetuated by railroad press agents and optimistic treasure hunters.

Serious historians doubt the existence of a man named Gasparilla but concede that one of the many Gulf Coast pirates might have borrowed the island's name. Others hold tenaciously to the legend, plying coastal sands with shovels and dredges in search of his ill-gotten booty.

wife, daughter of one of the Manatee planters, had 10 children and later went into cattle ranching and farming.

The year after the peace treaty was signed, a tribe of Seminoles attacked a settlement across the river from their village, on the same site as present-day Fort Myers. The Harney Point Massacre rekindled the war. Fort Harvie was built near the site of the violent attack. Chief Billy Bowlegs led his people in evasive tactics through the wild and mysterious Everglades, but by 1842 the government had captured 230 of his people and shipped them west. Further pursuit was abandoned. Only Fort Harvie and one other fortification remained operational. A new agreement contained the Seminoles along the Caloosahatchee and barred them from the islands to protect the fishermen and their families. The treaty made no mention of the swampland, probably because the government considered it useless; the Seminoles assumed the territory was theirs.

By 1848, three years after Florida's admission to the Union as the 27th state, there was a surge of interest in the wetlands. The government, envisioning drainage projects to create more land, offered the Seminoles $250 each to relocate in the West. When they refused, a systematic plan to conquer them went into effect. This plan included the repair of Fort Harvie, which was renamed Fort Myers after a U.S. colonel who had served for many years in Florida and was engaged to the commanding general's daughter. Manpower was increased there, and the fort was reinforced and enlarged. Scouting parties stalked the Seminoles but usually found only the remains of abandoned and burned villages when they arrived.

In December 1855, after soldiers destroyed Billy Bowlegs's prize banana patch, the Seminole chief and his people retaliated. Fort Myers became the center of war activity. The government placed a bounty on the head of any Seminole brought to the fort and offered $1,000 to each Seminole warrior ($100 to each woman and child) who agreed to leave the area. Finally, in 1858, after soldiers had captured his granddaughter and other women of the tribe, Billy Bowlegs capitulated, thus bringing an end to 37 years of killing and deception by the government and the military. Fort Myers was abandoned, and the remaining Seminole dispersed deep into the Everglades. Farmers, planters, fishermen, and cattlemen continued peacefully in their trades, although government vigilance against alliances with the Seminole forced some of the island fishing *ranchos* to close during the war's final years. Today the Seminole live on reservations, earning an income from tourism, fishing, and casinos.

In the late 1850s, Virginia planter Captain James Evans purchased Fort Myers on the auction block. He brought in his slaves to work the crops he envisioned—tropical fruits, coconut palms, coffee, and other exotic plants. But the Civil War interrupted his venture, sending him back home. Florida joined the Confederacy in 1861. West coast inhabitants generally remained uninvolved until a federal blockade at Key West cut off supplies, at which point they turned to the profitable business of blockade running.

CATTLE KINGS, CARPETBAGGERS, AND CRACKERS Jacob Summerlin epitomized the Florida cattle king. He dressed in a floppy hat, leather boots, and trail dust. Having established a steady trade between Florida and ports south before the Civil War, Summerlin was in a good position to provide the Confederate Army with contraband beef. Working with his blockade-running partner, James

McKay Sr., he drove his cattle from inland Florida to Punta Rassa, where the causeway from Sanibel Island makes landfall today. There he sold his scrub cattle, descendants of livestock left by the early Spaniards. The U.S. Navy eventually learned of these illegal dealings and stationed boats at Sanibel and Punta Rassa. Despite attempts to thwart their trade, however, Summerlin and McKay sold 25,000 steers to the Confederates between 1861 and 1865.

Jake Summerlin lived by the seat of his pants, driving cattle to Punta Rassa and collecting big bags of Cuban gold—which he spent at the end of the line on drinking and gaming. In 1874 he built the Summerlin House at Punta Rassa, where he and his men could bunk and invest the profits of the business in frivolity.

The rough, free-and-easy lifestyle of the cow hunter attracted young post–Civil War drifters. In addition, Summerlin's success lured Civil War officers into the prosperous life of the cattle boss, including Captain F. A. Hendry, founder of an ongoing Fort Myers dynasty. Between 1870 and 1880 stockmen sold 165,000 head of cattle at Punta Rassa for more than $2 million. Into the 1900s, the cow hunters drove their herds through the streets of downtown Fort Myers, past the homes of investors, bankers, and other wealthy settlers, including Thomas Edison.

Reconstruction brought other settlers to Florida's west coast. One notable rebel refugee, Judah P. Benjamin—who had served as the Confederacy's secretary of state—ducked indictment as a war criminal by hiding out in Florida. His weeklong asylum at the old Gamble plantation near Bradenton ensured the landmark's preservation by the United Daughters of the Confederacy.

The first postwar visitors to Fort Myers were the vultures who picked the fort clean of coveted building materials. Then came men who remembered the old fort in its heyday and hoped to settle with their families in this land of plenty. The first settler, Captain Manuel A. Gonzalez, had run a provisions boat from Tampa during the Seminole War. He and his family moved from Key West with another family named Vivas. Other war officers and refugees settled in and around the ruins of the old fort, planting gardens, opening stores, and living a blissful existence unknown elsewhere in the devastated South.

Captain James Evans returned to Fort Myers from Virginia to find his land comfortably occupied. After struggling in the courts to keep the land out of government hands, he split it with the squatters in exchange for a share of his legal fees. In 1872 the first school in Fort Myers was built. County government was centered 270 miles away, in Key West.

Some historians credit the cow hunters with contributing the name "Cracker" to early Florida settlers, which they say derives from the cracking of the long whips the cowmen used

STOCK LEFT ON FLORIDA SHORES GAVE HOOF TO LUCRATIVE CATTLE-DRIVING ENTERPRISES IN THE MID- TO LATE 19TH CENTURY.

to drive their herds. Others say it originated with the Georgia settlers who cracked corn for their hush puppies, corn pone, and fritters. Georgians did, in fact, drift down to southwest Florida, most notably the Knight clan, which founded a settlement at Horse and Chaise, named by seamen to describe a landmark clump of trees. (The name was changed to Venice in 1888 by developer Frank Higel, who was reminded of the Italian city by the area's many bayous and creeks.)

The Homestead Act, passed in 1862, entitled each settler in Florida to 160 acres of land, provided they built a home and tended the land for five years. As had been intended, the act brought a flood of intrepid settlers into the area from all over the eastern seaboard and Deep South. Traveling by foot or boat, they built rough palmetto huts, burned cow chips to ward off mosquitoes that carried yellow fever, ate raccoon purloo and turtle steaks, and stubbornly endured the heat, hurricanes, and freezes that stymied a number of enterprises: sugar refining, fish-oil production, and pineapple and citrus farming.

Florida's cow hunters eventually proved detrimental to the agriculturally based ventures associated with the Crackers of the Sarasota Bay region. They allied themselves with greedy land speculators who, by 1883, underhandedly nullified the beneficial effects of the Homestead Act. These speculators had discovered a loophole in Florida's land development legislation, namely the Swamp Land Act, which allowed them to purchase flooded land at rock-bottom prices while overriding homestead claims. They succeeded in declaring arable property swampland and ultimately bought up a good 90 percent of present-day Manatee County, much of which had been worked for years by hardy pioneers. Together the speculators and the cattlemen fought farmers' protests against "free ranging," the practice of letting herds roam and feed without restriction. A Sara Sota Vigilance Committee formed in opposition, and by the time the fighting ended, two men lay dead.

As thatch homes gave way to wooden farmhouses—the tin-roofed vernacular style today termed Cracker—Gulf Coast settlements entered a new era, an era that made "riffraff" out of Crackers, rich men out of schemers, and exclusive getaways out of crude frontier towns.

AT THE DROP OF A NAME When your first guests are Juan Ponce de León and Hernando de Soto, whom do you invite next? With such an impressive pair , it wouldn't do to host just anybody. So began west coast Florida's tradition of larger-than-life visitors with impressive names and pedigrees, all of whom just as impressively influenced the region's development. Thomas Edison, Henry Ford, Harvey Firestone, John and Charles Ringling, Charles Lindbergh, Teddy Roosevelt, Henry du Pont, Andrew Mellon, Rose Cleveland, and Shirley Temple were among the wide array of early southwest Florida winterers. Their fame and following quickly elevated the status of the lower Gulf Coast from crude and backward to avant-garde and exclusive, attracting the cutting-edge elite. They set national trends by declaring new hot spots—fresh, wild, unspoiled places about which no one else knew, especially the paparazzi. It was they who balanced the very wild coast with a very civilized clientele. The area's natural endowments of fish, fowl, and game attracted adventurers, fishermen, and hunters with the means to make the long, slow journey to it.

The first and most influential name in any Gulf Coast retrospective is Thomas Edison. Disappointed by the cold winters of St. Augustine, the ailing inventor embarked on a scouting cruise along the Gulf Coast in 1885, the same year Fort

Myers was incorporated. As Edison sailed along the Caloosahatchee River, he sighted a stand of bamboo trees. Then and there he decided to move to Fort Myers. And he wanted that property!

The bamboo worked well as filament in Edison's lightbulb experiments, and the climate bolstered his failing health, helping to add another 46 years to his life. On the banks of the Caloosahatchee the inventor fashioned his ideal winter home, Seminole Lodge, complete with laboratory and tropical gardens. Holder of more than a thousand patents, the genius experimented with rare plants in his quest to produce inexpensive rubber for his friend, tire mogul Harvey Firestone. So enamored with Fort Myers was Edison that he persuaded Firestone to spend his winters there. He also set up fellow visionary Henry Ford on an estate next to his. A self-styled botanist, Edison planted the frequently photographed row of royal palms lining the street that eventually ran past his home, McGregor Boulevard, thereby earning the town its nickname: City of Palms.

Meanwhile, the Florida Mortgage and Investment Company—connected with such notables as the archbishop of Canterbury and estate owner Sir John Gillespie—lured a colony of politically disgruntled Scotsmen to Sara Sota, a paradise of genteel estates, bountiful orange groves, and cheap land. Or so the brochures promised. But instead of the Garden of Eden and ready-made manor houses about which they had read, the newcomers found shortages of food and building materials. Only through the kindness of the Whitakers and other pioneers did they survive their first month. Then the Gulf Coast's unpredictable winter weather dealt another cold blow, causing most of the colonists to return to their homeland. Those who stayed, however, brought life to the struggling village and sparked it with a determined spirit.

Most influential among the Scottish ranks was John Hamilton Gillespie, son of Sir John. He built the city's first hotel, the De Soto, and introduced the game of golf to Florida. Gillespie initially transplanted the sport from his homeland by building a two-hole links down Main Street, near his hotel; he later built the area's

OLD FISH HOUSES, LIKE THIS ONE IN CORTEZ, SURVIVE FROM THE 1930S, WHEN FISHERMEN'S FAMILIES LIVED IN AND WORKED OUT OF THE STILTED STRUCTURES.

first real course and clubhouse nearby. When the town of Sarasota was incorporated on October 14, 1902, Gillespie became its first mayor.

It was an American woman, however, who firmly and definitively upgraded Sarasota's image. At the turn of the 20th century, the name Mrs. (Bertha) Potter Palmer stood for social elitism—not only in her hometown, Chicago, but also in London and Paris, where she kept homes and hobnobbed with royalty. When the widowed socialite decided to visit Sarasota in 1910, hearts palpitated: She could make or break the new town. Enchanted by the area's beauty and the town's quaintness, Mrs. Palmer immediately bought 13 acres that eventually grew to 140,000. She built her home, The Oaks, and a cattle ranch in a community south of Sarasota called Osprey and from there proceeded to spread the word.

Mrs. Palmer's much-publicized love affair with the Gulf Coast drew the attention of John and Charles Ringling, the youngest of the illustrious circus family's seven sons. The two brothers, in a contest of one-upmanship, began buying property around town. They became active in civic affairs, built bridges to Sarasota's islands, and stoked the economy by making the town the winter home for the Ringling Circus. John Ringling, especially, and his wife, Mable, brought to Sarasota a new worldliness born of their extensive travels and love of European art.

The fate of the Charlotte Harbor coast lay mostly in the hands of one powerful man, Henry B. Plant. The west coast's counterpart to Henry Flagler—builder of the east coast's railroad and great hotels—Plant brought the railway to Tampa, where he built a fabulous resort of his own, always in competition with Flagler. At the same time, another railway company extended its tracks to an unknown, unsettled spot in the wilderness of Charlotte Harbor's shores and erected the Hotel Charlotte Harbor. It reigned briefly as the latest posh outpost for wealthy sportsmen and adventurers, counting Andrew Mellon and W. K. Vanderbilt among its patrons. But in 1897, after Plant had acquired the railway to Punta Gorda, he decided that the town's deepwater port and resort posed too much competition for his Tampa enterprises. So he choked the life out of a thriving commercial and resort town by severing the rails to Punta Gorda's Long Dock.

Deepwater ports, railroads, and fabulous hotels went hand in hand in those days: Developers had to provide transportation before they could attract visitors. And at the end of the line, the visitors needed a place to stay. In Boca Grande, where a railroad had been built in 1906, the deep waters of Boca Grande Pass attracted Rockefellers, du Ponts, J. P. Morgan, and other industrialists who used the port for shipping phosphate from central Florida. To accommodate them, the graciously refined Gasparilla Inn was built in 1913.

Another man who was to influence the discovery and development of the Gulf Coast came to town in 1911. John M. Roach, Chicago streetcar magnate and owner of Useppa Island, introduced Barron Collier to the area. Collier eventually bought Useppa from his friend and there established the Useppa Inn and the Izaak Walton Club. Both attracted, according to local lore, tarpon-fishing enthusiasts such as Shirley Temple, Gloria Swanson, Mae West, Herbert Hoover, Zane Grey, and Mary Roberts Rinehart; the latter author then bought nearby Cabbage Key for her son and his bride.

Collier went on to infuse life into the southwest coast by underwriting the completion of the Tamiami Trail, stalled on its route from Tampa to Miami. He acquired land throughout the county that today bears his name after earlier attempts by Louisville publisher Walter Haldeman had failed to put Naples on the map.

Along the lower Gulf Coast of Florida, Collier bought more than a million acres, much of it under the infamous Swamp Act. Although he dreamed of development on the scale of Flagler and Plant, anticorporation outcry, hurricanes, the Depression, and war staunched his success. His sons inherited his kingdom, which they ruled with a heart for the unique environment their father so loved. Collier's influence increased awareness of the Gulf Coast as a refuge for crowd-weary stars and illuminati. Its islands still are popular with the rich and famous who seek anonymity.

But what about the ordinary people—Native Americans, fishermen, cattlemen, Crackers, pioneers, and common folk—who loved this land long before it became fashionable to do so? For the most part they lived side by side with this new brand of resident, called the "winterer" or "snowbird." (In Boca Grande they were termed "beachfronters" for their unusual-at-the-time idiosyncrasy of building dangerously close to the shore.) The locals became their fishing guides, cooks, and innkeepers. In some cases their heads were turned by brushes with great wealth. In other instances, heightened standards pulled the curtain on cruder lifestyles, especially that of the cow hunter, whose boisterousness and preference for free-running stock hastened his extinction.

Sometimes the common folk protested big-bucks development and were classified as riffraff. The "Cracker" label today, despite the culture's enriching influence on architecture and cuisine, is considered an insult by some native Floridians.

BOOMS, BURSTS, AND OTHER EXPLOSIONS

The Gulf Coast's resort reputation came of age at the turn of the 20th century. Sarasota's De Soto, the Hotel Charlotte Harbor, Boca Grande's Gasparilla Inn, the Useppa Inn, Fort Myers's Royal Palm Hotel, the Naples Hotel, and the Marco Inn pioneered in the hotel field, hosting visitors in styles ranging from bare bones to bend-over-backward. They sparked an era touched with Gatsby-type glamour, giddiness, and graciousness.

The Gulf Coast's halcyon days peaked in the early 1920s as the state entered a decade known as the Great Florida Land Boom. Growth came quickly to the young communities of Bradenton, Sarasota, Fort Myers, and Naples. In fact, the good people of the Gulf Coast grew dizzy with the whirl of growth and success.

According to the 1910 census, Sarasota's population was 840; before the 1920s drew to a close, almost 8,400 people called it home. In the

AN EXHIBIT AT MANATEE COUNTY AGRICULTURAL MUSEUM IN PALMETTO ILLUSTRATES THE IMPORTANCE OF COMMERCIAL FISHING TO THE REGION'S ECONOMIC DEVELOPMENT.

meantime the city shaped itself with sidewalks, streets, schools, a newspaper, a pier, an airfield, and the establishment of its own county, having split from Bradenton's Manatee County. A bridge to Siesta Key added a whole new element to the town's personality by plugging it into the gulf and attracting a seaside resort trade.

World War I briefly interfered. Prohibition brought to the coast yet another roguish character: the rumrunner. Homes and hotels popped up like toadstools after a summer rain shower. Increased lodging options opened the Gulf Coast to a wider range of vacationers. The average traveler could now afford Florida's Gulf Coast, no longer just a socialites' haven. A new class of winterer arrived in force, known as tin-can tourists for the trailers and campers they pulled behind their vehicles. Tourist camps sprang up overnight, and southwest Florida became an Everyman's paradise. Real estate profits added to the lure of tourism, and many visitors decided to remain permanently.

The 1920s created Charlotte County along the Charlotte Harbor coast. A bridge was built across the Peace River, connecting the pioneer towns of Charlotte Harbor and Punta Gorda, spurring growth, and spawning subdivisions by the score.

Fort Myers became the seat of a new county named for Confederate General Robert E. Lee. Between 1920 and 1930, the population grew from 3,600 to 9,000, boosted by the completion of the Tamiami Trail in 1928. Fort Myers evolved from a raucous cattle town into a modern city with electricity (thanks to Edison), telephone lines, and a railroad. The Royal Palm Hotel treated guests to a regal departure from the cow trails that ran adjacent to the property. A country club put Fort Myers on the golfing map, and a bridge to Estero Island's beautiful beaches (today Fort Myers Beach) further boosted tourism. Real adventurers took the ferry to Sanibel Island, to be accommodated at Casa Ybel or the Palm Hotel.

South of Fort Myers, the farming community of Survey was renamed Bonita Springs. In 1923 Naples—previously a well-kept secret among buyers from such faraway places as Kentucky and Ohio and distinguished vacationers from the upper echelons—became a city just in time to feel the effects of the tourism boom. The same year, Collier County seceded from Lee County. Everglades City became the first county seat; later, growing, thriving Naples took the honors. In 1927 the Naples Pier, which had served as a landing point for visitors and cargo since 1887, was replaced in importance by a railroad depot.

Gulf Coast skies had never been sunnier: Visitors spent lots of money. Residents prospered. Real estate prices soared. It seemed too good to be true. And indeed it was.

A 1926 hurricane hit Fort Myers, worsening a condition of already deepening debt. In Sarasota, John Ringling suffered severe financial losses from which he never recovered. On the southernmost coast, however, the national economy had little impact on the surge of interest sparked by the opening of the Tamiami Trail.

The Depression blunted the momentum with which the Gulf Coast had developed during the 1920s, but in many ways affected the region less drastically than it did other parts of the country. Since it most tragically affected the middle class, wealthy Gulf Coast residents were largely spared. Works Progress Administration (WPA) recovery projects built Fort Myers its waterfront park, yacht basin, and the city's first hospital. The WPA also funded the building of Bayfront Park, a municipal auditorium, and the Lido Beach Casino along the Sarasota Bay coast. And despite serious financial problems, Ringling kept his promises to build bridges and an art museum.

MINA'S MOONLIGHT AT THE EDISON & FORD WINTER ESTATES REFLECTS THE BOTANICAL
FASHION OF THE DAY, AS COMMISSIONED BY EDISON'S WIFE.

By the beginning of World War II, southwest Florida had firmly joined the 20th century, with modern conveniences that made it popular among retirees. New golf courses accommodated active seniors, who often participated in the civic affairs of their adopted communities more vigorously than they had in those of their home-towns. Professional golf tournaments were introduced, first in Naples and then along the coast, making the area golf's winter home. Later, spring baseball camps brought another spectator sport to this land of year-round recreation.

Heat seekers turned their attention to the Gulf Coast's islands and beachfronts. Golfing communities and waterfront resorts swallowed up local farming and fish-ing industries. High-rise condominiums replaced Cracker houses, posh resorts top-pled tourist fishing camps, and the Gulf Coast continued to grow—albeit not quite as loudly or erratically as in pre-Depression times.

Some areas learned to control their growth. Sanibel Island served as a model, taking grip of its fate after a causeway connected it to the mainland in 1963. It incorporated and introduced measures to protect wilderness areas and limit takeover by developers. The southward expansion of Interstate 75 during the 1970s and 1980s changed the Gulf Coast from a series of towns connected by two-lane roads to communities keeping pace with the world. Communication and transportation systems improved. Commercial development spread to the freeway corridor, leaving downtown areas to fade in bygone glory. Light industry and win-ter-weary entrepreneurs relocated. Postsecondary schools worked to prepare local youth for the changing marketplace, while the construction and tourism industries continued to prosper.

The Gulf Coast remained seemingly untouched by the fluctuations of the American economy. Urban blight was a distant reality. Northerners fled to the Gulf Coast to escape overcrowding, smog, and crime. In previous decades this had caused unnatural development in some of the metropolitan areas. The delicate bal-ance of infrastructure, human services, nature, heritage preservation, and the arts spun out of kilter. The coast lived very much in the present, deaf to the demands of residents, both human and otherwise.

Finally, though, the new trends of ecotourism and social responsibility amplified the voices of the few who had screamed over the decades for preservation of the environment against tourism and cultural sterility. While Sarasota and Naples served as cultural prototypes, Sanibel Island and Charlotte County provided environmental models. The 1990s brought an awareness of the frailty of the west coast's islands, wetlands, and shorelines. At the same time, interest in the area's history grew, and movements were launched to preserve architectural treasures that so far had been spared by the bulldozer. Eventually the dipping economic trends of the early 1990s and more recent years affected the Gulf Coast. Construction slowed its racing pulse, and unemployment figures jumped as Northerners continued to arrive, looking for jobs in this legendary land of treasure and youth.

All of these factors have contributed to the current perspective on the Gulf Coast. Economic fluctuations give city planners occasion to pause and rethink. Future growth is being mapped out with more care than ever before. Dying downtown neighborhoods and abandoned Cracker homes are being revitalized, now recognized as an important part of the area's heritage. Government is drawing into its blueprints the need for environmental preservation, cultural enrichment, and historic renovation. A new blight is having a profound effect on the pristine environment of Sanibel Island that once served as an environmental model. Nutrient runoff from sugar farming around Lake Okeechobee, in the center of the state, reaches the region's estuaries via the Caloosahatchee River when flooding occurred as it did in the wake of 2004's hurricanes. The resultant algae killed sea grasses, thereby diminishing fish and bird populations in the sanctuary island and its environs. Grass roots movements struggle to remedy the situation and make plodding headway. They have inspired the state to seek methods to buy out the Okeechobee sugar industry, hoping to reverse the damage before it's too late; hoping that the grain of sand and the mangrove pod from which this land was wrought will once again play a role in its future.

COASTAL CULTURE One of southwest Florida's great contradictions is that it lies more to the north than to the south on the cultural map. North of it or inland, you will find Deep South cookery, clog dancing, bluegrass music, and traditional Southern arts. In southwest Florida, however, Midwestern and Northeastern U.S. influences sway heavy. The only truly indigenous art forms have their origins in the Seminole Indian traditions of weaving, dancing, basket-making, and festivals. Other cultures have arrived through the centuries to create one of the nation's richest melting pots. African Americans, East Indians, Hispanics, Haitians, and Germans have most indelibly enriched the coastal makeup.

The arts have been heavily influenced through the years by the region's winter population. Many Northern-based artists have relocated here, lured by the sea and tropical muses. Others bring with them their appetite for culture, sparking the finest in visual, performing, and culinary arts.

SOUTHWEST FLORIDA ARCHITECTURE Years of simmering together Seminole, Cracker, "Yankee," and Caribbean traditions have yielded a unique southwest Florida style, particularly in architecture and cuisine. If one overall style could be said to represent local architecture, it would have to be Mediterranean—specifically,

Italian and Spanish-mission forms.

Lumped together under the label "Mediterranean Revival," these southern European influences are found primarily in public and commercial buildings constructed during the boom years of the Roaring Twenties. They're revealed in stucco finish, mission arches, red barrel-tile roofing, bell towers, and rounded step facades. Re-revived Mediterranean Postmodern—updated Mediterranean Revival blended with elements of tropical styles adopted from the Cracker era—serves as a popular style for upscale housing developments and commercial enterprises.

Cracker vernacular runs a close architectural second. Pure Cracker style began as folk housing. From the single-pen home—a wood-frame, one-room house featuring a shady veranda, a high tin roof, an elevated floor, and wood siding—grew more sophisticated interpretations of the style. With Gothic touches, Victorian embellishments, Palladian accents, and New England influences, the humble Cracker house evolved into a trendy, modern-day version termed "Old Florida." Boxy and built on stilts, its most distinctive characteristics include a tin roof and wide wraparound porch.

A SEMINOLE TRADEMARK, CHIKEE HUTS HAVE DOTTED THE EVERGLADES LANDSCAPE SINCE THE SEMINOLE WARS FORCED THE NATIVE AMERICANS INTO THE HOSTILE SWAMPLAND.

The latest influence on the Cracker house comes from the Caribbean and the Bahamas via the Keys. Since indigenous West Indian styles are greatly similar to Cracker, especially in their suitability to tropical weather, the convergence was inevitable. The result: sherbet colors and hand-carved fretwork—used as much for ventilation as for decoration—that add charm and whimsy to the basic unit.

Like the Cracker home, the Seminole Indians' chikee, or chickee (pronounced chi-KEY), hut conformed to the tropical climate with its high-peaked roof, wide overhangs, and open sides. Today the thatched roofing that is the chikee's most distinctive feature has become an art form. Still a popular style of housing for the Seminoles and Miccosukees of the Everglades, the chikee has evolved as a trademark of the Gulf Coast watering-hole tradition known as chikee, or tiki, bars.

With the mid-1920s influx of tin-can tourists, the mobile home replaced the Cracker house on the low end of the architectural totem pole. Mobile homes—homes that would "look a lot better as beer cans," according to an old Jimmy Buffett tune—still provide low-cost housing, mostly to part-time winter residents. The brutal winds of Hurricane Charley in 2004 went a long way toward eliminating many of the structures. But despite their unsuitability, many mobile homes still remain.

The concrete-block ranch, a popular residential style of the 1970s, was built to withstand hurricanes. The flood regulations of the 1980s raised these up on pilings; lattice and fretwork added interest. Art deco returned later in the decade, as Miami Beach's Art Deco District attracted attention.

Today's Gulf Coast towns are seasoned with period styles and spiced with contemporary looks that strive for compatibility with nature. Screened porches (often called lanais), windowed "Florida rooms," and lots of sliding doors let the outside in, taking full advantage of the unique, enviable climate and environment.

COASTAL CUISINE As for culinary *richesse,* southwest Florida has wowed hungry visitors since the first Europeans came ashore and discovered nature's abundantly stocked pantry. The seas were teeming with Neptune's bounty, and exotic fruits and vegetables flourished on land. In fact, one former Fort Myers newspaper columnist, Bob Morris, adheres to a theory that this was the original Paradise, and it was a sweet, luscious mango, not an apple, that caused Eve's downfall—hence the fruit's name: "Man! Go!"

Mangoes, though, are not actually native to southwest Florida, but grow plentifully along with other naturalized tropical fruit: bananas, coconuts, pineapples, avocados, sapodillas, carambolas (star fruit), and lychees. Citrus fruit, particularly oranges, is of course the region's most visible and profitable crop. Key lime trees grow mostly in backyards. Practically year-round producers, they are a standard part of any good Florida cook's landscaping scheme. Here on the Gulf Coast, as in the Florida Keys, where the tree got its name and fame, key lime pie is a culinary paradigm, and each restaurant claims to make the best. In the finest restaurants with the most extravagant dessert menus, key lime pie inevitably outsells the rest. The classic recipe, created by Florida cooks before refrigeration, uses canned sweetened and condensed milk and is elegant in its simplicity. The most important factor is the freshness of the limes—sometimes a problem for restaurants since the fruit does not lend itself to commercial farming. One sure sign of an inauthentic version is the color green. Key limes turn yellow when ripe and, unless the cook adds food coloring, should impart a buttery hue to the pie.

Historically, crop farming has provided coastal residents with economic sustenance. Weather conditions bless farmers with two growing seasons for most ground crops. As land becomes too valuable to farm, agriculture has been pushed inland. Pine Island, known for its tropical fruits, is the region's final bastion of the agricultural tradition.

Seafood is most commonly associated with Gulf Coast cuisine, including some delicacies unique to Florida. Our prize catch, the stone crab (Florida author Marjorie Kinnan Rawlings once described the taste as being "almost as rare as nightingales' tongues"), was discovered as a food source in the Everglades. They are in season from October 15 through May 15, and restaurants serve them hot with drawn butter or cold with tangy mustard sauce. Their aptly named shells are usually precracked to facilitate diners' enjoyment.

The gulf shrimp is an emblem of local cuisine. Look for labels telling you it's "wild shrimp," otherwise you might be buying Asian imports treated with antibiotics and other unregulated additives. Its poorer cousin, the rock shrimp, gets less publicity because of its hard-to-peel shell. More economical and with a flavor and texture akin to lobster, the rock shrimp is certainly worth tasting. Restaurants change their menus—or at least their daily specials—according to what's in season. Grouper, the most versatile food fish in the area, traditionally has been available year-round, but overfishing is limiting its availability. A large and meaty fish, its taste is so mild that you hardly know it's fish. Winter months bring red and yellow-tail snapper—my favorite—to diners' plates. Warmer weather means pompano, cobia, shark, and dolphinfish (also known as mahimahi). Tuna and flounder are caught year-round but sporadically. Some restaurants serve less well-known species, such as triggerfish and catfish, to offset spiraling costs caused by dwindling supplies of the more popular varieties. Fish farming also addresses these shortages. Catfish and a Brazilian fish called tilapia (which tastes similar to snapper) are culti-vated most commonly. Fresh fish from around the world supplement local bounty.

The best Gulf Coast restaurants buy their seafood directly from the docks of local commercial fishermen to ensure the utmost freshness. The traditional style of cooking seafood in Florida is deep-frying. Although constituting a mortal sin in this age of gourmet standards and health awareness, it is a true art when properly exe-cuted. There's a vast difference between what you find in the frozen food depart-ment at the supermarket and what comes hand-breaded, crunchy, and flavor-sealed on your plate at the local fish house.

New Florida style, at the other extreme, has evolved from so-called California, new American, new world, global, and eclectic styles of cuisine. This type also depends on freshness—of all its ingredients. For this reason it uses local produce prepared in global culinary styles. Regional cookery—sometimes termed Floribbean cuisine—prefers tropical foods and ingredients, inspired by the cuisines of New Orleans, Mexico, Cuba, Puerto Rico, Haiti, the Bahamas, Jamaica, and South America. Pacific Rim influences have become prominent in recent years. Depending on the cook, Deep South traditions take their place at the table, too. The outcome of all this blending, at its tamest, merely twists the familiar; at its most adventurous, it can treat your taste buds to a veritable bungee jump.

Between the two extremes of old and new Florida styles, Continental cuisine survives in both classic and reinvented forms. Along with restaurants that serve the finest in French and Italian haute cuisine, you will find others that represent the Gulf Coast's melting pot, with authentic renditions or interpretations of a wide variety of cuisines: Native American, Thai, East Indian, Iranian, German, Irish, Greek, Cuban, Jamaican, Amish, Jewish, Mexican, Puerto Rican, and Peruvian.

In its cuisine and cultural makeup as well as its history, the map of Gulf Coast Florida resembles a patchwork quilt. It blankets its people in warmth, checkers its past with colorful and contrasting patterns, and layers its character with intriguing, international textures.

TRANSPORTATION

The Gulf of Mexico and its mighty rivers and Intracoastal Waterway compose the region's oldest and lowest-maintenance transportation system. From the days when the Calusa paddled the streams and estuaries in dugout canoes, through the romantic steamboat era, and until 1927, when the railroad to Naples was completed, boat travel was the most popular means of getting around. Early homes lined the waterways, and historic houses face the water, not the roads that accommodate modern-day traffic. Even today the Caloosahatchee River, which empties into the sea along the Island Coast and connects to the east coast via canals and Lake Okeechobee, constitutes part of a major intercoastal water route.

The railroad first came to Charlotte County's deepwater port in 1886 and created the town of Punta Gorda—much to the chagrin of Fort Myers's leaders, who had tried for years to persuade company officials to extend their Florida Southern Railroad to the Caloosahatchee River. Instead, an unpopulated location was selected and a fabulous hotel built there, according to the custom of Florida's great railroad builders of the day. Besides transporting wealthy winterers to the nation's southernmost railroad stop, the trains hauled fresh fish, cattle, and produce.

A train nicknamed "Slow and Wobbly" ran between Bradenton and Sarasota from 1892 to 1894. The Seaboard Railroad built a more reliable version to Bradenton in 1902. In 1911 it was extended beyond Venice under the influence of Chicago socialite and major landholder Bertha Palmer. When Palmer named the railway terminus Venice, infuriated residents of the original Venice changed their town's name to Nokomis. Then the Charlotte Harbor and Northern Railway laid track in 1906 to ship phosphate from inland mines to the deep waters of Boca Grande Pass, off Gasparilla Island. Another refined resort came with it.

Fort Myers finally got its first railroad station in 1904. In 1922 the tres-

A GROWING MUSEUM GIVES NEW LIFE TO THE OLD NAPLES DEPOT, WHERE CELEBRITIES DISEMBARKED DURING THE ROARING TWENTIES.

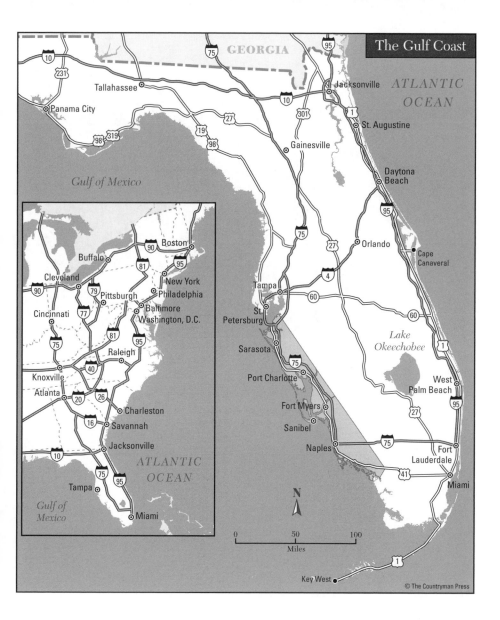

tles reached Bonita Springs and were later extended to Naples and Marco Island. Famous passengers such as movie stars Hedy Lamarr, Greta Garbo, and Gary Cooper rode the rails to vacation at the posh Naples Beach Hotel & Golf Club, one of Florida's first resorts to boast golf greens on the property.

The concept of Tamiami Trail made headway when, in 1923, a group called the Trail Blazers traveled the proposed route that would connect Tampa and Miami. Mules, oxen, and tractors were used to complete that first motorized crossing of the Everglades. Builders lived at the work site, and a whole body of legend grew

TAMIAMI TRAIL BRIDGES CROSS THE WIDE PEACE RIVER FROM PUNTA GORDA TO PORT CHARLOTTE.

up around the monumental task. Progress was slowed by dense jungles, forbidding swampland, devastating heat, and mosquitoes so thick that they covered exposed skin like a buzzing body glove. The project was further hampered by war and depletion of funds.

A special new dredge had to be invented to build the section across the Everglades, and before the trail was paved it had a sand surface. Summer rains caused flooding to the extent that old-timers remember getting out of the car to catch fish in the road while their parents worked to get their vehicle unstuck. Even after the rains subsided, jarring, muck-crusted ruts made the trip less than comfortable.

As the trail's west coast leg inched toward its destination, it changed the communities it penetrated. Thirteen years in the building, the Tamiami Trail was met with euphoria when it was completed in 1928, opening communities to land travel, trade, and tourism. Today, The Trail—also known as US 41—strings together the region's oldest towns and cities, and newer communities have grown up around it.

With the extension of parallel I-75, the Tamiami Trail has lost its role as the sole intercoastal lifeline. Nonetheless, it remains the backbone of the lower west coast. Probing both metropolitan interiors and rural vistas, it provides glimpses of a cross-section of life—as it was and as it is—in southwest Florida.

US 41 runs through the middle of the area covered in this book. At the Gulf Coast's northern and southern extremes, the highway edges close to the shoreline. In midsections it reaches inland to communities built along harbors and rivers.

I-75 draws the eastern boundary for this guide's coverage. The freeway glimpses, at top speed, Gulf Coast life as it zips into the 21st century. Although convenient and free of traffic lights, it misses the character that the more leisurely pace of the Tamiami Trail reveals. However, it does extend the boundaries of US 41's family of communities and create new ones.

more highly charged areas by both major conduits and small feeders. Tampa/St.
Petersburg lies at the Sarasota Bay coast's back door, via US 41, I-75, and I-275.
The Tamiami Trail ends here, but US 41 continues on. The interstate proceeds
north and connects to Orlando and the east coast via I-4. US 19 takes up the
coastal route in St. Petersburg, heading toward Georgia. FL 70 cuts across the
state above Lake Okeechobee to connect the east coast to the Sarasota Bay coast at
Bradenton, and at Sarasota and Punta Gorda via FL 72 and US 17 respectively.
These roads meander into Native American reservation territory, Arcadia's cowboy
country, and the expansive Myakka River State Park. The route runs jaggedly
among the Island Coast, the big lake, and West Palm Beach, following a series of
lazy two- and four-lane roads, including FL 80, US 27, US 441, and US 98.

Alligator Alley (I-75) crosses the Everglades with a certain mystique. Once a
two-lane toll road on which encounters with crossing gators and panthers were
common (tragically, cars inevitably fared better in such encounters), today I-75 has
been widened to four lanes, with underpasses for wildlife. At certain times of the
year, it continues to earn its name, and a sharp eye can spot hundreds of gators
sunning on water banks. But it's still a toll road and still less than user-friendly. Gas
up before you approach: Fuel station/restaurant exit breaks are few and far
between on the two-hour drive before it reaches the east coast at Fort Lauderdale.
US 41 takes you into Miami and branches off into US 1 to the Florida Keys.
By Plane: Two major airports service the lower Gulf Coast: Sarasota-Bradenton
International Airport (SRQ) and Southwest Florida International (RSW) in Fort
Myers. The Sarasota-Bradenton facility gives a proper introduction to the region,
with shark tanks and tropical orchids from local attractions, a two-story waterfall,
and works from its prolific artist community. Southwest Florida recently expanded
from 17 gates to 28, and a new runway is in the planning.

Smaller airports and fields service shuttle, charter, and private planes. The
Charlotte County Airport caters mainly to private craft, but does service two small
charter airlines. North Captiva Island and Everglades City have their own landing
strips for private planes, and seaplane service is available to some islands.

Sarasota-Bradenton International Airport (SRQ) (941-359-5200; www.srq
-airport.com), 6000 Airport Circle, Sarasota 34243. Air Canada, Air France, Air-
Tran, Alitalia, Delta, JetBlue, KLM, US Airways.

Charlotte County Airport (PGD) (941-639-1101 or 888-700-2232; www.flypgd
.com), 28000 A-1 Airport Rd., Punta Gorda 33982. Allegiant, Direct Air.

Southwest Florida International Airport (RSW) (239-768-1000; www.flylcpa
.com), 11000 Terminal Access Rd. #8671, Fort Myers 33913. Air Berlin, Air Canada, AirTran, American, Cape Air, Continental, Delta, Frontier, JetBlue, Midwest,
Northwest/KLM, Southwest, Spirit Airlines, Sun Country, United/United Express,
USA 3000, US Airways, WestJet.

Naples Municipal Airport (APF) (239-643-0733; www.flynaples.com), 160 Aviation Dr. N., Naples 34104. Gulf Coast Airways.

Marco Island Executive Airport (MKY) (239-394-3355; www.colliergov.net),
Collier County Airport Authority, 2005 Mainsail Dr. #1, Naples 34114.

By Bus: Greyhound Lines (www.greyhound.com) Depots are found along the west
coast at Bradenton (941-747-2986; 3028 First St. W.), Sarasota (941-955-5735; 575

N. Washington Blvd.), Port Charlotte (941-627-5836; 900 Kings Hwy.), Punta Gorda (941-875-2781; 26505 N. Jones Loop), Fort Myers (941-334-1011; 2250 Peck St.), and Naples (941-774-5660; 2669 Davis Blvd.).

GETTING AROUND THE GULF COAST *Best Routes by Car:* **The Tamiami Trail** (US 41) runs through the heart of the Gulf Coast's major metropolitan areas and provides north-south passage within and between them.

Sarasota Bay Coast

In Bradenton and Sarasota, US 41 runs along bay shores and converges with US 301, another major trunk road. Principal through streets for east-west traffic in this area are generally those with exits off I-75, north to south: Manatee Avenue (FL 64), Carter Road (FL 70), University Parkway (closest to the Ringling museums), Fruitville Road (closest to downtown and the islands), Bee Ridge Road (closest to Siesta Key), Clark Road (FL 72), and Venice Avenue.

Bradenton's 75th Street West (De Soto Memorial Highway) skims the town's western reaches close to the bay front. At exit 220, FL 64 travels straight into downtown and out to Anna Maria Island. From the south, take exit 217 and follow FL 70 to US 41. Head north on US 41, then turn west on FL 684 (Cortez Road/44th Avenue), which takes you across the south bridge. Both bridges lead to Gulf Drive (FL 789), the island's main road. Longboat Key lies to the south of Anna Maria Island, across a bridge, along Gulf of Mexico Drive. Lido Key is connected to Longboat Key by yet another bridge and also by bridge to the mainland in downtown Sarasota.

Streets hiccup through downtown Sarasota, starting and stopping without warning. Main Street runs east-west, crossed by Orange Avenue, one of the neighborhood's longest streets. Bayfront Drive arcs around the water and skirts a lot of the

EARLY GUESTS TO SANIBEL'S HISTORIC ISLAND INN ARRIVED BY WAGON, AS PORTRAYED IN THIS CIRCA-1910 PHOTO.

town's water-based recreation action. Bahia Vista intersects Orange at its southern extreme and constitutes a major route. To cross town from north to south between US 41 and I-75, take Tuttle Avenue, Beneva Road, McIntosh Road, or Cattlemen Road.

To get to St. Armands Key and Lido Key from downtown Sarasota, follow the signs on Tamiami Trail to cross the Ringling Causeway. To reach Siesta Key from I-75, take exit 205 (Clark Road) or 207 (Bee Ridge Road). From Bee Ridge Road, turn north on US 41 and west on Siesta Drive, which leads to the north bridge. Clark Road (FL 72) becomes Stickney Point Road and crosses the south bridge. On Siesta's north end, Higel Avenue and Ocean Boulevard are the main routes into the shopping district. Beach Road runs gulfside and merges with Midnight Pass Road, which travels to the island's south end, intersecting Stickney Point Road.

Take Venice Avenue off I-75 to get to Venice's beaches and old Mediterranean-influenced neighborhoods. US 41's business route splits from the Tamiami Trail at Venice and takes you to the older part of town. Harbor Drive travels north-south along the beaches. The Esplanade and Tarpon Center Road reach into waterfront communities.

Charlotte Harbor Coast

US 41 heads inland, running within miles of I-75 at some points. In these parts getting to the gulf entails crossing several bodies of water. Most of the routes qualify as back roads and are listed under that heading. A toll bridge links Gasparilla Island (Boca Grande) to the mainland; it costs $4 for cars to cross, $3.50 for motorcycles.

Island Coast

Bonita Beach is touted as the closest sands to I-75 in this area. US 41 again distances itself from its modern counterpart to take you into downtown business districts and past upscale golfing communities. In the area's northern regions, Pine Island Road, FL 78, diverges from the major arteries and crosses North Fort Myers and Cape Coral to reach Pine Island. Del Prado Boulevard and Cape Coral Parkway, which intersect, are Cape Coral's main commercial routes; downtown Cape Coral, which city officials are intent on defining these days, runs along Cape Coral Parkway north of Del Prado. Stringfellow Road, which lies at the end of Pine Island Road, is Pine Island's principal north-south artery.

On the south side of the Caloosahatchee Bridge, Fort Myers's main east-west connectors are Martin Luther King Jr. Boulevard, Colonial Boulevard (which feeds into the Mid-Point Toll Bridge—$2 toll to Cape Coral), College Parkway (which also crosses the river between Fort Myers and Cape Coral at Cape Coral Parkway with a $2 toll), Daniels Parkway/Gladiolus Drive, and Alico Road. The last two are also airport exits. Traveling roughly from north to south, historic and royal-palm-lined McGregor Boulevard (FL 867) follows the river past the old homes that line it. Summerlin Road (FL 869) and Metro Parkway run parallel, to the east. The Tamiami Trail, also parallel and sandwiched between Summerlin Road and Metro Parkway, becomes Cleveland Avenue.

Take McGregor or Summerlin west (they eventually merge) to get to Sanibel and Captiva Islands, land of no traffic lights. There's a $6 toll for crossing the bridge to Sanibel without a transponder gate-pass gizmo; stay in the right lanes unless you have one. The drawbridge was replaced by a high span in 2007. Periwinkle Way is

Sanibel's main drag and connects to Sanibel-Captiva Road via Tarpon Bay Road. Policemen wearing white gloves direct traffic at the main intersections during high-traffic hours. Sanibel-Captiva Road turns into Captiva Drive at the pass between the two islands.

San Carlos Boulevard off Summerlin Road takes you to Fort Myers Beach and the islands that lie to its south along County Route 865 (CR 865), known as Estero Boulevard in Fort Myers Beach, Hickory Boulevard in Bonita Beach. Alico Road, exit 128 off of I-75, takes you to San Carlos Park; Corkscrew Road (FL 850) exit 123, to the south, goes to Estero.

South Coast

Here, US 41 (also known as Ninth Street) closes in on the sea once again as it travels through Naples. At Bonita Springs, Old US 41 branches off toward the town's business district. Bonita Beach Road (exit 116) crosses US 41 to travel to Bonita Beach. I-75 exit 111 gets you to the Vanderbilt Beach/North Naples area via CR 846; exit 107 dumps into Pine Ridge Road, which leads to the north end of Naples. I-75 then swings east, so that CR 951 at exit 101 is closer to downtown Naples in a north-west direction but farther in an east-west direction. Depending on the time of year, you're sometimes better off taking exit 107 to US 41 when approaching from the north, then heading south to get downtown. When coming from the south, take exit 101 and hook up with US 41.

Parallel to US 41 in Naples, major city dissectors include Goodlette-Frank Road (CR 851) and Airport-Pulling Road (FL 31). East-west trunks are, from north to south, the Naples-Immokalee Highway (CR 846) at the north edge of town, Pine Ridge Road (CR 896), Golden Gate Parkway (CR 886), Radio Road (CR 856), and Davis Boulevard (FL 84) in town; and Rattlesnake Hammock Road (CR 864) at the southern extreme.

To get to Marco Island from the north, take CR 951 (interstate exit 101), which will take you to the main high bridge at the island's north end. CR 951 becomes Collier Boulevard and continues through the island's commercial section and along the gulf front. Bald Eagle Drive (CR 953) heads north-south to Olde Marco and midisland. It connects to San Marco Drive (CR 92), which crosses the south bridge. The south-end bridge is a better access if you're approaching from the east along US 41. Turn southwest off US 41 onto CR 92 to cross the south bridge.

FL 29 takes you from US 41 and I-75 to Everglades City. Take a right onto Camellia Street to get to School Drive along the river, lined with old fishing boats, stacks of crab traps, and fish houses. Copeland Avenue crosses the causeway to Chokoloskee Island.

ALTERNATE BACK ROADS AND SCENIC ROUTES This section of Gulf Coast has many scenic back roads that bypass traffic and plunge the traveler into timeless scenes and unique neighborhoods. These routes are especially good to know when you tire of counting out-of-state license plates during rush hour in high season.

Sarasota Bay Coast

Follow the snaking road through a string of barrier islands, from Anna Maria in the north to Bird Key at the end. FL 789 adopts a different name on each island: John Ringling Parkway, Gulf of Mexico Drive, and so on. To avoid US 41 traffic

ED FRANK (SECOND FROM RIGHT) INVENTED THE SWAMP BUGGY, AN AMPHIBIOUS FORM OF TRANSPORTATION ENGINEERED FOR TRAVEL IN THE EVERGLADES. HE POSES HERE IN 1947 WITH HIS BRAINCHILD AND HIS HUNTING BUDDIES.

between downtown Sarasota and Siesta Key, turn west onto Orange Avenue, follow it through scenic neighborhoods along McClellan and Osprey Avenues to Siesta Drive, and then turn west again. FL 758, along Siesta Key, makes a short, beachy bypass between Siesta Drive and Stickney Point Road. The drive through lovely Casey Key begins between Sarasota and Venice at Blackburn Point Road, off US 41, then proceeds south through Nokomis Beach and back to the mainland.

Charlotte Harbor Coast

To reach Englewood from Venice, cross quiet, out-of-the-way Manasota Key along FL 776 through Englewood Beach. Then follow CR 775 and CR 771 back to FL 776 for a scenic drive through the peninsula, separated from the mainland by Charlotte Harbor, or to get to Gasparilla Island. (It costs $4 to cross the causeway onto the island by car, $3.50 by motorcycle.) Park Avenue is the shopper's route in Boca; Gulf Boulevard takes you to the beaches. Staying on 776 takes you more directly to US 41. To skirt US 41's chain-outlet anonymity in the Port Charlotte area, take Collingswood Boulevard off 776 to Edgewater Drive (turn left) and back to 41.

Between Charlotte County and the Island Coast, CR 765, or Burnt Store Road, was once the locals' secret bypass, but it is becoming clogged with developments and the trucks it takes to build them. This connects to FL 78 (Pine Island Road), which leads to Pine Island when taken west or to US 41 and I-75 when followed east. To enter Cape Coral the back way, follow Burnt Store Road through the FL 78 intersection to Veterans Parkway, then to Chiquita Boulevard. Turn right on Chiquita and then left on Cape Coral Parkway.

Island Coast

The back roads along the Island Coast's shores plunge you briefly into the frenzied activity of Fort Myers Beach along FL 865 (San Carlos Boulevard) and CR 865 (Estero Boulevard), then carry you along at a more mellow pace as you cross into Lovers Key and Big and Little Hickory Islands, where CR 865 becomes Hickory Boulevard. Traffic creeps along this two-laner at high-season rush hours. The road returns you via Bonita Beach Road to US 41 at Bonita Springs.

On Sanibel Island you can avoid rush-hour clogs on main street Periwinkle Way by taking "the back way" on Middle Gulf Drive from Rabbit Road in the northwest; Tarpon Bay Road, Casa Ybel Road or Donax Street midisland; or Lindgren Boulevard at the causeway.

South Coast

Gulfshore Boulevard, which stops and starts to make way for Naples's waterways, is the town's most scenic route, skirting beaches and beautiful homes.

South of Naples, CR 951, CR 952, and CR 953 carry you to Isles of Capri, Marco Island, Goodland, and back to US 41 west of the Everglades.

CAR RENTALS Rental agencies with airport offices or shuttle service are listed below:

Alamo: 800-732-3232; www.alamo.com (SRQ, 941-359-5540; RSW, 239-768-2424)

Avis: 800-331-2112; www.avis.com (SRQ, 941-359-5240; RSW, 239-225-2702; APF, 239-643-4013)

Budget: 800-227-4503; www.budget.com (SRQ, 941-359-5360; RSW, 239-225-2802; APF, 239-732-0439)

SUNSET OVER THE NEW SANIBEL ISLAND CAUSEWAY.

Dollar: 800-800-3665; www.dollarcar.com (SRQ, 866-434-2226; APF, 239-213-1400)

Hertz: 800-654-3131; www.hertz.com (SRQ, 941-355-8848; RSW, 239-768-3100; APF, 239-643-1515)

National: 800-227-7368; www.nationalcar.com (SRQ, 941-355-7711; RSW, 239-561-7191)

Thrifty: 800-367-2277; www.thrifty.com (RSW, 239-337-9656; APF, 877-283-0898)

AIRPORT TAXIS/SHUTTLES Some hotels and resorts arrange pickup service to and from the airport. Taxi and limousine companies operate in most areas.

Taxi companies that provide transportation to and from the Bradenton-Sarasota airport include **Diplomat Taxi** (941-355-5155) and **Longboat Limousine** (941-383-1235 or 800-525-4661; www.longboatlimousine.com). **Blue Sky Airport Limo Service** (941-484-9796, 800-637-6358 out-of-state; www.blueskylimo.net) serves passengers arriving at SRQ and RSW. For more companies that service the Bradenton-Sarasota airport, call 941-383-1235 or 800-525-4661.

Boca Grande Limousine (239-964-0455 or 800-771-7433; www.bocagrande limo.com) provides 24-hour connections to all Florida airports. For a more dramatic arrival or departure, call **Boca Grande Seaplane** (941-964-0234 or 800-940-0234). **Charlotte Limousine Service** (800-208-6106 or 941-627-4494; www.charlottelimousine.com) will pick up from and deliver to all airports in the region. **Airport Limo & Car Service** (800-954-9404; www.airportlimoandcar service.com) has a fleet that includes Lincolns and SUVs. Lincoln Town Cars and vans pick you up when you call **Air-Port Shuttles & Transportation** (941-505-5054 or 866-956-5054; www.air-portshuttles.com).

From Southwest Florida International Airport in Fort Myers, **Aaron Airport Transportation** (239-768-1898 or 800-998-1898; www.aarontaxi.com) makes pick-ups and deliveries throughout the region. Or call **AAA Airport Transportation** (800-872-2711). **Pine Island Taxi** (239-283-7777) provides 24-hour service anywhere with advance notice.

In the south coast area, call **Naples Transportation Shuttle** (239-262-3006; www.experience-naples.com). Its new airport-to-hotel shuttle service is available for $30 per person. There's also **Checker Cab** (239-455-5555), **Naples Taxi** (239-643-2148), or, on Marco Island, **Classic Transportation** (239-394-1888 or 800-553-8294; www.classicluxurytransportation.com).

By Bus: The Sarasota Bay coast boasts dependable public transportation, with discounts for schoolchildren and seniors. Buses run every day but Sunday, 6 AM to 6 PM. A downtown trolley runs around Sarasota and St. Armands Circle. For route information, call Sarasota County Area Transit (SCAT) (941-861-1234; www.sgov .net/SCAT) or Manatee County Transit (MCAT) (941-747-8621; www.mymanatee .org/mcat).

On the Island Coast, city buses follow routes around Fort Myers, Cape Coral, and south Fort Myers. Call **Lee Tran** (239-533-8726; www.leetran.com) for schedules and information about trolley rides to and around Fort Myers Beach's beach accesses, including Lovers Key.

The **Naples Trolley** (239-262-7300; www.naplestrolleytours.com) conducts sight-seeing and shopping tours in the Naples area, with 23 scheduled stops.

The narrated **Trolley Tours of Marco Island** (239-394-1600) make 15 stops where you can deboard and reboard Monday–Saturday. **Collier Area Transit (CAT)** (239-596-7777; www.colliergov.net) travels throughout Naples and Marco Island.

By Train: The Seminole Gulf Railway (239-275-8487 or 800-SEM-GULF; www .semgulf.com), stationed at Colonial Boulevard and Metro Parkway in Fort Myers, does dinner trips, murder mystery tours, and other excursions throughout the area.

By Water: Water no longer provides functional transportation routes on the Gulf Coast, except to the unbridged islands. Today boat travel is mostly recreational. The region boasts two trademark water vessels: the noisy, power-driven airboat, designed especially for the shallow waters of the Everglades, and the swamp buggy, an all-terrain vehicle built to carry two to 20 passengers and travel on fat tire treads. In addition, pontoon boats offer a more conventional way to explore the Everglades and coastal shallows.

Numerous sight-seeing tours and charters originate daily at marinas and resorts. Some specialize in fishing, others in shelling or birding. Many include lunch at an exotic island restaurant, while a few serve meals on-board. All cater to the sight-seer. Most tour operators are knowledgeable about the sights and history of local waterways. These are all listed in the "To Do" section of each chapter.

By Other Means: **Billy's Bikes/Segway of Sanibel** (239-472-3620; www.billys rentals.com), 1470 Periwinkle Way, Sanibel Island. Two-hour tours of Sanibel's East End.

The **Naples Horse and Carriage Company** (239-649-1210), 5191 Coral Wood Drive, Naples. Provides evening tours of Old Naples, the beaches, and the fishing pier in season.

Segway of Naples (239-262-7300; www.experience-naples.com), 1010 Sixth Ave. S., Naples. Two-hour guided tours of historic downtown Naples three times daily.

Sarasota Bay Coast

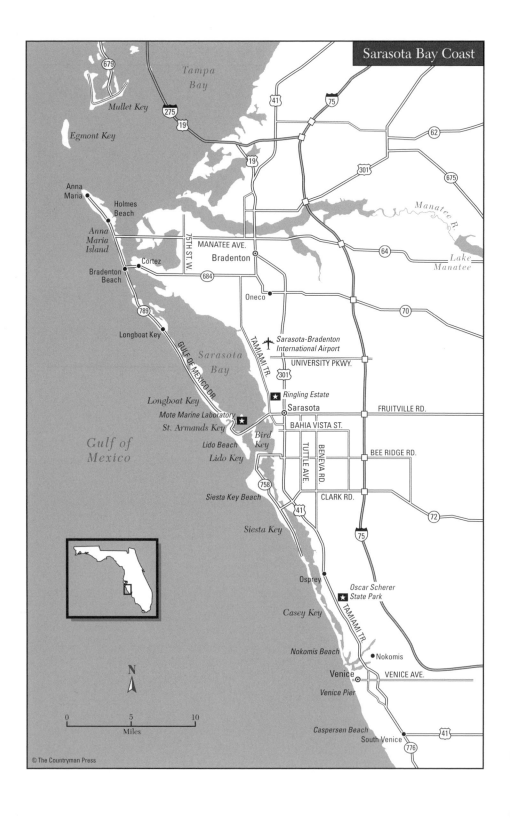

Sarasota Bay Coast

SARASOTA BAY COAST

SEASHORE SOPHISTICATE

The cities of Bradenton and Sarasota dominate the Sarasota Bay coast, an expanse of metropolitan sprawl barricaded behind sybaritic, beach-centric islands. History and a heritage of high culture add dimension to this world of sand and city streets.

Bradenton draws much of its historical identity from the supposed landing of Hernando de Soto on local shores. Old Hernando—scoundrel and sadist though he turned out to be—gives the town a reason to celebrate its heritage each year when it re-enacts his momentous arrival at a national park that honors the Indian-slaying conquistador.

Later in the history of Bradenton and the surrounding mainland communities, two pioneering influences dictated a low-key attitude and light development. The first, the wealthy plantation owners of the 1840s, ranked Manatee County as the largest area in the state for sugar and molasses production. Sugar's aristocratic families set the social standards of the town until the Civil War turned the sweetly lucrative industry sour. The second, 19th-century land speculators, exploited Florida's Swamp Act, which had a counterproductive, stunting effect on the area's development. By having homestead properties fraudulently declared wetlands, they prevented agricultural expansion and delayed its by-product, the building of railroads.

Wealthy social godparents guided Sarasota's early development. Mrs. Potter (Bertha Honore) Palmer, known as "queen of Chicago society," settled south of town in 1910, which eventually drew John Ringling and his circus to Sarasota. Though lesser known today, Mrs. Palmer exerted an influence equal to Ringling's in attracting attention to the area around Sarasota Bay. Sarasota continues to grow as a wealth-conscious town—not too big, not too small, just right. In past years, growth has been upward, as the downtown bayside skyline fills in with luxury condo and resort towers, the Ritz-Carlton and Renaissance among them. In 2006, the National Civic League included Sarasota County among its "All-American County" designations.

Most of **Bradenton's** modern growth has occurred since 1970, when tourism and shipping into deepwater Port Manatee became major income sources. Today, downtown waterfront restoration projects and a new artists' colony make Bradenton a vital city textured with an interesting past.

Across the Manatee River, preservation of the Gamble Plantation and original village structures, along with the development of long-sleepy, agriculturally driven **Palmetto,** extends Bradenton-area visitors' options to include more historic attractions and riverfront activity.

The village of **Cortez** lies southwest of Bradenton and several eras to the past. Fishing made this peninsular community, and fishing remains its livelihood. Along its southern waterfront, a working fishing operation and its toilers reside in a time-stilled setting.

Fishing, resorts, and heterogeneous neighborhoods mark the three incorporated towns of **Anna Maria Island: Anna Maria, Holmes Beach,** and **Bradenton Beach.** The first Anna Maria Island settlers of record, George Emerson Bean and his family, arrived around 1890. He developed the island in the early 1900s for tourists, who came by boat at the Anna Maria city pier. In 1921 the first bridge to the island was built from Cortez.

Longboat Key, to the south of Anna Maria Island, was mentioned often on the maps and journals of early Spanish explorers. It supposedly got its name from the longboats that Hernando de Soto's scouting party used to come ashore. Aside from one tucked-away village with a salty, local flavor, Longboat Key is known for its prim-and-properness. A series of seven historic markers relate Longboat Key's history as a 16th-century destination for Timucuan canoes and Spanish galleons, a World War II bombing target, and a major shipping port destroyed by the hurricane of 1921.

THE TOWN THE CIRCUS BUILT

The circus comes as close to being the world in microcosm as anything I know; in a way it puts all the rest of show business in the shade. Its magic is universal and complex.

—E. B. White, Ring of Times, 1956

Legend has it that Bird Key and St. Armands Key, two of Sarasota's barrier islands, became John Ringling's possessions in a poker game. Tales of the circus master's influence on the area's development have grown to mythic proportions: elephants that built bridges, midgets who built fortunes, and an eccentric who built himself an Italian palace. However true the legends, during the 20 years after John Ringling came to Sarasota to house his circus here in wintertime, he demonstrated a three-ring influence over the city and its barrier islands.

After falling in love with the fledgling mainland village and purchasing real estate offshore, Ringling erected his lavish mansion, Cà d'Zan ("House of John" in Italian), modeled after a Venetian palazzo. He also began the construction of a causeway to Lido Key by filling and dredging, and he

OLD FISHING TRADITIONS ENDURE IN THE VILLAGE OF CORTEZ.

Remote **Siesta Key** resisted settlement until the turn of the 20th century, when a hotel launched the island's reputation as a restful place. A bridge built in 1917 finally brought permanent residents to the island. Siesta Key has historically attracted creative types. One of its best-known citizens was prolific writer John D. MacDonald, most famous for his Travis McGee detective novels. It is believed that while living on Siesta Key he wrote more than 70 novels. Witty essayist E. B.

dreamed of a city park and a shoppers' haven on St. Armands Key. For Longboat Key he envisioned a world-class hotel. With unbridled fervor he set out during his worldwide travels to acquire a fine collection of Baroque art for public display in a museum.

The dreams Ringling failed to realize before he died in 1936 were not abandoned. The causeway was completed and donated to the state. St. Armands Circle today is famed for its shops. The steel skeleton of what was to be the world's finest hotel sat rusting on Longboat Key for years until it was reborn as a modern resort. The John and Mable Ringling Museum of Art encompasses acres of bayside estate, and its collection and grounds include Baroque statuary, original Rubens masterpieces, a rose garden, the restored Venetian Gothic mansion Cà d'Zan, circus museums, and an antique Italian theater.

Aside from John Ringling's concrete legacy to Sarasota, he bequeathed an undying commitment to beauty, fantasy, art, and showmanship. The circus remains an important industry in Sarasota—in fact, at the high school, circus is an extracurricular activity, like football. Theaters and galleries thrive, thanks to Ringling's patronage of the arts. Without his influence, the entire coast might well have remained a cultural frontier for many more decades.

White was a regular visitor around the 1940s. Pulitzer Prize–winning author MacKinlay Kantor and late abstractionist Syd Solomon also settled on the island, and Pulitzer Prize–winning cartoonist Mike Peters lived there for many years. Other cartoonists and artists have also found the area conducive to creativity. *Hagar the Horrible's* Dik Browne made his home in the area until his death in 1989; now his son Chris has moved in. *Garfield's* Jim Davis has wintered on Longboat Key. Surrealist Jimmy Ernst, son of Dada master Max Ernst, spent much time on Casey Key during his life. Artist Thornton Utz and jazz notable Jerry Jerome have also lived in the area.

The Webb family first arrived in the Sarasota area in 1867 to plant the seed for a town they named **Osprey** 17 years later. Here is where Bertha Honore Palmer headquartered when she arrived in 1910.

The original village of **Venice** sat where Nokomis does today. Venice moved south and seaward to its current location after the railroad bypassed it in 1922. Actually an island separated from the mainland by narrow waterways, the original Venice reflects the influence of John Ringling and visionary urban planner John Nolen, who was hired by the Brotherhood of Locomotive Engineers union after it purchased much of the town in the 1920s.

Casey Key was built on the principle that island real estate should be reserved for the well-to-do. This has kept it exclusive and lightly developed, particularly at its north end, where a narrow road snakes through a forest of mansions à la Palm Beach. Nokomis Beach, at the southern end, is a more casual, beachy, fishing-oriented resort area.

The Sarasota area has conveniently organized its environmental and historical attractions on a *Gulf Coast Heritage Trail* map, available at visitor information centers around town or by calling 941-359-5841.

✳ To See

Culture arrived on the Sarasota Bay coast with the early settlers of wealth and means. Eager at first to escape metropolitan ways for the simplicity of life on the beach, they eventually craved access to theater and fine arts, and so ensured the existence of both.

Sarasota benefited most from the generous cultural endowment of the Ringling brothers. Not only did the Ringlings bring circus magic to a quiet frontier town, they also exposed the pioneers to the wonders of Gilded Age European art and architecture. In their wake they left a spirit that is still palpable and entirely unique to Southwest Florida. Art schools and theater groups in Sarasota breed a freshness, vitality, daring, and avant-garde attitude that is unusual for a town of this size. Siesta Key, especially, has an atmosphere that has attracted writers, artists, actors, and cartoonists since folks began settling there.

Sarasota's cultural heritage began with an influx of Scottish settlers at the turn of the century. Now widely varied, its population includes a colony of Amish/Mennonite residents in a district known as Pinecraft, around Bahia Vista Street and Beneva Road. Here you'll see long-bearded men driving tractors or riding bikes down the streets, a Mennonite church, simple homes, a neighborhood park, and an Amish restaurant or two. The historic African American district is known as Rosemary District and lies between US 41 and US 301 and between 10th and Myrtle Streets.

ARCHITECTURE In the Bradenton area, the Greek Revival–style plantation house has left its mark. The best example of this style survives grandly at ❂ Gamble Plantation (see "Historic Sites"). Pioneer styles are preserved at the Manatee Historical Village, which includes a Cracker Gothic farmhouse, a one-room schoolhouse, and an early brick store. In downtown Bradenton you'll find a Mediterranean influence in commercial buildings such as the South Florida Museum. Old Florida–Victorian style survives in the homes of neighborhoods around downtown.

On **Longboat Key,** resorts and mansions are modern and ostentatious. In the village once known as Longbeach, one finds a return to comfortable, older styles and a bit of New England charm.

Sarasota's downtown and bay areas hold a smorgasbord of old European styles, from the lavish, Italian-inspired ❂ **Cà d'Zan** at the Ringling Estate to the recently renovated and expanded ❂ **Sarasota Opera House** downtown. Fine examples of old residential architecture are found on the fringes of the downtown area. In contrast, the Frank Lloyd Wright Foundation's ❂ **Van Wezel Performing Arts Hall** makes a big-purple-shell statement on the bay shoreline.

In the 1950s Sarasota revolutionized local architecture by developing a contemporary style suitable to the environment. Examples of the Sarasota School of Architecture are spread throughout the area. Often overlooked, **Venice** houses many architectural treasures created in the 1920s, when the Brotherhood of Locomotive Engineers selected it as a retirement center and subsequently built a model city in northern Italian style. Two shining examples of this style are the **Park Place Nursing Home**—originally the Hotel Venice—at Tampa Avenue and Nassau Street, and the nearby **Venice Mall,** once the San Marco Hotel, later the Kentucky Military Institute. The length of **West Venice Avenue** reveals stunning shops and homes in the prevailing Mediterranean Revival style, as does the **Venezia Park** neighborhood along nearby Nassau Street. You'll find architectural treasures throughout the city, which strives to preserve its treasures.

CINEMA **AMC 12 Theatres at Westfield Sarasota Square** (941-922-9609; westfield.com/Sarasota), 8201 S. Tamiami Trail, at Beneva Rd., Sarasota.

Burns Court Cinemas (941-955-3456; www.filmsociety.org), 506 Burns Ln., Sarasota. A bright pink movie theater showing art, foreign, and other mainstream and out-of-the-mainstream films on three screens.

Hollywood Stadium 20 (941-365-2000; www.regalcinemas.com), 1993 Main St. at Hwy. 301, Sarasota. State-of-the-art theaters with stadium seating and surround-sound stereo.

Regal Oakmont 8 (941-795-4106; www.regalcinemas.com), 4801 Cortez Rd. W., Bradenton.

In addition to run-of-the-mill movie theaters, Sarasota is also a hotbed for film, with its celebrated film festivals, alternative cinema, and ideal locations for filming.

Sarasota Film Society (941-364-8662, box office: 941-955-FILM; www.filmsociety.org), Burns Court Cinemas, 506 Burns Ln., Sarasota; P.O. Box 3378, Sarasota 34230) This group is devoted to screening quality international films, both first-run and classic, year-round. It sponsors the Cine-World Film Festival (see "Special Events" at the end of this chapter).

DANCE American International Dance Centre (941-955-8363), 556 S. Pineapple Ave., Sarasota. Ballroom dancing instruction and competition for adults and children.

Gotta Dance Studio (941-486-0326; www.gottadancestudio.net), 303 Tamiami Trail S., Nokomis. Classes in tango, children's ballroom, and more for beginners and experienced dancers.

Sarasota Ballet (941-351-8000 or 800-361-8388; www.sarasotaballet.org), 5555 N. Tamiami Trail, Sarasota. Classic and interpretative dance performances are staged by professionals at the FSU Center for the Performing Arts, Sarasota Opera House, and Van Wezel Performing Arts Center, from October to April.

Sarasota Dance Club (941-955-2224; www.sarasotadanceclub.com), 1646 10th Way, Sarasota. Dancing and classes from swing to salsa

GARDENS Historic Spanish Point (941-966-5214; www.historicspanishpoint .org), 337 N. Tamiami Trail, P.O. Box 846, Osprey. This multiera historic attraction (see "Historic Homes & Sites," below) features the ornamental and native gardens built by Sarasota matriarch Bertha Honore Palmer in the 1910s. The Duchene Lawn, the most dramatic, is lined with towering palms and holds a Greek-column portal that once framed a view of the sea. To create the lovely jungle walk, Mrs. Palmer built a miniature aqueduct system. A sunken garden and pergola, fern walk, and ornamental pond also provide oases of lush respite along the path at this 30-acre site. Open Monday–Saturday 9–5., Sunday noon–5. Admission: $10 adults, $8 seniors, $5 children ages 5–12. Docent tram tours $3 extra each.

Marie Selby Botanical Gardens (941-366-5731; www.selby.org), 900 S. Palm Ave., Sarasota. This 1920s residence on Sarasota Bay occupies 9.5 acres of gardens that wow plant-lovers with plots of palm, bamboo, hibiscus, tropical food plants, herbs, and other exotic flora. Selby is world renowned for its collection of more than 6,000 orchids and 3,600 bromeliads in a lush rainforest setting of bamboo, a koi pond, and rare tropical plants. Artsy interpretative signage tells the different

MARIE SELBY GARDENS SHOWS OFF MORE THAN 5,000 ORCHIDS IN ITS LUSH SETTING.

plants' stories, and a Children's Rainforest with a canopy walk and treehouse is forthcoming. Delightful shops and a café add to the natural pleasures. Open daily 10–5. Admission: $17 adults, $6 children ages 6–11, free for children ages 5 and younger.

Ringling Estate Rose Garden and Grounds (941-355-5101; www.ringling.org), 5401 Bay Shore Rd., on the Ringling Estate, Sarasota. Mammoth banyan trees (gifts from Thomas Edison, who had an estate in Fort Myers), a showy poinciana, statuesque royal palms, and a 1,200-bush rose garden planted in 1913 are the centerpieces of the lovely bayfront Ringling Estate. Near Cà d'Zan, family graves are situated in the Secret Garden, rediscovered 25 years ago and recently rededicated. The Dwarf Garden lies between the art museum and the visitors center. Open daily 10–5:30. Admission: free with admission to the Ringling complex.

✍ **Sarasota Jungle Gardens** (941-355-5305 or 877-861-6547; www.sarasota junglegardens.com), 3701 Bayshore Rd., Sarasota. Although this is largely a kiddie attraction, plant-lovers will enjoy the botanical gardens and cool, tropical jungle. Winding paved paths lead easily through the grounds' more than 10 acres, a hundred varieties of palms, and countless species of indigenous and exotic flora, all identified. Private nooks, arbored benches, and bubbling brooks make this a lovely spot for quiet reflection, especially in the early morning before the throngs arrive. Exotic birds and other attractions are gravy for the connoisseur of nature. (See "Kids' Stuff" in this section.) Snack bar and gift shop. Open daily 9–5. Admission: $15 adults, $14 seniors, $10 children ages 3–12.

HISTORIC HOMES & SITES Braden Castle Ruins, Braden Castle Dr. off 27th St. E. and FL 64, Bradenton. At the juncture of the Manatee and Braden Rivers, antebellum memories crumble gracefully in a setting recognized by the National Register of Historic Sites. Just short of spectacular, the plantation house ruins are surrounded by chain-link fences and posted with KEEP OUT, DANGER signs. They hide at the center of a historic retirement community in a riverside park that's not easy to find. A marker tells the story of Dr. Joseph Addison Braden from Virginia and his ill-fated, eponymous plantation. Open daily sunrise to sunset. Free admission.

Cà d'Zan (941-355-5101; www.ringling.org), 5401 Bay Shore Rd., on the Ringling Estate, Sarasota. A new visitors center with gift shop, restored 18th-century European theater, and restaurant welcomes you to the Ringling complex, which also contains the centerpiece art museum, a circus museum, miniature circus exhibit building, gardens, and John Ringling's fabulous *palazzo* Cà d'Zan. The 32-room showpiece is a gem of Gilded Age glory. Visitors can take a self-guided tour of the first floor or sign up for the $5 guided tour of the first two floors. For $20, you can get the private tour of upper floors and the tower. Using the Doges Palace in Venice as a model, circus king John Ringling spared no expense building this monument to success and overindulgence in the 1920s. He imported styles, materials, and pieces from Italy, France, and elsewhere around the world to embellish his eponymous (in Italian dialect) "House of John." Baroque, Gothic, and Renaissance elements, marble, colored tiles, and jesterlike, multicolor-tinted leaded windows contribute to a breathtaking, ornate Roaring Twenties opulence in the $1.5 million (nearly $17 million in today's currency) mansion on the bay at the John and Mable Ringling Museum of Art (see "Visual Arts Centers & Resources," below). Open daily 10–5:30. Admission: $25 adults, $20 seniors, $10 students and Florida teachers with ID, free for children under age 5; covers admission to all Ringling attractions.

Cortez Village, Cortez Rd. and 123rd St., Bradenton. Vital remnants of an 1880s fishing village include old tin-roofed fish houses, boat works, and seafood plants. Exhibits and painted murals throughout the salty district describe local culture and environmental practices. A new maritime museum complex (see "Museums") is developing to preserve the heritage of this community—once the largest fishing center on Florida's West Coast.

✪ ✿ ♪ **De Soto National Memorial** (941-792-0458; www.nps.gov/deso), 75th St. N.W., Bradenton. Somewhat off the beaten path, this is a place where you can imagine yourself back in the 16th century with conquistadores in heavy armor try-ing to survive among irate Native Americans, mosquitoes, and sweltering heat. Engraved plaques, a re-created Amerindian village and Spanish camp, and the Memorial Trail tell the story of Hernando de Soto's life and adventures here, where supposedly he first breached the shores of the Florida mainland to begin his heroic trek to the Mississippi River. A visitors center holds artifacts and shells, a 22-minute video presentation, and helmets and armor kids can try out. In the win-ter, rangers and volunteers dress up and play the parts of 16th-century inhabitants, demonstrating weaponry and methods of food preparation. Right outside the park's gates, Riverview Pointe Trail takes hikers to historic sites along the De Soto Expe-dition Trail. Visitors center open daily 9–5; park open daily sunrise to sunset. Free admission.

Downtown Bradenton, Main St. and Manatee Ave. (FL 64). Old Main Street and the city yacht basin are the historic downtown district's backbone. Because the area is compact, it's easy to walk and experience the old architecture, a fine muse-um, an intimate theater, park benches, sidewalk eateries, antique stores, pubs, and brick-paved crosswalks. Locals are trying hard to pump new life into a river town that died with the advent of the automobile. A riverwalk takes strollers along the Manatee River. Visit the shops on Main Street and have lunch, then stroll around nearby Point Pleasant for a taste of Bradenton's oak-canopied homeyness and her-itage. Every Saturday, October–May, visit the farmer's market.

Gamble Plantation Historic State Park (941-723-4536; www.floridastateparks .org/gambleplantation), 3708 Patten Ave., US 301 near I-75, exit 224, Ellenton. Major Robert Gamble, originally from Scotland, learned about sugar planting in Virginia and Tallahassee before he moved to the Manatee River. He eventually cleared 1,500 acres of jungle using slave labor and built a Greek Revival–style home. He constructed the mansion's crowning touch—18 Greek columns—with a mortar, known as tabby, made of crushed and burned seashells. The spacious (by the time's standards) palace was inhabited by bachelor Gamble alone, but served as the area's social hub until hurricane and frost damage and market losses forced the major to sell it in 1856. In 1925 the United Daughters of the Confederacy res-cued the mansion from decades of neglect. The site was declared a Confederate shrine for its role in sheltering Judah P. Benjamin, Confederate secretary of state, when he fled for his life after the Civil War. The United Daughters donated the monument to the state a couple of years later. Visitors can see the inside of the home only by a tour, which takes less than an hour. The two floors contain period furnishings and housewares, which the park ranger explains in lively, interesting

ROBERT GAMBLE'S GREEK REVIVAL PLANTATION HOME REFLECTED HIS VIRGINIA ORIGINS.

dialogue. You'll learn, for example, how such expressions as "hush puppy," "sleep tight," and "pop goes the weasel" came to be, and about the lives of 19th-century plantation owners and slaves. Note that the home is not air-conditioned, and can get extremely warm in the summer. The museum in the visitors center tells the plantation's story through the eras. A picnic shelter accommodates lunchers. Visitors center open 9–5; tours depart at 9:30, 10:30, 1, 2, 3, and 4; closed Tuesday and Wednesday. Admission: mansion tour, $6 adults, $4 children ages 6–12. Free admission to visitors center museum.

✪ ✿ **Historic Spanish Point** (941-966-5214; www.historicspanishpoint.org), 337 N. Tamiami Trail, Osprey. This historic site spans multiple eras of the region's past—from 2150 B.C. through 1918. Its importance lies not only in its historical aspects, but also in its environmental and archaeological significance. Assembled on the 30-acre Little Sarasota Bay estate, once owned by socialite Bertha Palmer, are prehistoric Indian burial grounds, a cutaway of a shell midden mound, the relocated homestead and family chapel of the pioneering Webb dynasty, Mrs. Palmer's restored gardens (see "Gardens" in this section), and a late Victorian pioneer home. Local actors give living-history performances on Saturdays and Sundays in the winter. Guided tours and docent-narrated tram rides are available; reserve ahead for both. Another tip: Bring mosquito repellent in warm weather. Open 9–5 Monday–Saturday, noon–5 Sunday. Admission: $10 adults, $8 seniors, $5 children ages 5–12. Docent tram tours $3 extra each.

♞ ✿ **Manatee Village Historical Park** (941-749-7165; www.manateeclerk.com/ ClerkServices/HisVill/village.htm), 1404 Manatee Ave. E., Bradenton. Several buildings with local historical significance have been restored and moved to a pleasant, oak-shaded park strongly representative of Bradenton's old wooded and winding neighborhoods. The County Courthouse, completed in 1860, is the oldest and also the oldest remaining building constructed as a county courthouse in

THE STEPHENS HOUSE REPRESENTS PIONEER HOME LIFE AT MANATEE VILLAGE HISTORICAL PARK.

Florida. Others include a circa-1889 church (the oldest congregation south of Tampa), a Cracker farmhouse, a one-room schoolhouse, a smokehouse, and a brick general store from the early 19th century. A museum of artifacts, photographs, and period furnished rooms is located in the general store. The Cracker-Gothic Stephens House is stocked with preserves, period kitchen items, furniture, and farm implements. Bat Fogarty Boat Works reflects Bradenton's boatbuilding heritage. Kids can climb aboard "Old Cabbage Head," a historic timber-hauling locomotive. The staff sometimes wears historically accurate dress. Across the street lies the Manatee Burying Ground, which dates from 1850. All in all, the park is a romantic site, grossly underrated and lightly visited. Open: 9–4:30 weekdays, 9-4 second and fourth Saturday of each month. Admission: Suggested donation $5 for adults, $4 for seniors, $3 for students.

Palmetto Historical Park (941-723-4991; www.manateeclerk.com/Clerk Services/HisVill/village.htm), 515 10th Ave. W., Palmetto. Check in at the circa-1914 Carnegie Library to visit historic museum exhibits and to gain admission to some of the village's other buildings, including a circa-1880 post office, a wedding chapel that is a composite of three Palmetto historic churches, a circa-1920 one-room schoolhouse, and the Cypress House Museum, which is devoted to military artifacts. Within the park, the Manatee County Agricultural Museum & Hall of Fame is a staffed facility housed in a barnlike structure; it holds hands-on and other displays demonstrating the importance of farming to Manatee County past and present. Open 10–noon and 1–4 Tuesday–Friday, the first and third Saturday of the month, and Monday by appointment. Free admission.

Sarasota Circus Heritage Trail (www.sarasotacircushistory.com), throughout Sarasota County. This Web site and trail map take visitors through the county's Big Top past via 10 sites, including "the church the circus built" (St. Martha's Catholic Church at 200 N. Orange Ave. in Sarasota), the Circus Ring of Fame at St. Armands Circle, the Ringling Estates complex, the home of Charles and Edith Ringling at New College of Florida (5800 Bayshore Rd. in Sarasota), the Sailor Circus Big Top, Venice's Circus Bridge, and a statue of famed animal trainer Gunther Gebel-Williams at the historic Train Depot in Venice (see below).

Venice Depot (941-412-0151; www.venicehistory.com), E. Venice and Seaboard Aves. Set in Railroad Park under the Business 41 bridge, this circa-1927 depot, the last remaining in the county, conducts tours of the Mediterranean Revival building in season. The depot has local significance because the Brotherhood of Locomotive Engineers owned much of Venice in the 1920s, and in the 1960s, when Ringling headquarters moved here, the Seaboard Railroad transported the circus. In the park, you can also visit the statue of circus trainer Gunther Gebel-Williams and a Seaboard railroad car. The depot hosts special events such as country dancing every Monday 7–9 (941-925-2242). Open by tour only, 10–3 Monday, Wednesday and Friday, November–April. Free admission; donations accepted.

KIDS' STUFF ✿ **Bayfront Park,** downtown Sarasota. Toddlers especially love the shallow pool, with its squirting fountains and sculptures of frogs, manatees, turtles, gators, and fish that they can climb. It's a good place for strolling, people-watching from a park bench, jogging, and shopping for boat charters. There's a small, inexpensive restaurant and water-sports concession within. Street sculpture exhibitions are year-round and feature artists from around the world. Free.

✿ **The Children's Garden** (941-330-1711; www.sarasotachildrensgarden.com), 1670 10th Way, Sarasota. This magical fantasy, an especially popular place for parties, uses recycled products and old-fashioned concepts to entertain children. Kids can dress up in their choice from a roomful of costumes; take the yellow brick road to play gardens where pirate ships, dragons, and an octopus lurk; find their way through the maze; visit the butterfly garden; and run, climb, jump, and make-believe. Open 10–5 daily. Admission: $10 adults, $9 seniors, $5 children ages 3–12.

✪ ✿ **G. Wiz** (941-309-4949; www.gwiz.org), 1001 Boulevard of the Arts, Selby Library Building, Sarasota. Its name about sums it up, as does "wow!" All shiny and high-tech, it offers hours of enrichment and entertainment in an uncrowded, gallerylike, glass geodesic structure. The state-of-the-art outdoor playground is free and includes much more than mere swings and slides. Inside, theme areas explore various scientific and artistic phenomena. Kids love to make timed dashes against one another and the jump measurer. EcoZone has live snakes, turtles, lizards, and tarantulas. We like the animation workstations best. Here kids can pose and click action figures and other toys one frame at a time to create a short film. For constructive play, this is the best place around to take the kids. Don't forget to stop in the gift shop (as if the kids would let you) for educational playthings. Open 10–5 Monday– Saturday, noon–5 Sunday. Admission: $9 adults, $8 seniors, $6 children ages 3–18.

✿ **Sarasota Jungle Gardens** (941-355-5305 or 877-861-6547; www.sarasotajungle gardens.com), 3701 Bayshore Rd., Sarasota. A birds-of-prey exhibit and show, reptile and rainforest-bird shows (starring *Ed Sullivan Show* star Frosty), a Meet the Keeper program, free-strolling flamingos you can hand-feed, a playground with a jungle theme, a bird posing area, pony rides ($3 each, $8 with photo, daily 11–2), monkeys, swans, wallabies, and other live animals and feathered friends make this one of the area's favorite children's attractions. Its peaceful, junglelike gardens appeal to others. (See "Gardens" in this section.) Open daily 9–5. Admission: $15 adults, $14 seniors, $10 children ages 3–12.

✿ **South Florida Museum & Bishop Planetarium** (941-746-4131; www.south floridamuseum.org), 201 10th St. W., Bradenton. This downtown museum has a designated Discovery Place for kids' hands-on enjoyment. In the regular museum, youngsters especially love the prehistoric skeleton casts, live manatees, and the drawers of artifacts in the "visible storage" area. Special first Saturday programs keep the museum open until 9 pm with manatee presentations, crafts, special tours, and planetarium shows. Open January–April, July, 10–5 Monday–Saturday, noon–5 Sunday; closed Monday during all other months. Admission: $15.95 adults, $13.95 seniors, $11.95 children ages 4–12. Half-price admission Saturday after 4.

✒ **Venice Little Theatre's Theatre for Young People** (941-488-1115; www .venicestage.com), 140 W. Tampa Ave., Venice. One of the most successful non-profit community theaters in the United States, Venice Little Theatre hosts off-season summer theatrical instruction (call 941-486-8679) and musical performances for youngsters October–May.

MUSEUMS During the month of September, the Sarasota area promotes its 30 Days of Discovery season (www.30daysofdiscovery.com), when local museums offer "buy one get one free" admission. (For art museums, see "Visual Arts Centers & Resources.")

✪ **Anna Maria Island Historical Museum** (941-778-0492; www.amihs.org), 402 Pine Ave., Anna Maria. A homey little museum inside a 1920s icehouse holds a heartwarming wealth of photos, maps, records, books, a shell collection, a logger-head turtle display, and vintage movies on video. Next door sits the old jail, its humorous graffiti worth a chuckle. The newest adjunct to the museum, circa-1920 Belle Haven Cottage, is filled with antiques and shares space with a natural garden. Open October–April, Tuesday–Saturday 10–4; May–October, Tuesday–Saturday 10–1. Donations accepted.

Florida Maritime Museum of Cortez (941-708-4935; www.manateeclerk.com/ ClerkServices/HisVill/village.htm), 4415 119th St. W., Cortez. Newly completed in fall 2007 in the 1912 Cortez Rural Graded Schoolhouse, this ongoing project explores the state's maritime heritage from Cedar Keys to the Florida Keys, with special emphasis on Cortez. Displays include artwork, models of boats that were once made in Cortez, artifacts, and photographs from prehistoric times to present. The circa-1890 Bratton Store has been moved next to the schoolhouse and is undergoing renovation for use as a library. Another facility for restoring historic watercraft and building models from historic plans will also be relocated on the premises. When completed, the complex will include a nature preserve with trails. Open Tuesday–Saturday 8:30–4:30.

THE FLORIDA MARITIME MUSEUM OF CORTEZ SCHOOLS VISITORS ON THE TOWN'S SALTY PAST AND PRESENT.

✪ ✒ **Ringling Circus Museum & Tibbals Learning Center** (941-355-5101; www.ringling.org), 5401 Bay Shore Rd., on the Ringling Estate, Sarasota. The circus museum was Florida's way of saying thank you to John Ringling back in 1948. Its re-creation of Big Top magic paid tribute to the man who bequeathed to the city a legacy of exotica, sophistication, and art appreciation. The museum reflects Ringling's seemingly contradictory interests. Fine-art displays counterbalance high-wire exhibits. Black-and-white photography is juxtaposed with gilded fantasy. Tasteful cloth mannequins model plumed and sequined costumes. The museum plays up Sarasota's role as winter headquarters for the circus and its part in

THE NEW TIBBALS LEARNING CENTER AT RINGLING ESTATES RE-CREATES THE MAGIC OF THE BIG TOP.

the filming of the movie, *The Greatest Show on Earth.* In 2006, Tibbals Learning Center opened next to the museum; the addition is a more modern tribute to the art and magic of the circus in a larger sense than Ringling and Sarasota. The experience begins with a short film of historic footage that deals with the logistics of the moving city known as a circus. The complexity of visiting 150 towns in one season with 100 railcars inspired Howard Tibbals to create a 3,800-square-foot miniature model of the circus—the largest in the world—that covers every aspect of the circus from its arrival in town by train to behind the scenes and the Big Top main event. This multisensory experience re-creates the sounds of the circus while the lighting turns the scene from day to night. Upstairs, you can look down upon the massive display. Other exhibits include another miniature circus, memorabilia, and a time line chronicling the circus from its ancient origins, through its Golden Age, and up to its modern incarnations. The museum and learning center are located on the grounds of the John and Mable Ringling Museum of Art (see "Visual Arts Centers & Resources," below). Open daily 10–5:30. Admission: $25 adults, $20 seniors, $10 students and Florida teachers with ID, free for children under age 5; cost covers admission to all Ringling attractions.

○ **Sarasota Classic Car Museum** (941-355-6228; www.sarasotacarmuseum.org), 5500 N. Tamiami Trail, Sarasota. About 100 antique, classic, muscle, and celebrity cars park under one roof here. See a DeLorean like the one from *Back to the Future;* four of the Beatles' cars, including John Lennon's psychedelic party Bentley '91; John Ringling's Rolls Royces and Pierce Arrow; and vintage motorized vehicles dating from 1903. The kids will get a kick out of the vintage games. Open daily 9–6. Admission: $8.50 adults, $7.50 seniors, $6.50 children ages 6–12.

♪ South Florida Museum & Bishop Planetarium (941-746-4131; www.south floridamuseum.org), 201 10th St. W., Bradenton. This two-story museum recently underwent a $5 million renovation that installed shiny, new, impressive displays and a planetarium so state-of-the-art there are only two more like it in the world. The museum's first floor focuses on ancient history and features prehistoric skeleton casts, realistic life-size Native American dioramas, and appropriate sound effects. One of the museum's most prized exhibits, the Tallant Collection, displays Amerindian artifacts excavated mostly from Manatee County. Upstairs holds collections of historic artifacts. The newest addition simulates different local environments and includes exhibits that virtually take you underwater in a river, mangrove forest, and the gulf. It segues into the re-created habitat of Snooty, the star of the museum and the oldest known manatee born in captivity (since 1948) in the U.S. You can watch him and his current playmate underwater through aquarium windows or from above at the Parker Aquarium, where interactive exhibits explain the plight of the endangered manatee, and educational presentations and feedings take place throughout the day. The outdoor Spanish Plaza holds a replicated 16th-century chapel. Bishop Planetarium shows include IMAX-like movies, a summer-long Thursday film series and other special events. Open January–April, July, Monday–Saturday 10–5, Sunday noon–5; closed Monday during all other months. Admission: $15.95 adults, $13.95 seniors, $11.95 children ages 4–12; half-price admission Saturdays after 4.

Venice Archives and Area Historical Collection (941-486-2487; www.venice gov.com/archives.htm), 351 S. Nassau St., Venice. The most interesting relic here is the building that houses the facility. A 1927 Italianate structure with a triangular base and a Renaissance tower, it once was called the Triangle Inn. Stop for a peek at whatever exhibit is showing, a room full of local fossils, and another room honoring city father Dr. Fred Albee, whose operating table you'll find among the other memorabilia. A city park lies across the street. Open May–December, Monday and Wednesday 10–4; January–April, Monday–Wednesday 10–4. Admission is free or by donation.

MUSIC & NIGHTLIFE Thanks to its population of college students, Sarasota dances with action throughout the week and especially on weekends. Local bands and up-and-coming stars appear in theaters, cabarets, and nightclubs. Cores of activity include downtown and posh St. Armands Circle. Every Friday check the *Sarasota Herald-Tribune's* "Ticket" and *Bradenton Herald's* "Weekend" to learn what's happening in area clubs.

Bradenton

The Distillery (941-739-7845; www.thedistillery.com), 108 44th Ave. E., Bradenton. Live Southern rock, '80s tunes, and more.

Bradenton Beach

Beachhouse (941-779-2222; www.groupersandwich.com), 200 Gulf Dr. N., Bradenton Beach. Live reggae and island music most evenings.

Nokomis

Pelican Alley (941-485-1893; www.pelicanalley.com), 1009 W. Albee Rd., Nokomis. Live music from 7–10 every Friday evening.

Cha Cha Coconuts (941-388-3300; www.chacha-coconuts.com), 417 St. Armands Circle, Sarasota. Cover bands Thursday–Sunday and some Wednesdays.

Sarasota

Concerts at Ringling (941-359-5700; www.ringling.org), John and Mable Ringling Museum of Art, 5401 Bay Shore Rd., Sarasota. Local and international musicians perform seasonally in the courtyard and in the Rubens Galleries.

❧ **Five O'Clock Club** (941-366-5555; www.5oclockclub.net), 1930 Hillview St., Sarasota. The hottest thing going away from downtown, it hosts live bands nightly in an old (circa 1955), plain neighborhood bar setting. Happy hour here lasts from 11 AM to 8 PM!

Florida West Coast Symphony (941-953-3434; www.fwcs.org), 709 Tamiami Trail N., Sarasota. Besides holding classical symphony concerts in Bradenton and Sarasota from September to May, this group sponsors June's Sarasota Music Festival, a chamber orchestra, and other special performances.

✪ **The Gator Club** (941-366-5969; www.thegatorclub.com), 1490 Main St., Sarasota. One of the hottest places downtown, in historic digs with a pressed-tin ceiling and straw ceiling fans. Live music nightly.

Jazz Club of Sarasota (941-366-1552 or hot line 941-316-9207; www.jazzclub sarasota.org), 330 S. Pineapple Ave., Suite 111, Sarasota. This organization dedicates itself to the perpetuation and encouragement of jazz performance by presenting various monthly and annual events, members' concerts, special presentations, and youth programs. It also has a musical instrument lending library and sponsors the weeklong Sarasota Jazz Festival in March (see "Special Events").

Sarasota Concert Band (941-364-2263), 1345 Main St., Sarasota. This ensemble's 50-some members perform from October–May at Van Wezel Performing Arts Hall and other venues, and at outdoor concerts throughout the area.

Sarasota Friends of Folk Music (941-377-9256; www.sarafolk.org), 3874 Wolverine St., Sarasota. This group specializes in Florida folk music and performs free monthly concerts on City Island at the Sarasota Sailing Squadron.

Siesta Key

✪ **Beach Club** (941-349-6311), 5151 Ocean Blvd., Siesta Key. Once a rowdy college bar, this pool hall–nightclub has been hosting local rock, jazz, and reggae groups nightly since 1947.

❧ **Siesta Key Oyster Bar** (941-346-5443; www.skob.com), 5238 Ocean Blvd., Siesta Key. In the midst of Siesta Key Village hubbub, it's open-air component and nightly live music make it a popular pub crawl stop.

Venice

Crow's Nest (941-484-9551; www.crowsnest-venice.com), 1968 Tarpon Center Dr., Venice. Features live soloists and duets on a changing calendar Thursday–Saturday.

Venice Symphony (941-488-1010; www.thevenicesymphony.org), P.O. Box 1561, Venice. Classical and pops concerts December–April at Church of the Nazarene (1535 E. Venice Ave.) and a free outdoor pops concert in March.

SPECIALTY LIBRARIES Family Heritage House (941-752-5319; www .familyheritagehouse.com), Manatee Community College, 5840 26th St. W., Bradenton. Part of Florida's Black Heritage Trail, it contains children's books, videotapes, audiotapes, adult books, magazines, and other materials relevant to the Underground Railroad and to black heritage, arts, and culture.

John and Mable Ringling Museum of Art Research Library (941-359-5700, ext. 2701; www.ringling.org), 5401 Bay Shore Rd., Sarasota. One of the largest art libraries in the Southeast, it specializes in Italian and European Baroque art, Peter Paul Rubens, and decorative art. Open to the public Wednesday and Friday 1–5, or by appointment.

Manatee County Central Library (941-748-5555; www.co.manatee.fl.us/library/ master.html), 1301 Barcarrotta Blvd. W., Bradenton. The Eaton Room contains a collection of state and county historical photographs, newspapers, books, census records, and articles.

✔ **Selby Public Library** (941-861-1100; www.suncat.co.sarasota.fl.us/Libraries/ Selby.aspx), 1331 First St., Sarasota. The city's central and most impressive-looking library, it schedules cultural events throughout the year. Arranged in a circular design, the library features an exciting youth wing that you enter through a glass aquarium arch.

Verman Kimbrough Memorial Library (941-359-7587; www.lib.rsad.edu), Ringling College of Art and Design, 2700 N. Tamiami Trail, Sarasota. Art history and instruction.

THEATER Anna Maria Island Players (941-778-5755; www.theislandplayers .org), 10009 Gulf Dr. at Pine Ave., Anna Maria Island. October–May, community theater in an Old Florida–style building for more than 60 years.

FLORIDA STATE UNIVERSITY'S DRAMA BRANCH IS AT HOME IN SARASOTA'S ASOLO CENTER FOR THE PERFORMING ARTS, ON THE GROUNDS OF THE RINGLING ESTATES.

❂ **Asolo Center for the Performing Arts/Florida State University Acting Conservatory** (941-351-8000 or 800-361-8388; www.asolo.org), 5555 N. Tamiami Trail, across from the Ringling Estate, Sarasota. The original Asolo Theatre was built in Italy in 1798 as part of a queen's castle. It ended up on the Ringling Estate in the 1940s, where it was reconstructed and, in 1965, designated the State Theater of Florida. The building has been restored and is part of the Ringling visitors center across the street from the new Asolo center, which was built in the early 1980s. The new Asolo incorporated into the interior of one of its venues a different dismantled, historic European theater: a circa 1900 Scottish opera house. Carved box fronts, friezes, and ornate cornice work from the old theater decorate the new, lending it an aura of Old World heritage. Opened in 1989, the 500-seat Harold E. and Esther M. Mertz Theatre hosts the excellent, nearly 50-year-old Asolo Repertory Theatre troupe November–May. Free tours are available November–May, Wednesday–Saturday at 10 and 11 AM. A separate, more intimate, 161-seat theater, called the Jane B. Cook Theatre, is the home of Florida State University's graduate actor training program. Its season runs concurrently with the Mertz's.

Banyan Theater (941-358-5330; www.banyantheatercompany.com), P.O. Box 49483, Sarasota 34230. Professional theater group that performs the classics during the summer season at the Asolo and the Ringling Estate.

✪ ✑ **Circus Sarasota** (941-355-9335; www.circussarasota.org), 8251 15th St. E., Sarasota; performances at 12th St. and Tuttle Rd. This troupe resurrects Sarasota's deeply entrenched Big Top tradition with a February schedule of performances. Conceived by Sarasota native Dolly Jacobs (daughter of the late, great circus clown Lou Jacobs), it's a not-for-profit, educational organization hosting clown-arts seminars and a kids' club.

Florida Studio Theatre and Cabaret Club (941-366-9000; www.fst2000.org), 1241 N. Palm Ave., downtown Sarasota) A major testing ground for budding playwrights and new works, Florida Studio Theatre's professional troupe performs in its Mainstage and experimental Stage III theaters October–June and hosts a summertime Florida Playwrights Festival (see "Special Events" at the end of this chapter). There are musical revues, improv, and other light entertainment, plus full-service dining, in the Parisian-style Cabaret Club.

Glenridge Performing Arts Center (941-552-5300 or 888-999-4536; www .theglenridge.com), 7333 Scotland Way, Sarasota. In addition to live theater, this 267-seat state-of-the-art facility hosts films and concerts from chamber music to jazz.

Golden Apple Dinner Theatre (941-366-5454 or 800-652-0920; www.thegolden apple.com), 25 N. Pineapple Ave., downtown Sarasota. Year-round Broadway dinner entertainment since 1971.

Historic Ringling Asolo Theatre (941-355-5101; www.ringling.org), 5401 Bay Shore Rd., Sarasota. Recently restored and merged into the Ringling Estate's new visitors center, it hosts a couple performances each season from the new Asolo Center's (see above) repertoire. Docents give tours of the theater five times daily, hourly beginning at 11 AM. The tour includes a 37-minute film, *The Life and Times of John and Mable Ringling*. Tour cost is $5 per person.

Manatee Players Riverfront Theater (941-748-0111, box office: 941-748-5875; www.manateeplayers.com), 102 Old Main St., Bradenton. Community theater in an intimate, historic setting. Also theatrical performances for children and families.

The Players of Sarasota (941-365-2494; www.theplayers.org), 838 N. Tamiami Trail, Sarasota. Community theater group that stages Broadway musicals, plus live music and other programs year-round.

Powel Crosley Theater (941-722-3244; www.powelcrosleytheatre.com), 8374 N. Tamiami Trail, Sarasota. In the setting of a gorgeous historic estate, this troupe performs unique adaptations from the world's best authors: Dickens, Poe, Shakespeare, Oscar Wilde, and more.

✪ **Sarasota Opera House** (941-366-8450; www.sarasotaopera.org), 61 N. Pineapple Ave., downtown Sarasota. Don't even try to park or dine downtown on opera opening nights during the January–March season. Southwest Florida's oldest opera company's opening galas are popular events that require ticket purchase months in advance. In operation for more than 50 years, the Sarasota Opera Association stages all the classic and rare works in its beautifully restored, 1926 Mediterranean Revival-style structure, located in the Theater and Arts District. You can tour the facility (and see the chandelier from the set of *Gone With the Wind*) every Monday at 10:30 for $12.

✪ **Van Wezel Performing Arts Hall** (941-953-3368 or 800-826-9303; www .vanwezel.org), 777 N. Tamiami Trail, Sarasota. The Van Wezel, that purple eye-catcher radiating outward like a scallop shell from the shores of Sarasota Bay, was designed by the Frank Lloyd Wright Foundation and hosts name comedians, musicians, and dance groups; Broadway shows; major orchestras; ethnic music and dance groups; and chamber and choral music. In the off-season, May–October, the hall hosts Friday Fest on the Bay one Friday a month from 5 to 9 PM, featuring live music from country to reggae.

Venice Theatre (941-488-1115; www.venicestage.com), 140 W. Tampa Ave., downtown Venice. This community-theater company has spread to two venues. In its Mediterranean Revival structure, the troupe performs six main-stage shows October–May, four contemporary plays at Stage II November–April, plus occasional cabarets and concerts. It conducts theater classes, workshops, and summer camp for adults and kids (call 941-486-8679).

VISUAL ARTS CENTERS & RESOURCES The canvas of Sarasota Bay arts reveals a complex masterpiece, layered with the diverse patterns and local color of its many communities. With its backdrop of artistic types dating back to avid collector John Ringling, Sarasota leads the region to avant-garde heights.

The following entries introduce you to opportunities for experiencing art as either an appreciator or a practicing artist. A listing of commercial galleries is included under "Shopping," below.

ArtCenter Manatee (941-746-2862; www.artcentermanatee.org), 209 Ninth St. W., Bradenton. It hosts changing monthly exhibitions, an artists' market, classes, and workshops.

Art Center Sarasota (941-365-2032; www.artsarasota.org), 707 N. Tamiami Trail, Sarasota. Exhibition and sales galleries feature the paintings, jewelry, sculpture, pottery, and enamelware of local and national artists. Art instruction and demonstrations are available. The gallery features an outdoor sculpture garden. Open Tuesday–Saturday, 10–4.

Artists' Guild of Anna Maria Island (941-778-6694), 5414 Marina Dr., Holmes Beach. Local artists meet and display in the gallery.

Art League of Manatee County (941-746-2862; www.almc.org), 209 Ninth St. W., Bradenton. Classes and demonstrations in all media for all ages; sales gallery.

The Fine Arts Society of Sarasota (941-953-3368 or 941-955-7676; www .vanwezel.org/aboutUs/ guidedTours.cfm), Van Wezel Performing Arts Hall, 777 N. Tamiami Trail, Sarasota. Van Wezel houses a permanent collection of prominent Florida artists' works on loan from the society, which conducts tours at 10 AM the first Tuesday of each month, October–May. Cost is $5 per person.

✪ ✿ ♪ **The John and Mable Ringling Museum of Art** (941-355-5101; www .ringling.org), 5401 Bay Shore Rd., Sarasota. Sarasota's pride and joy, and designated the State Art Museum of Florida, this is not only an art museum, but also the nucleus of tourism activity and the heart of the local art community. It shares its 66-acre bayfront estate with Ringling's extravagant Cà d'Zan palace (see "Historic Homes"), a circus museum and learning center (see "Museums"), a rose garden (see "Gardens"), and a visitors center with an extensive gift shop (see "Shopping"), restaurant, and restored historic Italian theater. The art collection, much of which was purchased by Ringling, covers 500 years of European art and specializes in late-medieval and Renaissance Italian works. The Old Masters collection contains five original Rubens tapestries as well as Spanish Baroque, French, Dutch, and northern European works (mostly portraits of a religious nature). The museum continually augments its collection of American and contemporary works in three wings and the Education Conservation Complex that opened in 2007 to house traveling exhibits. The lushly landscaped courtyards feature reproductions of classic statues and Italian decorative columns, which Ringling originally purchased for the hotel he hoped to build on Longboat Key. The museum is open daily 10–5:30; the grounds are open 9:30–6. Admission covers all Ringling property attractions and a tour of the art museum: $25 adults, $20 seniors, $10 students and Florida teachers with ID, free for children under age 5. Admission to the museum only is free every Monday.

Longboat Key Center for the Arts (941-383-2345; www.lbkca.org), 6860 Longboat Dr. S., Longboat Key. Hidden from mainstream traffic, here is a find for the buyer and would-be artisan. Galleries sell works mostly by Florida artists. Changing and permanent exhibits feature local, emerging, and experimental artists. A crafts shop sells wares made at the center's surrounding workshops, where classes are taught in basketry, watercolor, jewelry making, metal craft, pottery, and more. In season, second Tuesdays bring jazz concerts to the center.

The Manatee Arts Council Gallery (941-746-2223; www.manateearts.org), 926 12th St. W., in Village of the Arts, Bradenton. It hosts monthly shows by local artists on a rotating basis.

Selby Gallery (941-359-7563; www.ringling.edu/selbygallery), 2700 N. Tamiami Trail, at the Ringling College of Art and Design, Sarasota. This intimate, modern space exhibits the works of contemporary students, faculty, and local, national, and international artists and designers. Free admission. Open September–April, Monday–Saturday 10–4, Tuesday 10–7; May–August, Monday–Friday 10–4.

✪ ✿ **Towles Court Artist Colony** (www.towlescourt.com), 1943 Morrill St., Sarasota. A delightful, blossomy village of restored and brightly painted tin-roofed bungalows turned art colony. Showings, studios, and galleries. Third Friday gallery walks, 6–10 PM.

Venice Art Center (941-485-7136; www.veniceartcenter.com), 390 S. Nokomis Ave., Venice. Local artists' exhibitions, gift shop, café, and art instruction.

✪ ✿ **Village of the Arts** (941-747-8056; www.villageofthearts.com), 18-block radius around 12th St. and 11th Ave. W., Bradenton. Officially welcomed in January 2001, this artist colony revitalized a former drug neighborhood, turning it into a point of pride for the community. More than 35 artists and artisans from all disciplines—visual arts, healing arts, culinary arts—have moved into the neighborhood

BRADENTON'S VILLAGE OF THE ARTS BRIGHTENED A DRUG-INFESTED NEIGHBORHOOD
WITH THE STUDIOS AND WORKSHOPS OF WORKING ARTISTS.

to work and sell their art and services. Most are concentrated on 12th Street and open October–May, Friday and Saturday 11–4; look for banners with bright appliqués in front of participating houses. Artwalks take place the first Friday (6–10) and Saturday (11–4) of the month. One of my favorites is **The Baobab Tree Gallery** (941-447-3795; 1113 12th St. W.). The village hosts a First Weekend Art Fest each month. In 2006, the Village mounted a gecko auction, and you can still see the colorfully decorated fiberglass creatures crawling the sides of buildings around town.

✳ To Do

Known both for its superlative white sand beaches and as the birthplace of Florida golfing, Sarasota and its environs draw lovers of the outdoors to their year-round playgrounds.

BEACHES The Sarasota area claims more than 35 miles of sandy seashore. Island beaches are, for the most part, highly developed, with lots of facilities and concessions. Recent years have seen a concession of another sort—to nature—as boardwalks and sea oat plantings restore the dunes. On the islands, erosion takes its toll and beaches must be periodically renourished. This stretch of the Gulf Coast boasts some of the whitest beaches this side of the Florida Panhandle—and some of the darkest. Like most Southwest Florida beaches, gulf waters here are typically calm and inviting. Parking is free at all area beaches. Pets (except where noted) and glass containers are prohibited. So is walking across dune vegetation any way but on the boardwalk crossovers.

🐾 ✒ **Anna Maria Bayfront Park,** northeast end of Anna Maria Island. One of the region's more secluded beach parks, this one is narrower than the rest of the island's beaches. You get a magnificent view of St. Petersburg's Sunshine Skyway

Bridge from the bay. A historical marker tells about the island's early settlers. Heed danger signs that mark where heavy tidal currents make swimming perilous. Facilities: picnic areas, restrooms, showers, playground, recreational facilities, fishing pier.

Brohard Beach (941-316-1172), 1600 S. Harbor Dr., Venice. This wide, dark-flecked sand beach threads under the Venice Fishing Pier and around covered picnic tables. Folks come here to fish, hang out at the pier tiki bar, and hunt for shark teeth. Facilities: picnic areas, restrooms, showers, fitness trail, fishing pier, bait shop, restaurant, volleyball.

Caspersen Beach (941-316-1172), South end of Harbor Dr., Venice. At the end of the road lies natural Caspersen Beach, where a series of boardwalks cross scrub-vegetated dunes onto diminishing dark sands. It's popular with shark-tooth hunters and young beachgoers. From here you can walk to Manasota Key Beach to the south. On the bay side, the county has built a new bike path, fishing pier, and kayak launch along the Venetian Waterway. Facilities: picnic areas, restrooms, showers, nature trail, covered playground, bike path, bayside fishing pier, kayak launch. Open daily 7–8.

Coquina Beach, southern end of Gulf Dr., Bradenton Beach, Anna Maria Island. This large and popular park boasts plump, wide sands edged in Australian pines and small, sea-oat dunes. Several jetties poke out into the gulf. Waters at the south end provide good snorkeling. The park continues on the bay, where swimming should be avoided because of currents and boat traffic. The Coquina Bay-Walk takes you to environmentally restored 30-acre Leffis Key. Facilities: picnic areas, restrooms, showers, lifeguard, café, volleyball, playground, concessions, boat ramps (bayside).

Cortez Beach, Gulf Dr., Bradenton Beach, Anna Maria Island. Here's a long stretch of revamped sand at the end of the Cortez Bridge. It meets up with Coquina, its more popular cousin. Surfers like it here. It's convenient for the heavily laden beachgoer because you park right along the sand's edge. Facilities: picnic tables, restrooms, showers, lifeguard.

Crescent Beach (941-316-1172), south of Siesta Public Beach on Midnight Pass Rd., access near Stickney Point Rd. intersection, Siesta Key. Less populated than the main public beach, but with the same award-winning sand, it's a little tricky to find. It lacks the facilities and ease of parking of the main beach. At its south end, Point of Rocks is popular with snorkelers and fishermen because of an accumulation of rocks that attracts marine life.

Lido Beach (941-316-1172), 400 Benjamin Franklin Dr., Lido Key. Heavily developed and popular, this is

FOR A CHANGE, TRY MAKING SAND ANGELS—IN SIESTA KEY'S HEAVENLY WHITE SAND.

the main beach on Lido Key. Canvas cabanas and stylish, umbrella-shaded lounge chairs may be rented along the stretch of sand carpeted with small shells and shell hash. South of the pavilion at the Lido Beach Resort, you'll find water-sports equipment rentals. In 2001, residents rallied to save the circa-1926 community pool on the beach, a throwback to the glamour days of John Ringling and friends. Facilities: picnic areas, restrooms, showers, lifeguards, historic swimming pool, snack bar, swings, volleyball, beach wheelchairs. Pool admission is $4 for adults, $2 for seniors and children ages 4–11.

Longboat Key, public accesses at Broadway St. on the north end of island. Long-boat Key has beautiful beaches, mostly enjoyed by resort guests and waterfront residents. Public accesses are marked subtly with blue signs at Atlas Street, Gulf-side Road, and Broadway Street. Parking is limited, and there are no facilities or lifeguards. But the beach stretches wide as well as long and has fluffy white sand and dramatic sunset views.

✪ 🐾 ✎ **Manatee Public Beach** (941-778-0784), 4000 Gulf Dr. at 40th St., Holmes Beach. The hot spot of Anna Maria Island beachgoing, this park appeals to families because of its full complement of facilities. The beach is wide enough to accommodate rows and rows of beach towels. Australian pines shade picnic areas, and the café is popular for breakfast and ice cream. Facilities: picnic area, restrooms, showers, lifeguard, playground, restaurant, ice cream shop, beach rentals, volleyball.

✪ 🐾 ✎ **Nokomis Beach** (941-861-5000), Casey Key Rd. at Albee Rd., Casey Key. Remote and exclusive Casey Key gives way to beachy abandon toward its southern end. In the midst of the town's action, it is a popular destination, prettily land-scaped and inviting. A series of parking lots provides public access, and a long boardwalk runs parallel between two of them. Facilities: picnic area and shelters, restrooms, showers, lifeguards, beach wheelchairs.

🐾 ✎ **North Jetty Park** (941-861-5000), south end of Casey Key Rd. at Albee Rd., Casey Key. The town of Nokomis Beach is a fisherman's haven, and North Jetty, at its southernmost point, lures anglers. (South Jetty lies across the pass on Venice Beach.) A bait shop keeps fishermen supplied. The beach's wide sands, festooned with Australian pines and sea grape trees, are well loved by serious local beachgo-ers. When the waves kick up, the surfing crowd heads here. Fast-moving pass waters can make swimming treacherous. Facilities: picnic area and shelters, rest-rooms, showers, lifeguards, concessions, boat ramps, beach wheelchairs.

North Lido Beach (941-316-1172), end of John Ringling Blvd., Lido Key. The beach less traveled on Lido, this one extends from the main beach up to New Pass. A lack of facilities and limited parking keep the throngs away at this naturally maintained park. It is wide, with fine, spic-and-span sand, plus trails for hiking and running.

Palma Sola Causeway Beach, Anna Maria Bridge, FL 64. Fairly narrow sands edge the causeway between the mainland and Anna Maria Island. They gain some character from Australian pines and are popular with windsurfers and jet-skiers. Facilities: picnic area, restrooms, restaurant, water-sports rentals.

Service Club Park (941-316-1172), S. Harbor Dr., Venice. An extensive system of boardwalks crosses scrub pinelands (watch for rare scrub jays and gopher tortoises) and provides picnic nooks off the beach. This is quieter than neighboring Brohard

Park and its fishing pier, but within walking distance of both. Facilities: picnic areas and shelters, restrooms, showers, tot play area, volleyball.

✪ ☙ ✐ **Siesta Key County Beach** (941-861-2150), Midnight Pass Rd. at Beach Way Dr., Siesta Key. Siesta Key's sand was once judged "the finest, whitest beach in the world" by the Woods Hole Oceanographic Institute. (Anna Maria Island's beach placed third.) In 2003 the Travel Channel named it the "Best Sand Beach in America." The blinding whiteness comes from its quartz (99 percent) origins; the sand's fineness comes from Mother Nature's efficient pulverizer, the sea. Unfortunately, these facts have not been kept secret. The park averages about 20,000 visitors a day. Arrive early to find a parking space. Condos and motels line the wide beach. Swimming is wonderful because the beach has gradually sloping sands and usually clear waters. Public accesses along Beach Road to the north provide more seclusion, but parking is on the street and limited. On Sunday evenings, a drum circle starts an hour or two before sunset. Facilities: picnic areas and shelters, restrooms, showers, lifeguard, snack bar, playground, volleyball, tennis, ball fields, soccer field, fitness trail, sundecks, beach wheelchairs.

South Brohard Park (941-316-1172), S. Harbor Dr., Venice. South of Brohard Park, parking and boardwalks over mangrove wetlands provide access to the beach that is away from noise, fishhooks, and crowds. The undeveloped natural beach appeals to escapists, who are nonetheless within walking distance of facilities at Brohard. One acre of its 22 acres is a designated dogs-allowed beach and is outfitted with fenced areas for doggies and owners. Facilities: picnic table, restrooms.

South Jetty (941-486-2626), 2000 Tarpon Center Dr., Venice. Also known as Humphris Park, the jetty at Casey's Pass—a favorite of fishing types—is shored with huge boulders. Past them stretches a span of condo-lined beach that's popular with surfers and sailboarders. Here, people while away time eating lunch and watching boat traffic through the pass. Across the pass lies Nokomis Beach's North Jetty. Facilities: restrooms, picnic tables, food concession.

South Lido Beach Park (941-316-1172), 2201 Benjamin Franklin Dr., Lido Key. A wide, natural beach wraps around the tip of Lido Key from the gulf to the bay, facing Siesta Key to the south. Picnic areas are overhung with Australian pines and carpeted by their needles. Within its 100 acres several Florida ecosystems thrive on different waterfronts. Squirrels are the most evident wildlife throughout the park, which is smoke- and pesticide-free. Hiking trails lead you along the mangrove worlds of Little Grassy and Big Grassy lagoons. Brushy Bayou is a good place to kayak. Swift waters in the pass make swimming treacherous but fishing fine. Facilities: picnic areas, restrooms, showers, playground, volleyball, ball fields, horseshoes, soccer field, fitness trail, nature trail, canoe trail.

☙ ✐ **Turtle Beach,** south end of Blind Pass Rd., Siesta Key. The sands become coarser, darker, and more shell studded at Siesta's lower extremes as the high-rise buildings become scarcer. Along here and Midnight Pass Road the island's upper echelon resides behind iron gates. Less crowded than the other Siesta beaches, it's sports- and family-oriented but without lifeguards. If you walk southward, you'll reach ✪ **Palmer Point Beach** (otherwise only reachable by boat), where Midnight Pass between Siesta and Casey keys has filled in and shark teeth are easy to find. Facilities: picnic areas, restrooms, showers, small playground, volleyball, boat ramps, horseshoes; restaurants and bars across the street.

✪ ⚘ ✍ **Venice Beach** (941-316-1172), 100 The Esplanade, Venice. This beach feels cramped and more urban than Venice's spacious south-end beaches. Buildings border the sands, which spread wide here. Wooden benches provide places to gaze at the normally calm sea. This beach is especially popular with divers because a reef fronts the sands a quarter mile out. Facilities: restrooms, showers, food concession, lifeguards, volleyball, beach wheelchairs.

BICYCLING Sarasota's best bikeways lie on barrier islands, in parks, and in rural areas to the east. Most biking elsewhere is on the sides of roads or sidewalks.

By state law, bicyclists must conduct themselves as pedestrians when using sidewalks. Where they share the road with other vehicles, they must follow all the rules of the road. Children under 16 must wear helmets.

Best Biking: The ✪ **Historical Manatee Riverwalk** takes in downtown Bradenton for strollers and cyclists. It zigzags through downtown and crosses the Green Bridge (Business 41) to Palmetto. Brochure maps are available through the local Chamber of Commerce. In Palmetto, **Emerson Point Preserve** offers a pleasant bike ride on an almost 3-mile, partially paved path that runs along waterfront vistas.

✪ **Longboat Key's** 12 miles of bike path and lane parallel Gulf of Mexico Drive's vista of good taste and wealth on both sides of the road. Bike paths travel through parts of **Lido Key** and **Siesta Key.** The **Venetian Waterway Park** in Venice runs along both sides of the Intracoastal Waterway and stretches for nearly 10 miles from the train depot on Venice Avenue, one of seven trailheads for **Legacy Trail** (941-861-7245 or 941-861-5000; www.legacytrailfriends.org), which follows the old railroad route to Potter Park in the north. **Oscar Scherer State Park** provides a more natural backdrop for biking on nearly 15 miles of trails. In Sarasota, county buses are equipped with bike racks for pedal-and-ride passengers.

Rental Shops: Resorts and parks often rent bikes or provide free use of them.

Bicycle Center (941-377-4505), 4084 Bee Ridge Rd., Sarasota. Offers pickup and delivery on mountain bike and beach cruiser rentals.

Island Scooter Rentals (941-726-3163; www.islandscooters.com), Silver Surf Resort, 1301 Gulf Dr. N., Bradenton Beach. Rents bikes to the public by the hour, day, and week. Customer pickup and drop-off available.

Legacy Bike Shop & Coffee (941-412-3821), 127 Tampa Ave. E. #10, Venice. Rentals, repairs, and sales. Located near the Venetian Waterway Park and its Legacy Bike Path.

Siesta Sports Rentals (941-346-1797; www.siestasportsrentals.com), 6551 Midnight Pass Rd., Southbridge Mall, Siesta Key. Beach cruisers, speed bikes, kid bikes, tandems, surreys, jogger strollers, and beach stuff.

BOATS & BOATING

Canoeing and Kayaking: In addition to the outlets listed below, many resorts and parks rent canoes and kayaks. Best trails include those that run along the Myakka and Manatee Rivers and in intracoastal waters.

Almost Heaven Kayak Adventures (941-504-6296; www.kayakfl.com), 7134 87th Ln. E., Palmetto. Offers tours in and around the islands, bays, and rivers of Sarasota and Bradenton; lessons included. One 2½-hour tour in Longboat Key waters stops for lunch at Mar-Vista Restaurant, where participants receive a 20 percent discount. Daily and weekly rentals and drop-off and pickup service.

Enticer Watersports (941-366-7245), 5 Bayfront Dr., at Bayfront Park, Sarasota. Rents kayaks, paddleboats, small sailboats, and WaveRunners by the half-hour or hour.

Native Rental (941-778-7757), 5416 Marina Dr., Holmes Beach. Quality rentals and guided and self-guided tours through bay waters and bird islands.

✪ **Oscar Scherer State Park** (941-483-5956; www.floridastateparks.org/oscarscherer), 1843 S. Tamiami Trail, Osprey. Canoe rentals and launch and tidal creek paddling along scrubby and pine flatwoods. River otters and alligators inhabit the waters; scrub jays, bobcats, and bald eagles inhabit the land.

Siesta Sports Rentals (941-346-1797; www.siestasportsrentals.com), 6551 Midnight Pass Rd., at Southbridge Mall, Siesta Key. Rents single and double kayaks, plus snorkels, boogie and skim boards, and other beach equipment.

Silent Sports (941-966-5477; www.adventuresinflorida.net/silentsportsoutfitters.htm), 2301 Tamiami Trail, Nokomis. Rents kayaks and canoes and leads three-hour tours.

Snook Haven (941-485-7221; www.snookhavenretreat.com), 5000 E. Venice Ave., Venice. Canoe launch (closed during concerts) and rentals on the Myakka River.

Tropical Kayak Rentals (941-779-7426; www.tropicalkayakrentals.com) Free delivery and pickup for rentals. Also offers sunset, fishing, birding, and Lido Key mangrove tours.

Personal Watercraft Rental/Tours: Florida law now requires operators between ages 18 and 21 to have a boater safety card. Many rental agents can qualify you for the card.

Enticer Watersports (941-366-7245), 5 Bayfront Dr., at Bayfront Park, Sarasota. Rents kayaks, paddleboats, sailboats, and WaveRunners by the half-hour, hour, day, or week.

Siesta Key Jet Ski (941-346-3000; www.siestakeyjetski.com), 1249 Stickney Point Rd., at CB's Saltwater Outfitters, Siesta Key 34242. One- to four-hour rentals.

Powerboat Rentals: **Bradenton Beach Marina** (941-778-2288; www.bradentonbeachmarina.com), 402 Church Ave., Bradenton Beach. Runabouts, center-console fishing boats, and pontoons.

Cannons Marina (941-383-1311; www.cannons.com), 6040 Gulf of Mexico Dr., Longboat Key. Rentals by half-day, day, and week; runabouts, deck boats, and water skis.

CB's Saltwater Outfitters (941-349-4400; www.cbsoutfitters.com), 1249 Stickney Point Rd., Siesta Key. Runabouts, center console boats, pontoons, and deck boats; also rod and reel rentals, fishing licenses, tackle shop, and fishing guides.

Sarasota Boat Rental (941-951-0550; www.sarasotaboatrental.com), 2 Marina Plaza, at Marina Jack, Sarasota. Center console fishing boats, deck boats, and pontoons by the half or full day. Also water skis, kneeboards, and fishing equipment.

Public Boat Ramps: **City Island,** Ken Thompson Pkwy. Three ramps.

Coquina Beach Bayside Park, Gulf Blvd., Bradenton Beach. Two ramps, plus picnic and recreational facilities; restrooms nearby.

Higel Park, Tarpon Center Dr., Venice Beach, Venice Inlet.

Kingfish Ramp, FL 64 on causeway to Anna Maria Island. Picnic facilities.

Marina Boat Ramp Park, 215 E. Venice Ave., Venice.

Nokomis Beach, Venice Inlet.

Palma Sola Causeway, Palma Sola Bay and FL 64. There are three ramps along the causeway, plus restrooms and picnicking.

Palmetto, Riverside Park on Riverside Dr., just west of the Green Bridge. One ramp on the Manatee River, picnicking.

Turtle Beach, Blind Pass Rd., Siesta Key. Two ramps.

Sailboat Charters: **The Enterprise Sailing Charters** (941-951-1833 or 888-232-7768; www.sarasotasailing.com), 2 Marina Plaza, in Bayfront Park, Sarasota. Morning, afternoon, and sunset sails, lasting two to four hours, on a tall-masted Morgan 41-footer.

Key Sailing (941-346-7245; www.siestakeysailing.com), 1219 Southport Dr., at Marina Jack, Sarasota. Two-hour to full-day sail-away adventures aboard a 41-foot Morgan Classic.

Sara-Bay Sailing (941-914-5132; www.sarabaysailing.com), City Island, at New Pass Grill & Bait Shop, Sarasota. Captained charters by the half-day or full, sailboat rentals, and American Sailing Association (ASA) certification courses.

Spice Sailing Charters (941-704-0773; http://charters2.tripod.com), 902 Bay Blvd. S., at the Galati Yacht Basin, Anna Maria. Half-day and sunset sails to Egmont Key aboard a 30-foot vessel. Sailing lessons available.

Spindrift Yacht Services (941-383-7781; www.spindrift-yachts.com), 410 Gulf of Mexico Dr., Longboat Key. Sailing ventures for up to 12.

Sailboat Rentals & Instruction: Many resorts have concessions that rent Hobie Cats and other small sailboats. Instruction is often available with the rental. For something more sophisticated, try:

Coastal Watersport Rentals (941-778-4969), 1301 Gulf Dr., Bradenton Beach. Free lessons with catamaran rentals; also rents WaveRunners and kayaks.

Sara-Bay Sailing (941-914-5132; www.sarabaysailing.com), City Island, at New Pass Grill & Bait Shop, Sarasota. ASA-certification courses.

Sight-Seeing & Entertainment Cruises: Look under "Wildlife Tours & Charters" for nature excursions.

✔ **Just Ducky** (941-485-6366), 1011 S. Tamiami Trail, one block south of Captain Eddie's Seafood Restaurant, Nokomis. Explore dry and wet scapes on this wacky amphibious tour of the Venice area.

✔ **LeBarge Tropical Cruises** (941-366-6116; www.lebargetropicalcruises.com), 2 Marine Plaza, at Marina Jack in Bayfront Park, Sarasota. Island-style crooning, an aquarium bar, and live on-board coconut palms put the tropical in this excursion. Sight-seeing, dolphin, nature, and sunset-party cruises depart daily. Light snacks and drinks available.

Terry's River Tours (941-255-0400), Snook Haven, 5000 E. Venice Ave., Venice. One-hour narrated trips on the Myakka River, Wednesday–Sunday in season.

THE FLYING FISH FLEET MEETS EVERY ANGLER'S NEEDS.

FISHING Nonresidents 16 and older must obtain a license unless they are fishing from a vessel or pier that's covered by its own license. You can buy inexpensive, temporary, nonresident licenses at county tax collectors' offices and most Kmarts, hardware stores, marinas, and bait shops.

Snook are so plentiful in the Intracoastal Waterway between Sarasota and Venice, it's been dubbed "Snook Alley." The Bradenton area is known for its mammoth grouper (formerly known as jewfish). Other fine catches include mangrove snapper, sheepshead, and pompano in backwaters, and grouper, amberjack, and mackerel in deep seas. Check local regulations for season, size, and catch restrictions.

Deep-Sea Party Boats: **Flying Fish Fleet** (941-366-3373; www.flyingfishfleet .com), 627 Avenida del Norte, at Marina Jack in Bayfront Park, Sarasota. Half-day to 12-hour deep-sea charters and party-boat excursions.

Fishing Charters/Outfitters: To find fishing guides, check with major marinas such as Marina Jack's in downtown Sarasota. Capacity is smaller and prices higher than for party-boat excursions.

Big Catch (941-366-3373; www.flyingfishfleet.com/bigcatch.html), 627 Avenida del Norte, at Marina Jack's in Bayfront Park, Sarasota. Four- to eight-hour party-boat excursions and fishing charters.

CB's Saltwater Outfitters (941-349-4400; www.cbsoutfitters.com), 1249 Stickney Point Rd., Siesta Key. Light-tackle fly and spin sportfishing charters in Sarasota Bay, the gulf, Snook Alley, and Charlotte Harbor. Four to eight hours. Fly-casting instruction available. Orvis endorsed.

Charter Boat Shark (941-365-2161; www.charterboatshark.com), 2 Marina Plaza, at Marina Jack, Sarasota. Catch tuna, kingfish, mackerel, shark, and more offshore aboard an air-conditioned, 41-foot boat.

Cortez Fishing Center (941-795-6969 or 888-844-4140; www.cortezkat.com), 12507 Cortez Rd. W., Cortez. Here's your one-stop place for fishing licenses, bait, deep-sea fishing, backwater fishing, and sight-seeing charters. Deep-sea fishing trips aboard the *Cortez Kat* party boat last four to six hours.

Lucky Dawg Charters (941-951-0819 or 941-587-9852 (cell); www.sarasota fishingcharters.com), 2576 Hillview St., Sarasota. Light-tackle sportfishing the flats, backcountry, and inshore for snook, trout, redfish, and tarpon. Half-day, six-hour, and full-day trips.

Spindrift Yacht Services (941-383-7781; www.spindrift-yachts.com), 410 Gulf of Mexico Dr., Longboat Key. Half-day offshore and bay-fishing excursions.

Stray Dog Charter Boat (941-794-5615; www.straydogcharters.com), 12507 Cortez Rd. W., Cortez. One of several guide charters docked along "Charter Row" at Cortez Fishing Center (see above), it takes fishermen offshore on a 43-foot custom boat with private head.

Fishing Piers: **Bradenton Beach City Pier,** Bridge St., Bradenton Beach. Reaching into Intracoastal waters, the pier was originally part of the first bridge from the island to the mainland. Rotten Ralph's Restaurant (see Anna Maria Island restaurants) and bait concession.

Green Bridge Pier, Business 41 over the Manatee River, downtown Bradenton.

Historic Anna Maria City Pier, Pine Ave., Anna Maria Island. It juts 678 feet into Anna Maria Sound at the south end of Bayshore Park.

Ken Thompson Pier (941-316-1172), 1700 Ken Thompson Pkwy., City Island. Three small piers into New Pass.

BOATS BOB IN SARASOTA BAY—A SCENIC, SERENE DOWNTOWN BACKDROP.

○ **Nokomis Beach's North Jetty** (941-316-1172), south end Casey Key Rd., Nokomis Beach. Man-made rock projection into the gulf. Beach and picnic area.

Osprey Fishing Pier, west end of Main St., Osprey. A neighborhood pier in an off-the-beaten-path area; no parking.

Rod & Reel Pier (941-778-1885), 875 North Shore Dr., Anna Maria. A privately owned fishermen's complex extending 250 feet into Tampa Bay. Includes a café and bait shop.

Tony Saprito Fishing Pier, Hart's Landing, Ringling Causeway Park en route to St. Armands Key. Bait store across the road. For 24-hour tide and fishing information, call the hotline at 941-366-TIDE.

○ **Venice Fishing Pier,** 1600 S. Harbor Dr., at Brohard Park, Venice. It's 740 feet long, complete with restrooms, showers, bait shop, rod and reel rentals, and restaurant. Admission to the pier is free.

Venice's South Jetty (941-316-1172), Tarpon Center Dr., Venice. A stretch of boulder buffer with a paved walkway at Venice's north end.

GOLF In 1902 Sarasota's founder and first mayor, a Scotsman, built a two-hole golf course in the middle of town. This is believed to have been Florida's first golf course. Through the years the sport has grown in Sarasota, and today there are more courses than you can swing a club at. The majority are private or semiprivate. Several large resorts have their own greens or arrange golf-around programs at local links. In winter season, rates are highest and greens are the most crowded. Carts are often required. Make tee times well in advance.

Golf Centers: **David Leadbetter Golf Academy** (941-752-2661; www.imga academies.com), IMG Academies, 5500 34th St. W., Bradenton. A highly respected full-time boarding school that also offers summer and weeklong lesson programs.

Evie's Golf Center (941-377-0990), 4735 Bee Ridge Rd., Sarasota. Practice sand traps, chipping and putting greens, lessons with PGA pros, miniature golf.

Mark Reid Golf School (941-273-1800; www.summergolfschool.com), The River Club, 6600 River Club Blvd., Bradenton. One-hour to weeklong programs for juniors and adults.

Public Golf Courses: **Bobby Jones Golf Course** (941-955-8041; www.bobby jonesgolfclub.com), 1000 Circus Blvd., off Beneva Rd. or 17th St., Sarasota. Sarasota's only municipal course, it has 36 holes plus a nine-hole executive course, practice range, and chipping and putting greens. Restaurant and lounge. Named for one of the sport's late greats, who personally dedicated the course in 1927.

Lake Venice Golf Club (941-488-3948; www.lakevenicegolf.com), 1801 Harbor Dr. S., Venice. A par-72 18-hole course and par-36 nine-hole course. Walk or ride the course; snack bar.

❦ **Manatee County Golf Course** (941-792-6773; www.co.manatee.fl.us/golf .html), 6415 53rd Ave. W., Bradenton. One of the county's most popular courses. Eighteen holes, par 72 with five different sets of tees. Clubhouse and restaurant. Reasonable rates; afternoon and twilight discounts apply.

❦ **Sarasota Golf Club** (941-371-2431), 7280 N. Leewyn Dr., Sarasota. Public course with 18 holes, par 72, and driving range. Restaurant, snack bar, and bar. Reasonable rates, especially in summer.

HEALTH & FITNESS CLUBS **Arlington Park & Aquatic Complex** (941-316-1346), 2650 Waldemere St., Sarasota. City-owned, county-operated facility with swimming pool, fitness center, tennis, racquetball, and basketball.

✄ **Babe Weiller Branch YMCA** (941-366-6778; www.sarasota-ymca.org), 1991 Main St., Suite 200, Sarasota. Weight machines, sauna and steam room, classes. Daily, weekly, and monthly memberships available and transferable to other Sarasota Y's.

✄ **Evalyn Sadlier Jones YMCA** (941-922-9622; www.sarasota-ymca.org), 8301 Potter Park, Sarasota. With an Olympic-sized pool and children's water park, this Y goes beyond fitness to fun. For workouts, there are classes, a weight room, an indoor track and pool, an outdoor 50-meter pool, diving boards, and a Jacuzzi area. At the water park families will enjoy the activity pool, slides, water cannons, fountains, and other cool stuff, plus there's an adjacent climbing tower. A child-watch program supervises the little ones while parents work out. Daily, weekly, and monthly memberships available and transferable to other Sarasota Y's.

Lifestyle Family Fitness (941-921-4400; www.lff.com), 8383 S. Tamiami Trail, Sarasota. Exercise equipment, sauna, whirlpool, lap pool.

✄ **South County Family YMCA** (941-492-9622; www.veniceymca.com), 701 Center Rd., Venice. Wellness center with strength-building and extensive cardio equipment, plus two racquetball courts, massage therapy, baby-sitting, and a food court.

HIKING **Emerson Point Conservation Preserve** (941-748-4501; www.my manatee.org/conservation.html), 5801 17th St. W., Palmetto. This lovely chin of land on Snead Island lays out trails up ancient Indian mounds, along the river and bay, and through thick woods. Bring your binoculars for some spectacular birding.

✪ **Oscar Scherer State Park** (941-483-5956; www.floridastateparks.org/oscars cherer), 1843 S. Tamiami Trail, Osprey. A combined 15 miles of six level-ground nature trails, including a half-mile barrier-free trail. An audio device introduces the scrub habitat of the marked, 5-mile Yellow Trail.

Sarasota Bay Walk, 1550 Ken Thompson Pkwy., next to Mote Marine Aquarium, City Island. Self-guided nature hike.

South Lido Nature Park (941-316-1172), south end of Benjamin Franklin Dr. at Taft Dr., Lido Key. Adjacent to South Lido Beach Park, it has nature trails into the wetlands of Brushy Bayou.

HUNTING For information on hunting licenses, permits, and seasons, visit www .myfwc.com/hunting.

Knight Trail Park (941-486-2350), 3445 Rustic Road, Nokomis, east of I-75 at exit 195. Public facility maintained by the Sarasota Parks and Recreation Department. Trap and skeet, pistol and rifle range, archery range, picnic areas.

KIDS' STUFF *✄* **Evalyn Sadlier Jones YMCA** (941-922-9622; www.sarasota -ymca.org), 8301 Potter Park, Sarasota. Water park families with activity pool, slides, water cannons, fountains, and climbing tower.

✄ **The Fish Hole** (941-778-3388), 115 Bridge St., Bradenton Beach. A welcome new addition to Bradenton Beach's family friendliness. Its 18 holes of mini golf are open daily.

⚓ **G.T. Bray Park** (941-742-5974), 5502 33rd Ave. Dr. W., Bradenton. Safety equipment is required. Dedicated BMX hours.

⚓ **Holmes Beach Skateboard Park,** 5801 Marina Dr., Holmes Beach. Open to BMX bikers, skateboarders, and inline skaters. Also playground and shuffleboard.

⚓ **Smuggler's Cove Adventure Golf** (941-756-0043; www.smugglersgolf.com), 2000 Cortez Rd. W., Bradenton; and (941-351-6620), 3815 Tamiami Tr., Sarasota. Eighteen holes of "adventure-style" miniature golf and live gators, with a pirate motif. Admission is per player per game.

RACQUET SPORTS Anna Maria Youth Center, Magnolia Ave., Anna Maria Island. Two lit tennis courts.

Bayfront Park (941-316-1980; www.longboatkey.org/departments/rec/rec.htm), Longboat Key.

C. V. Walton Racquet Center (941-742-5973; www.co.manatee.fl.us), 5512 33rd Ave. Dr. W., at G. T. Bray Park, Bradenton. Eight each of cement, clay, and racquetball courts, plus a tennis practice wall and pro shop.

Gillespie Park (941-316-1172), 710 N. Osprey Ave., Sarasota. Three unlit tennis courts.

Glazier Gates Park, Manatee Ave. E., Bradenton. Two unlit, cement, public tennis courts.

Hecksher Park (941-316-1172), 450 W. Venice Ave., Venice. Six tennis courts with lights. Also, shuffleboard.

Holmes Beach Courts, near City Hall, Holmes Beach. Three lit tennis courts.

Jessie P. Miller, Ninth Ave. and 43rd St. W., Bradenton. Four lit cement tennis courts and one handball court.

Nick Bollettieri Tennis at IMG Academies (941-752-2476, 941-752, 2477 or 800-872-6425; www.imgacademies.com), 5500 34th St. W., Bradenton. Training camp for adults and juniors. Includes state-of-the-art tennis, 72 courts (six of them indoors), swimming pools, a sports-therapy care center, and high-tech sports center. Andre Agassi, Venus and Serena Williams, Anna Kournikova, and other pros have trained here.

Siesta Key County Beach (941-861-2150), Midnight Pass Rd. at Beach Way Dr., Siesta Key. Four tennis courts with lights.

South County Family YMCA (941-492-9622; www.veniceymca.com), 701 Center Rd., Venice. Two racquetball courts, plus workout and fitness rooms and classes.

SHELLING Though not comparable to the coast's southern beaches for shelling, the islands of Bradenton and Sarasota do yield some unusual finds. Venice Beach, for instance, is known for its shark teeth, which come in all sizes and various shades. Manasota Beach and the south end of Siesta Key also boast toothy waters, but Venice's beaches have the best pickings.

Sharks continually shed teeth and grow new ones. Most of what you find is prehistoric. The white ones are recent sheddings. Teeth range in size from 1/8 inch to a rare 3 inches. Some resorts provide "Florida snow shovels"—screen baskets fastened to broomsticks for sifting through the sand. You can also buy them in local hardware stores. Digging for specimens is taboo.

SPAS Body & Spirit (941-921-1388; www.bodyandspirit.net), 500 Southgate Plaza, Sarasota. A luxury day spa with massages, body treatments, facials, salon services.

Island Wellness (941-779-6836 or 941-782-1123; www.amislandwellness.com), 109 First St. N., Bradenton Beach. Holistic spa for massage, body wrap, acupuncture, and yoga on the beach.

The Key Spa & Salon (941-349-9005; www.siestakeyspa.com), 5150 Ocean Blvd., Suite A, at Tropical Breeze Resort, Siesta Key. Complete massage, skin care, and beauty treatments, plus lunch packages, in a charming island setting.

Mandala Medi Spa & Yoga Sanctuary (941-927-2278, www.mandalamedispa .com), 1715 Stickney Point Rd. Indonesian body treatments, massage, salon services, acupuncture, and medical aesthetics.

The Met (941-388-1772; www.themetsarasota.com), 35 S. Blvd. of Presidents, St. Armands Circle, Sarasota. Up a sweeping staircase from a posh clothing store in an elegant setting, The Met offers full spa and beauty facilities and treatments, including wraps, massages, and facials. Also offers a spa lunch.

Ocean Salon and Spa (941-364-3322), 1812 Hillview St., Sarasota. A complete menu of facials, massages, scrubs, polishes, and body masks, as well as manicures, pedicures, waxing, air-brush tanning, and other salon services.

A RECENT MAKEOVER ADDS ANOTHER CHAPTER TO THE LONG HISTORY OF WARM MINERAL SPRINGS.

Warm Mineral Springs (941-426-1692; www.warmmineralsprings.com), 12200 San Servando Ave., south of Venice near North Port. Water of a rare quality attracts health seekers to a 1.4-acre lake fed by 9 million gallons of mineral water each day. If you know your spas, you will appreciate the springs' chemical analysis of 19,870 parts per million of fixed solid minerals, the third highest in the world. The lake, which maintains a year-round temperature of 87 degrees, has soothing and, some believe, healing powers that attract people from around the world. Folks bathe at a roped-off beach and children's area, and sun on a grassy lawn. Opened in 1940, the facilities are under new ownership and are undergoing an extensive renovation. There's talk of building a resort and expanding beyond its mostly European clientele. Archaeologists have discovered artifacts in the lake suggesting that Native Americans came here for a bit of mineral-washed R&R 10,000 years ago. Some claim this was the Fountain of

Youth Ponce de León sought but never found because of his untimely death from an arrow inflicted nearby. Massages, acupuncture, and spiritual readings are available at the springs' spa facility, along with an on-site cafeteria. Admission is $20 per person, $14 for students, and $8 for children ages 12 and younger. Ten-day passes are available. Open daily 9–5.

SPECTATOR SPORTS

Greyhound Racing: **Sarasota Kennel Club** (941-355-7744; www.sarasotakennel .com), 5400 Bradenton Rd., Sarasota. Greyhound night and matinee racing from November to mid-April. Parimutuel betting, Texas Hold 'Em, and matinee and evening shows year-round. Thoroughbred horse racing is simulcast from Miami and other tracks year-round. Closed Sunday. Admission. Must be 18 or older to enter.

Polo: **Sarasota Polo Club** (941-907-0000; www.sarasotapolo.com), 8201 Polo Club Ln., 3.5 miles east of I-75 exit 213, Sarasota) Watch from the grandstands or bring a tailgate picnic. Game time is 1 PM every Sunday, mid-December–Easter. Admission.

Pro Baseball: **Ed Smith Stadium** (941-954-4101), 2700 12th St., Sarasota. Spring-training home (March and early April) of the Baltimore Orioles (888-848-BIRD; http://baltimore.orioles.mlb.com) and off-season home of the Sarasota Reds (941-365-4460). Plans are under way for a new stadium.

McKechnie Field (941-748-4610; http://pittsburgh.pirates.mlb.com), Ninth St. and 17th Ave. W., Bradenton. Site of the Pittsburgh Pirates' exhibition games during March and into April; a small but fun park.

🌱 **Pirate City** (941-747-3031; http://pittsburgh.pirates.mlb.com), 1701 27th St. E., Bradenton. Spring-practice field for the Pittsburgh Pirates' major and minor leagues. Catch the major leaguers during spring season working out from 10 AM to 1:30 PM. The minor leaguers train here in March and early April.

Waterskiing: 🌱 **Sarasota Ski-A-Rees Show** (941-388-1666; www.skiarees.com), Ken Thompson Park adjacent to Mote Marine Aquarium, Sarasota. Free amateur water-skiing and wakeboarding performances in the bay at 2 pm Sundays, February–April (except Easter). See Web site for off-season show schedule.

WATER SPORTS

Parasailing & Waterskiing: **Fun & Sun Parasail** (941-795-1000 or 888-778-8322), 135 Bridge St., Bradenton Beach. Fly single, double, or triple over Anna Maria Island.

Siesta Key Parasailing (941-586-1972), 1265 Old Stickney Point Rd., at Dockside Marine, Siesta Key. Single, double, and triple rides.

Sailboarding & Surfing: Sailboarders find fine conditions all along the coast.

Kiteboarding, one of the newest water sport to hit Florida seas, requires extensive training and lots of cash.

As far as Florida's west coast surfing reputation goes—which isn't very far— Bradenton Beach is one of the prime spots for surfing, especially in winter when cold fronts approach or in summer before and after tropical storms. Look in the "Beaches" section for other surfing and windsurfing venues.

Island Style Wind & Watersport (941-954-1009), 2433 N. Tamiami Trail, Sarasota. Offers kiteboarding lessons.

Snorkeling & Scuba: Of all the southern Gulf Coast, this region generally boasts the best visibility for underwater exploration, especially in spring. Man-made reefs make up for the lack of natural reefs on Florida's west coast. At Venice Beach, a natural reef lies just a quarter-mile from the beach, making shore dives possible. South of Crescent Beach, at the island's central zone, rocks, underwater caves, and coral formations make good submerged sightseeing at Point of Rocks beach.

At Bradenton Beach, the sunken sugar barge *Regina* houses various forms of marine life.

Both snorkelers and divers look for shark teeth fossils.

Dolphin Dive Center (941-922-9671; www.floridakayak.com), 6018 S. Tamiami Trail, Sarasota. Local charters, instruction, snorkel and scuba rentals.

Scuba Quest (941-366-1530; www.scubaquestusa.com), 1129 S. Tamiami Trail, at Bahia Vista St., Sarasota. With several locations in Florida, this company offers NAUI certification classes, charters, and equipment sales.

SeaTrek Divers (941-779-1506; www.seatrekdivers.com), 105 Seventh St. N., Bradenton Beach. Located across the street from the barge wreck, this firm offers two-tank, near-shore dives and scuba certification courses.

WILDERNESS CAMPING ✪ **Oscar Scherer State Park** (941-483-5956; www.floridastateparks.org./oscarscherer), 1843 S. Tamiami Trail, Osprey. This nearly 1,400-acre natural oasis provides 98 full-service campsites in a wooded, creekside setting of palmettos, pines, and venerable moss-draped oaks. The threatened Florida scrub jay seeks refuge here, along with bald eagles, bobcats, river otters, gopher tortoises, and alligators. You can swim in a freshwater lake or enjoy a bird walk, nature and canoe trails, picnicking, and fishing. To reserve a campsite or cabin, call 800-326-3521 or go to www.reserveamerica.com.

WILDLIFE SPOTTING *Birds:* The Sarasota coast is the least natural of the Gulf Coast's four regions. Determined bird spotters can find feathered friends at parks and refuges such as the Passage Key sanctuary north of Anna Maria Island (bring binoculars—landing ashore is forbidden); Rookery Islands north of Siesta Key (also approachable by boat only); Venice Area Audubon Rookery at the end of Annex Road in South Venice, a half-mile south of the junction of US 41 and FL 776; and Oscar Scherer State Park in Osprey, home of the endangered Florida scrub jay. Look for feral peacocks roaming the streets of the village on Longboat Key.

Dolphins: Dolphins often follow in the wake of tour boats, but they're unpredictable. You can't plan on them; you can only be thrilled and charmed when they do appear. If you learn their feeding schedules, you have a better chance of catching their act.

Manatees: Named after the lovable creatures, Bradenton's Manatee County has erected MANATEE WATCH signs at manatee-frequented areas: on the bridges and city pier of the Manatee River, on the Palma Sola Causeway, and on Anna Maria Island at Bayfront Park, Coquina Beach and Boat Ramp, and Kingfish Boat Ramp.

Nature Preserves & Eco-Attractions: ✪ ✿ **Mote Marine Laboratory Aquarium** (941-388-4441 or 800-691-MOTE, ext. 536; www.mote.org), 1600 Ken Thompson

HOLY SEA COWS!

Today we know them as Florida manatees: 1,300-pound blimps, with skin like burlap and a face only a nature buff could love. They also go by the name sea cows, although they are more closely related to the elephant. In days of yore, many a sea-weary sailor mistook them for mermaids.

Well, Ariel they're not, but bewitching they can be. Gentle and herbivorous—consuming up to 100 pounds of aquatic plants daily—they make no enemies and have only one stumbling block to survival: man. Being mammals, manatees must surface for air, like whales and dolphins. Their girth makes them a prime target for boaters speeding through their habitat. Warning signs designate popular manatee areas. Instead of zipping through these waters and further threatening the seriously endangered manatee population, boaters can benefit by slowing down and trying to spot the reclusive creatures as they take a breath. It requires a sharp eye, patience, and experience. Watch channels during low tides, when the manatees take to deeper water. Concentric circles, known as "manatee footprints," signal surfacing animals. They usually travel in a line and appear as drifting coconuts or fronds.

To report manatee deaths, injuries, harassment, or orphans, call 941-332-6972.

A SCULPTURE AT BRADENTON PIER PAYS HOMAGE TO THE COUNTY'S NAMESAKE.

Pkwy., on City Island, northeast of Lido Key, Sarasota. Mote Marine is known around the world for its research on sharks, marine mammals, and environmental pollutants. Its two visitors centers here educate the public on projects and marine life. A 135,000-gallon shark tank centerpieces the original facility and is kept stocked with sharks and fish typical of the area: grouper, snook, pompano, and snapper. Dozens of smaller aquariums and a touch tank hold more than 200 varieties of common and unusual species. Colorful signs challenge kids to ponder and learn about aquarium denizens. The original visitors center has expanded its shark focus in the new millennium with a sensory *Shark Attack* cinema, a *Sharktracker* interactive exhibit, and the entirely cool new Immersion Cinema, where visitors use individual touch screens to make their way through an underwater adventure. A 1,500-gallon *Remarkable Rays* touch tank sits outside in a chikee hut, and a mollusk exhibit features a preserved 25-foot giant squid from 2,000 feet down off the coast of New Zealand. In the Marine Mammal Visitors Center, the main attraction is a floor-to-ceiling glass tank that holds manatees Hugh and Buffett. The center also features a marine mammal rehabilitation tank and a sea turtle exhibit, which host some of the world's most fascinating sea creatures. Open daily 10–5. Admission: $17 for adults, $16 for seniors, $12 for children ages 4–12.

MOTE MARINE LABORATORY AQUARIUM BUILT ITS REPUTATION ON SHARK AND OTHER MARINE-CREATURE RESEARCH.

✪ ✐ **Oscar Scherer State Park** (941-483-5956; www.floridastateparks.org /oscarscherer), 1843 S. Tamiami Trail, Osprey. Home of the threatened Florida scrub jay plus bald eagles, bobcats, river otters, gopher tortoises, and alligators. Experience wildlife in a canoe along a saltwater tidal creek or by hiking an extensive system of nature trails. Take heed: If you swim in the freshwater lake, you may become more closely acquainted with an alligator than you would care to. Also, signs warn of amoeba threats in the warm summer months. The 1,384-acre park offers camping, swimming, canoeing (with rentals and a launch), fishing, and picnicking. Open sunrise to sunset. Admission: $5 per vehicle of two to eight people; $4 per single-occupant vehicle; $2 per pedestrian, cyclist, or extra passenger.

Quick Point Nature Preserve (www .longboatkey.org/parks/quick_point .htm), 100 Gulf of Mexico Dr., south end of Longboat Key. The town of Longboat Key worked to restore the natural environment of this 34-acre plot, once covered over and nearly destroyed by sand dredged from New

Pass. Park on the west side of the road and follow a boardwalk under the pass bridge to get to the trails through beach, uplands, mangrove, and lagoon habitats. It's a popular spot for ospreys, egrets, ibises, and shorebirds. Open daily. Free admission.

Sarasota Bay Walk, 1550 Ken Thompson Pkwy., on City Island, next to Mote Marine Aquarium, Sarasota. Take a quiet, self-guided walk along the bay, estuaries, lagoons, and uplands to learn more about coastland ecology. Boardwalk and shell paths lead you past mangroves, old fishing boats bobbing on the bay, egrets, and illustrated signs detailing nature's wonders. Free admission.

Wildlife Tours & Charters: ♪ **Sarasota Bay Explorers** (941-388-4200; www .sarasotabayexplorers.com), Mote Marine Laboratory Aquarium, 1600 Ken Thompson Pkwy., on City Island, Sarasota. A marine pontoon tour takes you into the Intracoastal waters between City Island and Siesta Key. Features include trawl-net tossing, binocular study of rookery islands, and a marine-biologist narration. Kids love the hands-on quality of this educational tour. It also offers custom and kayak tours. Packages with Mote Marine are available.

✳ Lodging

Most vacationers on the Sarasota Bay coast gravitate toward the barrier islands. On Siesta Key you won't find chain hotels; however, you will find accommodations large and small by the score. The other islands have their chains but more mom-and-pops, B&Bs, inns, destination resorts, and privately owned places. On the mainland, especially around the airport, business travelers find no-nonsense franchise and small motels. A couple of luxury options have opened in recent years: a Ritz-Carlton in 2001 and Hotel Indigo, the boutique branch of Inter-Continental Hotels Group, in 2006. With downtown Sarasota's renewal, more and more vacationers are choosing mainland accommodations.

Privately owned second homes and condominiums provide another source of accommodations along the Sarasota Bay coast. Vacation brokers who match visitors with such properties are listed under "Home and Condo Rentals" at the end of this section.

I've listed here a well-rounded selection of Sarasota-area accommodations, including a few of the better chain hotels. Toll-free 800, 888, 866, or 877 reservation numbers, where available, are listed after local numbers.

Pricing codes are explained below. They are normally per person/double occupancy for hotel rooms and per unit for efficiencies, apartments, cottages, suites, and villas. The range spans low- and high-season rates. Many resorts offer off-season packages at special rates and free lodging for children. Pricing does not include the 6 percent Florida sales tax or Sarasota County's 4 percent tourist tax, which is allotted to beach revitalization, arts funding, and tourism promotion. Some large resorts add service gratuities or maid surcharges.

Rate Categories

Inexpensive	Up to $100
Moderate	$100 to $200
Expensive	$200 to $200
Very Expensive	$300 and up

An asterisk after the pricing designation indicates that the rate includes at least a continental breakfast in the cost of lodging and possibly more extensive meal service as noted in the listing.

Note that under the Americans with Disabilities Act (ADA), accommodations built after January 26, 1993, and containing more than five rooms must be usable by people with disabilities. I have indicated only those small places that do not make such allowances.

ACCOMMODATIONS

Anna Maria

Emerald by the Sea Rod & Reel Motel (941-778-2780; www.rodandreelmotel.com), 877 North Shore Dr., 34216. This motel sits prettily on a narrow slab of bayside beach, with flowery landscaping, shuffleboard, picnic facilities and barbecue grills, a sunning deck, and a tiki-roofed pavilion. Each of the 10 one-room efficiencies is fully furnished with a kitchenette (microwave, stove top, and refrigerator), granite counters, dishware and cooking utensils, an ironing board, couch, wicker dining room chairs, and spic-and-span housekeeping, but no telephones. Conveniently for fishing types, the motel is next to the independently owned Rod & Reel Pier. Moderate.

Bradenton

Courtyard by Marriott Bradenton Sarasota Riverfront (941-747-3727 or 866-624-1658; www.marriott.com/srqbd), 100 Riverfront Dr. W., 34205. Formerly a Holiday Inn, the property reopened in December 2008 fully transformed but for its old Spanish-style architecture, fountained courtyards, and riverside views. Completely modernized, the lobby holds a media center with free use of Wii games, fashionable furnishings, a little market with microwave oven, and a sleek bistro that serves Starbucks coffee, breakfast, lunch, and dinner. The courtyard outside drips with hibiscus and oleander blossoms. Here you'll also find the pool and whirlpool. The hotel also has a fitness center and free wireless Internet access. All 153 rooms (57 of them suites) in the five-story hotel have narrow private balconies that overlook the river (rooms) or courtyard (suites) and come with flat-screen TVs, clean lines, and earthy tones. Moderate.

The Londoner Bed & Breakfast (941-748-5658 or 941-465-9636 (cell); www.thelondonerinn.com), 304 15th St. W., 34205. The 1926 home sits behind a picket fence as if it were built just to be a B&B. Six rooms are named for London neighborhoods, such as the Kensington, which has a Lady Di theme. Like two of the other rooms, it has its own bath across the hall and a communal refrigerator stocked with snacks and beverages. The three suites have bathrooms and fridges inside the room. Flat-screen TVs, robes, Gilchrist & Soames toiletries, pillow-top mattresses, and Wi-Fi add homey, convenient touches to all of the rooms, which are furnished in individual style to reflect their name, such as the Victorian furnishings in the Victoria suite. Rates include full breakfast in the sunny breakfast room. Traditional English afternoon tea convenes Monday–Saturday 11:30–3:30, but is not included and is open to the public. The delightful B&B is an easy walk to downtown's shops, restaurants, and other attractions. Moderate.°

Bradenton Beach

Bridgewalk (941-779-2545 or 866-779-2545; www.silverresorts.com) Bridge St., 34217. Key West–Caribbean in look, it colorfully houses 28 studio suites, town houses, and mini apartments in three tin-roofed low rises along the town's historic district. Units are comfortably spacious with full or mini kitchens. Deluxe touches include granite countertops, Jacuzzi tubs in some units, and gulf views from one of the buildings. The resort also houses upscale shops along the street. The beach is a short walk across the street, and a heated pool in the parking area cools off guests. Its restaurant serves up sunset views with cocktails to match. Moderate to Expensive. No handicap access.

✈ (ᵚ) **Seaside Inn & Resort** (941-778-5254 or 800-447-7124; www.seasideresort.com), 2200 Gulf Dr. N., 34217. Like the rest of Bradenton Beach, things are constantly looking better here. Spotless and decorated with charm, the six efficiencies and three rooms (all newly remodeled in July 2008) have tiled bathrooms, private patios, and modern kitchen facilities: toasters, refrigerators, and microwaves, with stove tops in the efficiencies. The penthouse (Expensive to Very Expensive) has a separate bedroom and luxury appointments, and it can connect to two other rooms for large family gatherings. Each room looks out on the gulf with a patio or deck balcony, and the inn has its own private seawalled beach above the public beach. Use of kayaks is complimentary to guests. It's a good value for beachside lodging with pleasant amenities. Moderate to Expensive.

Holmes Beach

🍴 **Cedar Cove Resort & Cottages** (941-778-1010 or 800-206-6293; www.cedarcoveresort.com), 2710 Gulf Dr. N., 34217. You have to love this place's casual, carefree beachside attitude, but what I like most is its sense of humor. As you walk up to the office, a sign offers the day's special—free margaritas—adding in small print, YESTERDAY. The Nut House out back looks like a Gilligan or Moondoggie kind of place to hang out. Hammocks, swinging benches, and a tub of beach toys keep guests on the beach. Every one of the 22 one- and two-bedroom suites comes

with a kitchen or kitchenette, along with surprises such as the scope and the pinball machine in the two-bedroom villa. Run by a Florida native, the resort has a feel that is right on and conducive to its two rules: "zero stress, 100 percent relaxation." Moderate to Expensive.

✪ **Harrington House B&B** (941-778-5444 or 888-828-5566; www.harringtonhouse.com), 5626 Gulf Dr., 34217. One of Florida's loveliest and best-maintained bed & breakfasts, Harrington adds to its homey, historic allure with a beachfront. Built in 1925 of local coquina rock and pecky cypress with Mediterranean flourishes, the Main House was refurbished with casual elegance and magical touches. Each of the six rooms—such as Renaissance, Birdsong, and Sunset—is labeled with a needlepoint door sign. Room sizes vary from spacious, with a king-sized bed, to comfortably cozy. Each guest room has its own bathroom, refrigerator, and TV. Six other rooms plus an assortment of suites are distributed throughout the Carriage House and beach houses. An eclectic collection of handpicked antique furniture enhances guests' comfort. A dramatic cut-stone fireplace dominates the sitting room, where classical music recordings are interrupted only by an occasional piano solo and homemade chocolate chip cookies in the afternoon. Guests enjoy gourmet home-cooked breakfasts at individual tables amid Victorian pieces and filmy white curtains. Outdoor areas include sundecks, a pool, a wide beach, and colorful landscaping around picket fences and arched alcoves. Bikes and kayaks are available for guests' use. No smoking or children younger than age 13 are allowed. Moderate to Very Expensive (two-night minimum weekends and holidays).

Lido Key

🐚 **Historic Gulf Beach Resort Motel** (941-388-2127 or 800-232-2489; www.gulfbeachsarasota.com), 930 Ben Franklin Dr., Sarasota 34236. Just a couple of doors down from the towering Lido Beach Resort, Gulf Beach takes you to a circa-1950 era of Florida vacationing. All 49 rooms of this "condo-tel" are privately owned and therefore decorated with individual personality. They range from tiny motel rooms with mini fridges, microwaves, and coffeemakers to roomy, two-bedroom, gulf-front apartments with all the comforts of home. Three one- and two-story cement-block buildings file between the main beach drag and the wide sands of Lido. There's a homey feel here. Owners have been coming for years, taking advantage of the welcoming pool, grilling area, shuffleboard, and sunset-perfect view. In 2003 Lido Key businesspeople saved this, Lido's first motel, from demise and high-rise takeover by getting it designated a historic landmark. Inexpensive to Moderate.

✑ **Lido Beach Resort** (941-388-2161 or 800-441-2113; www.lidobeachresort.com), 700 Ben Franklin Dr., Sarasota 34236. Located next to Lido Key's public beach, the 223-unit, smoke-free resort provides attractive accommodations furnished in sand and sea tones, and a full range of water sports in the thick of beach activity. Its tower holds 14 floors, a city-view restaurant named Lido Beach Grille, and business facilities. Between it and the original four-story hotel squirms a goldfish creek crossed by wooden walkways with tin-roofed gazebos. The two pools sit on the shell-scattered beach and have their own beach bar. Another café offers guests lunch and dinner in the lobby. Modern, nicely furnished rooms come with or without full kitchens.

Some have a small refrigerator and microwave instead; all have coffeemakers; the resort provides a complimentary shuttle to shopping at St. Armands Circle. Moderate to Expensive.

Longboat Key

✪ ♂ ✑ ((ᵖ)) **Colony Beach and Tennis Resort** (941-383-6464 or 800-4COLONY; www.colonybeachresort.com), 1620 Gulf of Mexico Dr., 34228. The Colony ranks among Florida's finest resorts, a place where you could hide indefinitely behind security gates without ever having to face the real world. It stakes its reputation on top-notch tennis and dining: Ten of the 21 tennis courts have state-of-the-art soft surfaces. *Tennis* magazine named it the top U.S. tennis resort for eight consecutive years. The Colony Dining Room, one of the property's two dining spots, also consistently wins awards. The other, ✪ The Monkey Room, features comical monkey murals and great martinis, plus there's a deli-market. The 18-acre oleander-trimmed resort occupies a stretch of broad private beach. Complimentary kids' recreational programs take young guests to the courts, beach, pool, and off-property attractions. The Colony rents out 104 units ranging from beach houses to family-friendly one- or two-bedroom suites. All units contain modern kitchen facilities, Murphy beds, a mixed bag of furnishings, and marble master baths. Guests have free use of tennis courts as well as a spa and a professionally staffed health club with a fitness studio. Very Expensive.

✪ ((ᵖ)) **Rolling Waves Beach Cottages** (941-383-1323; www.rollingwaves.com), 6351 Gulf of Mexico Dr., 34228. What more could you ask of a beach vacation than a cute little 1940s cottage furnished modernly in bright colors, containing a modern full kitchen and bath, and complete with glass patio tables, umbrellas, classic-style painted metal chairs, a grill, sea grapes, huge pink hibiscus blossoms, and a quiet beach outside the door? Rolling Waves' eight cottages are kept meticulous and are decorated with touches of character: clay-tile kitchen floors, rag rugs over wood floors in a couple of the cottages, full-sized futons in the living room, DVDs, and an exterior paint job that evokes the chattel houses of the Caribbean. Maid service is not provided. Located in Longboat Key's old, historic section, it escapes the glitz and the throngs with classic class. Moderate to Expensive. No handicap access.

🐾 **Sandpiper Inn** (941-383-2552; www.sandpiperinn.com), 5451 Gulf of Mexico Dr., 34228. Barefoot beach vacations are my favorite, and Sandpiper Inn manages to shut out the world—effectively blocking the low-rise next door from the one-story, 11-room property's view with clever vegetation and a focus on the sea. A paver walkway leads past the efficiencies, each set up with a rock pad for its chaise lounge and patio table with umbrella. It passes a picnic area with gas grills and a rock fountain on its way to a tin-roofed gathering area and the beach, fringed with palms, sea oats, and other vegetation. Rattan and white wicker furnish the tiled rooms with their fully equipped kitchens and palm tree accents. Recently fully renovated (it was formerly The Riviera), its appliances gleam, though there are a few rough edges. The beauty lies in the details—your name posted on a plaque as you arrive, cushions on the lounge chairs, beachy art in the rooms, and innkeepers who greet you like family, sit you down at a table for check-in, and pay individual attention to all. Neat, orderly, and quiet, Sandpiper is everything you want in a beach escape. Small pets are allowed. Daily house-

ON LONGBOAT KEY, ROLLING WAVES PROVIDES GUESTS WITH THE ULTIMATE BEACH-COTTAGE VACATION.

keeping is extra. Moderate to Expensive.

Nokomis

((ᵞ)) **A Beach Retreat** (941-485-8771 or 866-232-2480; www.abeachretreat .com), 105 Casey Key Rd., 34275. A Beach Retreat owns efficiencies and apartments on both the beach and the bay. Fancied up with a jaunty yellow paint job and lattice trim, it also has a swimming pool on the bay side, where boat docks and 10 units accommodate guests and their vessels. The gulfside rooms, mostly ground level, are steps from a lovely, natural beach, but because the wonderful tall sea oats block views of the water, they cluster around a tropically vegetated courtyard and shuffleboard courts. The 26 units—from studios to three-bedroom suites—all have their own look and layout that is largely modern but with some imperfections that lend beach character. All but two have full kitchens. Moderate to Expensive.

Sarasota

❂ ((ᵞ)) **The Cypress** (941-955-4683; www.cypressbb.com), 621 Gulfstream

Ave. S., 34236. Details make a bed & breakfast inn, and The Cypress's attention to special touches, flourishes, and minutiae place it among the top in its genre. Notice the antique ice cream table with swivel-out stools in the sunny breakfast room, the fireplace, the vintage Edison phonograph and the piano in the living room, the exquisite crown molding throughout, the fresh flowers in each of the five individually decorated rooms, the multi-course gourmet breakfasts, and the happy-hour cocktails and hors d'oeuvres alfresco at 6 PM. In short, the innkeepers spoil their guests. A trio of talent—Vicki Hadley and Robert and Nina Belott—took over a 1940s home that the original owner's daughter refused to sell out to encroaching condos, making The Cypress—named for its sturdy building material—a flower in the shadow of high rises. Still, the location is quite enviable. From the front deck guests can watch the sun set over the masts of yachts in the marina across the way. Downtown's Palm Avenue district of galleries, sidewalk cafés, and specialty shops, meanwhile,

is a short stroll away. Moderate to Expensive.°

✪ (ᵞᵖ) **Hotel Indigo** (941-487-3800 or 866-2-INDIGO; www.hotelindigo .com), 1223 Boulevard of the Arts, 34236. From the people who bring you Holiday Inn and Crowne Plaza, this new concept and brand made its Florida debut here in 2006. Hotel Indigo provides a stimulating environment in a boutique setting. Trademarks of the brand include lobby and room murals that change with the season. The lobby is even scented with seasonal aromas, such as cinnamon apple in fall. Oversized wooden Adirondack-style beach chairs decorate the lobby, where you'll also find Phi, a bright little café serving breakfast, lunch, and dinner. The hotel's 95 rooms (12 of which are suites) are inviting and decorated beach cottage style with hardwood floors, sleeper sofas, and glassed-in shower stalls (no bathtubs). Two large whirlpools—one hot, one cold—are the centerpieces of an outdoor lunching and sunning deck. A coffee-pastry counter and fitness room complete the description of this so-called lifestyle

ARTISTIC AND GRACIOUS, THE CYPRESS BED & BREAKFAST BLENDS WELL WITH SARASOTA'S DOWNTOWN PERSONALITY.

hotel. Adjacent to the new Renaissance residential development, it is also close to Van Wezel Center, G.WIZ, and downtown attractions. Moderate to Expensive.

((♥)) **Hyatt Regency Sarasota** (941-953-1234 or 800-233-1234; www .sarasota.hyatt.com), 1000 Blvd. of the Arts, 34236. Inside the 10-story Hyatt unfolds a world of modern decor, contemporary comfort, and bayside splendor. In 2008, it underwent a $22 million renovation inspired by the Florida-style clothing design of Lilly Pulitzer. The decor is all asplash in her pinks, lime greens, oranges, and floral bursts. A soaring atrium makes way for a clubby lounge and refined restaurant Currents, with windows overlooking the water. At the front desk, staff in crisp uniforms are efficient and helpful. Spaciousness and good taste characterize the 12-story hotel's 294 rooms and 12 suites. They come equipped with flat-screen TVs and iPod docking stations. All have a view of Sarasota Bay or the hotel's marina, which has 32 boat slips, plus boat rentals and fishing charters. The full fitness center (which thoughtfully provides refrigerated towels), a zero-entry swimming pool with rock-arched waterfalls and its own grill-bar, and close proximity to Van Wezel Performing Arts Hall and downtown attractions make this long-standing landmark a favorite with business travelers. Inexpensive to Moderate.

✪ ♂ ✎ ((♥)) **Ritz-Carlton Sarasota** (941-309-2000 or 800-241-3333; www .ritzcarlton.com), 1111 Ritz-Carlton Dr., 34236. One of the first in the Ritz-Carlton line to offer living quarters, this hotel has 266 rooms and suites that deliver all the luxury you expect from the name. Perched on the edge of downtown, it's more of a city hotel than other Ritz-Carlton Florida properties, but it has its own off-site beach

club. Some rooms have views of Sarasota Bay, others overlook a neighboring marina. White marble bathrooms, oversized rooms in butterscotch tones, wonderful beds, and wireless Internet and Ethernet hook-ups make it equally accommodating for leisure and business travelers. Available on the main campus are a spa and fitness center, as well as a swimming pool and burger bar, a fine American regional cuisine restaurant, and a sophisticated bar called the ✪ **Cà d'Zan Lounge.** The full-service spa's fitness center requires a daily fee or membership. Small touches such as a free shoeshine service and over-the-top service define the inimitable Ritz experience. For the ultimate experience, book on the club floors and take advantage of the complimentary food and drink services. Nine floors of the 17-story high-rise are devoted to resort guests; the rest, plus two other buildings on the mainland and beach, are residential units. An hourly shuttle transports guests to shopping on St. Armands Key and the Ritz's Members Beach Club on Lido Key, which includes a kids' club, pool, locker rooms, and a tropical-cuisine restaurant. A shuttle also transfers guests to the private Ritz-Carlton Golf Course, which lies about 13 miles to the east. Expensive to Very Expensive.

Siesta Key

Many of Siesta Key's accommodations require a minimum stay (usually one week) during season. The majority of beach accommodations are condos, villas, or homes.

((♥)) **Siesta Key Bungalows** (941-349-9025 or 888-5-SIESTA; www.siestakey bungalows.com), 8212 Midnight Pass Rd., 34242. Appealing to birders and seclusion-seekers, these 10 individually decorated, one-bedroom bungalows on Heron Bay feature full kitchens (some with dishwashers), white wicker and rattan furnishings, and double pillow-top mattresses. Hand-painted murals and accents match each bungalow's fitting name, such as Hibiscus, Catamaran, and Dolphin. The living room areas contain sleeper sofas, making the bungalows convenient for families. Kayak and canoe use is complimentary, plus there's a swimming pool and a makeshift sand beach. Moderate to Expensive.

☃ (ᵖ) **Turtle Beach Resort** (941-349-4554; www.turtlebeachresort.com), 9049 Midnight Pass Rd., 34242. One of Sarasota's Small Superior Lodgings, this place is a real find at the southern, quiet end of the island, a three-minute walk from Turtle Beach. Ten cottages on the bay contain studio, one-bedroom, or two-bedroom accommodations, plus a private hot tub. Each cottage has its own personality, reflected in names such as Rain Forest, Montego Bay, and Southwestern. Modern designer furniture and lamps, objets d'art, and other decorative pieces carry out the themes. Ten new units across the street at The Inn at Turtle Beach, designed in a Tommy Bahama mode and also with private outdoor whirlpools, are ideal for couples. Most rooms at both properties have sleeper sofas; all come with kitchen facilities. Bathrobes, TVs, CD and DVD players, and sherry are provided in each of the cottages, which spread along a lushly landscaped strip. The well-planned property provides private nooks and hammocks along waterside docks and two pools. Use of washers and dryers is free after 4 PM, and bicycles, canoes, kayaks, rowboats, and beach gear are complimentary for guests' enjoyment. Very romantic, the original resort is nonetheless conducive to families, and pets are permitted. Expensive to Very Expensive (minimum stay required in season; housekeeping is extra).

Venice

(ᵖ) **Banyan House** (941-484-1385; www.banyanhouse.com), 519 S. Harbor Dr., 34285. In the mid-1920s architects designed Venice in accordance with its Italian name; homes and buildings are modeled after northern Mediterranean styles. The town's first community swimming pool was located in the backyard of one of the original

A TOUCH OF THE OLD WORLD AT BANYAN HOUSE, A VENERABLE BED & BREAKFAST IN VENICE.

homes, next to a fledgling banyan tree. Today that small pool, with its now-sprawling tree, resides at the same home, a red-tile-roofed B&B known as the Banyan House. Classic statuary, fountains, multihued blossoms, a courtyard, a sundeck, a billiard and fitness room, and a hot tub share the property. Five rooms, each with a private bath, exert their individual personalities. The Palm Room has a fireplace. The Laurel Room features an outdoor balcony. The Tree House includes a sunny sitting room overlooking the pool. The Sun Deck has a separate entrance. The Palmetto Room offers hardwood floors and lavender hues. All units contain at least a small refrigerator; three are efficiencies. Two rooms and one apartment are also available in the carriage house, rented by the month. Deluxe touches include bathrobes in the closet and wine in the fridge. Susan serves homemade gourmet breakfast in a solarium off the formal sitting room, the latter furnished with an antique Italian fireplace, a circa-1890 hoop-skirt bench, and other Victorian period pieces. Pecky cypress, wood-beam ceilings, terra-cotta slate tiling, and wrought-iron banisters are all original. Free use of bicycles allows guests to explore old Venice's nearby shopping mecca and beach. Smoking is not allowed in any of the rooms. Moderate* (minimum two-night stay required). No handicap access.

((ᵞ)) **Inn at the Beach** (941-484-8471 or 800-255-8471; www.innatthebeach .com), 725 W. Venice Ave., 34285. This modern resort was built to include Mediterranean architectural overtones and contemporary Florida comfort and decor. Located across the street from the public access to Venice Beach, the hotel has 49 units; many of the second-floor ones overlook the gulf. Its well-maintained rooms have a clean white, light wood, understated floral motif

with plantation shutters and tile floors. All contain at least a microwave, coffeemaker, and mini fridge; efficiencies and one- and two-bedroom suites add full refrigerators, stove tops, dishwashers, dishware, and pans. A small pool with spa and sundeck is tucked behind the hotel in the parking lot—not high on atmosphere. I'd opt for the beach. Continental breakfast is included in the rate. Moderate to Very Expensive*.

((ᵞ)) **Venice Beach Villas** (941-488-1580 or 800-542-3404; www.venice beachvillas.com), 501 W. Venice Ave., 34285. A short walk to downtown and quick drive to the beach, this refitted retro property lends itself to exploring the best of Venice. An evening walk takes you to many of the best local restaurants and around a neighborhood canopied with huge oaks carrying armfuls of Spanish moss. Its 13 units range from studios to two-bedroom units (Expensive in season) and come complete with modern kitchen facilities. One sign of their circa-1940 age is the colorful wall tiles in the bathrooms. A pretty pool, free use of bikes and "Florida snow shovels" for shark-toothing, and barbecue grills provide the necessaries for a Venice vacation. Its sister property at 505 Menendez holds 10 more units and the same pedigree. In season, minimum stay may apply. No housekeeping. Inexpensive to Moderate.

HOME & CONDO RENTALS Anna Maria Gulf Coast Rentals (941-778-3699 or 800-865-0800; www.amgc rentals.com), 5319 Gulf Dr., Holmes Beach 34217. Anna Maria Island is a hot market for home and condo rentals, from charming beach cottages to swank condos and multiroom homes.

Anna Maria Island Accommodations (866-264-2226 or 941-779-0733;

www.annamariaparadise.com), 5604-B Marina Drive, Holmes Beach 34217. More than 200 homes to rent by the week or month.

A Paradise Rental Management (941-778-4800 or 800-237-2252; www.aparadiserentals.com), 5201 Gulf Dr., Holmes Beach 34217. Rental condos and homes on Anna Maria Island for short and long term, starting under $1,000 for a week.

Beckmann Properties (941-346-3500 or 888-437-3500; www.stayonsiesta.com), 6604 Midnight Pass Rd., Siesta Key 34242. Condos, villas, and homes to rent on the island.

Resort Quest Southwest Florida (239-992-6620; www.resortquest.com), 26201 Hickory Blvd., Bonita Springs 34134. Rentals from Venice to Anna Maria Island.

RV RESORTS Camp Venice Retreat (941-488-0850; www.camp venice.com), 4085 E. Venice Ave., Venice 34292, at exit 191 off I-75. This campground near Snook Haven park and restaurant has full hook-ups and waterfront sites, plus tent sites and cabin rentals. Amenities include security gates, a heated swimming pool, shuffleboard, horseshoes, a nature trail, fishing, boat and canoe rentals, a laundry room, and a supply store.

Horseshoe Cove (941-758-5335 or 800-291-3446; www.horseshoecove .net), 5100 60th St. E., Bradenton 34203. This 60-acre oak-grove riverfront site includes a 12-acre island with a pavilion and nature and biking trails. The resort has a heated pool and spa, a postal facility, hook-up to phone and cable, lighted fishing docks on the Braden River, shuffleboard courts, and other recreational facilities. Musical jam sessions happen regularly.

Linger Lodge (941-755-2757; www.lingerlodgeresort.com), 7205 85th St.

Ct. E., Bradenton 34202. By dint of its old-Florida-style character and slightly bizarre restaurant, this place has gained a reputation for funky. RV sites lie along or near the Braden River. Amenities include a boat ramp, fishing, and laundry.

Sarasota Bay Travel Trailer Park (941-794-1200 or 800-247-8361; www.paradisebay-sarasotabayrvpark.com), 10777 44th Ave. W., Bradenton 34210. Located on the bay and having full hook-ups, a boat ramp and dock, fishing, horseshoes, exercise room, recreation hall, and entertainment, this park for seniors caters mostly to permanent abodes, with some spots for transients. This is an exceptionally well-kept and scenic facility.

Turtle Beach Campground (941-349-3839), 8862 Midnight Pass Rd., Sarasota 34242. Forty sites for tents and RVs near the beach. Electric and cable TV hookups.

✷ Where to Eat

Bravo! Sarasota's individually owned restaurants have banded together to fight chain-restaurant homogeneity and build their promotional muscle. Look for restaurants that display the "Fresh Originals" logo (www.fresh originals.com).

For Sarasotans, eating out is as much a cultural event as attending the opera. It is often an inextricable part of an evening at the theater or a gallery opening. Sarasotans take dining out quite seriously and keep restaurants full, even off-season. Their enthusiasm for newness makes local kitchens more innovative than those of their neighbors to the south. (Out of about 70 Golden Spoon winners awarded in 2009 by *Florida Trend* magazine, eight—Beach Bistro, Euphemia Haye, Michael's on East, Colony Dining Room, Derek's, Maison Blanche, Selva

Grill, and Vernona at the Ritz-Carlton—are found in this region.) The town also counts one of the highest concentrations of Zagat-rated restaurants in Florida. Sarasota slides along the cutting edge of New World cuisine while maintaining classic favorites that range from rickety oyster bars to French cafés.

The following listings span the diversity of Sarasota Bay coast cuisine in these price categories:

Inexpensive	Up to $15
Moderate	$15 to $25
Expensive	$25 to $35
Very Expensive	$35 or more

Cost categories are based on the range of dinner entrée prices or, if dinner is not served, on lunch entrées. Those restaurants listed with "Healthy Selections" usually mark such on their menu.

Note: Florida law forbids smoking inside all restaurants and bars serving food. Smoking is permitted only in restaurants with outdoor seating.

Anna Maria Island

🦞 ✨ ♿ **Rotten Ralph's** (941-778-3953; www.rottenralphs.com), 902 Bay Blvd. S. Also at the Anna Maria Yacht Basin: (941-778-1604), 200 Bridge St., on the Historic Bridge Street Pier, Bradenton Beach. The atmosphere here is due entirely to the setting. It's a place that locals frequent and is full of character and characters. The laminated place mat menu describes several finger food selections (steamed shrimp, oysters Rockefeller, chicken wings, nachos), Old Florida fried seafood standards, fish and chips (all you can eat for $9.99), sandwiches, and pasta. I inevitably order the blackened grouper sandwich, which is totally fresh and well seasoned. We've always found the food fresh and tasty, but, truthfully, we enjoy the view more. A couple of years ago, the restaurant opened a second place in Bradenton Beach, a long-awaited replacement for a previous restaurant on the pier. Inexpensive to Moderate. No reservations.

Bradenton

➕ 🦞 ♿ **Alvarez Mexican Food** (941-729-2232), 1431 Eighth Ave. W., Palmetto. Across the river from Bradenton, Palmetto is the seat of Manatee County's huge agricultural industry. That means a heritage of fresh produce and Hispanic cuisine. Alvarez has ruled the latter category since 1976. Farm workers mingle with white-collar tomato brokers for the real thing in Mexican. The dining room is small, kitsch, and worn, but the patio has more of a festive air and is the first choice when weather allows. The menu spans all the Tex-Mex favorites along with Alvarez specialties: *huevos rancheros* for breakfast, *camarones al Diablo* (spicy shrimp), *barbacoa* (Mexican barbecue), and rich *mole* with either pork or chicken. Daily lunch specials and "speedies" combinations offer bargains. Beware of the salsa: It appears simple but packs a wallop and tastes entirely of fresh tomatoes. Inexpensive. No reservations.

ALVAREZ MEXICAN FOOD SERVES THE REAL THING AND HAS SINCE 1976.

🦐 ⅙ **Fav's Italian Cucina** (941-708-3287; www.favsitaliancucina.com), 419 Old Main St. Restaurants come and go in struggling downtown Bradenton, but this one has endured, and it's not difficult to reckon why. Simple: good food, easy-to-swallow prices. Packed into a tiny storefront corner of an arcade, it spills onto the arcade and sidewalk out front. The counter/kitchen bustles with the activity of locals coming in to pick up their take-out, chat with the staff, or sit down at a table topped with butcher block paper. Lots of windows mean a bright atmosphere inside or out. The menu is crammed with Italian favorites, hot and cold subs, and wraps. Order anything topped with Fav's homemade red sauce, because it's perfect. The subs come on homemade Italian flat bread baked daily on-site, and that adds a whole new twist to the taste and texture. I tried the meatball subs—garlicky, not-too-crazy-big meatballs smothered in mozzarella. It rates #1 in a lifetime of loving meatball subs. Hand-tossed pizzas include deep dish, meatball, and a lunch special where you can order two slices and a soft drink for $4.50. Dinner entrées, most of which are not available until after 5, made my mouth water, especially the gnocchi and baked tortellini with tomato cream sauce, sausage, mushrooms, and mozzarella. Inexpensive. No reservations.

Bradenton Beach

🦐 ⅙ **Island Crêperie** (941-778-1011), 127 Bridge St. Crêpes, of course, are the main draw at this tiny, 10-table eatery. Buckwheat crêpes—filled with such tasty combinations as ratatouille with egg and bacon or so-called chorizo (actually pepperoni), smoked salmon with artichoke and sour cream, or proscuitto with blue cheese and walnuts—are a specialty at breakfast and lunch. Salads, sandwiches, and quiche are also offered breakfast through lunch. At dinner, which is booked months in advance during the winter season, chef-owner Olivier Rose does a set of classic French dishes such as beef bourguignon, shrimp à la provençale, or pork in Gorgonzola sauce, served with a choice of starters—marvelous blue-cheese salad, onion soup, champagne country pâté, garden salad, or smoked salmon salad—and potatoes au gratin for only $16.90. Such a deal! Twenty-three different dessert crêpes take their inspiration from Cape Cod (apple sauce with caramel), the Black Forest (red fruits with chocolate sauce), Jamaica (banana, cinnamon, flambé with white rum), and beyond. Inexpensive. Closed Sunday dinner.

⅙ **Sun House Restaurant & Bar** (941-782-1122; www.thesunhouse restaurant.com), 111 Gulf Dr. S., at BridgeWalk resort. Hiked up on the second floor of the colorful Bridge-Walk resort, Sun House keeps in tropical theme with such creative inventions as Bahamian lobster and ravioli, pan-seared grouper with spinach and key lime beurre blanc, coconut pecan chicken, and the popular chipotle burger. Come for a sunset cocktail and munchies (the salsa has won awards and comes with a mélange of tropical chips) or stay for a full-blown meal; you won't be disappointed, no matter what. But be sure to budget in a frozen key lime pie cocktail or double crème brûlée dessert. Inexpensive to Moderate. No reservations; preferred seating.

Casey Key

✪ 🦐 🐚 ⅙ **Casey Key Fish House** (941-966-1901), 801 Blackburn Point Rd., Osprey. Casey Key does not attempt to dazzle its boat- and drive-in customers with pretensions. Everyone's happy to find good food reasonably priced, a perennially cheerful staff, fresh seafood with little fuss but lots of freshness, and a view of the water and a great blue heron or two for atmosphere. Well, to be fair, there is an aquarium and a mounted dolphinfish as "decorator touches," but this place is about the seafood. The laminated, all-day menu warns that patience is a virtue if you wish food cooked to order. It then goes on to list standard Florida fish-house fare such as baskets of crab-cakes, battered shrimp, fish and chips, and grouper sandwiches. Dinners dress it up a little with such choices as diver scallops provençal or fresh grilled salmon with cucumber-dill sauce. The blackboard lists the day's catches, which are available after 4 PM and are served with toasted white bread, white rice, and steamed veggies on a plastic plate. Don't be fooled by these simplicities. My recent affair with a grouper special resulted in a wonderfully sautéed fillet topped with black beans and corn off the cob in a limey butter sauce—a totally unexpected pleasure. If you can't fit it in, take some key lime pie to go because it's way up there on the "best" scale with just the right balance of sweet to tart and a light, creamy consistency. Inexpensive to Moderate. No reservations.

Holmes Beach

✪ **Beach Bistro** (941-778-6444; www.beachbistro.com), 6600 Gulf Dr. The talk of connoisseurs for many years, this little bit of gourmet heaven has fewer than 20 tables in its main dining area, a two-room cottage. (Most of them cluster around picture windows in a room with one of the best local-dining views of the sunset.) On every occasion we've visited, servers attended us with skilled timing and pleasant surprises. In recent years, it has added small plate and cocktail menu options for those who can't

afford its specialty items in the $50 to $70 range. Dinner begins with herbed bread and a marvelous dip of tomatoes and basil, The exacting menu showcases the chefs' quirky talents, which are difficult to define but easy to enjoy. The "lobstercargots" appetizer, for instance, replaces those "chewy little slugs" with succulent morsels of Florida lobster in bubbling garlic butter and spinach. We had a hard time letting them cool before we ate them, they were that tantalizing. Bouillabaisse with lobster, calamari, and fish is a signature ($46 to $56, depending on portion size), as is the "Food Heaven" marvel—lamb crowned with lobster and foie gras on brioche bread pudding ($52 to $68). Each dish is executed to perfection. The vegetable accompaniments to our main courses were delicious enough to fight them for attention. And our wine by the glass was poured from the bottle, a touch I always appreciate. In short, if you hear critics and regular folks raving about Beach Bistro, it's all true. Serving dinner only. Moderate to Very Expensive. Handicap access is limited; close quarters and no bathroom wheelchair access.

Lido Key

✪ 🦐 **New Pass Grill & Bait Shop** (941-388-3050; www.newpassgrill .com), 1498 Ken Thompson Pkwy., Sarasota, on City Island at New Pass Bridge. Here's a place to grab a quick breakfast or lunch if you're out boating or visiting Mote Marine Aquarium. Step up to the window; order your burger, hot dog, clam basket, fish and chips, sub, or other cold sandwich; then meander off to settle onto a jumbled selection of picnic tables and dock counter space along the water at New Pass. Watch the fleets of herons, egrets, pelicans, and boats while you wait for your name to be called. The

SEAFOOD DOESN'T GET ANY FRESHER OR MORE AFFORDABLE THAN AT NEW PASS GRILL.

burgers are legendary and the prices are unbeatable. Afterward, troll the bait-shop tanks and shelves for fishing supplies and leave with the satisfaction that a place such as this still exists (and has since 1929!). Inexpensive. No reservations or handicap access.

✪ ✂ ♿ **Old Salty Dog** (941-388-4311; www.theoldsaltydog.com), 1601B Ken Thompson Pkwy., Sarasota, on City Island. A spin-off of the Siesta Key original, this one has a more properly salty setting: a tin-roofed, red stucco building tucked into a marina in the shadow of the Longboat Key bridge. If you sit outside on the breezy patios, you'll be entertained by boaters, WaveRunners, and water-skiers. The menu lists such fun casual eats as Buffalo wings with dill sauce, New England clam chowder, deep-fried clams, peel-and-eat shrimp, burgers, fish and chips, coconut shrimp, baby back ribs,

fresh catch dinners (char-broiled, blackened, deep-fried, or the trademark Salty Dog—beer-battered and deep-fried, and not for the faint of heart). We like the wide selection of beer it offers, on tap as well as bottled. My son likes that we don't have to wait long for our food. Inexpensive to Moderate. No reservations.

Longboat Key
♿ ✂ **The Colony Dining Room** (941-383-5558; www.colonybeach resort.com), 1620 Gulf of Mexico Dr., at Colony Beach Resort. Judging by the black-peppered ahi tuna panini I enjoyed for lunch not long ago, excellence and details are what have kept this resort restaurant at the top of its game for more than 40 years. That and the incredible beach view! Wasabi mayo, beefsteak tomatoes, and Havarti cheese elevated my meal above mere "sandwich." Other luncheon offerings include littleneck clams with pancetta over linguine, a bleu filet open-face sandwich, and pizza with mushroom, pineapple, hot peppers, and feta. At dinner, start with the lavender-honey breast of duck or roasted yellow beet salad, then choose from seafood and meat dishes such as blackened grouper with key lime beurre blanc and avocado-papaya salsa, seared snapper with lump crab, or veal medallions with jumbo shrimp and béarnaise sauce. The Colony Classic key lime pie does it Key West style, with fluffy meringue atop custardlike filling. For something lighter and more affordable, the adjacent Monkey Bar serves seafood wonton tacos, Mediterranean chicken wings and burgers (Inexpensive to Moderate) all day long. Moderate to Very Expensive. Reservations accepted.

✪ **Mar-Vista Dockside Restaurant & Pub** (941-383-2391; www.grouper sandwich.com), 760 Broadway St., in the Village. Locals still refer to it as the Pub, a hangover from years gone by. Casual at its best, it has that lovely, lived-in, borderline ramshackle look on the outside, crowned by an appropriately rusting tin roof. Inside, tables don't match, napkins are paper, historic photos and sailors' dollar bills adorn the wall, boaters hoist beers at the bar, and a view of the harbor dominates the decorator's scheme. There's also seating on plastic chairs on the patio, which has heaters when it's cool and fans when it's hot. The seafood is fresh and prepared with signature twists: vegetable and conch fritters, a fresh-catch Rueben sandwich, grouper quesadilla, Longbeach bouillabaisse, sesame ahi tuna, and Caribbean grilled chicken. A steamer pot brims with shellfish and vegetables, plus other steamed seafood dinners satisfy the urge for simplicity. The key lime pie is creamy, dreamy, and authentic. We've enjoyed the well-executed cuisine and laid-back atmosphere here many times. Moderate to Expensive. No reservations; preferred seating. Handicap access in the restaurant but not the restrooms.

Nokomis

✪ 🦐 🌊 ♿ **Captain Eddie's Seafood Restaurant** (941-484-4623), 107 Colonia Ln. E. Ask anyone around the Venice-Nokomis-Osprey area where to get fresh seafood, and nine out of 10 will recommend, without pause, Captain Eddie's. The restaurant began as a fish market that took over a convenience store and set up a few picnic tables to fill the space. Those picnic tables came to be in such great demand that the market eventually grew into a restaurant where the locals know they can get their money's worth in fresh fish. A couple of years ago, to keep up with the demand, Eddie's expanded to a new adjacent dining

room and tiki bar. The renovation covered the walls in rough-hewn wood siding and added a modern look, but the long tables and casual atmosphere abide. This is a true Florida fish house—my favorite brand of dining. The hostess calls most of the patrons by name. The menu carries a lot of fried-fish items such as shrimp, catfish, and oysters (but fried right and in canola oil) as well as broiled options. After an appetizer of alligator bites, I tried a broiled grouper sandwich that was the best I've tasted since my husband came home from a deep-sea fishing trip. Broiled grouper can be bland, but this was tastefully prepared, served on a yummy hoagie in a plastic basket. The lone dessert, key lime pie, is the real thing, though with a discernible "off flavor" that sometimes comes from bottled lime juice. (But then again, I have my own lime tree and am something of a snob!) Inexpensive to Moderate. No reservations.

St. Armands Circle

✪ ♿ **Café L'Europe** (941-388-4415; www.cafeleurope.net), 431 St. Armands Circle. Café L'Europe remains a shining star—after 35 years—that offers French classics with a New Age tweak. Dark woods and redbrick archways set an atmosphere that's warm in an inviting way, yet offers a cool, cellarlike break from Florida heat. When the weather allows, you can also sit outdoors on the patio to sip your French pinot blanc and sample such stunning selections as the flambéed shrimp Pernod appetizer, bourbon pecan salad, key lime grilled salmon, signature brandied duckling, pan-seared scallops with sweet potato hash, lobster-stuffed shrimp, potato-crusted grouper, or tableside chateaubriand for two. Expensive to Very Expensive. Reservations accepted for both lunch and dinner.

&. **Cork on the Circle** (941-388-2675; www.corkonthecircle.com), 29 N. Blvd. of the Presidents. Its two components give diners a choice of a casual, side-walk, or bar-fly setting in the Bot-tleshop, or upstairs where ultramodern metal, terrazzo, orange porcelain tile, and wood floors combine for sophisti-cation. Naturally the wine list is exten-sive, with more choices in the Bottleshop you can purchase and open for a $25 corkage fee. The downstairs lunch and dinner menus are affordable (inexpensive for a few entrées) with sandwiches, creative salads (fennel and spinach, for instance), pizza, meat loaf, eggplant Parmesan, scampi, and other pasta, seafood, and meat dishes. There's some crossover on the upstairs dinner menu, such as the so-fresh-tasting Heirloom & Hothouse Gazpacho, Mediterranean salmon with crisp polenta and artichoke-olive tapenade, grilled hangar steak with potato risotto, and oven-roasted chicken. Some of its exclusive dishes boldly go, including the green apple duck, porchetta osso bucco, grilled gulf snapper with braised fennel, and bouillabaisse. Desserts demonstrate equal creativity. Try the deconstructed s'more with homemade square marshmallows, hazelnut croquant, and giandua—it leaves the Girl Scout version in the dust. Designed by an acclaimed local minimalist architect, this is one of the Circle's smartest, hippest spots these days. Moderate to Very Expensive.

Sarasota

&. **Bijou Café** (941-366-8111; www .bijoucafe.net), 1287 First St., at Pineapple Ave. Situated in the midst of the theater and arts district, the Bijou is the pick of the pre- and post-theater crowd and upper-echelon business community of Sarasota. Small and sim-ply decorated, only lacy curtains, some heavily framed paintings, lavish crown

molding, and a few stylish vases (here you'd pronounce that *vah-zes*) embel-lish. Linen dresses the tables, even at lunch, when the clientele is equally dressed up. The eclectic menu offers choices from Continental, New Orleans, and American cuisine, from fruit soup to duck. One of my favorite dishes, shrimp Piri-Piri, is a classic example of how chef/owner Jean-Pierre Knaggs perfectly balances fla-vors to create entirely fresh taste sensations. It is mildly spicy with citrus tones, and appears on both the lunch and dinner menus. Other dinner spe-cialties include roast duckling, salmon crusted with grain mustard and dill, veal sweetbreads saltimboca, and braised lamb shanks in Burgundy and wild mushrooms. The pommes gratin Dauphinois with Gruyère is a signature side dish, available à la carte. Desserts, made in-house, have an excellent repu-tation. Lunch draws a brisk business crowd and can include dishes such as handmade spinach and ricotta ravioli, pecan-crusted chicken with bourbon-pear sauce, crabcakes remoulade, chicken manchego sandwich on focac-cia, and the like. Moderate to Expen-sive. Reservations recommended. Closed Sunday in summer, Saturday and Sunday for lunch year-round.

Café Baci (941-921-4848; www.cafe baci.net), 4001 S. Tamiami Trail. Affordably dressy, Café Baci has a porte cochere out front and linens on the tables (even at lunch) inside; the business clientele and older crowd wear nice clothes; and the Tuscan-Roman specialties dwell in the realm of fine cuisine. Yet its location on ple-beian South Tamiami Trail, away from Sarasota's centers of chichi, allows for a reasonably priced menu. Lunch is especially popular with locals, who squeeze the parking lot full to capacity. I enjoy lunch there, too; it imparts a bit of affordable elegance in the middle of a hectic day alongside a road-rage street. Soothing and stylish in atmosphere, its food has kept it at the head of growing Italian competition since it opened in 1991. Many of the dinner entrées are available in smaller portions and prices at lunchtime. Dishes we have tried and loved include Italian wedding soup; a tasty meatball dish on special the last time we visited; ravioli di funghi, exquisite homemade half-moon pasta pockets filled with delicately creamed wild mushrooms and topped with a buttery tomato cream sauce; pollo Baci, a divine version of chicken francese with bursts of flavor from sundried tomatoes and lemon wine butter sauce; and fluffy tiramisu. Both lunch and dinner menus touch on the four major Italian food groups: pasta, veal, chicken, and seafood. These are tended with a creative hand. Here's a taste: grilled salmon with spinach pesto risotto; a sampler of veal francese, marsala, and sarda; and Tuscan fisherman's stew with risotto. Seasonal luncheon and early dinner specials add to the value of this experience. The extensive wine list has received the *Wine Spectator* Award of Excellence. Moderate to Expensive. Reservations recommended for dinner. Closed for lunch Saturday and Sunday, also all day Monday during the summer. Handicap access in the restaurant but not the restrooms.

○ ⌗ ⌀ ⌙ **Captain Brian's Seafood & Market Restaurant** (941-351-4492), 8421 N. Tamiami Trail. When fresh seafood is priority one and affordability priority two, go see Captain Brian. I'm not sure such a person actually exists, but the T-shirted staff here can quickly fix you up with the best seafood available. The first thing you notice when you enter the inconspicuous storefront is that it looks like a seafood market, but it doesn't smell like one. Clean as humanly possible with an attractive

aquarium centerpiece, it makes seafood relishing totally appealing. The daily lunch offers typical fish-house fried shrimp baskets, fish sandwiches, crabcakes, seafood combo platters, and the day's fresh catches. Dinner adds specialties such as the mixed grill, shrimp scampi, and the seafood combo platter. The decor is simple: tables and booths, seafood-motif oilcloths, and fish. Keep your eye peeled for this local secret just north of the airport. Inexpensive to Moderate. No reservations. Closed Sunday.

○ **Derek's Culinary Casual** (941-366-6565; www.dereks-sarasota.com), 514 Central Ave., in the Rosemary District. After my second try, it's now official: This is my Sarasota favorite. Before you even think of ordering your opening courses, decide to save room for the poached pear dessert. Simmered with lavender and honey, then topped with goat cheese ice cream and minced mint in a pool of homemade black pepper caramel, it is totally original and amazing. It gives you an idea of the gutsy creativity that goes on in the display kitchen of this corner of spare urbanity. Servers, who are at the top of their game, served the soup of the day when I first dined there by presenting a bowl with a dollop of yogurt on the bottom sprinkled with toasted almond. Atop it they poured a puréed blend of tomatillo and cucumber that was wonderfully sweet, garlicky, and refreshing. My main course, the grouper cheeks, came with wedges of chorizo sausage and plump little corn fritters in a sweet-tangy sauce flavored with red peppers and parsley. Derek's is so fresh and cutting-edge, it has its own vocabulary, defined on the back of the menu. Whet your appetite on "Caesaresque" salad with caramelized anchovy vinaigrette or foie gras with pomegranate gelée and pink peppercorn and grapefruit vinaigrette.

Then tuck into a mole pulled pork sandwich on chorizo cornbread with fried pickle, duck two ways (seared breast and pecan-crusted leg confit with creamed spaetzle, bacon braised greens, and burnt honey jus), chocolate braised rabbit, or something similarly out-of-the box. My latest near-religious experience at Derek's? A Prince Edward Island mussels dish that was at once rustic, elegant, smoky, and surprising in its broth of chorizo, garbanzos, and grilled tomato butter. Grab a seat at the kitchen counter to watch your meal in the making and kitchen craft at its finest. Moderate.

♿ **Libby's Café + Bar** (941-487-7300; www.libbyscafebar.com), 1917 S. Osprey Ave., Sarasota. The Hawaiian yellowfin tuna tartar cold plate at this place goes into my taste buds' hall of fame. It's one of those dishes you cannot stop eating, although it was meant to be a starter, and I knew it would steal pleasure from my entrée. It could have been a meal, and that's the way I would prefer dining at Libby's— noshing from a variety of its "small" cold and hot plates such as Asian pear salad, sturgeon caviar deviled eggs, roasted sweet corn and blue crab chowder (delicious!), truffled wild mushroom torte, and boneless Wagyu beef shortribs, to name a few. In the interest of comprehensive coverage, we also ordered the grilled jumbo scallop Caprese and grouper Oscar, both excellent dishes. The scallops rested on a bed of marinated heirloom tomatoes, grilled veggies, greens, and kalamata olives with a light but authoritative golden balsamic vinaigrette. The Oscar was classically flawless. Other interesting selections: simply grilled sustainable salmon, Maine lobster Bolognaise, snapper and whitewater clam pan roast, grilled lamb chops with butternut squash risotto, and sautéed veal paillard with focaccia crumb crust.

Lunchtime brings a selection of $9 meals with a cup of organic tomato soup, unusual sandwiches such as the ginger teriyaki yellowfin tuna burger, simply grilled selections, and specialties such as rock shrimp scampi over penne. Key lime pie with gummi bears tempted us for dessert, but we settled on the fried chocolate and peanut butter "potstickers" with toasted coconut ice cream, which was tasty despite our overindulgences. I most like Libby's commitment to the organic/sustainable movement, its cheesy biscuits, and its easy atmosphere of conviviality. Superb in every way: If you don't believe me, consider that *Florida Trend* magazine named it among the state's 17 best newcomers in 2009. Moderate to Very Expensive. Reservations accepted.

✚ ♿ **Michael's on East** (941-366-0007; www.bestfood.com), 1212 East Ave. S., in Midtown Plaza at Bahia Vista St. and Tamiami Trail. Michael Klauber is a well-respected name in Sarasota culinary circles. He learned successful restaurateuring early in life as a member of Longboat Key's Colony Beach Resort family. He created an immediate sensation when he opened his own place back in 1987, and Michael's on East remains the pinnacle of cutting-edge cuisine and atmosphere. Oh so art deco, its wavy motif is completely devoid of square corners. You can dine around the circular bar or in two other rooms separated by scrims and etched glass (wavy, of course, and très chic). On the lunch menu, the best value is one of the $11.95 combinations, where you have your choice of any two of the following: duck spring rolls, Caesar salad, angel-hair onion rings, chef's soup, seasonal salad, calamari, or a half turkey wrap. If your idea of calamari has anything to do with rubber bands, try Michael's cornmeal-battered, hand-breaded version—tender to a T and complemented with a wonderful sauce and corn-pancetta relish. The lunch menu also features a lengthy selection of glorious salads, like warm chicken on greens with dried cranberries, candied pecans, and goat cheese. Such are the touches that make Michael's a consistent winner. Specialties on the dinner menu include espresso-crusted yellowfin tuna with lobster-papaya slaw, porcini-rubbed rack of lamb, broiled Maine lobster, and pan-roasted crabcakes with truffle-roasted potatoes. For dessert, try the fresh peach cobbler made to order with cream cheese ice cream and praline sauce, or key lime tart. Michael's is also known for its extensive wine list, which features a generous selection of wines by the glass, including sparkling varieties. Moderate to Very Expensive. Reservations recommended for lunch and dinner.

🦞 🍴 ♿ **Phillippi Creek Village Oyster Bar** (941-925-4444; www.creek seafood.com), 5353 S. Tamiami Trail. In Sarasota they call their fish houses "oyster bars," and Phillippi Creek is one of the oldest. Combo pots for two are the specialty of the house and include pans full of steamed oysters, shrimp, corn on the cob, and a selection of specialty items (clams, crab, or scallops). You can also order individual pots or platters of one type of shellfish. The seafood is so fresh, it ought to be slapped. We've eaten here on several occasions; it's my husband's first choice for casual dining when we're in town. He loves the gooey-thick clam chowder and fried oyster sandwich. I typically pick the blackened grouper sandwich, which comes with a mustardy tartar sauce. You have your choice of settings here, either indoors, glassed-in with a boathouse motif, or out in the breeze on the dry dock. Either way you get a backwater view and the kind of service that puts you at ease. Inexpensive to Expensive. No reservations. Closed Monday.

✪ ♿ **Selva Grill** (941-362-4427; www .selvagrill.com) 1345 Main St. This downtown sensation and *Florida Trend* Golden Spoon winner claims Peru as its country of culinary inspiration, but the good looks of its exotic dining rooms, clientele, and kitchen art bespeak much deeper dimensions. Of course, there is the ubiquitous selection of ceviches, a signature Peruvian creation. The Triologia presents three different mixtures of fish and shrimp served in three large spoons with wisps of fried plantain and yucca. Other starters include tuna tartare in tamarind vinaigrette and yucca in garlic sauce. Meat and seafood get equal time on the entrées menu. The menu describes *arroz con pato* as a gourmet version of a traditional duck-breast dish of northern Peru with green pea and beer risotto, and most of the dishes are likewise Peruvian dressed up for discriminating American palates. The mirin-roasted sea bass, for instance, demonstrates both the Eastern influence and the prevalence of corn in the diet with a smooth, slightly sweet corn custard. The silky creaminess of the fish nearly matched that of the flan. Dessert tempts with such selections as *pastel de tres leches,* and peaches and cream bread pudding with bourbon. In the main dining room, the atmosphere is lively with the backdrop of a swirly wall that changes color thanks to the lighting. Moderate to Very Expensive. Resesrvations accepted.

♿ **Verona** (941-309-2000; www.ritz carlton.com), 1111 Ritz-Carlton Dr., at The Ritz-Carlton Sarasota. Amid soothing European-style trappings and fine art, overattentive servers leave you wanting for nothing. Chef Greg Howe has made a commitment to local, organic, healthy cuisine that bursts with creativity, flavor, and finesse. For the best experience of his talents, sample one of his four-course tasting plates, which might include his incredible popcorn crab bisque, foie gras torchon with vanilla gelée, organic fuji apple salad, or sashimi tuna with yuzu. If you prefer à la carte, the dinner menu covers a lot of territory: crispy squash flowers or lobster macaroni and cheese with truffle cream for starters; beer-braised veal cheeks with sweet potato spaetzle, wild Florida cobia with red quinoa, and Kobe beef short ribs for entrées; and key lime pie with cilantro-lime sauce and citrus-ginger soup with lime-vanilla sorbet for dessert. There's also an early dining menu for seatings between 6 and 6:30. At lunch, the three-course $19 menu lets you select from several starters, main courses, and desserts. Salads, sandwiches, pizza, and dishes such as rock crab sliders complete the menu. Sunday brunch, a grand affair, fills the room (and the stomach) with everything from sushi and dim sum to seafood and malted waffles for $69 per person. Expensive. Reservations accepted.

♣ ♂ & **Yoder's** (941-955-7771; www
.yodersrestaurant.com), 3434 Bahia Vista St. A happy outgrowth of the Amish/Mennonite community in Sarasota, homestyle restaurants throughout the area feature comfort-food goodness. These folks are principally farmers, so you can expect farmhouse-style freshness at their table. Yoder's sits squarely in the midst of the Pinecraft Amish community, and you know it's the real thing because many of the patrons are wearing long beards and suspenders or white bonnets and full-body aprons over their plain dresses. Amish photography, art, quilts, and other handiwork decorate the dining room, which is almost always full. Although you'll find typical sandwiches and hamburgers, Midwestern comfort food predominantly makes up the all-day menu and its daily specials: fried chicken, liver and onions, turkey and dressing, pulled smoked pork, meat loaf, and roast beef. There's no replacement for homemade goodness, and even my meat loaf sandwich benefited from red juicy tomatoes and home-baked bread. At breakfast, who could resist the apple fritter French toast? Pies are the claim to local fame here, and there's a window where fans come to pick up their whole cream or baked pies. I can vouch for the rhubarb; tart and encased in a crumbly, sugar-glazed crust, it is the perfect ending to a meal like my mother would have made. Inexpensive. No reservations. Closed Sunday.

Siesta Key

♣ ♂ & **Captain Curt's Crab & Oyster Bar** (941-349-3885; www.captain curts.com), 1200 Old Stickney Point Rd. Captain Curt's complex takes up a good part of the block here near the south bridge in Siesta. Besides the blessedly air-conditioned main restaurant, there's a tiki bar, backroom saloon, and gift shop. It claims to be the island's oldest restaurant and to have the best clam chowder in the world. I can attest only to the latter. Besides my thumbs-up, it has won the International Great Chowder Cook-Off in Newport, Rhode Island. As for its age, it's been serving typical Old Florida–style (i.e., raw and fried) seafood since 1979. It does some non-seafood items, including a good old Midwestern pork tenderloin sandwich (try it with a dousing of Curt's hot sauce) and ribs. On the fancier side, there's crawfish-stuffed snapper, seafood combos, and steamers. The atmosphere is organized chaos, picnic tables, and friendly. Inexpensive. No reservations.

✪ & **Ophelia's on the Bay** (941-349-2212; www.opheliasonthebay.net), 9105

Midnight Pass Rd. For 20 years and counting, this lovely spot on Little Sarasota Bay at Siesta Key's quiet southern end has meant fine dining with a creative streak. The Caesar salad, for instance, comes with white truffle croutons, tomato salsa, and, upon request, white anchovies. The menu changes nightly, often using a template of proteins whose preparation the kitchen varies. My bigeye tuna was rare-seared, sliced, arranged upon a slab of grilled watermelon, and topped with Meyer lemon pesto. The U-8 diver scallops on that occasion came with sweet corn coulis, shallot marmalade, roasted garlic and tomato concasse, and herb risotto. Kobe beef, jumbo shrimp, black Angus filet mignon, Norwegian salmon, and veal tenderloin receive equally alluring treatments. Save room for the key lime pie—the best in my experience—a creamy round molded atop a coconut crumb crust with mango and raspberry coulis and lots of fresh whipped cream. Wow! Expensive. Reservations suggested.

Venice

🦐 ♿ **The Back Eddy Bistro** (941-244-2643; www.backeddybistro.com), 239 W. Miami Ave., downtown. The new kid in town, Eddy Glennon has served as private chef for Jimmy Buffett, Neil Young, and other celebs. To Venice he brings a flair for classic and innovative combined in such dishes as achiote cornmeal-crusted tilapia, creole-marinated shrimp with coconut curry sauce, Thai beef salad with ginger-chile lime dressing, roasted rack of lamb, and the like. For lunch, there's the expected and surprises: smoked marlin pâté, almond-crusted warm goat cheese, Reuben sandwich, grilled steak sandwich, and crab salad tostaditas. Chocolate pecan torte with crème anglaise or key lime pie entice for dessert. The smart setting blends classic chairs and oil paintings with a butcher-paper bistro setting. The select, mostly California wine list is as affordable as the menu. Inexpensive to Moderate. Reservations accepted. Closed Monday.

BACK BAY VIEWS SWEETEN THE DINING EXPERIENCE AT OPHELIA'S ON THE BAY.

✪ ♿ **The Crow's Nest** (941-484-9551; www.crowsnest-venice.com), 1968 Tarpon Center Dr. A seaworthy Venice institution, it serves the finer side of fresh seafood, including specialties such as roasted Bahamian lobster tail, walnut-crusted salmon, crabcakes, and shrimp and scallops Alfredo. Meatlovers can choose from ale-marinated rib eye, chicken picatta, and surf-and-turf selections. Service is sometimes a little off, but a lot can be forgiven when you're staring out at yachts bobbing in the harbor. The two-story, window-lined dining room has a stateroom-level nautical feel. Downstairs in the faintly lit tavern, you can order sandwiches and pub fare all day, plus there's a daily lunch menu of sandwiches and entrées such as a grouper sandwich, pan-roasted chicken with citrus sauce, and fajita-seared tenderloin tips salad. In season, be sure to make reservations well in advance, because this place has a big local following. Moderate to Expensive.

✪ ♪ **Snook Haven** (941-485-7221; www.snookhavenfl.com), 5000 E. Venice Ave., exit 191 off I-75. For a poignant taste of rural Old Florida close to the interstate, visit Snook Haven for good, affordable eats and live country music on the banks of the wild and scenic Myakka River. Hear the legend of the killer turtles (a leftover from the 1940s on-site filming of Tarzan's *Revenge of the Killer Turtles*). If you find you can't leave the peace, you may be able to rent one of the old, rustic cottages at the retreat, part of a county park. At lunch, pick from burgers, a barbecued pork sandwich, pot roast, grouper, catfish, and other seafood dishes. Choose the degree of casual seating: at the stretch tables and plastic chairs in the air-conditioned interior, on the screened porch, or at a picnic table on the riverside deck. Afterward, rent a canoe and paddle as slowly as time moves in these parts. It's truly a "y'all come" kind of place. Inexpensive to Moderate. Reservations accepted. Handicap access in the restaurant but not the restrooms.

♣ ♪ ♿ **The Soda Fountain** (941-412-9860), 349 W. Venice Ave. Reward yourself with a downtown shopping break at this treat. Your inner and outer child(ren) will thank you. Decorated like an old-fashioned soda fountain, with black-and-white checked floors and chrome-edged swivel stools at the counter, it serves all-American sandwiches and burgers. These, however, are secondary to the main course: ice cream. Have it scooped up in a cone, slathered with syrup in a sundae, or whizzed in a canister as a shake or malted. During happy hour, 4–7 Monday–Saturday, you can get two ice creams for the price of one. The menu lists 16 varieties of quarter-pound beef hot dots, including the Hawaiian dog with pineapple and the sloppy dog. Other offerings range from wraps and traditional sandwiches to chicken Caesar salad. Inexpensive. No reservations.

BAKERIES **Bakery d'Europa** (941-795-1719), 6753 Manatee Ave. W., at Northwest Promenade, Bradenton. A true bakery, with luscious cakes, cookies, desserts, pastries, muffins, bagels, sandwiches, and fragrant coffees.

The Broken Egg (941-346-2750; www.thebrokenegg.com), 140 Avenida Messina, Siesta Key. Yummy cinnamon swirls, muffins, coffee cakes, and pies.

C'est La Vie (941-906-957), 1553 Main St., Sarasota. This authentic French bakery holds showcases full of breads, pastries, tarts, cake, and other sweets. It also serves breakfast and lunch at sidewalk tables and inside the café.

Ginny's & Jane E's Café & Bakery (941-778-7370; www.annamariacafe.com), 9807 Gulf Dr., Anna Maria.

Rustic breads, cakes, pies, muffins, pastries, and cookies baked fresh. Also breakfast, sandwiches, coffee, and smoothies.

Pastry Art (941-955-7545; www.pastry artonmain.com), 1512 Main St., Sarasota. Exquisite pastries, cakes in every flavor, tortes, truffles, cookies, cheesecakes, European-style fruit tarts, French-press coffees, espressos, and sandwiches and salads.

BREAKFAST Blue Dolphin Café (941-383-3787; www.bluedolphin cafe.com), 5370 Gulf of Mexico Dr. #101, at the Centre Shops, Longboat Key; and (941-388-3566), 470 John Ringling Blvd., at St. Armands Circle, Sarasota. Stylish eatery serving muffins, banana granola pancakes, Belgian waffles, omelets (try the spinach-feta). Breakfast and lunch are served throughout its open hours, 7–3.

✪ **The Broken Egg** (941-346-2750; www.thebrokenegg.com), 140 Avenida Messina, Siesta Key. Huge and yummy pancakes in a dozen varieties, seven types of Benedicts, six omelets. Also bakery goods and lunch. (Serves dinner Wednesday–Saturday.)

🍴 ✪ **Café on the Beach** (941-778-0784), 4000 Gulf Dr., at Manatee County Park, Holmes Beach. Locals know this as one of the most affordable and scenic places to start the morning. Belgian waffles are a specialty, and the all-you-can-eat pancakes with sausage ($5.95) are a draw. Also lunch and dinner.

✪ 🍴 **Gulf Drive Café** (941-778-1919), 900 Gulf Dr., Bradenton Beach. A longtime, wildly popular spot for affordable hotcakes, eggs, or Belgian waffles on the beach, all day long. Also lunch and dinner.

CANDY & ICE CREAM Bently's Homemade Ice Cream (941-486-

1816), 720 Albee Rd., Nokomis. Hard and soft-serve ice cream, sorbet, gelato, and ice cream cakes.

Big Olaf Creamery (941-349-9392), 5208 Ocean Blvd., Siesta Key. A vintage purveyor of fresh fudge, handmade waffle cones, homemade ice cream, skinny dips (low-fat frozen desserts), espresso, and cappuccino.

✒ **Joe's Eats & Sweets** (941-778-0007; www.joeseatsandsweets.com), 219 Gulf Dr. S., Bradenton Beach. Forty gourmet flavors of ice cream (cotton candy and Nerds, key lime cheesecake, cappuccino crunch, and pineapple coconut among them) made on the premises, including sugar-free, lactose-free, and fat-free varieties, plus low-fat yogurt. Homemade fudge in dozens of unusual flavors, sodas, creative sundaes (raspberry truffle cheesecake, latte crème, apple pickers, and wet walnut, for instance), shakes, espresso, and cappuccino.

Mermaids Ice Cream (941-807-6830), 5263 Ocean Blvd., Siesta Key. Homemade ice cream and luncheon sandwiches.

ScoopDaddy's (941-388-1650; www .scoopdaddys.com), 19-C N. Blvd. of the Presidents, at St. Armands Circle, Sarasota. Combines the nostalgia of a soda fountain and retro '50s entertainment; features a jukebox and reproduction gifts.

Two Scoops (941-779-2422), 101 S. Bay Blvd. #A2, Anna Maria. Near the city pier, this has become the talk of local sweet-tooth types. Offers scrumptious sundaes; a long line of ice cream flavors, such as birthday cake and muddy sneakers; an espresso bar; teas; plus muffins, bagels, breakfast, and luncheon wrap sandwiches.

COFFEE & TEA 🎧 **Back Alley** (941-778-1800), 121 Bridge St., Bradenton Beach. Coffee, frappés, smoothies, and Wi-Fi in the back of a funky little gift shop with a back patio.

(ꟼ) **The B'Towne Coffee Co.** (941-745-3100), 440 Old Main St., Bradenton. Joffrey's coffee and espresso, plus ice cream, bakery treats, and wireless Internet access.

Island Gourmet (941-484-3667), 201 Venice Ave. W., Venice. Buy gourmet coffee by the bag or cup at the espresso bar. Also teas, wine, spices, and hard-to-find gourmet food items.

Java Jazz (941-748-1676), 1001 Third Ave. W., Bradenton. So much more than a coffee shop, its espresso bar nonetheless impresses with specialty creations such as Almond Joy mocha and Peppermint Patty latte. A full complement of breakfast and lunch dishes, baked goodies, smoothies, and iced drinks.

(ꟼ) **Local Coffee & Tea** (941-870-2671; www.localcoffee.com), 5138 Ocean Blvd., in Siesta Key Village, Sarasota. Espresso, lattes, more than 20 loose-leaf teas, smoothies, and bakery goods. Free Wi-Fi access.

The Londoner Tea Rooms (941-748-5658 or 941-465-9636 (cell); www.thelondonerinn.com), 304 15th St. W., Bradenton. The Londoner serves authentic English afternoon tea Monday–Saturday 11:30–3 in a prim little B&B parlor. All of the scones and other goodies are made from scratch daily. Reservations recommended.

DELI & SPECIALTY FOODS

Columbia Gift Shop (941-388-1026; www.columbiarestaurant.com), 411 St. Armands Circle, Sarasota. Dressings, black-beans mix, sangria jelly, cookbooks, coffee, wine, cigars, and other items sold in the renowned Spanish restaurant.

Geier's Sausage Kitchen (941-923-3004 or 888-743-4377; www.geiers-sausage.com),7447 S. Tamiami Trail, Sarasota. European-style sausage and smoked meats, prime fresh meats, imported cheeses, beer, wine, pastries, and other gourmet items.

The Gourmet Market (941-953-9101 or 888-953-9101; www.thegourmetmarket.com), 1469 Main St., Sarasota. A delightful place full of good smells, cheeses, Godiva chocolates, pastas, oils, vinegars, coffees, wine, and hot sauces.

Greenleaf Wisconsin Cheese (941-923-9750; www.greenleafcheese.com), 4521 Tamiami Trail, Sarasota. More than 140 artisan cheeses, brats and other meats, fresh curds, and gift boxes.

✪ **Morton's Market** (941-955-9856; www.epicureanlife.com), 1924 S. Osprey Ave., at Southside Village, Sarasota. The ultimate gourmet's delight, it sells hot and cold prepared items for take-out, fresh produce, deli and fresh meats, seafood, coffees, shelves of gourmet products—you name it.

St. Armands Gifts & Winery (941-388-5330 or 800-591-5330; www.starmandswinery.com), 466 John Ringling Blvd., Sarasota. Tropical fruit wines are the specialty here, but it also sells other tasty treats, such as rum cake and bottled sauces.

✪ **Sarasota Olive Oil Company** (941-366-2008; www.sarasotaoliveoil.com), 514 Central Ave., Sarasota. A very cool little "tongues-on" place in the Rosemary District. Taste a couple dozen different kinds of seasonings from the salt and pepper bar or multiple types of olive oil from around the world, including some flavored with garlic, jalapeño, basil, navel orange, and more. It's also the place to buy coffee, intriguing condiments such as artichoke sauce or cider confit with apples and calvados, and vegetarian and nonvegetarian sandwiches.

Southside Deli (941-330-9302), 1825 Hillview St., Sarasota. Popular spot for a take-out or eat-in lunch. Breakfast, luncheon sandwiches and salads, smoothies.

Too Jay's (941-362-3692; www.toojays .com), Westfield Southgate, 3501 S. Tamiami Trail, Sarasota. This import from the Tampa area is the ultimate in deli food: sandwiches, hot comfort-food dishes, and the real thing in New York cheesecake.

FRUIT & VEGETABLE STANDS

Albritton Fruit (941-923-2573 or 800-237-3682; www.albrittonfruit .com), 5430 Proctor Rd., Sarasota) Albritton is a well-known name in citrus.

Hunsader Farms (941-322-2168; www.hunsaderfarms.com), 5500 Co. Rd. 675, 10 miles east of I-75, Bradenton. A bit of a drive from Bradenton's tourist attractions, but worth it if you're in the market for fresh produce. U-Pick and We-Pick crops from September to June. Also a petting zoo and playground.

Mixon Fruit Farms (941-748-5829 or 800-608-2525; www.mixon.com), 2712 26th Ave. E., Bradenton. A large, old, family-owned business specializing in citrus. Tram tours of the grove and processing plant, a wildlife preserve, free samples, shipping, and a gift shop selling fruit, fudge, ice cream, wine, and jellies. Closed Sundays and the first two weeks in September.

Sarasota Farmer's Market (941-225-9256; Lemon Ave. between First St. and Main St., downtown Sarasota. The biggest and best in the region: Florida fruits, vegetables, organic products, flowers, plants, seafood, and honey. Every Saturday, 7 AM–noon.

Yoder's Fresh Market (941-955-7771; www.yodersrestaurant.com), 3434 Bahia Vista St., Sarasota. In addition to fresh produce, it sells home-made jams, jellies, cheeses, and baked goods.

INTERNET CAFÉS (ᵒᵖᵒ) **Bella Luna Café** (941-488-3089; www.bellaluna cafeofvenice.com), 200 Miami Ave., Venice. Coffee and pastries. Wireless access but no electric plug-ins.

(ᵒᵖᵒ) **Local Coffee & Tea** (941-870-2671; www.localcoffee.com), 5138 Ocean Blvd., in Siesta Key Village, Sarasota. Free Wi-Fi; coffee drinks, teas, smoothies, and bakery goods.

NATURAL FOODS **Good Earth Natural Foods** (941-795-0478 or 800-638-5201; www.goodearthfoods.com), 6717 Manatee Ave. W., Bradenton. A full line of organic produce and healthy food products. Two other Bradenton locations where licensed nutritional counselors are on-site.

The Granary Natural Foods Market (941-924-4754), 1930 Stickney Point Rd., east of the Siesta Key bridge, Sarasota. A full-service mart with a juice bar, hot and cold deli, salad and burrito bar, and a large fresh produce and grains area.

TROPICAL FRUITS ADD AN EXOTIC FLAVOR TO THE SARASOTA FARMER'S MARKET.

Richard's Whole Foods (941-966-0596; www.richardswholefoods.com), 1092 Tamiami Trail S., Osprey. One of several area locations, it carries a good stock of bulk natural foods and organic groceries.

PIZZA & TAKE-OUT **Anna's Restaurant & Deli** (941-349-7990; www.surfersandwich.com), 217 Avenida Madera, Siesta Key; and (941-349-4888), 6535 Midnight Pass Rd., Siesta Key. Famous for its swirled rye bread and tall stack sandwiches such as the Surfer with ham, turkey, Swiss, and cucumber.

Crusty's Pizza (941-366-3100), 3800 Tamiami Trail S. #29, at Paradise Plaza, Sarasota. Stuffed, pan, or Chicago-style thin-crust pizza. Also wings, soups, salads, sandwiches, and pasta dishes to go.

Main Bar Sandwich Shop (941-955-8733; www.themainbar.com), 1944 Main St., Sarasota. A long list of sandwiches, hot and cold, plus salads and desserts at this circa-1958 landmark. Specialties include the Aztec sandwich with roast beef, provolone, and jalapeño dressing, and the New Orleans Muffuletta and Veggiletta.

✪ Morton's Market (941-955-9856; www.epicureanlife.com), 1924 S. Osprey Ave., at Southside Village, Sarasota. Wildly popular (practically legendary), Morton's sells hot prepared items, pizza, deli sandwiches, salads, bakery goods, and homemade desserts for take-out, plus fresh produce, deli and fresh meats, seafood, coffees, and gourmet products.

Vertoris Pizza House (941-751-0333; www.vertorispizza.com), 6830 14th St. W., Bradenton. It specializes in brick-oven-baked thin-crust pizzas and gluten-free and vegan pies.

SEAFOOD **Captain Brian's Seafood Market** (941-351-4492), 8421 N. Tamiami Trail, Sarasota. Fresh local and imported seafood in a large, dine-in venue.

Captain Eddie's Retail Market (941-484-4623), 107 Colonia Ln. E., Nokomis. "Stone crab headquarters," it proclaims. Fresh seafood of all varieties in a restaurant venue.

Fish Market (941-567-6130; www.thefishmarketami.com), 5604 Marina Dr., Holmes Beach. Local seafood, organic produce, take-out salads and chowders, desserts, beer, and wine.

✪ Star Fish Company (941-794-1243; www.starfishcompany.com), 12306 46th Ave. W., Cortez. To get any closer to the source, you'd have to get wet. This long-standing tradition is the anchor of Cortez village's working waterfront, where crusted old fishing and shrimp boats pull up, and murals and plaques deliver lessons on history and heritage. Buy fresh, fresh fish in the market to take home, or order it off the menu to enjoy on dockside picnic tables.

✱ Selective Shopping

In season you may well be tempted, like everyone else, to save shopping and sightseeing for rainy, cold, off-beach days. Don't. You'll lose your diligently attained good beach attitude by the time you've found your first parking spot. Go in the morning for best results and the most relaxing experience.

Sarasota's **St. Armands Circle** is known far and wide for its arena of posh shops, galleries, and restaurants. **Downtown Sarasota** has a nice mix of one-of-a-kind shops interspersed with restaurants. Nearby **Southside Village,** at Hillview Street and Osprey Avenue, has grown into an intriguing little shopping and dining destination. On the islands you'll find fun shops and beach boutiques that blend with the sand and sun.

SHOPPING CENTERS & MALLS
De Soto Square (941-747-5868; www.desoto-square.com), 303 Hwy. 301, Bradenton. Some 700,000 feet of shop-till-you-drop opportunities in more than 100 stores, including Sears, Macy's, and JCPenney.

◐ Downtown Sarasota (941-366-7040; www.discovermainstreet.com) One of the Gulf Coast's most successful downtown restoration projects has returned Sarasota's vitality to Main Street and its environs. The area encompasses approximately 1.5 square miles and is centered at Five Points, where Main Street intersects with four other streets. Renovated old buildings house galleries, clothing boutiques, antique shops, restaurants, sidewalk cafés, clubs, and gift shops. October–May, First Friday Nights bring live music and outdoor wine bars. Palm Avenue holds a preponderance of galleries while Historic Burns Square (Pineapple and Orange Avenues) has its share of antique and specialty shops.

Downtown Venice (941-484-6722), at Venice Ave. W. and adjacent streets, Venice. Down a Mediterranean-type, date-palm-lined boulevard you'll find shops and restaurants to fit every budget. Wander a block to the south for antiques and secondhand collectibles. A Third Thursday Stroll takes place every month from 5:30 to 8 PM. Centennial Park runs along Venice Avenue across from its shops. Here musicians often entertain at the gazebo, and children splash in the interactive fountains. North of the park, Venice Mall holds history and more options for shoppers.

Longboat Key. You'll find a smattering of interesting shops and galleries at The Centre Shops (5370 Gulf of Mexi-

co Dr.) and Avenue of Flowers (off Gulf of Mexico Dr.).

◐ St. Armands Circle (941-388-1554; www.starmandscircleassoc.com), 300 Madison Dr., on St. Armands Key, Sarasota. On one of the Sarasota barrier islands that he owned, John Ringling envisioned a world-class shopping center, complete with park-lined walkways and Baroque statuary. He would be gratified by St. Armands Circle. On a scale with Beverly Hills's Rodeo Drive and Palm Beach's Worth Avenue, it was named for developer Charles St. Amand (whose name was misspelled "Armand" in later land deeds—and it is this spelling that persists). Its spin-off formation is suited geographically to the pancake shape of the island. Four sections arc off the circular center drive. "The Circle," as it is known in local shorthand, is a hub of activity for the entire region, encompassing shops of the most upscale nature, galleries, restaurants, clubs, and specialty boutiques. International style is well represented. People dress in finery just to shop here, but don't feel obligated. Parking is free on the street and in a garage nearby.

Siesta Key (www.siestakeychamber .com/shopping.htm). Located in the village along Ocean Boulevard, Siesta Key's shopping district has a refreshingly barefoot atmosphere with a touch of beach bawdiness. Mixed in with the shops is a generous dose of casual eateries and daiquiri bars. You'll find a more refined collection of shops around Stickney Point Road.

Southgate (941-955-0900; http://west field.com/southgate), 3501 S. Tamiami Trail, at Bee Ridge Rd., Sarasota. Smaller than Sarasota Square, this one houses Macy's, Dillards, and Saks Fifth Avenue, plus an above-average food court.

Westfield Sarasota Square (941-922-9609; www.westfield.com), 8201 S.

Tamiami Trail, at Beneva Rd., Sarasota. Your choice of four major department stores, movie theaters, and more than 140 specialty shops and eateries.

ANTIQUES & COLLECTIBLES

Antique shops are plentiful and easy to find in and around Sarasota. You'll find a row of them on Pineapple Street and another on Fruitville Avenue, both downtown. In Venice, look along Miami Avenue, parallel to the main shopping drag, Venice Avenue. Pick up a copy of the *Sarasota Antique Guide & Locator Map* from the Sarasota Visitors Center.

Antiques and Chatchkes Fine Antique Mall (941-906-1221), 1542

PRETTY PALMS AND HISTORIC ARCHITECTURE MAKE DOWNTOWN VENICE SHOPPING PAINLESS.

Fruitville Rd., Sarasota. Mainly furniture and things for the home.

Jack Vinales Antiques (941-957-0002; www.jackvinalesantiques.com), 539 Pineapple Ave. S., Sarasota. More contemporary than most of Sarasota's antique stock, this shop concentrates on nostalgia of the '40s and '50s, art deco, pottery, lamps, and Bakelite and Fiesta ware.

Lucia's Antiques (941-412-1939), 225 W. Miami Ave. #2A, Venice. Fine estate wares; a little bit of everything, from furniture to crystal.

Memory Lane Antiques & Collectibles (941-812-6894), 306 Old Main St., Bradenton. Fine dishware and glass, books, vintage-looking signs, and other just used pieces.

Sarasota Art & Antique Center, 640 S. Washington Ave., Sarasota. This huge pink building holds a number of fine antique galleries, including **Crissy Galleries** (941-957-1110; www.crissy.com), selling quality furniture, jewelry, and art; **Sarasota Rare Coin Gallery** (941-366-2191 or 800-447-8778; www.sarasotacoin.com); and **Sarasota Estate & Jewelry** (941-364-5158), specializing in vintage diamond jewelry.

The Sea Hagg (941-795-5756; www.seahagg.com), 12304 Cortez Rd. W., Cortez. It's impossible to pigeonhole this into one shopping category, but it fits here with its stock of antique periscopes, sextants, rods and reels, and other nautical and fishing memorabilia. Browse its two shops and yards for everything from old crab traps to sea glass by the scoop and metal bird and fish sculptures. This is a place to buy a piece of Cortez maritime heritage.

Shadow Box (941-957-3896), 1522 Fruitville Rd., Sarasota. Along Fruitville Road, which runs on the edge of downtown, you can find antique shops mixed among thrift and consignment outlets. These antique shops are generally more affordable than mainstream downtown's. This one carries a nice collection of 18th-century, Victorian, art deco, and modern home furnishings and decoratives.

BOOKS **Circle Books** (941-388-2850; www.circlebooks.net), 478 John Ringling Blvd., at St. Armands Circle, Sarasota) Small but packed with books for all ages, plus puzzles and games for kids; features regular author signings.

Venice Newsstand (941-488-6969), 329 W. Venice Ave., Venice. An old-fashioned newsstand selling cigars, greeting cards, magazines, out-of-town newspapers, and paperbacks.

CLOTHING

Captain's Landing (941-485-2329), 319 W. Venice Ave., Venice. High-quality Hawaiian, golf, and sporty fashions for men.

Dream Weaver (941-388-1974; www.dreamweavercollection.com), 364 St. Armands Circle, Sarasota. Fine woven wear—in silk, suede, and other extravagant materials—that crosses the line into fabric art.

Ivory Coast (941-388-1999), 15 N. Blvd. of Presidents, at St. Armands Circle, Sarasota. Outstanding imported women's fashions, jewelry, and decorative items inspired by Africa.

Little Bo-Tique (941-388-1737), 367-A St. Armands Circle, Sarasota. Adorable and stylish children's wear for boys and girls.

The Met (941-388-3991; www.themetsarasota.com), 35 S. Blvd. of Presidents, at St. Armands Circle, Sarasota. Expensive dressy and casual designer fashions for men and women in a divine setting.

Nana's (941-488-4108), 223 W. Venice Ave., Venice. Quality kids' clothes, books, and toys.

SunBug (941-485-7946; www.venicemainstreet.com/sunbug), 141 W. Venice Ave., Venice. The most fun in women's fashions, from dressy to casual. Great cotton styles, swimsuits, and unusual, comfortable dresses.

Venice Tropical Shop (941-483-4533), 213 W. Venice Ave., Venice. Standout, tasteful women's fashions, flirty and sexy in style; handcrafted jewelry; evening wear.

CONSIGNMENT/THRIFT In Sarasota buying secondhand is not the embarrassment that it is in some places. In fact, recycled apparel is the "in" thing among the young and artistic. Because of the wealth and transient nature of its residents, the area offers the possibility of great discoveries in its consignment shops. Fruitville

A SAMPLING OF COLORFUL WARES AT BRADENTON'S VILLAGE OF THE ARTS.

Road is a good place to shop for recycled goods. Some of the stores benefit local charities.

Divine Consign (941-488-3219), 203 W. Miami Ave., Venice. Benefits a local church. Furniture, housewares, ladies' clothing, and jewelry.

🐘 The Elephant's Trunk Thrift Shop (941-483-3056), 595 Tamiami Trail, behind the Chamber of Commerce, Venice. Lots of furniture and other household goods, including discontinued merchandise. Operated by Healthcare Volunteers of Venice.

Encore & More (941-953-4222; www .thewomensresourcecenter.org), 1439 Main St., Sarasota. It sells women's clothing and accessories, furniture, and art to benefit the Women's Resource Center.

Restyled Rags (941-750-0032), 417 Old Main St., in the Jennings Arcade, Bradenton. It sells women's clothing and accessories to benefit the Women's Resource Center.

🐘 Woman's Exchange (941-955-7859), 539 S. Orange Ave., downtown Sarasota. Furniture, family clothing, antiques, housewares, and china. Profits support local arts.

FACTORY OUTLET CENTERS
Prime Outlets (941-723-1150 or 888-260-7608; www.primeoutlets.com), 5461 Factory Shops Blvd., at I-75 exit 224, Ellenton. More than 130 shops, a nice food court, and a children's playground in a Caribbean setting. Besides the typical kitchen and clothing stores, it boasts some top designer names, such as Brooks Brothers, Liz Claiborne, and others.

FLEA MARKETS & BAZAARS
The Dome Flea & Farmer's Market (941-493-6773; www.thedome fleamarket.com), 5115 FL 776, Venice. A 300-booth indoor market open Friday, Saturday, and Sunday 9–4.

Red Barn Flea Market (941-747-3794 or 800-274-FLEA; www.red

CORTEZ'S SEA HAGG TAKES SHOPPING INTO A TREASURE-HUNTING DIMENSION.

barnfleamarket.com), 1707 First St. E., Bradenton. More than 600 stores and booths selling everything from baseball cards to car parts in an air-conditioned facility. Fully open Friday, Saturday, and Sunday 8–4 (also Wednesday, November–April); mall-area stores (about 40) are open Tuesday–Sunday 10–4.

GALLERIES Art Uptown Gallery (941-955-5409), 1367 Main St., Sarasota. One of downtown's more affordable galleries, this nonprofit cooperative carries the various media of local artists. Lots of vibrancy.

Everything But the Girl (941-954-8800; http://shopebtg.com), 430 Central Ave., Sarasota. Art and gifts by local artists and designers—from paintings to circus-inspired bead earrings to herbal food products.

Galleria Silecchia (941-365-7414 or 888-366-7414; www.galleriasilecchia .com), 12 and 20 S. Palm Ave., Sarasota. These two storefronts contain some of the most interesting art we've seen in all of Sarasota: large and small bronze sculptures, the exquisite glass lamp works of Ulla Darni, and strikingly colorful porcelain art bowls by Doug Randall. Pieces sell in the four- to five-figure range.

O Gallery (941-228-2627), 240 W. Tampa Ave., at Venice Mall, Venice. Local artists create everything from local scenes to stunning abstracts.

Pagliacci (941-955-8785; www.clowns 4u.com), 1429 Main St., Sarasota. Just what you'd expect in Sarasota—a gallery that specializes in clowns in all media; also masks and cartoon and TV nostalgia.

R & R Bond Galleries (866-579-DALI or 941-338-221; www.rrbond galleries.com), 18 S. Blvd. of the Presidents, at St. Armands Circle, Sarasota. Dalí works dominate this impressive gallery, but also Frederic Hart, Royo,

Tuan, M. L. Snowden, and other fine international artists whose work ranges into the six-figure category.

Ten Thousand Villages (941-316-0120; www.tenthousandvillages .com), 45 S. Palm Ave., downtown Sarasota. You may have seen one of these wonderful galleries in other cities; the organization's mission is to provide Third World artisans with a fair marketplace for their works. The brochure describes them as "handicrafts," but the quality is fine art—from baskets and ceramics to lamps and furnishings.

❂ Towles Court Artist Colony (www.towlescourt.com), 1938 Adams Ln., off US 301, Sarasota. A charming district of restored and brightly painted bungalows has been turned into an art colony. It features the galleries and working art studios of artists in all media. The Towles Court Art Center contains several galleries and a café. It is the colony's headquarters, and other studio-galleries are scattered around it.

The **Katharine Butler Galleries** (941-955-4546; www.kbutlergallery .com), 1943 Morrill St., Sarasota, carries the artist's diverse work plus that of 17 other artists. Third Friday art walks, 6–10 PM, include live music.

Venice Gallery & Studio (941-486-0811 or 888-999-9113; www.clyde butcher.com), 237 Warfield Ave., Venice. Search out this off-the-beaten-path home to Clyde Butcher, Florida's unofficial photographer laureate. Here are his darkroom and workshops, plus a collection of his limited-edition and giclée black-and-white portraits of Florida and other scenic locations. He is known for his large-format photography and is often compared to Ansel Adams.

GIFTS Some of the best gifts and souvenirs are found in attraction gift shops, especially those at the Ringling museums, Sarasota Jungle Gardens, G.WIZ, and the South Florida Museum.

Artisans (941-388-0082), 301 John Ringling Blvd., at St. Armands Circle, Sarasota) Inexpensive, flirty, and unusual handbags, jewelry, and home art.

🐌 **Artisans' World Marketplace** (941-365-5994), 128 S. Pineapple Ave., Sarasota. This not-for-profit has made a commitment to selling the work of below-poverty-level artisans and features such items as crèches from Peru, metal-drum sculptures from Haiti, Indonesian pottery, sculptures of recycled materials from South Africa, and stone sculptures from Zimbabwe. The resourcefulness reflected in the delightful scope of work is remarkable.

Back Alley (941-778-1800), 121 Bridge St., Bradenton Beach. Fun place to browse for beach art, jewelry, and T-shirts, and enjoy a coffee while you're at it.

Elysian Fields (941-361-3006; www.elysianfieldsonline.com), 1273 Tamiami Trail S., at Midtown Plaza, Sarasota. This shop's subtitle tells it succinctly enough: "books and gifts for conscious living." It's filled with wonderful New Age accoutrements, aromatherapy supplies, feng shui books and items, cards, candles, and books.

Exit Art Gallery (941-387-7395 or 800-833-0894; www.exit-art.com), 5380 Gulf of Mexico Dr., at the Centre Shops, Longboat Key. Artistically designed home and office tools, pop art, colorful tableware, jewelry, and clothes.

Giving Tree Gallery (941-388-1353; www.thegivingtreegallery.com), 5 N. Boulevard of Presidents, at St. Armands Circle, Sarasota. Beautiful inset and sculpted wood art, unique jewelry, glassware, and other fine and unusual gifts.

Hurricane Rita (941-346-7712; www.hurricaneritas.com), 5212 Ocean Blvd., Siesta Key Village, Siesta Key. Island-style gifts and home decor items at affordable prices.

Toy Lab (941-363-0064), 1529 Main St., Sarasota. Don't look for PlayStation games here. Playmobil, yes; PlayStation, no. This tiny, tightly packed, old-fashioned toy shop has educational toys and games, puppets, stuffed animals, and puzzles.

Yoder's Amish Gift Shop (941-366-3208; www.yodersrestaurant.com), 3434 Bahia Vista St., Sarasota. Besides Amish-made items such as baskets, bonnets, aprons, jams, and children's clothing, Yoder's carries more typical jewelry and home decorations.

JEWELRY Bridge Street Jewelers (941-896-7800), 129 Bridge St., Bradenton Beach. Pretty custom and other beach-inspired jewelry—rings, bracelets, necklaces, and gemstones.

Coffrin Jewelers (941-366-6871), 1829 S. Osprey Ave., at Southside Village, Sarasota. Fine creations in gold, silver, and platinum; specializing in original designs. Also a vendor of hand-painted French Quimper tableware.

Heitel Jewelers (941-488-2720), 347 W. Venice Ave., Venice. Buy your shark teeth jewelry, including gold tooth-shaped charms, here; also sea-motif charms, gold, diamonds, and other fine pieces.

Jewelry by Cole (941-388-3323 or 800-572-9375), 7 N. Blvd. of Presidents, at St. Armands Circle, Sarasota. Lovely set gems; a wide variety of the usual to the unusual in sea-themed pieces; custom work.

June Simmons Designs (941-388-4535), 68 S. Palm Ave., Sarasota. Artistic, exclusive-edition jewelry and custom work.

Michael & Co. Jewelers (941-349-5478; www.siestakeyjewelers.com), 5221 Ocean Blvd., Siesta Key. Specializing in nautical pieces, diamonds, and creative jewel settings.

Tilden Ross Jewelers (9941-388-3338; www.tildenrossjewelers.com), 410 St. Armands Circle, Sarasota. All that glitters! Damiani, Patek Lombardi, and other top designers provide a showroom of exquisite sparkle, from pearls to gems to pale-blue beaded collars to unusual gold rings.

KITCHENWARE & HOME DÉCOR

Annabelle's Home & Kitchen (941-552-0339; www.epicureanlife.com), 1924 S. Osprey Ave., Sarasota; and (941-782-0918), 8130 Lakewood Main St. #104, Lakewood Ranch. Connected to Morton's Market (see "Deli & Specialty Foods"), it sells the finest in kitchen- and tableware.

Artisans (941-388-0082), 301 John Ringling Blvd., at St. Armands Circle, Sarasota. Fun glassworks, jewelry, painted furniture, neon art, and more.

Garden Argosy (941-388-6402), 361 St. Armands Circle, Sarasota. Gifts for the home and garden: an extensive selection of candles, frames, painted wood bowls, garden statues, and fountains.

Main Street Traders (941-373-0475; mainstreettraders.com), 1468 Main St., Sarasota. "Everything for the Home" from silly cocktail napkins to art to retro and antique reproduction furnishings.

Restoration Hardware (941-952-9666), 105 Southgate Mall, Sarasota. Those familiar with the chain need no introduction to its smooth and classy line of furnishings, home accessories, and, yes, hardware—that is, the fancy kind, such as drawer pulls and light fixtures.

Rolling Pin Kitchen Emporium (941-925-2434; www.myrollingpin.com), 8201 S. Tamiami Trail, at Westfield Sarasota Square, Sarasota. German cutlery and fine kitchenware; also offers cooking classes.

The Tabletop (941-485-0319; www.thetabletop.com), 205 W. Venice Ave., Venice. Hand-painted and other fun barware, kitchen and table accessories, coffee and espresso paraphernalia, and gourmet items.

❦ **Tervis Tumbler Outlet** (941-966-8614 or 800-237-6688; www.tervis.com), 928 S. Tamiami Trail, Osprey. Floridians know the only way to keep their drinks cool is with Tervis Tumblers, which are made locally and sold throughout Florida. You'll find the widest selection here at the original factory store. The insulated acrylic tumblers are guaranteed for life, and you can exchange defective or broken merchandise at this outlet.

SHELL SHOPS Beach Bazaar (941-346-2995), 5211 Ocean Blvd., Siesta Key. A one-stop mart for seashells, toys, beach clothes, boogie and skim boards, sunglasses, and other vacation must-haves.

Raders Reef (941-778-3211), 5508 Marina Dr., Holmes Beach. Specimen and craft shells, handmade Christmas ornaments and other shell crafts, sponges, jewelry.

Sea Pleasures and Treasures (941-488-3510), 255 Venice Ave. W., Venice. Quantity, not necessarily quality: sea-theme gifts, shells, jewelry, shell craft supplies, and shark teeth.

SPORTING GOODS *Note:* This listing includes general sports outlets only. For supplies and equipment for specific sports, please refer to "To Do" in this chapter.

CB's Saltwater Outfitters (941-349-4400; www.cbsoutfitters.com), 1249 Stickney Point Rd., Siesta Key. Fishing gear and sportswear.

Cook's Sportland (941-493-0025), 4419 Tamiami Trail, Venice. Equipment for archery, golf, camping, and fishing; also fishing licenses, tackle repair, sportswear, shoes, and western clothing.

✳ Special Events

For a complete listing of local cultural events, visit www.sarasota-arts.org or call 941-365-5118.

January: **Arts Day Festival** (941-365-5118), downtown Sarasota. A gala confluence of Sarasota's visual and performing arts that spills from the galleries and theaters onto outdoor stages and sidewalks. One day mid-month. **Manatee County Fair** (941-722-1639; www.manateecountyfair.com), 1303 17th St. W., Palmetto. Ten days midmonth.

February: **Cortez Commercial Fishing Festival** (941-794-1249; www.fishpreserve.org), village of Cortez. Food vendors, music, net-mending demonstrations, arts and crafts, boat tours, and educational exhibits describing the community of Cortez's 100-year-old fishing industry. Third weekend of the month. **Forks & Corks** (www.freshoriginals.com/forksandcorks). This four-day festival, presented by The Sarasota-Manatee Originals group of nonfranchised restaurants, includes interactive seminars, vintner and brewmaster events, and The Grand Tasting at Ringling Estates. **Greek Glendi Festival** (941-355-2616 or 877-355-2272; www.stbarbara-church.org/glendi.html), St. Barbara's Greek Orthodox Church, 7671 N. Lockwood Ridge Rd., Sarasota. Greek food, dancing, and arts and crafts on four days near Valentine's

Day. ○ **Ringling Medieval Fair** (877-334-3377; www.renaissancefest.com), 3000 Ringling Blvd. at Sarasota County Fairgrounds. Two weekends in the month benefit the Ringling Estates by entertaining throngs with kingly entertainment.

March: **Anna Maria Island Springfest** (941-778-2099; www.islandartleague.org), Holmes Beach City Hall Park. A celebration of island arts featuring artist and craft booths, local entertainment, and food concessions. Two days early in the month. **Manatee Heritage Month** (941-749-7165) The entire month is devoted to the celebration of local history and traditions throughout Bradenton and Manatee County. Special tours are arranged by local attractions, and demonstrators weave, quilt, and make baskets and doilies. **Palmetto Heritage Day** (941-723-4991), Palmetto Historical Park, 515 10th Ave. W., Palmetto. Live entertainment, a chicken-and-yellow-rice luncheon, and one-day postage cancellations at the historic post office highlight this open house. **PAL Sailor Circus** (941-361-6350; www.sailorcircus.org), 2075 Bahia Vista St., Sarasota. Proof that the circus is still in the blood of many Sarasota families. Students from grades three to 12 perform professional circus feats during a two-week season. Also Christmastime performances. **Run For the Turtles** (941-388-4441; www.mote.org), Siesta Beach Pavilion, Siesta Key. One-day 5K race to benefit Mote Marine Aquarium. **Sarasota County Fair** (941-365-0818; www.sarasotafair.com), Sarasota Fairgrounds, 3000 Ringling Blvd., Sarasota. Traditional county fair with midway and carnival areas, exhibits, and entertainment. **Sarasota Film Festival** (941-364-9514; www.sarasotafilmfestival.com), 1991 Main St., Suite 108, Courtyard of the Stars next to Regal Cinemas on Main St., downtown Sarasota. More than 200 film screenings, national celebrities, outdoor screenings, and live entertainment. Ten days late March to early April. **Sarasota Jazz Festival** (941-366-1552; www.jazzclubsarasota.com), throughout Sarasota. Big-name jazz players lead a slate of big bands and jazz combos at indoor and outdoor venues. Plus there are jazz appreciation lectures and a jazz trolley route. One week. **Scottish Highland Games & Heritage Festival** (941-342-0509; www.sarasotagames.org), held at the Venice Airport, Venice Rd., Venice. Traditional dancing as well as competitions and entertainment for one day midmonth.

April: **Florida Heritage Festival** (941-747-1998), Bradenton. The monthlong schedule of events (starting at the end of March) includes an illuminated night parade, seafood festival, children's parade, Easter egg hunt, and plastic-bottle boat regatta. **Florida Winefest and Auction** (941-952-1109 or 800-216-6199; www.floridawine fest.com), various locations in the area. A prestigious event featuring food and wine seminars, tastes from the area's finest restaurants, top entertainment, a black-tie dinner, and a fine-wine auction. Four days. **La Musica International Chamber Music Festival** (941-366-8450, ext. 3; www.lamusica festival.org), held at the Sarasota Opera House, 61 N. Pineapple Ave., Sarasota. Five classical music concerts held during two weeks in April. ✪ ♪ **Shark's Tooth & Seafood Festival** (941-412-0402), Airport Festival Grounds, Venice. A bacchanal of seafood bounty, the festival gets its name also from its reputation among shark teeth collectors. One weekend midmonth. **Siesta Fiesta** (941-349-3800), Siesta Key. A weekend of fine art shows, food, and live musical and kids' entertainment late in the month.

May: **New Play Festival** (941-366-9000; www.fst2000.org), Florida Studio Theatre, 1241 N. Palm Ave., downtown Sarasota. Premieres the works of emerging playwrights from Florida and around the nation, launching almost 70 main-stage productions. Late May–early June. **Sand Sculpting Contest** (941-349-3800; www.siestakeychamber .com), Siesta Key Public Beach. A 35-year competition with adult and youth divisions.

June: **Sarasota Music Festival** (941-953-3434 or 866-508-0611; www.sarasota musicfestival.com), Florida West Coast Symphony, 709 N. Tamiami Trail, Sarasota. Presents classical and chamber music by promising musicians from around the world. Sponsored by the Florida West Coast Symphony, the program includes lectures for participants. The public is welcome at the performances. Three weeks. **Savor Sarasota** (www.sarasotafl.org/spirit), 10 days of tasting the award-winning fare of 30 local restaurants. Early in the month. **Suncoast Super Boat Grand Prix** (941-371-8820, ext. 1800; www.suncoastoffshore.org), Sarasota Bay and other county locations. A national attraction more than 25 years old, it features fishing and golf tournaments, parties, a boat parade (on land), a car show, and fireworks as well as the headline powerboat races. Eleven days at month's end through July 5. **Venice Art Festival** (941-484-6722), downtown Venice. Artisans from around the U.S. gather for one weekend.

July: **De Soto Fishing Tournament** (941-747-1998), Bradenton Yacht Club, Palmetto. Inshore and offshore divisions. Entry fee and cash prizes. Takes place one weekend midmonth.

October: **Ringling International Arts Festival** (800-660-4278; www .ringlingartsfestival.org), John and Mable Ringling Museum of Art,

Sarasota. Theater, dance, music, and visual arts all fall under the umbrella of this world-class festival. Five days early in the month.

November: **Blues Fest** (941-954-4101, ext. 5454; www.sarasotabluesfest.com), Ed Smith Stadium Complex, 2700 12th St., Sarasota. Blues musicians of world renown. One day early in the month. **Cine-World** (941-364-8662, box office: 941-955-FILM; www.film society.org), Burns Court Cinemas, 506 Burns Ln., downtown Sarasota. Independent film screenings. One week early November. **St. Armands Circle Art Festival** (941-388-1554), 411 St. Armands Circle. Features more than 200 national artists for one weekend midmonth. **Venice Art Festival** (941-484-6722), downtown Venice. Artisans from around the U.S. gather for one weekend.

December: **Winterfest** (941-778-2099; www.islandartleague.com), Holmes Beach City Hall Park. Two days of arts and crafts shows, live entertainment, and food. ✐ **Winter Wonderland** (941-932-9400, ext. 449), Old Main Street, downtown Bradenton. Two mounds of snow, kids' craft fair, lit-boat parade, food, and entertainment. Held three evenings the first weekend of December.

Charlotte Harbor Coast

2

CHARLOTTE HARBOR COAST

WILD AND WATERY

As one of Florida's largest bays and its second largest estuary (17th largest in the United States), 270-square-mile Charlotte Harbor supplies a huge gulp of nature and a place to play on many waterfronts—a total of 830 miles of shoreline. The region has remained the most isolated and undeveloped of any in southwest Florida, primarily because its beaches—glorious though they might be—are so far removed from main highways. The fact that 84 percent of Charlotte Harbor shoreline is preserved land ensures that the Charlotte coast will retain its quiet, natural temperament and still hold on to fishing as a way of life and livelihood.

This chapter begins where the last left off, on twisty, out-of-the-way **Manasota Key,** a refuge for wealthy isolationists at its north end and the site of the unpretentious, underappreciated resort community of **Englewood Beach** at its south.

On the mainland's Cape Haze peninsula—bounded by the Myakka River and Charlotte Harbor—small residential communities such as ✪ **Englewood, Grove City, Cape Haze, Placida,** and **Rotonda West** hold Amerindian mounds, fishermen, retirees, golf-course communities, and families. Placida is the jumping-off point for **Gasparilla Island,** which has built its reputation and character on one fish in particular: the tarpon. Phosphate shipping and legends of bygone buccaneers first attracted attention to the area. Later the Silver King, prize of the fishing world, drew millionaires to the island community of **Boca Grande.** They're still around; the town reportedly has a median household income of more than $164,000, and its 33921 ZIP code was listed in *Forbes's* list of 500 most expensive in 2009. Privately owned **Little Gasparilla** and **Palm Islands** and mostly state-owned **Don Pedro Island** have run together with shifts of tides and time. They remain three of Florida's most pristine barrier islands.

Inland, across the harbor, **Port Charlotte** is a new city that was built around Tamiami Trail, principally as a retirement community. The town of **Charlotte Harbor** was settled shortly after the Civil War by farmers and cattle ranchers. Facing it across the Peace River's widest point, ✪ **Punta Gorda** boasts a past as deep as its harbor. The southernmost station for the Florida Southern Railroad in 1886, this deepwater port town enjoyed a bustling era of commerce and tourism before railroad builder Henry Plant decided to shut it down in favor of further

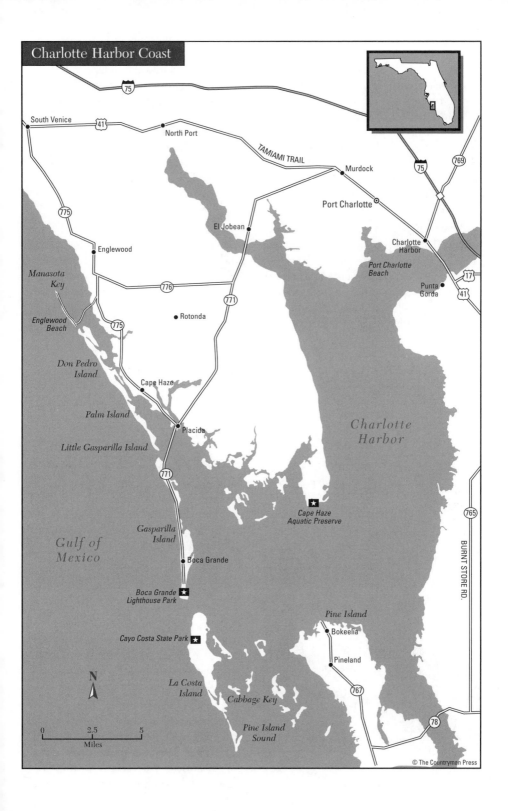

Charlotte Harbor Coast

developing Tampa Bay. Ice making, turpentine stilling, pineapple growing, and especially commercial fishing continued to earn local citizens a living for some time. Today Punta Gorda is working to recover its past glories through downtown and riverfront restoration. Residential-retail developments are replacing old shopping centers and rubble left in the wake of 2004's Hurricane Charley, which hit Punta Gorda squarely.

Money magazine regularly declares Punta Gorda one of America's most desirable places to live. Home of Ponce de León Park, where the explorer is believed to have met his death, it hosts subdivisions of modern-day youth seekers. Its heyday train depot has been restored to its old glory and today houses a small museum and an antique mall.

✳ To See

The Charlotte Harbor coast is small town—even in its larger, urban-sprawl-infected communities. Long considered a refuge for the retired, the region is not known for a vibrant arts scene or cultural diversity. Overall, it has a Midwestern flavor in coastal areas but is definitely Old Florida in inland rural parts. Awareness of the arts has developed slowly and on a hobby level. For information on local arts and culture, contact the Arts & Humanities Council of Charlotte County, 941-764-8100.

ARCHITECTURE In the smaller towns around Charlotte Harbor, single examples of historic character appear serendipitously in the midst of concrete-block homes. Downtown Englewood, a destination off the beaten path of the Tamiami Trail, holds a few such treasures that have been reincarnated as shops, boutiques, and galleries.

MODERN BOCA GRANDE ARCHITECTURE TAKES CUES FROM MEDITERRANEAN STYLES INTRODUCED BY THE WEALTHY INDUSTRIALISTS WHO DEVELOPED AND SETTLED THE ISLAND.

Punta Gorda sprinkles its architectural prizes—old homes, commercial buildings, and churches—along **Marion Avenue, Olympia Avenue, Retta Esplanade,** and side streets such as **Sullivan Street** and the **Punta Gorda History Park** on Shreve Street. Along the **Esplanade,** look for impressive newly restored homes, the jewels of the old riverfront district. In and around the town's historic section, an eclectic array of architecture ranges from old shotgun cigar workers' homes and tin-roofed Cracker shacks to Victorian mansions and a neoclassical city hall. Watch for historic murals and street sculptures along the way.

Boca Grande's most noteworthy examples of architecture, aside from the grande dame **Gasparilla Inn,** are four historic churches, each with their own style, located in a four-block area downtown. The Catholic church takes its inspiration from Spanish missions; the other three occupy early-20th-century wood-frame buildings and serve Episcopal, Baptist, and Methodist congregations.

A few blocks away, on **Tarpon Avenue,** spruced-up old Cracker homes slump comfortably in a district once called **Whitewash Alley.** For a taste of wealthy eccentricity, check out the **Johann Fust Library** on Gasparilla Road. It was built of native coquina, cypress, and pink stucco.

CINEMA Regal 16 Cinema (941-623-0114; www.regalcinemas.com), 1441 Tamiami Trail, in the Port Charlotte Town Center, Port Charlotte.

DANCE Aki's Dancesport Centre (941-624-4001), 3109 Tamiami Trail, Port Charlotte. Dancing socials, competitions, and lessons in swing, merengue, salsa, lindy, fox-trot, and waltz.

THE HISTORIC COURTHOUSE IN PUNTA GORDA, BUILT CIRCA 1928, REFLECTS NEOCLASSICAL STYLE WITH GREEK AND ROMAN INFLUENCES.

Country Line Dance Lessons (941-575-8188; www.fishville.com), 1200 W. Retta Esplanade, in Fishermen's Village, Punta Gorda. Every Wednesday night, 7 to 9; $3 per person for lessons.

HISTORIC HOMES & SITES ✪ The A. C. Freeman House (941-639-2222), 311 Retta Esplanade, Punta Gorda. Docent tours Monday and Thursday starting at 11. Donations suggested. Newly moved to the riverfront, this house was once occupied by Punta Gorda's mayor and mortician. Narrowly escaping the wrecking ball in 1985, the lovely clapboard Queen Anne mansion was saved and restored by the people of Punta Gorda as a memento of gracious pioneer lifestyles. Kids especially enjoy the kitchen out back, the room under the stairwell à la Harry Potter, and the girls room and toys. Period and nonperiod pieces furnish the home, which also houses the Charlotte County Chamber of Commerce. The first Friday of each month, the Chamber holds a free Friday coffee at 8 AM.

✪ The Blanchard House Museum (941-639-2914; www.blanchardmuseum.org), 406 Martin Luther King Blvd., Punta Gorda. Open Tuesday–Friday and the first Saturday of the month 10–2, other times by appointment; closed June–September. Donations suggested. The 1925 home of an African American steamboat pilot and his mail-order bride, the museum displays photographs, documents, and artifacts relating to Punta Gorda's black population and its history, which dates back to the town's settling in 1886 by seven African Americans and eight white folks. Tours are by docent or self-guided. A garden commemorates those who gave their lives in

THE BOCA GRANDE LIGHTHOUSE IS ONE OF THE STATE'S MOST PICTURESQUE.

military service. It resides in the Trabue Woods community, a historic African American neighborhood.

🦐 **Boca Grande Lighthouse Museum** (941-964-0060; www.barrierislandparks society.org), Gasparilla Island State Park, Gulf Blvd., Boca Grande. Open November–May, Monday–Saturday 10–4, Sunday noon–4; the rest of the year closed Monday and Tuesday; closed all of August.. $3 per vehicle of eight ($2 pedestrians, cyclists, and extra passengers) for state park; donation of $1 requested. This 1890 structure—the most photographed and painted landmark on the island—was renovated in Old Florida style and put back into service in 1986 after 20 years of abandonment. You can self-tour both the lighthouse and the museum, which explores its history and Boca Grande bygones—from ancient Calusa civilizations through railroad and industrial eras to the island's modern-day reputation as a tarpon-fishing mecca. Historic cisterns, the assistant lighthouse keeper's home, and a struggling native vegetation garden compose the fenced-in complex. It overlooks the beach within Gasparilla Island State Park.

Ponce de León Historical Park, 4000 W. Marion Ave., Punta Gorda. A rock shrine encasement, chipped-paint statues, and historic plaques commemorate Ponce de León's supposed 1513 landing here and his subsequent death caused by an Indian attack. The park has a wildlife and recreational area on the harbor, plus a boat ramp, picnic facilities, a small seawalled beach, a playground, two fishing piers, and a nature trail into the mangroves and along a creek where you'll often see herons. The park is home to the Peace River Wildlife Center rehabilitation facility.

🦐 **Punta Gorda History Park** (941-391-4446), 501 Shreve St., Punta Gorda. So far this gathering of historic buildings in a pretty two-acre park setting amounts to three old homes. Stop in first at the old Trabue office (closed Mondays and July and August), where Punta Gorda's founder conducted his land sales business. Today it houses an art gallery gift shop and a small exhibit on the history of the two-year-old park and its buildings. Ask for a tour of the Cigar Cottage, where the town's tobacco industry was once headquartered, and learn about Punta Gorda's hibiscus-growing fame. The third structure, Punta Gorda's first jail, is not open for touring. The fountain from the old Punta Gorda Hotel also graces the grounds, now a quarter wishing well. Several gardens beautify the park, including The Harry Goulding Hibiscus Gardens, named for a local man who hybridized 600 varieties.

Punta Gorda Train Depot, 1009 Taylor St., Punta Gorda. Signs marked COL-ORED and WHITE are telltale relics of the late 1920s era when this Atlantic Coast Line station was in operation. It is the only one of six built in Mediterranean style that survives. You can see the original ticket windows and historic photographs and artifacts that have previously been the traveling exhibit at the Blanchard House (see above). On the depot's backside, an antique mall raises funds for the historical society (look under "Shopping: Antiques & Collectibles"). Across the street, one of the town's historic murals illustrates its railroad days.

MUSEUMS ✐ **Charlotte County Historical Center** (941-629-7278; charlotte-countyfl.com/historical), 22959 Bayshore Rd., Charlotte Harbor. Open 10–5 Tuesday–Friday; 10–3 Saturday. $2 adults, $1 children ages 12 and younger. Located at a gorgeous spot on the river, next to the Bayshore Pier, the roomy facility is geared toward children with programs, signage, showcases, and interactive exhibits that illuminate facets of local history. Permanent exhibits are devoted to Calusa natives, fishing heritage, fossils, Spanish explorers, turpentine camps, and more. About five changing exhibits cycle through yearly.

✪ **Gasparilla Island Maritime Museum** (941-964-GIMM), at Whidden's Marina on Harbor Dr., Boca Grande. Hours vary. Admission by donation. Some might call it a shed full of old junk, but to the citizens of Boca Grande, it represents Americana and a way of life that has survived in contrast to the mansions and yachts that surround it. Part of Whidden's Marina, the museum features photo albums that remember a day when the nation's top industrialists sailed here to fish and winter. Odd parts of boats and fishing gear lie strewn around the old, peeling fish shack, listed on the National Register of Historic Places. Still in operation, the marina and its store make it difficult to tell where the museum ends and the present begins.

Military Heritage & Aviation Museum (941-575-9002; www.mhaam.org), 1200 W. Esplanade #48, at Fishermen's Village, Punta Gorda. Open Monday–Saturday 10–8; Sunday noon–6. This collection of wartime memorabilia spans the Civil War to Desert Storm with photographs, uniforms, weaponry, documents, medals, field equipment, and more—constantly rotating to reflect the private collections of local veterans who lend their items.

Rick Treworgy's Muscle Car City (239-941-5959; www.musclecarcity.net), 3811 Tamiami Trail, Punta Gorda. Open 9–5 Tuesday–Sunday.

ROWS OF GLEAMING CLASSIC CARS FILL THE NEW MUSCLE CAR CITY.

$10; children ages 11 and younger are admitted free with a paying adult. Lined up in orderly, glistening rows, Corvettes, Camaros, Chevelles, Pontiac GTOs, Oldsmobile Cutlass 422s, Impalas, et al pose with their hoods open, exposing gleaming, spotless engines. The museum, which opened in March 2009, claims at least one Corevette for every year from 1954 to 1975. Some of the pieces in the collection reflect the owner's nostalgic side, such as older models like the 1927 Chrysler and 1929 Chevrolet Woody. Besides cars, memorabilia including the RCA dog, vintage ice coolers, gas pumps, and a Budweiser racing boat and hauling rig demonstrate the breadth of Treworgy's collecting affliction. Those who share the affliction can purchase nostalgia and car-related gifts, including a $3,000 gas pump, in the impressively sprawling Speed Shop and Memorabilia Store. Even vintage cars are for sale in the Car Corral. The nostalgia theme carries over to the Muscle City Diner, a clever '50s-style diner complete with black-and-white tiled floors and a jukebox.

MUSIC & NIGHTLIFE

Boca Grande

South Beach (941-964-0765), 777 Gulf Blvd., Boca Grande. Contemporary bands play weekend nights. Sunset plays (almost) every evening. Even when neither of those events are happening, it's a pleasant place to hoist a few with the locals and take in the game within eyeshot of the gulf.

Englewood

Englewood Performing Arts Series (941-473-2787) Fine cultural entertainment from around the nation, mid-November–mid-April.

Junior's Cabaret (941-474-8730), 2643 Placida Rd., Englewood. You'll find the locals here—eating, shooting pool, drinking, and dancing.

Saturday Nite Live on Dearborn Street (941-473-8782; www.oldenglewood .com), W. Dearborn St., Englewood. Live entertainment and free refreshments augment the lively shopping experience here on the second Saturday of the month.

White Elephant Pub (941-475-6801), 1855 Gulf Blvd., Englewood Beach. It hosts live bands on the weekends.

Port Charlotte

Charlotte County Jazz Society (941-766-9422; www.ccjazz.org), P.O. Box 495321, Port Charlotte 33949. Sponsors several jazz concerts each year at the Cultural Center Theater (see below). Call or visit the Web site for information on jam sessions.

Charlotte Symphony Orchestra (941-205-5996; www.charlottesymphony.com) Performs at the Charlotte Center for Performing Arts (see below), November–March.

Gatorz Bar & Grill (941-625-5000), 3816 Tamiami Trail, Port Charlotte. Live music—jazz and Top 40—throughout the week in an indoor-outdoor, purely Florida swamp-culture setting along the main highway.

Visani Comedy Dinner Theater (941-629-9191; www.visani.net), 2400 Kings Highway, Port Charlotte. National comedians perform as well as murder mysteries and other entertainment; dinner menu available, but dining is optional.

Bin 82 (941-916-9581; www.bin82tastingroom.com), 258 W. Marion Ave., downtown Punta Gorda. A lively, sophisticated spot with live music on Friday and Saturday nights.

Charlotte Center for Performing Arts (941-505-SHOW for box office), 701 Carmalita St., Punta Gorda. This modern 869-seat facility hosts youth theater, symphony, chamber orchestra, and other performances.

Downtown Hookah (941-639-0004; www.downtownhookah.com), 307 E. Marion Ave., Punta Gorda. Belly dancing Friday and Saturday nights; special Mediterranean entertainment dinner shows the second Saturday of each month (reservations required).

Downtown Punta Gorda Gallery Walk (941-575-9979) Galleries and restaurants host free entertainment on the third Thursday of each month.

Fishermen's Village (941-575-3007; www.fishville.com), 1200 W. Retta Esplanade, Punta Gorda. Live entertainment most Friday and other evenings, with country line dance lessons on Wednesday evenings.

Gilchrist Park (Retta Esplanade) Local musicians gather for impromptu jamming on Thursday nights at 6 PM, and the public is invited.

THEATER Cultural Center of Charlotte County (941-625-4175; www.the culturalcenter.com), 2280 Aaron St., Port Charlotte. Home of the Charlotte Players (941-255-1022; www.charlotteplayers.org) community theater group and other theatrical and musical groups.

Lemon Bay Playhouse (941-475-6756; www.lemonbayplayhouse.com), 96 W. Dearborn St., Englewood. Home of the Lemon Bay Players community-theater group. Performances September–July.

Royal Palm Players (941-964-2670; www.royalpalmplayers.com), 333 Park Ave., Suite 4, Boca Grande. A community theater group sponsoring plays, guest-artist performances, children's performances, and concerts October–April.

VISUAL ART CENTERS & RESOURCES Punta Gorda lost many of its historic and educational murals to hurricanes and development, but the Punta Gorda Historical Mural Society is making headway in replacing them and today the number is back to 23 murals, the pre-hurricane number.

A listing for commercial galleries is included in the "Shopping" section of this chapter.

Arts & Humanities Council (941-764-8100), 2702 Tamiami Trail, Port Charlotte. Hosts art displays and events.

Englewood Art Center (941-474-5548), 350 S. McCall Rd., Englewood.

Hermitage Artist Retreat (941-465-1098; www.hermitage-fl.org), 6650 Manasota Key Rd., Englewood. This beachfront historic building (once part of a nudist resort) houses self-supporting artists.

Visual Arts Center (941-639-8810; www.visualartcenter.com), 210 Maud St., near Fishermen's Village, Punta Gorda. Home of the Charlotte County Art Guild. Exhibit halls, gift shops, library, darkroom, state-of-the-art pottery studio, computer lab, and classes.

✳ To Do

More behind-the-scenes than the touted playgrounds of its flanking neighbors, the Charlotte Harbor coast's greatest claim to recreational fame is its fishing—particularly for that king of all sport fish, tarpon.

BEACHES You must drive way off the beaten path to find the beaches of Charlotte County. Though less convenient, that keeps them more natural, less trodden.

❧ **Blind Pass (Middle) Beach** (941-861-1980; www.scgov.net/ParksandRec reation/Parks), FL 776, midisland on Manasota Key. Sixty acres of lightly developed shoreline attract those drawn more to seclusion than to the sports and activities of Manasota Key's other beaches. Low dunes edge wide salt-and-pepper sands. Next door you'll see one of the island's first buildings. Known as Hermitage House, it was once a nudist resort. Today it's a retreat for visiting artists. The skyline along the beach is low to the ground and unobtrusive—a great beach for long walks. From the parking lot you can follow a nature boardwalk trail into the mangroves. If there's surf to be found in the area, you'll find it here. Facilities: restrooms, showers, playground, nature trail, canoe launch.

❂ **Don Pedro Island State Park** (941-964-0375; www.floridastateparks.org/ donpedroisland), south of Palm Island, accessible only by boat. This secluded beach occupies a 129-acre island getaway. Once separated from Palm Island and Little Gasparilla, Don Pedro Island is now connected to the two to form one long, lightly developed barrier island. Don Pedro, the most natural component, is in the middle, with a pretty beach that attracts water birds. Contact Grande Tours (see Grande Tours under "Wildlife Tours & Charters") for information on ferry service. Facilities: picnic area/shelters, restrooms, showers, boat docks, nature trails. $2 per person.

❧ **Englewood Beach at Chadwick Park** (941-681-3742; www.charlottecounty fl.com/Parks/beaches.asp), FL 776, south end of Manasota Key at Englewood Beach. Popular with families, its facilities include a boardwalk, pirate-theme playground, basketball hoop, and picnic shelters. Shops and restaurants huddle around the area, which keeps activity levels high. Facilities: picnic areas/shelters, restrooms, showers, volleyball, beach wheelchairs. Parking: 75 cents per hour.

Lighthouse Beach/Gasparilla Island State Park (941-964-0375; www.florida stateparks.org/gasparillaisland), along Gulf Blvd., Boca Grande, Gasparilla Island. Marked by a historic lighthouse with a museum inside, the park edges the deepwater tarpon grounds of Boca Grande Pass. Its plush sands encompass 135 acres, although in some parts the beach gets quite narrow. Swimming is not recommended because of strong currents through the pass. A historic chapel in the same park has been restored for weddings and other private functions. Facilities: picnic tables, restrooms, interpretative center/museum. Parking: $3 per car for up to eight people, $2 for pedestrians, cyclists, and extra passengers.

❧ **Manasota Beach** (941-861-1980; www.scgov.net/ParksandRecreation/Parks), north end of FL 776, Manasota Key. This lively, 14-acre sunning and shelling venue connects to Venice's Caspersen Beach, about 1½ miles to the north. It also has a reputation—but not as pointed as Venice's—for shark teeth. The sands are somewhat narrower here than to the south, and a scenic boardwalk runs along the edge. Facilities: picnic area/shelters, restrooms, showers, lifeguard, historical marker, boat ramp.

THE BEACH AT BOCA GRANDE BECKONS.

✦ **Port Charlotte Beach Park** (941-627-1628), 4500 Harbor Blvd., Port Charlotte. A highly developed recreational center that sits where the Peace River meets Charlotte Harbor along a man-made beach, this is a good place to go if you (or the children) like to keep busy at the beach. It's better for sunning than swimming, however, as bacteria levels are sometimes high. Stick to the swimming pool. A boardwalk runs along the beach and connects to the fishing pier. It looks across the way at Punta Gorda. Facilities: picnic areas; restrooms; showers; concessions; boccie, basketball, volleyball, and tennis; playground; horseshoes; boat ramps; fishing pier; canoe and kayak launch; heated swimming and kiddie pools. Open: 6–9 daily; pool open 9–4 Tuesday–Friday, 11–5 Saturday–Sunday; pier and ramp open 24 hours. Swimming admission: $2.68 adult, $1.61 children ages 3–15 (pool phone: 941-629-0170). Parking: 75 cents per hour.

✪ **Stump Pass Beach State Park** (941-964-0375; www.floridastateparks.org /stumppass), south end of Gulf Blvd., Englewood Beach on Manasota Key. This uncrowded beach offers lovely, unspoiled seclusion. Traditionally, the 255-acre park has been a magnet for fishermen who cast into Lemon Bay. Follow the 2-mile wooded trail to the south, and you'll find nice areas to spread a towel and dip your toes. The park stretches all the way to Stump Pass in a skinny strip of black-specked sand fringed by sea oats. Facilities: restrooms, nature trail, picnic tables. Parking: $3 per car with up to eight passengers, $2 for bikers, pedestrians, and extra passengers

BICYCLING The Charlotte Coast region, with its abundance of back roads and wide-open spaces, gives cyclists an opportunity to pedal in peace. Many of its favored bikeways are on-road or designated bike lanes, which are separated from motor traffic by only a painted white line. According to state law, bicyclists who share the road with other vehicles must heed all the rules of the road. Children under age 16 are required to wear helmets.

Best Biking: Glimpse wild turkeys and lake views while pedaling along the 37 miles of trails at **Babcock-Webb Wildlife Management Area** (941-575-5768; www .myfwc.com), 29200 Tuckers Grade, Punta Gorda.

✪ **Cape Haze Pioneer Trail** (941-625-7529; www.charlottecountyfl.com) runs 5.5 miles parallel to County Route 771 (CR771) along a former rail bed. When completed in spring 2011, it will total 8.5 miles.

About a mile past Gasparilla Island's causeway (which can be crossed by bicycle for $1, but this is not recommended because of high winds), the **Boca Grande bike path** starts. Here you pedal along old railroad routes. Seven miles of pathway travel the island from tip to tip along Railroad Avenue and Gulf Boulevard. These paths are shared by golf carts, which you can rent and drive about the island as long as you are 14 or older. Many of Boca's downtown streets are also designated golf-cart trails.

FL 776 through Englewood and Englewood Beach is shouldered with a bike lane that ends at the Sarasota County line. In Punta Gorda, **Gilchrist Park's bike path** runs along green space overlooking the Peace River on Retta Esplanade. Bike riding on city sidewalks is legal throughout the county.

For a map of Charlotte County bikeways, call the Charlotte County–Punta Gorda Metropolitan Planning Organization at 941-639-4676.

Rental Shops: **The Bicycle Center** (941-627-6600; www.bicyclecentercc.com), 3795 Tamiami Trail, Port Charlotte. Bikes fitted to your size and experience. Also schedules biking events and rides.

Bikes and Boards (941-474-2019), 966 S. McCall Rd., Englewood Beach. Bike and kayak rentals, sales, delivery, and service.

Island Bike 'N Beach (941-964-0711), 333 Park Ave., Boca Grande. Rents bikes, golf carts, and beach stuff.

BOATS & BOATING Charlotte Harbor Coast offers many waterfronts for adventure: the gulf, harbor, Peace River, Myakka River, Lemon Bay Aquatic Preserve, and a number of creeks and canals. Charlotte Harbor has been named among the nation's top 10 sailing destinations by *Sail* magazine.

Canoeing & Kayaking: For information on paddling trails, contact the Charlotte County Parks and Recreation Department at 941-625-7529 or www.charlotte countyfl.com and request a copy of the *Blueway Trails* map and listing of 57 trails covering 200 miles. The Woolveton Trail, my favorite, takes you down small, quiet creeks tunneling under mangrove canopies. See Grande Tours under "Wildlife Tours & Charters."

Florida Paddlesports (941-621-2502; www.floridapaddlesports.net), 25010 Harborside Blvd., Punta Gorda. Rentals, kayak fishing rigs, instruction, and tours out of south Punta Gorda.

Personal Watercraft Rental/Tours: **Island Jet Ski** (941-474-1168), 1450 Beach Rd., at Englewood Bait House on the south bridge, Englewood Beach. Hourly and daily rentals; tours available.

Powerboat Rentals: **Bay Breeze Boat Rentals** (941-475-0733), 1450 Beach Rd., at Englewood Bait House on the south bridge, Englewood Beach. Rents pontoon boats and fishing skiffs.

Boca Boats Rentals (941-964-1333 or 888-416-BOAT; www.bocaboat.com), 5800 Gasparilla Rd., at Uncle Henry's Marina, Boca Grande. Rents powerboats, kayaks, hydrobikes, and golf carts.

Holidaze Boat Rental (941-505-8888; www.holidazeboatrental.com), 1200 W. Retta Esplanade, at Fishermen's Village, Punta Gorda. Rents 17.5- to 31-foot fishing boats, pontoons, and deck boats by the hour, half day, or full day. Also jet skis.

Public Boat Ramps: **Indian Mound Park,** Englewood Recreation Center, 101 Horn St., downtown Englewood. Two newly renovated ramps on Lemon Bay. Access to Stump Pass, picnic pavilion, restrooms, and nature trails.

Laishley Park Marina, Marion Ave. and Nesbit St., Punta Gorda. A newly renovated facility with a surf shop and a huge, on-site restaurant. The park next door has picnic facilities and a playground with an interactive fountain.

Manasota Beach, Manasota Beach Rd., Manasota Key. One public boat ramp across the street from a county park.

Placida Park, Causeway Blvd., Placida.

Ponce de León Park, west end of Marion Ave., Punta Gorda. One boat ramp on the harbor.

Port Charlotte Beach (941-627-1628), 4500 Harbor Blvd., southeast end of Harbor Blvd., Port Charlotte. Beach recreational area, access to Charlotte Harbor. Two boat ramps.

Sailboat Charters, Rentals & Instruction: **Paradise Sailing** (941-932-4232; www.paradisesailing.com), 4071 Key Largo Ln., Punta Gorda. Captained cruises, bareboat charters, and American Sailing Association (ASA) sailing courses.

Southwest Florida Yachts/Florida Sailing & Cruising School (239-656-1339 or 800-262-SWFY; www.flsailandcruiseschool.com), 3444 Marinatown Ln. N.W., Suite 19, North Fort Myers. ASA-certification courses and bareboat charters provide excellent adventures out of Burnt Store Marina (southwest of Punta Gorda) into Charlotte Harbor for live-aboard experiences.

Sight-Seeing & Entertainment Cruises: Look under "Wildlife Tours & Charters" for nature excursions.

Boca Boat Cruises & Charters (941-964-1333 or 888-416-BOAT; www.bocaboat.com), 5800 Gasparilla Rd., at Uncle Henry's Marina, Boca Grande. Twice weekly Cabbage Key lunch tours, and sunset cruises five days a week.

✪ ✧ **Grande Tours** (941-697-8825; www.grandetours.com), 12575 Placida Rd., Placida. Boat tours: sunset, kid fishing, wildlife, and shuttle to Don Pedro State Park. Also kayak nature and fishing tours and rentals.

✪ **King Fisher Cruise Lines** (941-639-0969; www.kingfisherfleet.com), 1200 W. Retta Esplanade, at

PASSENGERS ABOARD KING FISHER FLEET'S PEACE RIVER NATURE CRUISE POP UP AT AN ALLIGATOR SIGHTING.

Fishermen's Village Marina, Punta Gorda. Excursions to Cayo Costa and Cabbage Key and along the Peace River aboard a double-deck head boat. Also sunset, harbor sight-seeing, and dining cruises.

Ko Ko Kai Charter Boat Service (941-474-2141; www.kokokai.com), 5040 N. Beach Rd., Englewood Beach. Takes you island hopping to Gasparilla, Palm, Cayo Costa, Cabbage Key, Upper Captiva, and Captiva Islands, as well as on lunch, fishing, and shelling charters.

FISHING Tarpon reigns as the king of southwest Florida fish—the Silver King, to be exact, named for its silver-dollar-like scales. ✪ **Boca Grande Pass** is one of the most celebrated spots in the world for catching the feisty fighter. But the tarpon is hardly alone on its throne: A National Wildlife Federation study in 2006 reported 256 species of salt and freshwater fish in Charlotte Harbor. The harbor encompasses more than 200 square miles of fishable water.

Nonresidents age 16 and older who wish to fish must obtain a license unless fishing from a vessel or pier covered by its own license. You can buy inexpensive temporary-nonresident licenses at county tax collectors' offices and most Kmarts and bait shops. Check local regulations for season, size, and catch restrictions.

Fishing Charters/Outfitters: **Boca Grande Fishing Guides Association** (941-964-2559; www.bocagrandefishing.com), P.O. Box 676, Boca Grande 33921. Organization of more than 50 qualified charter guides especially knowledgeable about tarpon.

Captain Jack's Charters (941-475-4511; www.sunstate.com/captjack), 1450 Beach Rd., at the Englewood Bait House, Englewood Beach. Half-day, full-day, night, overnight, and weekend trips.

Fishing Unlimited (941-964-0907 or 800-4-TARPON; www.4tarpon.com), 431 Park Ave., Boca Grande. Outfitters, fly shop, guides, and charters. Authorized Orvis dealer.

King Fisher Fleet (941-639-0969; www.kingfisherfleet.com), 1200 W. Retta Esplanade, at Fishermen's Village Marina, Punta Gorda. Deep-sea back-bay fishing; owner Capt. Ralph Allen is the local expert on fishing and fishing conditions.

Tarpon Hunter Guide Service (941-743-6622), 265 Lomond Dr. #B, Port Charlotte. Charters aboard the *Tarpon Hunter II* in Charlotte Harbor and backwaters. Specialties include fly and light-tackle fishing.

Fishing Piers: **Bayshore Fishing Pier,** 22967 Bayshore Dr., Charlotte Harbor. At the mouth of the Peace River next to the Charlotte County Historical Center.

Bayshore Live Oak Park (941-629-7278; charlottecountyfl.com/Parks/Park Pages/bayshorepark.asp), 23157 Bayshore Dr., Charlotte Harbor. Another pier extends into the river just east of the Bayshore pier in a park setting with picnic facilities and a canoe launch.

Englewood Beach (Anger) Pier, along Beach Rd. east of the drawbridge.

Gasparilla Fishing Pier South (941-627-1628), near Courtyard Plaza, north end of Gasparilla Rd., Gasparilla Island. An old railroad bridge.

Gilchrist Park, W. Retta Esplanade, Punta Gorda. Cast into the brackish waters where the Peace River empties into the gulf.

Laishley Park Piers, 100 Nesbit St., Punta Gorda. Two quiet spots for fishing along the Trabue Harborwalk.

Myakka Fishing Pier North & South (941-627-1628), FL 776, El Jobean. Two piers into the Myakka River.

Ponce de León Park, 4000 W. Marion Ave., Punta Gorda. Two piers reaching into the mouth of the Peace River at Charlotte Harbor.

Port Charlotte Beach Park (941-627-1628), 4500 Harbor Blvd., Port Charlotte, southeast end of Harbor Blvd. Part of a beach and pool recreational center.

GOLF *Public Golf Courses & Centers:* **Deep Creek Golf Club** (941-625-6911; www.deepcreekgc.com), 1260 San Cristobal Ave., Port Charlotte. Semiprivate; 18 holes, par 70; driving range, putting green, and snack bar.

Duffy's Golf Center (941-697-3900), 12455 S. Access Rd., Port Charlotte. An 18-hole executive course (nine holes lit) and lit practice range. PGA professionals, golf shop, and Duffer's Tavern serving food and beverages.

Lemon Bay Golf Club (941-697-3729; www.lemonbaygolfclub.com), 9600 Eagle Preserve Dr., Englewood. Semiprivate; 18 holes, par 71; restaurant. A certified Audubon Society course.

Port Charlotte Golf Club (941-625-4109), 22400 Gleneagles Terrace, Port Charlotte. Semiprivate; 18 holes; full practice facilities, restaurant, and lounge.

HEALTH & FITNESS CLUBS ✔ **Charlotte County Family YMCA** (941-629-9622; www.charlottecountyymca.com), 19333 Quesada Ave., Port Charlotte. Aerobics, body shaping, yoga, volleyball, basketball, golf tournaments, youth sports competitions, steam room, and kiddie facilities and programs.

The Club Punta Gorda (941-505-0999; www.puntagordaclub.com), 2905 Tamiami Trail, Punta Gorda. Nice, modern facility offering cardiovascular equipment, golf-enhancement program, free weights, yoga, spinning, weight machines, tennis courts, baby-sitting, coffee-juice shop, massage, spinal health clinic, and other spa services. Daily, weekly, monthly, and yearly rates.

Cultural Center of Port Charlotte (941-625-4475, ext. 263; www.thecultural center.com), 2280 Aaron St., Port Charlotte. Full fitness facilities, classes, and personal trainers. For $10 a month, you can work out during "happy hour" Monday–Friday 5–7 and Saturday 8–4.

HIKING Babcock Ranch Preserve (800-500-5583; www.babcockwilderness .com), 8000 FL 31, Punta Gorda. The Footprints Trail takes you either 2 or 4.7 miles into Florida backcountry. The Eco-Trail is 1.8 miles long. On either of them, you may see deer, wild hogs, bald eagles, hawks, wood storks, and other birds.

Charlotte Harbor Environmental Center (941-575-5435; www.checflorida .org), 10941 Burnt Store Rd., Punta Gorda. Four miles of nature trails depart from this center.

Charlotte Harbor Preserve State Park (941-575-5861; www.floridastateparks .org/charlotteharbor), 12301 Burnt Store Rd., Punta Gorda. This park encompasses 80 miles of shoreline along Charlotte Harbor, spreading into two counties. In this region, two short trails delve into its diverse habitat of hammocks, pine and palmetto flatlands, and wetlands. The **Old Datsun Trail** next to the park office is about 2 miles long—a little shorter October–May, when you must detour for nesting eagles. North of Placida off CR 771, the **Catfish Creek Trail** travels approximately 1.5 miles.

Fred C. Babcock–Cecil M. Webb Wildlife Management Area (863-648-3200), 29200 Tucker Grade, Port Charlotte. The domain of endangered red-cockaded woodpeckers, this preserve attracts birders along its 37 miles of unpaved hiking and biking trails, once used in logging operations. Sandhill cranes, white-tailed deer, and warblers also favor the diverse habitat found within its 79,013 acres. Avoid trails during peak of the hunting season, late October to mid-November.

⚲ **Kiwanis Park** (941-627-1628), 501 Donora St., at Victoria Ave., Port Charlotte. Here's a nice place to hike or jog while the kids entertain themselves on the playground. Nature and fitness trails thread through the woods and alongside a creek where turtles swim.

Myakka State Forest (941-460-1333), 2000 S. River Rd., Englewood. With access off US 41 south of North Port, it opens 14 miles of multiuse trails along the Myakka River from sunrise to sunset.

Punta Gorda Riverwalk, downtown Punta Gorda. From Gilchrist Park to Laishley Park and the Trabue Harborwalk, 2½ miles of pathways follow the Peace River.

HUNTING Given southwest Florida's heightened environmental consciousness, most shooting of wildlife is done with a camera. But the Charlotte Harbor coast's wilderness does provide opportunities for hunting various species. The most popular game animals are wild hogs, deer, doves, snipe, quail, turkey, duck, and coot.

For information on hunting licenses, permits, and seasons, visit www.myfwc.com/hunting.

Cypress Lodge at Babcock Wilderness Adventure (941-637-0551 or 800-500-5583; www.babcockwilderness.com), 8000 FL 31, Punta Gorda. Experienced guides take guests hunting for wild turkey, quail, and wild hogs.

Fred C. Babcock–Cecil M. Webb Wildlife Management Area (941-575-5768; myfwc.com), 29200 Tucker Grade, Port Charlotte. With some 79,000 acres, this is one of Florida's 62 designated hunting preserves. Advance permission is required. There is a public shooting range on the property, accessible from Tucker Grade via Rifle Range Road. The range is open daily during daylight hours.

KIDS' STUFF ⚲ **Captain Don Cerbone Memorial Skate Park** (941-575-9253), 6905 Florida St., at Carmalita Park, Punta Gorda. Small park with ramps and half-pipes; playground and BMX track are part of the complex. Skate park admission is $3.

⚲ **Fish Cove Adventure Golf** (941-627-5393), 4949 Tamiami Trail, Port Charlotte. Two 18-hole putt-putt courses and a bounce house. Open Sunday–Thursday 10–10, Friday–Saturday 10–11. Admission for 18 holes of golf is $8 to $9.50. Playground and picnic facilities.

⚲ **Kidstar Park** (941-235-3131), 18505 Paulson Dr., at Sun Flea Market, Port Charlotte. Go-cart rides, a rock-climbing wall and giant slide, Ferris wheel and other children's rides, laser tag, motion ride, Waltzing Waters, small games arcade, and snack bar and restaurant. Open weekends only.

✔ **Laishley Marina Park** (941-575-0142; www.laishleymarina.com), 120 Laishley Ct., Punta Gorda. A new interactive fountain next to the playground keeps kids cool and entertained at this riverfront recreational area with picnic facilities. A riverwalk path leads to the park, crossing beneath the US 41 bridge.

✔ **Tringali Recreational Complex Skating** (941-473-1018), 3460 N. Access Rd., Englewood. Weekly skate parties for elementary and middle school kids and families; also basketball, tennis, a walking trail, a gym, and picnic grounds.

RACQUET SPORTS Boca Grande Community Center (941-964-2564), 131 First St. W., Boca Grande. Two lighted tennis courts are located on Wheeler Street.

The Club Punta Gorda (941-505-0999; www.puntagordaclub.com), 2905 Tamiami Trail, Punta Gorda. Seven courts, six of them clay; hitting wall and lessons. Fees.

McGuire Park, 32236 McGuire Ave., Port Charlotte. Four lighted hard-surface tennis courts.

Tringali Recreational Complex (941-473-1018), 3460 McCall Rd. S., Englewood. Four outdoor lit tennis courts.

SHELLING You'll find some shells on the beaches along the Charlotte Harbor coast, but if you're a serious beachcomber, you'll head south to the Island Coast.

Shelling Charters: **Ko Ko Kai Charter Boat Service** (941-474-2141), 5040 N. Beach Rd., at Ko Ko Kai Resort, Englewood Beach. Shelling excursions on and around the islands of Gasparilla, Palm, Cayo Costa, Cabbage Key, Upper Captiva, and Captiva.

AN INTERACTIVE FOUNTAIN ADDS TO THE FUN STUFF LANDSCAPE AT RIVERFRONT LAISHLEY MARINA PARK.

SPAS **Charles of the Village Salon & Day Spa** (941-639-6300 or 888-753-6115; www.charlesofthevillage.com), 1200 W. Retta Esplanade, at Fishermen's Village, Punta Gorda. Massages, polishes, facials, and beauty services. Packages available.

Skintopia by Bina (941-575-0721; www.skintopiabybina.com), 208 Tamiami Trail, Suite 116, Punta Gorda. An organic Aveda spa offering facials and nutritional counseling.

WATER SPORTS

Sailboarding & Surfing: **Island Bike 'N Beach** (941-964-0711), 333 Park Ave., Boca Grande. Rents boogie and skim boards.

Snorkeling & Scuba: The best underwater sightseeing lies offshore some distance, where divers find a few wrecks and other man-made structures.

WILDLIFE SPOTTING The Charlotte Harbor coast is a haven for many of Florida's threatened and endangered species, including Florida panthers (a relative of the mountain lion that is yellow, not black, and characterized by a kink in its tail), bobcats, manatees, brown pelicans, wood storks, and black skimmers. Manasota Key hosts the largest nesting sea turtle population on the Gulf Coast. White pelicans migrate to the region in winter. Look for them on sandbars and small mangrove islands in the bays and estuaries. They congregate in flocks and feed cooperatively by herding fish. The Cape Haze area between Englewood and Boca Grande is known for its nesting ospreys and bald eagles. Lemon Bay Park and Cedar Point Environmental Park afford the best opportunities to see the nests. Look for sandhill cranes on golf courses and in other grasslands.

At **Babcock Ranch,** a massive preserve east of Punta Gorda, you can see native sandhill cranes and contained Florida panthers along with lots of alligators (which are farmed there). Adjacent **Babcock-Webb Wildlife Management Area** shelters the endangered red-cockaded woodpecker among other species of woodpeck-

FLUTED CYPRESS TREES STALK TELEGRAPH SWAMP AT BABCOCK RANCH.

ers, warblers, and shorebirds. It, along with **Amberjack Environmental Park, Cedar Point, Charlotte Flatwoods Environmental Park, Charlotte Harbor Environmental Center, Charlotte Harbor Preserve State Park,** and **Tippecanoe Environmental Park** are plotted on the South Florida section of the **Great Florida Birding Trail** (www.floridabirdingtrail.com).

Nature Preserves & Eco-Attractions: **Audubon-Pennington Nature Walk** (www .peaceriveraudubon.org), Alton Rd. at Peachland Blvd., Port Charlotte. A bit tricky to find tucked into a residential neighborhood, this eight-acre site provides a ¾-mile loop trail with species identification signs through hardwood hammock. No facilities. Free admission.

✔ **Cedar Point Environmental Park** (941-475-0769; www.checflorida.org), 2300 Placida Rd., off FL 775, Englewood. Bald eagles, marsh rabbits, bobcats, gopher tortoises, and great horned owls are the stars of this 115-acre preserve, where free guided nature walks are offered at 9 AM Saturday and Sunday, and other days by appointment. It borders the Lemon Bay Aquatic Preserve. Free admission.

✔ **Charlotte Harbor Environmental Center (CHEC) at Alligator Preserve** (941-575-5435; www.checflorida.org), 10941 Burnt Store Rd., Punta Gorda. Open Monday–Saturday 8–3, Sunday 11–3; guided trail walks June–September, 10 AM weekdays; September–May, 10 AM Saturday and Sunday; and by appointment in summer. The center conducts guided tours around 4 miles of nature trails that wind through pine and palmetto flatlands, hammocks, and freshwater marshes where alligators and bobcats live. On one there's a bird blind—a little shack with a picture window and field guides for watching the birds it attracts to a water feature. Its educational exhibits about local wildlife are geared toward students and groups. The center conducts various tours and programs both on and off campus. The free Wading Adventure at Ponce de León Park January–May is particularly engaging and informative for adults and children alike. Free admission.

Lemon Bay Park & Environmental Center (941-474-3065 or 941-861-5000; www.scgov.net/ParksandRecreation/Parks), 570 Bay Park Blvd., Englewood. Its more than 200 acres of mangrove forest, wetlands, pinelands, and scrub are home to bald eagles and other creatures of the sky, woods, and water. Experience its nature trails, butterfly garden, indoor environmental displays, educational programs, and guided walks. Free admission.

✔ **Peace River Wildlife Center** (941-637-3830; www.peaceriverwildlifecenter.com), 3400 W. Marion Ave., at Ponce de León Park, Punta Gorda. Open 11–4 daily. Donations requested. You can self-tour or take a guided tour of the outdoor bird aviary. A board lists the current rehabilitating and recently released patients. It accepts nearly 1,400 orphaned, displaced, and injured creatures each year.

Wildlife Tours & Charters: ✪ ✔ **Babcock Wilderness Adventures** (941-637-0551 or 800-500-5583; www.babcockwilderness.com), 8000 FL 31, Punta Gorda. Tours by reservation only; call for times. $19.95 adults, $12.95 children ages 3–12 (plus tax). Advance reservations required. On a 90-minute swamp-buggy-bus ride through Crescent B Ranch and Telegraph Cypress Swamp you'll spot Old Florida wildlife, including white-tailed deer, fenced-in panthers, wild turkeys, sandhill cranes, squirrels, and alligators. The driver gives an on-board demonstration with a live baby gator and leads a boardwalk hike through a cypress swamp. The adventure takes place on an actual ranch that dates back to the cow-hunting era. Cracker cattle are still raised here, as well as alligators. A restaurant, live snake display, gift shop, and a small natural history museum set in a cabin used in Sean Connery's movie *Just Cause* (filmed partly on-site) provide other activities at this, one of Charlotte Harbor coast's finest attractions.

✪ ✎ **Grande Tours** (941-697-8825; www.grandetours.com), 12575 Placida Rd., Placida. Most tours arranged daily. Informative naturalists lead kayaking tours of Myakka River, Charlotte Harbor Aquatic Preserve, and Blueway Trail. Eco, dusk, and moonlight tours are among those available. The wildlife tour takes you on a pontoon boat in search of dolphin, manatees, and birds.

King Fisher Peace River Nature Cruise (941-639-0969; www.kingfisherfleet .com), 1200 W. Retta Esplanade, at Fishermen's Village Marina, Punta Gorda. 1 PM Wednesday and Saturday. You'll likely see alligators, pelicans, egrets, ibises, and cormorants on the 3½-hour journey upriver and back in time. You may also spot manatees, roseate spoonbills, river otters, and great blue herons. Volunteers from Charlotte Harbor Environmental Center knowledgeably narrate as the double-decker boat chugs leisurely along.

✳ Lodging

Accommodations along the Charlotte Harbor coast tend to exude personality. Sure, you have your Best Western and Budget Inn, but the remainder are either old-money polished, new-money luxurious, or money's-not-the-issue sporting. From beach cottages to the grand old Gasparilla Inn, the Charlotte Harbor coast promises something special in the way of lodging.

During high season, which begins shortly before Christmas and ends after Easter, rates may rise anywhere from 10 to 100 percent above those charged during the off-season. Some resorts schedule their rates based on as many as six different seasons, and the highest rates apply from mid-February through Easter. Reservations are recommended during these months. Some resorts and rental services require a minimum stay, especially during the peak season.

The following selection includes some of the coast's greatest lodging characters. Where available, toll-free 800, 888, 866, or 877 reservation numbers are listed after local numbers.

Pricing codes are explained below. They are normally per person/double occupancy for hotel rooms and per unit for efficiencies, apartments, and cottages. Many resorts offer off-season packages at special rates. Pricing does not include the 6 percent Florida sales tax or Charlotte County's 5 percent bed tax. Some large resorts add service gratuities or maid charges.

Rate Categories

Inexpensive	Up to $100
Moderate	$100 to $200
Expensive	$200 to $200
Very Expensive	$300 and up

An asterisk (*) after the pricing designation indicates that the rate includes at least continental breakfast in the cost of lodging; one establishment follows the American Plan, pricing all meals into the room rate.

Note that under the Americans with Disabilities Act, accommodations built after January 26, 1993, and containing more than five rooms must be usable by people with disabilities. I have indicated only those small places that do not make such allowances.

ACCOMMODATIONS

Boca Grande

⊕ ♂ ((ᵧ)) **Gasparilla Inn & Club**
(941-964-4500 or 800-996-1913; www
.gasparillainn.com), 500 Palm Ave.,
33921. With subtle grandeur the Gasparilla Inn sits on her throne of lush
greenery. Dressed in pale yellow clapboard with white columns, Georgian
porticos, and Victorian sensibilities, the
inn has been a town anchor and social
emblem since 1913. The region's oldest surviving resort, the Gasparilla first
opened its doors as a retreat for such
families as the Vanderbilts and Du
Ponts, whose descendants still visit,
along with the Bushes and other illuminati. Not that the accommodations
are ultraelegant: The 142 rooms reflect
the era of their construction, with
exposed pipes, tasteful cabana
nuances, and fine but understated furnishings; the cottages are more modern and roomy. In recent years, a
renovation and menu overhaul have
brought the resort into the 21st century. The inn itself offers bars, lounges,
libraries, generous porches, and various nooks and crannies where guests
can socialize or get away. A white-linen
dining room and two other restaurants,
a beauty salon and spa, a top-rated 18-
hole golf course, a croquet lawn, tennis
courts, a playground, a beach club with
fitness facilities, and two pools round
out the amenities. It's said that the
Gasparilla Inn in quiet Boca Grande is
where Palm Beach socialites came to
escape charity balls and the perpetual
fashion show of their glittery hometown. Rates include a variety of meal,
golf, and spa plans in season. Expensive to Very Expensive. Closed
July–mid-October (cottages available
during that time).

🐾 **The Innlet** (941-964-2294; www
.innletonthewaterfront.com), 1251
12th St. E., 33921. Little stepsister to
the Gasparilla Inn, the Innlet is also
painted yellow, to fit in with the family.
Fancy lattice touches and renovations
pretty up a motel remake. The name is
a double entendre on its sub-inn status
and its bayou location with a ramp and
docking, handy for boating and fishing
types. It has a nice little pool, playground, and 33 rooms and efficiencies
(with stove top, microwave, and fridge)
in modern, tasteful attire. Guests share
communal porches and balconies. An
on-site restaurant, The Outlet, is popular for breakfast. Moderate.

Cape Haze

⊕ ♪ ((ᵧ)) **Palm Island Resort** (941-
697-4800 or 800-824-5412; www.palm
island.com), 7092 Placida Rd., 33946.
A true island getaway in grand style,
Palm Island occupies the northernmost
point of a slab of sand above Gasparilla
Island. One must boat in; a car ferry
runs at least every half-hour from the
mainland, where the resort owns one-
bedroom harborside condos in which
you can also stay. On the island, Old
Florida–style villas front a wide, isolated apron of sea oats-fringed beach and
come with fully equipped kitchens,
laundries, one to three bedrooms,

THE GASPARILLA INN, DOYENNE OF THE
GULF COAST.

Palm Island Resort

PALM ISLAND RESORT: THE ULTIMATE ISLAND HIDEAWAY.

exquisite appointments, and screened porches overlooking more than 2 miles of deserted beach. The 160-unit (counting the mainland accommodations) property has five pools and 12 tennis courts, plus a restaurant and bar (another on the mainland), an island store, a full-service marina, boat rentals, charter services, nature programs, kids' programs, playgrounds, plus bicycles, golf carts (the main mode of transport on the island), kayaks, canoes, and beach equipment rentals—all the makings for an "I'm-never-leaving-this-island" vacation. What it doesn't have is roads, cars (you park outside resort gates), stress, and rigorous time schedules. Moderate to Very Expensive.

Englewood Beach
❀ ✍ ☀ **Weston's Resort** (941-474-3431; www.westonsresort.com), 985 Gulf Blvd., 34223. Taking up a good block at Englewood Beach's southern end, Weston's spreads from bay to beach to please both fishing and sand-loving types. For the former, it rents boats, motors, and gear, and provides boat slips, fishing docks, and freezer storage. Free for the use of all guests are tennis courts, barbecue grills, and two swimming pools. Accommodations on the 83-unit property range from studio efficiencies to three-bedroom apartments (Expensive) in cement-block buildings, all modernly outfitted. The rooms are clean and well kept, but no maid service or resupplying of paper products is provided. In some rooms, Murphy-style beds flip up into closets for more space. Some also have large, modern kitchens. Beach rooms look beyond seawalls to eroding beach. One pool sits in the middle of an asphalt parking lot. There's nothing luxurious about the resort, but its rates and beach location at the quiet end of the island make it a good choice for people who love water and water sports. The resort supplies only limited linens and paper supplies. Moderate to Expensive.

Manasota Key
✪ ✍ **Manasota Beach Club** (941-474-2614; www.manasotabeachclub.com), 7660 Manasota Key Rd., Englewood 34223. A tiny, low-impact sign whispers MANASOTA BEACH CLUB. And although it occupies 25 acres of Manasota Key, the resort itself is just as unobtrusive. The unadvertised property preserves the island's natural attributes with a low-key attitude, wooded paths, and an often deserted beach. Guests have reported seeing 92 bird species about the grounds. Fifteen beachy-woodsy-style cottages of various ages and configurations; the dining room; the bottle club (no alcohol is sold on the premises); and a library

display Old Florida charm. The 50-year-old resort appeals to the "sink into oblivion" type of vacationer who wishes to hide out among natural, gnarly vegetation. The property—which has a summer-camp feel to it—also appeals to the sportsperson, with three tennis courts; a swimming pool; boccie, shuffleboard, and basketball courts; a playground; croquet; bicycling; sailing, windsurfing, and kayaking; and a children's program. A private 18-hole golf course nearby is available to guests. During social season (February–March), cottage-room guests receive three meals a day on the American Plan; a Modified American Plan (two meals) is in effect Thanksgiving–January and in April. May–mid-November, the resort rents out entire cottages with kitchens and provides no meals. Expensive to Very Expensive° (two-day minimum stay).

Port Charlotte

🦐 🐟 🌴 **Banana Bay Waterfront Motel** (941-743-4441; www.banana baymotel.com), 23285 Bayshore Rd., off US 41, 33980. Along Bayshore Drive in Charlotte Harbor, the feeling is Old Florida, relaxed, and fishy. Across the wide mouth of the Peace River lies Punta Gorda. Down the way, free fishing piers jut into waters flush with fish, and there are boat docks out back. A few inexpensive motels in this neighborhood serve the stay-away-from-the-crowds crowd, and Banana Bay is one of the prettiest, with its banana-tree murals on its one-story stucco rooms and one-bedroom efficiencies. The 13 rooms have a clean, perky, tropical look. Efficiencies have small fridges, stove tops, and microwaves. Along the bay, shuffleboard courts, grills, a little beach, and picnic tables put the focus outdoors on the fetching water view. Families like the mini golf attraction next door. Inexpensive.

Punta Gorda

🦐 📶 **Four Points By Sheraton** (941-637-6770; www.fourpointspuntagorda .com), 33 Tamiami Trail, 33950. Punta Gorda's newest lodging option (opened May 2009) falls between the Wyvern and Vacation Villas (see below) to present an affordable downtown stay that both business and leisure guests appreciate for its proximity to restaurants, shops, and the convention center. It has its own breakfast and dinner restaurant tucked into its open, light wood lobby. A library at the other side of the lobby invites lounging or multitasking with its computers, televisions, and fireplace. The restaurant spills out on the terrace, where a small pool and fountain create atmosphere.

WHIMSICAL MURALS ADD COLOR TO RIVERFRONT BANANA BAY.

The hotel's riverside location adds to the ambiance, and the town's River-walk is steps away. The lobby's sleek, clean lines continue in the hotel's 106 rooms and suites, designed to suggest a ship's cabin with blues, portholes, nautical throw pillows, and the most original decor I've seen in a chain hotel—in any hotel, for that matter—in a long time. (It is a prototype for future Four Points.) The nicest rooms have river views, but others on the lower floors face a condo next door. Inexpensive to Moderate.

♣ ((ᵠ)) **Vacation Villas & Resort** (941-639-8721 or 800-639-0020; www.fish ville.com), 1200 W. Retta Esplanade #58, 33950. This is one of the Gulf Coast's best lodging bargains. These spacious time-share units—all decorated in modern taste and all with a view of the water—contain two bedrooms, a loft, a living area, a big full kitchen with counter bar and stools, and one bath. They are above the shops, restaurants, and courtyard hubbub of Fishermen's Village, but the rooms are well soundproofed. Guests have free use of a swimming pool, tennis courts, shuffleboard, and bicycles. They are close to all the action there is to find in Punta Gorda, on land and on water. Convenient for boat-in guests, Fishermen's Village fronts a yacht harbor and a 111-slip full-service marina. Moderate.

((ᵠ)) **Wyvern Hotel** (941-639-7700; www.thewyvernhotel.com), 101 E. Retta Esplanade, 33950. Owner operated, the boutique 63-room standout exerts individual style at only-in-Punta-Gorda reasonable rates. It touts its fashionable Nuevo Latin restaurant, LuLu, named for the owner's daughter. Sleek Euro-style rooms in earthy tones and dark wood are stocked with Frette linens, Gilchrist & Soames amenities,

an iPod docking alarm, and marble baths. Tip-top service includes free (optional) turndown service and shoe shines. In the small fitness center, some of the cardio machines have iPod hook-ups. Rooftop, the view from the pool and its deck and bar (with tapas and other food service) takes in the Peace River and downtown Punta Gorda, whose historic district is regenerating into a dining refuge and lively nightlife scene. Both LuLu and the rooftop scene have become popular with the locals, but Wyvern protects guests' security and privacy with a special key-scan system that allows only them to access room floors. Moderate.

HOME & CONDO RENTALS Boca Grande Real Estate (941-964-0338 or 866-302-0338; www.bocagrandereal estate.com), 430 W. Fourth St., Boca Grande 33921. Large selection of vacation and seasonal accommodations.

Conch Out Vacation Rentals at Manasota Key Realty (941-474-9536 or 800-870-6432; www.englewoodfl .com), 1927 Beach Rd., Englewood 34223. Grand mansions, beachside cottages, condos, and bayside homes.

Place in the Sun Vacation Rentals (941-475-6888; www.placeinthesun .com), 2670 S. McCall Rd. #12, Englewood 34224. Luxury three- and four-bedroom homes.

RV RESORTS Most of the area's RV accommodations lie east of I-75.

((ᵠ)) **Water's Edge RV Resort** (941-637-4677 or 800-637-9224; www .watersedgervresort.com), 6800 Golf Course Blvd., Punta Gorda 33982. Full hook-ups, recreation hall, pool, Jacuzzi, fishing lake and dock, convenience store, and rural setting. For adults (ages 55 and older) only.

✳ Where to Eat

Local cuisine smacks of Midwestern influence, but in recent years Floribbean and other exotic flavors have livened things up. Fishing crews bring just-hooked seafood to the table, but that doesn't mean some restaurants won't try to pawn off frozen products. Here I've tried to include a few eateries that believe in freshness and fanfare at the dining table.

The following listings sample all the variety of Charlotte Harbor Coast feasting in these price categories:

Inexpensive	Up to $15
Moderate	$15 to $25
Expensive	$25 to $35
Very Expensive	$35 or more

Cost categories are based on the range of dinner entrée prices, or, if dinner is not served, on lunch entrées.

Note: Florida law forbids smoking inside all restaurants and bars serving food. Smoking is permitted only in restaurants with outdoor seating.

Boca Grande

✪ ⅋ **PJ'S SEAGRILLE** (941-964-0806; www.pjseagrille.com), 321 Park Ave., in the Old Theatre Building. PJ's is one of Boca Grande's most popular fine-dining experiences. Family-owned and operated for some 22 years, it exudes an air of island familiarity, and regulars return year after year. Dinners offer linen and candlelight; lunch is more casual, and both are in the setting of unfinished wood and aquariums. The menus change according to fish availability and Chef Jim's creative mood swings. At lunch, you'll find standard fare with sporadic flares of creativity, such as pita chicken sandwich with pesto mayo and grilled onions, or black beans and rice with cornbread. At dinner, PJ's shines with an ever-changing menu featuring what the local fishermen caught that day. Some sure bets if you see them: the cucumber-wrapped

spicy tuna tartare roll, Thai sweet-and-sour soup (exceptionally well-seasoned), tomato basil bisque with lump crab, char-grilled yellow fin tuna with berry sauce and wasabi, and pan-fried snapper with garlic, lemon, and white wine (much more complex in flavor than it sounds). The sides battle for attention. Try the regularly featured cheese grits or, when available, the curried acorn squash with almonds. Save room for homemade dessert. The key lime pie and chocolate cake with coconut frosting are winners. Fishtales Lounge offers more casual fare and ambiance. Expensive. Reservations recommended for dinner. Closed Sunday and mid-July–September.

Englewood

⅋ **Mango Bistro** (941-681-3500; www.mangobistro.com), 301 W. Dearborn. You've come to a happy place here: a dozen tables scattered among cheerful yellow walls further brightened by local art for sale and more tables on the porch outside. The comforting waft of coffee greets you before the attentive wait staff with its headquarters behind the coffee bar. Crêpes are a specialty here—savory eggplant and mozzarella, chicken with brie, shrimp a l'orange, and lobster and shrimp with creamy lobster sauce for lunch or dinner, and sweet caramelized apples or Reese's crêpes for dessert. For my lunch, however, I decided upon the lobster bisque, for which they seem to be famous because the menu announces they now sell it by the quart, and a hummus wrap. The bisque, laced with sherry and a swirl of cream on top, couldn't be more intoxicating, and I'm not talking about the sherry. It made me want to lick the bowl; I restrained myself. And how do they make hummus taste THIS good? Fresh pesto, feta, cucumbers, and a cucumber-wasabi sauce help with the flavor factor. It tastes so fresh, it has ruined me for hummus wraps ever again. The pretzel bread sandwiches are another unusual specialty, but there's a lot to choose from, including bagel sandwiches and egg crêpes at breakfast, grilled paninis at lunch, and grilled wraps such as the Thai chicken wrap with peanut sauce, coconut, and baby spinach for dinner. If you're not in the mood for a dessert crêpe, there are smoothies and fresh-made sweets such as cheesecake du jour and coconut cream pie spiked with dark rum. Inexpensive. No reservations. Closed Sunday.

Englewood Beach

♿ **Gulf View Grill** (941-475-3500; www.gulfviewgrill.com), 2095 N. Beach Rd. In recent years, this has come to be my favorite Manasota Key restaurant. To start with, there's the drop-dead view from its stilted glass-cage perch; its new sunset deck takes full advantage. On my most recent visit, I was encouraged by the number of locals filling the tables and ultimately thrilled by the chef's special that I ordered: spinach and Gorgonzola tortellini topped with perfectly cooked shrimp and a superb creamy tomato sauce. On the regular lunch menu, shrimp and pasta, shrimp and scrambled eggs on ciabatta, and pecan-crusted tilapia join the typical burgers, fish sandwiches, wraps, seafood baskets, and fish tacos. For dinner, a multi-paged menu features the day's fresh catches simply prepared, either grilled and basted with garlic and lemon butter or sautéed in natural pan juices with the chef's sauce of the day. Or choose from specialties such as filet mignon, bouillabaisse, crab Alfredo, pan-fried pork tenderloin with rum and pineapple sauce, or caramelized salmon. For something lighter, try a deep-fried or grilled grouper sandwich or a Caesar salad topped with grilled tuna. Inexpensive to Expensive. Reservations accepted.

Placida

🐦 ✂ ♿ **The Fishery Restaurant** (941-697-2451; www.sunstate.com /fishery), 1300 Fishery Rd., Gasparilla

FISHING BOATS DOCKED OUT BACK LET YOU KNOW THAT WHAT YOU'RE GOBBLING AT THE FISHERY RESTAURANT IS AS FRESH AS CAN BE.

Sound. Take a side trip to Old Florida as you drive or boat in to this waterside shanty with a view of mangroves, an old fishing boat, and the dilapidated fish packing plant next door. Scenes from Denzel Washington's *Out of Time* were filmed in the restaurant, where locals and boaters belly up to the bar outdoors on the dock or inside in the plain dining room where the glass walls are the focal point. The menu reflects what's fresh from local waters, prepared both in Cracker style and classic Continental. Start with a garlic shrimp appetizer or a bowl of "Famous Fishery Gumbo," then try a basket of gator bites with hush puppies or pan-sautéed grouper with hollandaise and shrimp. For meat-eaters, there are a couple cuts of steak, cheesesteak sandwiches, or chicken picatta. It's all good, hearty, unpretentious fare. Inexpensive to Moderate. Reservations accepted. Closed Monday in summer.

Port Charlotte

✪ ⛐ Portofino Waterfront Dining (941-743-2800), 23247 Bayshore Rd. Great view: check. Creative Italian cuisine: check. Gorgeous decor: check. Top service: check. This new sensation on the Peace River has all that plus an artistic setting of beautiful wood and tiles. Three-tiered dining and the outdoor Deck 360 allow everyone an eyeful of water as they enjoy the finest ingredients magically worked into a cross-section of Italian favorites. Southern Italy, with its seafood and spice, is well represented with a marriage of local and imported fish: tuna piccante, fried mixed platter, crabcakes, fried grouper with roasted garlic tartar sauce, *frutti di mare fra diavolo*, shrimp and scallops Alfredo with spinach, and pan-seared salmon with lemon-caper cream sauce. Traditional dishes include minestrone, lasagna al forno, veal marsala, and chicken

parmigiana. To please every palate, the dinner menu also offers fine Angus steaks and some of its own creations, such as a killer wild mushroom ravioli with silky Gorgonzola cream sauce; and grilled chicken with portobello mushrooms, caramelized onions, and asiago and mozzarella cheese. The lunch menu, equally extensive, goes from an eggplant parmigiana sandwich and portobello panini to pizza, Gorgonzola burger, and pasta primavera. Try the shrimp avocado over linguini for special lunchtime indulgence. Moderate to Expensive. Reservations accepted. Closed inside for Sunday lunch.

Punta Gorda

⛐ Amimoto Japanese Restaurant (941-505-1515), 2705 S. Tamiami Trail, at Towles Plaza. Soothing and authentic, Amimoto satisfies the spirit as well as the stomach. The decor is simple, contemporary, and clean, decorated with tasteful Eastern art and arranged around the faux-wood Formica sushi bar. The sushi menu itself presents nearly 50 choices of raw fish and rolls in four categories: raw, vegetable, cooked, and preserved (smoked)—all expertly prepared. Cooked options range from fried shrimp to kobe beef rolls. The steamed *gyoza* dumplings with mustard sauce are also a tasty way to start off the meal. The lunch and dinner menus list dozens more options for appetizers, such as the light miso soup with tofu and enoki, fried softshell crab, and seaweed salad for starters. *Obento* box combinations, a Japanese improvement on box lunches, are popular midday choices, as are rice or noodle bowls. For dinner, the menu describes grilled sea bass, breaded pork loin, and shrimp teriyaki with Asian sauces. Ginger shrimp is one of its most popular dishes, and sushi combinations are another dinner option.

For a refreshing sweet after-dinner indulgence, try the pretty plum wine ice cream. Moderate to Expensive. Reservations accepted. Closed for lunch Saturday and Sunday.

✿ �&. **Downtown Hookah** (941-639-0004; www.downtownhookah.com), 307 E. Marion Ave. And now for something completely different—not just for Punta Gorda, but for Southwest Florida as a whole: Its subtitle is A Mediterranean Café, but that so doesn't tell the story. Specifically Middle Eastern (its owner is from Jerusalem), it brings an exotic element to the neighborhood not only by its food but also its hookah pipes, belly dancing (every Friday and Saturday night), and hafla parties with a dinner show (second Saturday of each month). But let's get back to the food. The menu is fairly simple, and you've probably heard of most of the dishes—hummus, baba ganoush, stuffed grape leaves, and falafel on the appetizer menu; shish and other kabobs on the entrées, and house-made baklava for dessert. Then there are the mysteries, such as the puréed lentil soup and *musabahha* I sampled. The latter layered hummus, garlicky ground beef, yogurt sauce, and toasted sliced almonds atop a foundation of pita chips—sort of a Middle Eastern nacho platter—for a new taste treat. The kabobs come in beef tenderloin, veggie, lamb, tuna, and other flavors. Lunch gives you a more well-rounded selection, adding hot and cold sandwiches to the mix. The hookahs? Fork over $16 to $19 for an hour's worth of group toking on your choice of 22 flavors—from cinnamon and Sunkist to bubble gum and rose, and combinations thereof. Order a Turkish coffee to go along with that for the ultimate hookah buzz. Inexpensive. Reservations accepted; recommended for belly dancing and hafla events.

&. ((·)) **LuLu** (941-639-7700; www.thewyvernhotel.com), 101 E. Retta Esplanade, in Wyvern Hotel. It's genius the way LuLu insinuates Cuban nuances into its inventive cuisine. Signature items go so far as coconut lobster chowder, sweet plantain vegetarian lasagna, mussels over fries with pineapple vinegar cream, and an incredible guava and feta crème brûlée. It's a bit Miami, but in a good way. The intimate space feels homey and stylish at the same time, with soft reds, white tablecloths, cushiony microfiber chair seats, and Latin music. Open for breakfast (the eggs Benedict are served on a baguette with Serrano ham), lunch, and tapas, it fulfills all needs of its hotel guests, but also draws in the locals. Service can be a bit slow at times, so don't come in a rush. Especially popular, the rooftop pool deck bar serves small bites such as pork kabob with papaya mojo. Moderate. Reservations accepted.

✿ &. **Peace River Seafood & Crab Shack** (941-505-8440), 5337 Duncan Rd., 1.5 miles east of I-75 exit 164. Kelly Beall and her husband Jimmy, a crabber of nearly 20 years, rescued a circa-1926 Cracker shack in the early 2000s in an attempt to also rescue the local crabbing industry, which foreign imports had just about decimated. Jimmy and 16 other crabbers provide the restaurant with a steady supply of its specialty—steamed blue crab. Servers cover your table with newspaper, arm you with a hammer and crab cracker, and you're ready to go. Other seafood comes from other parts of Florida such as Apalachicola oysters, Horseshoe Beach clams, gulf shrimp, and Keys lobster. Kelly's gator gumbo is a belly-buster with shrimp, sausage, crab, and rice. The menu stays the same throughout the day and includes a cheeseburger, catfish or grouper sandwich, and a lobster tail-sirloin

PEACE RIVER SEAFOOD SEALS IN THE FLAVOR OF OLD FLORIDA WITH ITS CIRCA-1926 DIGS AND CRABBING HERITAGE.

combo (Expensive). Inexpensive to Moderate. No reservations.

✪ ⅃ **The Perfect Caper** (941-505-9009; www.theperfectcaper.com), 121 E. Marion Ave. This local toast of connoisseurs serves fine, ingenious cuisine in a burnished bistro setting with an exhibit kitchen. Every meal I've eaten here scores A+. A James Beard Award semifinalist, Chef Jeanne Roland is gaining a national reputation. Recently, the duck on my lunch of duck salad came medium-rare as ordered, tender and juicy, served on greens and dressed deliciously with cherry vinaigrette. A square of herbed focaccia accompanied. Other intriguing meat-and-greens salads plus an array of entrées and sandwiches, such as ham and brie on a baguette or focaccia, complete the lunch menu. For dinner, a seasonally changing menu offers such delights as a crisp pork belly and steamed buns, homemade mozzarella and heirloom tomato salad with Serrano ham, pan-roasted mahi with grilled pineapple salsa and blood orange butter, udon noodle hot pot, and dry-aged New York strip with wild French mushrooms and white truffle oil. The chef also offers a prix fixe two-course menu for an affordable $20 each. Dessert presents a tough choice, but you won't regret the chocolate bread pudding with vanilla-caramel sauce or the hand-churned ice cream, sorbet, and gelato of the day. Don't miss this place for Charlotte County's most cutting-edge cuisine. Moderate to Expensive. Reservations accepted. Serving lunch Thursday and Friday only, dinner Tuesday–Saturday.

BAKERIES Boca Grande Baking Co. (941-964-5818; www.bocagrande bakingco.com), 384 E. Railroad Ave., Boca Grande. Homemade breads, creative muffins, scones, pastries, cakes, and other desserts in an inviting setting; complete coffee bar; also pizza, sandwiches, and other eat-in or take-out items.

Sugar Island Cupcakes (941-639-3030; www.sugarislandcupcakes.com), 322 Sullivan St., Punta Gorda. Small and filled large cupcakes (think PBJ, Boston crème, and strawberry short-cake). Buy individually or by the batch.

BREAKFAST 3rd Street Cafe (941-964-0155; www.thirdstcafe.com), 310 E. Railroad Ave., Boca Grande. Formerly Loons on a Limb: I mourn the loss of the fun, longtime name, but welcome the interesting menu of gravlax Benedict with dill hollandaise, cheese grits with corn salsa, brioche French toasts, fresh baked goods, and the like.

(•) **Café Ruelle** (941-575-3553; www.caferuelle.net), 117 W. Marion Ave., downtown Punta Gorda. Coffee is the buzzword, but muffins, pastries, and breakfast sandwiches provide a quick, tasty repast at this alleyway secret, whether alfresco or inside. Also lunch and weekend light dinner and live entertainment.

CANDY & ICE CREAM Cubby's Homemade Ice Cream (941-637-9600), 264 W. Marion Ave., Punta Gorda. Sandwiches, wraps, Cuban sandwiches, and salads in addition to hand-dipped ice cream.

✿ **The Loose Caboose** (941-964-0440), 433 W. Fourth St., Boca Grande. Known for its homemade ice cream and smoothies in many flavors, served in the town's historic depot.

Swiss Chocolate (941-639-9484; www.swissconnectionsusa.com), 403 Sullivan St., #112, Punta Gorda. Norman Love Chocolates (see the Sanibel and Fort Myers chapter), imported Swiss chocolate, coffee, mille feuilles, and other European pastries.

COFFEE Café Ruelle (941-575-3553; www.caferuelle.net), 117 W. Marion

Ave., downtown Punta Gorda. Enjoy coffee, tea, espresso, muffins, scones, lunch items, wine, and desserts in the little café or its courtyard.

Mango Bistro (941-681-3500; www.mangobistro.com), 301 W. Dearborn St., downtown in Olde Englewood Village, Englewood. There's a lot more going on here than coffee (see "Where to Eat"), but it's still a good place to stop by for your morning buzz in a pleasant setting with a free used book exchange.

The "Ornery" Attitude (941-639-2809; www.fishville.com), 1200 W. Retta Esplanade, at Fishermen's Village, Punta Gorda. Specialty coffees, espresso, cappuccino, smoothies, ice cream, lunch items.

(•) **Village Gifts & Gallery** (941-473-2300), 425 W. Dearborn St., Englewood. Roasters Coffee Bar serves fresh roasted coffee and ice cream.

DELI & SPECIALTY FOODS Gill's Grocery & Deli (941-964-2506), 5800 Gasparilla Rd., at The Courtyard, Boca Grande. Freshly made sandwiches, salads, and heat-up entrées, plus grocery items, ice cream, party trays, and bakery goods. Delivery available.

Grapevine (941-964-0614), 321 Park Ave., in the Old Theatre Building, Boca Grande. It has a loyal following for its specialty wines, imported cheese, fish, prepared dishes, sandwiches, gourmet products, and baked goods. Closed Sunday.

Hudson's Grocery (941-964-2621), 441 Park Ave., Boca Grande. Organic and other fresh produce, fish, meats cut to order, deli, seafood, and hot meals.

Kallis German Butcher Sausage Kitchen (941-627-1413), 2420 Tamiami Trail, Port Charlotte. Wursts of every variety, many of which you've probably never heard of; also fine cuts of meat, rouladen, cheese, hams, and gourmet European imports. This place is a lot of fun.

Pies & Plates (941-505-7437; www .piesandplates.com), 2310 Tamiami Trail, Suite 3117, at Punta Gorda Crossing, Punta Gorda. Prep your own meals, take a cooking class, buy prepped meals, and shop for bulk whole-leaf tea, gourmet products, and kitchen accessories.

Presseller Delicatessen (941-639-3990; www.deli-life.net), 209 W. Olympia Ave., downtown Punta Gorda. Part art gallery, it serves breakfast, smoothies, salads, sandwiches named for artists (Renoir, Dalí, and so on), pizza, soup, and homemade desserts to eat in or take out. Also sells deli meats, imported beer, wine, and other gourmet groceries.

FARMS & FARMER'S MARKETS
Greenmarket at Fishermen's Village (941-638-8721), 1200 W. Retta Esplanade, in Fishermen's Village, Punta Gorda. November–April, Wednesday 9:30–1:30. Featuring Worden Farm products.

🍠 **Punta Gorda Farmer's Market** (941-639-3990), Taylor St. and Herald Ct., Punta Gorda. Year-round every Saturday 8–2.

Worden Farm (941-637-4874; www .wordenfarm.com), 34900 Bermont Rd., Punta Gorda. Tractor-drawn hayrides tour this 55-acre organic produce and livestock farm, one of the region's most highly respected, every Saturday at 10 AM; November–March by reservation only. Cost is $10 per adult, $7 for children ages 2–11.

NATURAL FOODS Reid's Nutrition Center (941-474-1115), 1951 S. McCall Rd., at Palm Plaza, Englewood. Mostly vitamins, but also some

organic products; vegetable juice and fruit smoothie bar; certified nutritionist on staff.

PIZZA & TAKE-OUT Angelo's Pizza (941-474-2477), 2611 Placida Rd., Englewood. Pizza and Italian specialties. Take-out and delivery.

Boca Grande Baking Company (941-964-5818; www.bocagrande bakingco.com), 384 E. Railroad Ave., Boca Grande. Sandwiches, quiche, homemade pizza, lasagna, breads, desserts, and other take-out items.

Old Monty's Restaurant & Pizzeria (941-637-0008), 2310 Tamiami Trail #3101, Punta Gorda. Besides pizza, there's pasta dishes, hero sandwiches, amaretto tartufo, cannoli, and rum cake.

The Philadelphian (941-766-0555), 2320 Tamiami Trail, at Midtown Plaza, Port Charlotte. Famous, it claims, for its cheesesteaks and hoagies, the latter of which come in eight varieties.

SEAFOOD Miss Cindy's Placida Fish Market (941-697-4930), 13010 Fishery Road, Placida. Besides local and imported fresh and frozen seafood, Miss Cindy's sells homemade soups, salads, and spreads along with gourmet items.

✳ Selective Shopping
SHOPPING CENTERS & MALLS
Boca Grande (Park Ave.). Despite the millionaires and power brokers who make Boca Grande their winter home, shopping here is low-key and affordable, with shades of historic quaintness. The restored railroad depot houses gift and apparel boutiques; there's more in back at Railroad Plaza. Across the street you'll find an eccentric general store and a department store that's been there forever, both of which set a somewhat funky

tone. Sam Murphy Park presents a serene place to rest alongside a gentle waterfall pool and under shade trees. Don't visit in August and September, when the town literally closes down.

Downtown Punta Gorda. Centered around Marion and Olympia Avenues, both one-way streets, between Nesbit Street and Tamiami Trail South, you'll find a quiet historic downtown that underwent a recent renaissance. Restaurants and galleries occupy many of the old buildings. Streetscaping includes old-fashioned streetlamps, alley arcades, historic murals, and park benches. A new major residential-retail development taking up a city block was recently completed. The weekly Think Thursday event runs different themes and shops stay open later. Every third Thursday from 5 to 8 PM the theme is **gallery walk** with live music, demonstrations, art, food, and a chance to meet local artists.

Fishermen's Village (941-639-8721 or 800-639-0020; www.fishville.com), 1200 W. Retta Esplanade, Punta Gorda. More than 40 shops and restaurants occupy a transformed fish-

packing plant. This is Punta Gorda's most hyper center of tourism activity and the site of festivals and social events. There's docking, lodging, charter boats, and fishing from the docks, along with shopping and dining, geared generally toward seniors. A preponderance of nautical clothing and gifts reflect the motif.

✪ **Olde Englewood Village** (941-473-9795; www.oldeenglewood.com) Dearborn Street is downtown Englewood's main drag despite the fact it has no traffic lights; its historic buildings hold fun-to-browse galleries, gift shops, and restaurants. The second Saturday of the month it hosts the Saturday Nite Live Street Walk from 6 to 9 PM.

Port Charlotte Town Center (941-624-4447; www.simon.com), 1441 Tamiami Trail, Port Charlotte. An indoor megamall with movie theaters and more than 90 commercial enterprises, including Burdines, Sears, and other chain outlets and specialty shops.

ANTIQUES & COLLECTIBLES
Blue Pineapple (941-474-1504), 445

FISHERMEN'S VILLAGE COMBINES THE PLEASURES OF WATER SPORTS AND SHOPPING.

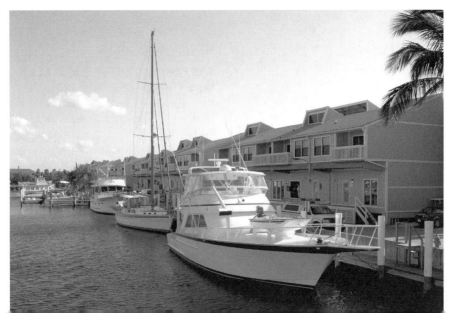

W. Dearborn St., Englewood. Unusual, high-end antique and modern home furnishings and accessories from England and France.

Esther's Antiques (941-460-8114), 446 Dearborn St., Englewood. It specializes in nostalgia, fine glass, jewelry, and decorative items, but you'll find a little bit of everything in this crowded space.

Oodles (941-769-2805), 403 Sullivan St. #11, Punta Gorda. A delightful and deliberate collection of antique books, new and old jewelry, art, and other gifts and collectibles.

Train Depot Antique Mall (941-639-6774), 1009 Taylor St., Punta Gorda. Sales of its wide range of memorabilia benefit the Punta Gorda Historical Society. It also holds flea markets. Closed July and August.

BOOKS Hooked on Books (941-637-8002; www.fishville.com), 1200 W. Retta Esplanade #4, at Fishermen's Village, Punta Gorda. Used and new books, Florida books, cards, and CDs.

Ruhama's Books in the Sand (941-964-5800), 333 Park Ave., Boca Grande. Books of local interest and for beach reading; cards, needlepoint supplies, and gifts.

CLOTHING Captain's Landing (941-637-6000; www.fishville.com), 1200 W. Retta Esplanade #24, at Fishermen's Village, Punta Gorda. Men's casual clothing with a nautical, tropical, and fishing flair; also formal wear.

Courtyard Boutique & Gift Shop (941-637-1226; www.fishville.com), 1200 W. Retta Esplanade #9, at Fishermen's Village, Punta Gorda. Kicky women's fashions and accessories for both casual and dressy occasions.

Fat Point Board Shop (941-205-2425), 150 Laishley Cr. #112, Punta

Gorda. Surfing themed and other youthful fashions.

Giuditta (941-639-8701), 322 Sullivan St., downtown Punta Gorda. Exotic patterns and finely tailored styles for the sophisticated woman; mostly formal and dress-up fashions.

Ltl. Ariel (941-964-2899), 360 Park Ave., Boca Grande. Pricey, fine clothing and gifts for kids.

Nichole's Collections (941-575-1911; www.fishville.com), 1200 W. Retta Esplanade #12, at Fishermen's Village, Punta Gorda. Fine cotton and casual women's fashions.

Tiki's (941-639-4310; www.tikis clothing.com), 105 W. Marion Ave., Punta Gorda. Distinctive casual and tropical fashions, bags, shoes, Brighton jewelry, and other accessories.

GALLERIES Arts Alliance of Lemon Bay (941-475-7141; www .artsallianceoflemonbay.org), 477 W. Dearborn St., Englewood. A wonderfully varied collection of local co-op art, including painted furniture, bronze sculpture, photography, jewelry, oil paintings, ceramics, and wood vases. Also offers art classes.

Gallery Dragonfly (941-505-0240; www.fishville.com), 1200 W. Retta Esplanade #22, at Fishermen's Village, Punta Gorda. Glass art and jewelry, fish wall sculptures, paintings, and prints with local appeal.

Paradise! (941-964-0774), 340 Park Ave., Boca Grande. Small but containing Boca's best selection, this gallery carries works by island artists and artisans as well as emerging Florida and national artists.

Presseller Gallery (941-639-7776; www.pressellergallery.com), 213 W. Olympia Ave., downtown Punta Gorda. Punta Gorda's most sophisticated gallery, carrying local photography, paintings, and sculptures—and a deli to feed the body along with the soul.

Sea Grape Artists Gallery (941-575-1718; www.seagrapegallery.com), 113 W. Marion Ave., Punta Gorda. Displays and sells the fine art and affordable paintings, pottery, jewelry, beadwork, and other three-dimensional art of co-op members, who staff the gallery, so you have a chance to meet the artists.

Smart Studio & Art Gallery (941-964-0519; www.smart-studio-fl.com), 370 Park Ave., Boca Grande. Shows and sells paintings of prolific wintering artist Wini Smart as well as other one-of-a-kind decorative arts. Closed in the off-season, when the artist tends her gallery in Maine.

GENERAL STORES Gill's Grocery & Deli Market (941-964-2506), 5800 Gasparilla Rd., at The Courtyard, Boca Grande. Beach needs, clothes, gifts, wine, deli items. Delivery available.

GIFTS Beach Road Boutique (941-474-6564), 1350 Beach Rd., on the causeway, Englewood Beach. Everything you're looking for in tasteful high-end beach souvenirs—from nice T-shirts to jewelry, bags, and home accessories.

Laff Out Loud (941-505-2067; www.fishville.com), 1200 W. Retta Esplanade #14, at Fishermen's Village, Punta Gorda. Whimsical toys for all ages: stuffed animals, dolls, puppets, lava lamps, and other nostalgic memorabilia and tropical souvenirs.

Margaret Albritton Gallery (941-698-0603), 13020 Fishery Rd., Placida. After lunch at The Fishery (see "Where to Eat"), browse this delightful shop for everything from kitsch pink flamingo gifts to fine art.

Papillon (941-205-2800; www.papillon online.net), 212 W. Virginia Ave.,

Punta Gorda. New Age books, crystals, music, jewelry, and other gifts.

Pirate's Ketch (941-637-0299; www.fishville.com), 1200 W. Retta Esplanade #44, at Fishermen's Village, Punta Gorda. Tasteful nautical clocks and lamps, weather vanes, seashell kitsch, framed sea charts, original art and prints.

Pomegranate & Fig (941-205-2333), 117 W. Marion Ave. #111, Punta Gorda. Unusual accessories for the home, women, and little girls with religious undertones—jewelry, ballet skirts, ceramic crosses, and wooden "rugs."

Village Gifts & Gallery (941-473-2300), 425 W. Dearborn St., Englewood. Original art, jewelry, gifts, a free used book exchange, and coffee.

JEWELRY ✪ Al Morgan (941-637-0946), 119 W. Marion Ave., downtown Punta Gorda. Showcases of custom, select, one-of-a-kind rings, bracelets, and necklaces—designed with a "chunky philosophy"—for men and women.

Bijoux (941-639-1676; www.mimi albright.com), 1200 W. Retta Esplanade #31, at Fishermen's Village, Punta Gorda. Silver, glass, and other beads and jewelry-making supplies, plus candles, scarves, home decorative items, women's clothing—all cool stuff.

Dearborn Street Jewelry & Repair (941-460-1750), 480 W. Dearborn St., Englewood. Small but well-stocked with affordable silver and gold charms, bracelets, toe rings, necklaces, and earrings.

Fine Things Jewelry (941-964-2166), 321 Park Ave., at Serendipity Gallery, Old Theater Building, Boca Grande. Designer jewelry.

Paradise Jewelers (941-475-2396), 3700 N. Access Rd., Englewood. Custom designs, nautical pieces, diamonds, gems, and repair.

KITCHENWARE & HOME DÉCOR

Bamboo Farm and Pottery Express (941-505-8400; www.potteryexpress .com), 25370 Zemel Rd., off Burnt Store Rd., Punta Gorda. A museum of Asian sculpture and Mexican folk art where all the pieces are for sale. Collections include detailed floral-painted Mexican pottery known as talavera, Vietnamese jars, pottery water fountains, and Buddha statues.

The Caged Parrot (941-637-8949; www.fishville.com/shops), 1200 W. Retta Esplanade #1, at Fishermen's Village, Punta Gorda. Garden accessories, wood-block models of Punta Gorda buildings, fanciful wall hangings, tin sculpture wall animals, and wind chimes.

Daylilies (941-473-1840; www.day liliesfl.com), 452 W. Dearborn St., Englewood. My first stop downtown, it carries a wide selection of artsy furniture and decorative items in tropical-jungle and marine-life motifs.

Holly's Island Shop (941-964-2767; www.hollysofbocagrande.com), 383 Park Ave., Boca Grande. Fun, beachy decorative items, plus jewelry and gifts.

Pies & Plates (941-505-7437; www .piesandplates.com), 2310 Tamiami Trail #3117, at Punta Gorda Crossing, Punta Gorda. Kitchen gadgets, dining wares, specialty foods, and gifts, plus a breakfast and lunch café and meal prep operation.

✳ Special Events

February: **Black Culture Festival** (941-637-7782), Gilchrist Park, Punta Gorda. One day midmonth devoted to African, Caribbean, and African American music and dance. Includes kids'

activities. **Charlotte County Fair** (941-629-4252), Charlotte Sports Park, 2333 El Jobean Rd., Port Charlotte. Rides, games, food, concerts, and shows for 10 days starting early in the month. **Charlotte Harbor Regatta** (941-639-0969; www.CharlotteHarborRegatta .com) Races in various boat classes with up to 100 participating boats and more than 400 sailors. Spectators can watch the action either from land or aboard a special sight-seeing boat. Four days early in the month. **Lemon Bay Festival & Cracker Fair** (941-474-5511 or 800-603-7198; www.lemonbayfest.com) Eight days of historical programs and nature cruises culminating in an all-day Cracker Fair at Pioneer Park on Dearborn Street. **Peace River National Arts Festival** (941-639-8810; www .visualartcenter.org), Laishley Park, Punta Gorda. Waterfront art show with food, beverages, entertainment, and kids' activities. One weekend at the end of the month. **Punta Gorda Wine & Jazz Festival** (941-639-3720; www .puntagordachamber.com), Lishley Park, Punta Gorda. One day of local and national artists plus food from local restaurants and, of course, wine.

March: **Florida Frontier Days** (941-629-7278; http://charlottecountyfl.com /historical/FloridaFrontierDays), Bayshore Live Oak Park, Charlotte Harbor. Re-enactors, artisans, storytelling, old-time games, music, and hands-on activities. One weekend late in the month. **Florida International Air Show** (941-639-1101; www .floridaairshow.com), Charlotte County Airport, Punta Gorda. A thrilling display of aerial feats including the Blue Angels. One weekend mid-month. **Placida Rotary Seafood Festival** (941-697-2271), Fishery Restaurant, Placida. Besides fresh fish, there are crab races, sculptures, and arts and crafts. Two days midmonth. **Rotary Spring Fine Arts Festival**

(941-474-5511 or 800-603-7198; www .englewoodchamber.com), W. Dearborn St., downtown Englewood. A late-month weekend of art from around the U.S., live entertainment, and refreshments.

April: **Punta Gorda Block Party** (941-639-3200; www.puntagordablock party.org), Punta Gorda. Community celebration with music, food, crafts, and a variety of events. One day mid-month.

May: **Emancipation Day Celebration** (941-575-7518), Blanchard House Museum, 406 Martin Luther King Blvd., Punta Gorda. Celebrating freedom from slavery with barbecue and chicken dinners. ✇ **Kids Cup Redfish Tournament** (941-766-8180; www .kidscuptournament.com), Fishermen's Village, Punta Gorda. One day mid-month devoted to kids age 10 to 16 who love to fish. **Ladies Day Tarpon**

Tournament (941-964-0568; www .bocagrandechamber.com) All-woman, all-release competition held on Mother's Day weekend.

June: **Punta Gorda Hibiscus Festival,** Gilchrist Park. Celebrating the town's reputation as "City of Hibiscus," it includes an evening concert, plant show and sale, kids' activities, secret garden trolley tour, and bike rides. One weekend midmonth.

July: **Fourth of July**, various locations. Independence Day in Charlotte County means swimming across the Peace River for some. Parties take place at Fishermen's Village, Bayshore Park, and Laishley Park with fireworks on the river come nightfall.

December: **Christmas Peace River Lighted Boat Parade** (941-639-3720) A procession of vessels in holiday attire. Saturday evening early in the month.

Sanibel Island & the Fort Myers Coast 3

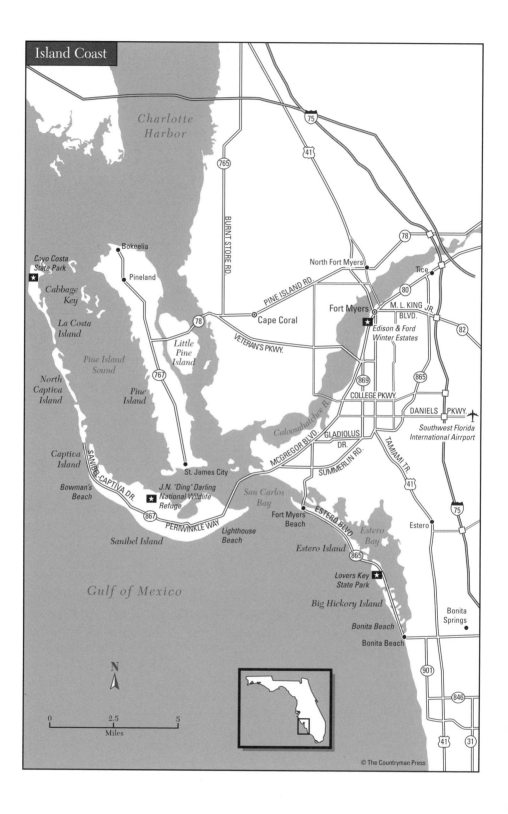

Island Coast

Charlotte Harbor

Bokeelia

Cayo Costa State Park

Pineland

Cabbage Key

La Costa Island

Little Pine Island

North Captiva Island

Pine Island Sound

Pine Island

Captiva Island

St. James City

Bowman's Beach

J.N. "Ding" Darling National Wildlife Refuge

Sanibel Island

Lighthouse Beach

Gulf of Mexico

BURNT STORE RD.

PINE ISLAND RD.

Cape Coral

VETERAN'S PKWY.

North Fort Myers

Tice

Fort Myers

Edison & Ford Winter Estates

M. L. KING JR. BLVD.

Caloosahatchee R.

COLLEGE PKWY.

DANIELS PKWY.

Southwest Florida International Airrport

MCGREGOR BLVD.

GLADIOLUS DR.

SUMMERLIN RD.

TAMIAMI TR.

San Carlos Bay

Fort Myers Beach

ESTERO BLVD.

Estero Bay

Estero

Estero Island

Lovers Key State Park

Big Hickory Island

Bonita Beach

Bonita Springs

Bonita Beach

N

0   2.5   5
Miles

© The Countryman Press

SANIBEL ISLAND &
THE FORT MYERS COAST

SAND, SHELLS, AND SERENITY

A dreamy, tropical land adorned with a necklace of islands, this slab of coastline resembles, more than any of its neighboring regions, the laid-back islands of the Keys, Bahamas, and Caribbean. Tourism pundits brand it "The Beaches of Sanibel and Fort Myers" to capitalize on its most reputable parts. More developed than its Charlotte Harbor neighbors and more relaxed than what lies to the south and at the Sarasota end of things, the Island Coast gives us the leafy greenery for the southwest Florida sandwich. It is considered one of Florida's most ecology-minded resort areas. How it balances its dual roles as wildlife preserver and tourism mecca has served as a model for state ecotourism.

At their northern extreme, the islands are mired in an Old Florida time frame. **Cabbage Key, Useppa Island, Cayo Costa,** and **Pine Island** gave birth to the Gulf Coast's legacy of fishing lifestyles, back when the Calusa lived off the sea. On Pine Island, fishing, crabbing, and shrimping are still a way of life and survival. Many commercial fishermen have turned to charter captaining in the wake of net-ban legislation in 1994. In 2003, *Field & Stream* editors named Pine Island among the 25 hottest American fishing destinations. Protected from rampant resort development by its lack of beaches, Pine Island clings to an older way of life like a barnacle to a mangrove prop. **Cayo Costa,** mostly state-owned, and **North Captiva** remain the uncut jewels in the Fort Myers coast necklace. **Useppa Island** and **Cabbage Key** preserve another era of island bygones, days graced by celebrity sporting types in search of escape, adventure, and tarpon.

Out in San Carlos Bay, to the south, the islands of **Sanibel** and **Captiva** developed quietly but steadily through the years. At various times in the past, the islands have supported a government lighthouse reservation, citrus and tomato farms, communities of fishermen (who sometimes dealt in rum-smuggling on the side), and a coconut plantation. From 1910–1940, wealthy notables made their way to the islands, intent on the relative anonymity that the wilds afforded them. Teddy Roosevelt discovered Captiva Island in 1914. Charles Lindbergh and his wife, Anne Morrow Lindbergh, visited often, inspiring her to pen her well-loved essays in *Gift from the Sea*, which uses seashells as a metaphor for the different stages in a woman's life. In more recent years, maverick artist the late Robert Rauschenberg called Captiva home. Pulitzer Prize–winning cartoonist and conservationist Jay N. "Ding" Darling gained national attention for Captiva and Sanibel Islands by fighting for the preservation of their natural attributes during his winter visits. His efforts sparked the development of the coast's environmental conscience.

Fort Myers Beach on San Carlos and Estero islands is synonymous with gulf shrimp, beach bustle, and spring breakers. Most of the bustle happens around Times Square, a pedestrian zone where retail meets the beach. The square's restaurants and shops have undergone a recent renaissance that nevertheless retains the island's ultra-casual vibe.

Southward, the maze of islands that includes **Lovers Key** and **Mound Key** is reminiscent of the coast's earliest times, with primeval estuaries, intact shell mounds, whispers of buried pirate treasure, and fishing lifestyles.

On the mainland, **Cape Coral** once served as a hunting refuge for steel magnate Ogden Phipps, who vacationed in Naples. The second-largest Florida city in the area, it was something of a developer's folly. The young city was cleared, canalled, and platted in 1970 and is slowly growing into itself. A downtown revitalization effort is currently under way, and a huge new marina, housing developments and resorts have recently appeared on horizon. **North Fort Myers,** rural in character, borders it on the east, and the Caloosahatchee River defines it on the south.

Across the river from North Fort Myers and Cape Coral, **Fort Myers** has evolved from its fort status of Seminole Wars time into the hub of communications, government, and transportation for the region. Cattle barons gave the community its early wild temperament; Thomas Edison and his class of successful entrepreneurs elevated it above its cow-trail streets.

Most unusual circumstances created the small community named **Estero,** along Tamiami Trail south of Fort Myers. The 19th-century religious cult that called itself the Koreshan Unity first settled there, led by Cyrus Teed, or Koresh (the Hebrew version of his name). The Koreshans believed that the earth clings to the inside of a hollow globe like coconut meat to its shell. Members practiced celibacy and communal living. They also experimented with tropical gardening, bringing the mango and the avocado to southwest Florida. The site of their brief stay has been preserved and re-created by the state, together with their buildings and the natural Florida they discovered there.

THOMAS EDISON PUT FORT MYERS ON THE MAP WHEN HE BUILT HIS WINTER HOME THERE IN THE LATE 1880S.

Edison & Ford Winter Estates

Between Fort Myers and Estero, **San Carlos Park** escalated to booming status with the genesis of a state university more than a decade ago. On its shirttails came massive shopping centers, restaurants, and other commercial enterprises that fill in the gap that once existed between quiet towns.

✳ To See

For many years the region was considered a cultural limbo, void of strong artistic or regional identity except for a certain retiree/Midwestern influence. Still lagging behind Sarasota and Naples in that department, the region nonetheless is making inroads toward "artsification." The population, furthermore, is diversifying in terms of ethnicity and age.

The residents of Cape Coral and North Fort Myers include many nationalities that share their customs at social clubs, restaurants, festivals, and other venues. Throughout Fort Myers, African Americans, Asians, East Indians, Europeans, and other ethnic groups heighten the cosmopolitan flavor. Flashes of Southern and Cracker spirit survive in the less resortlike areas of North Fort Myers and Pine Island.

The islands along the coast have inspired their share of creativity. Singer Jimmy Buffett has frequented Cabbage Key and Captiva Island. His brand of beachy folk song is the closest thing the Gulf Coast has to homegrown music. A Sanibel musician named Danny Morgan affects that same style and has been entertaining the islands for decades.

One of the few arts that residents can truly call their own is shell art, a form that flourishes on Sanibel Island, Florida's ultimate shell island. In its highest form, shell art can be stunning and delicate; its lowest can result in some pretty tacky shell animals.

Wealthy visitors to Sanibel and Captiva have exerted an influence on the fine arts through the years. The illustrious roll call began in the 1920s with Charles and Anne Morrow Lindbergh. Edna St. Vincent Millay's original manuscript for *Conversation at Midnight* burned in a Sanibel Island hotel fire. And the late Robert Rauschenberg, a pioneer in the field of photographic lithography, lived for many years on Captiva Island before his death in 2008.

ARCHITECTURE Fort Myers is home to some lovely architecture downtown and along McGregor Boulevard. Thomas Edison's home was perhaps Florida's first prefab structure: Because wood and materials were scarce (most newcomers made do with palmetto huts), Edison commissioned a Maine architect to draw up plans and construct sections of the home to be shipped down and pieced together on-site. Downtown, the **Richard Building,** circa 1924, boasts an Italian influence, while the courthouse annex

ONCE A ONE-ROOM SCHOOLHOUSE, CAPTIVA'S CHAPEL-BY-THE-SEA HOSTS INTERDENOMINATIONAL SERVICES AND MANY A WEDDING.

KORESHANS STATE HISTORIC SITE PRESERVES AND RE-CREATES A TIME WHEN A RELIGIOUS COMMUNITY GREW UP ALONG THE BANKS OF THE ESTERO RIVER.

superbly represents Mediterranean Revival. So do the Miles Building, built in 1926 by Dr. Franklin Miles, the "Father of Alka-Seltzer," and **Patio De León,** a restored and burgeoning entertainment and shopping complex on First Street. The newer Harborside Convention Center and other recent constructions echo the motif.

Pine Island possesses the best, most concentrated collection of preserved vernacular architecture, especially in ✪ **Matlacha.** Pineland's mound-squatting homes are also prime examples, occasionally dressed up with latticework and vivid paint jobs. In **Bokeelia,** the entire Main Street is designated a historic district. Notice especially the Captain's House, a fine example of slightly upscale folk housing of the early 1900s, with French Provincial elements. Nearby Turner Mansion represents a higher standard of living and is reminiscent of New England styles. The club at **Useppa Island** exhibits another prime collection of Old Florida styles, both traditional and revival.

CINEMA Beach Theater (239-765-9000; www.ftmyersbeachtheater.com), 6425 Estero Blvd., Fort Myers Beach. A new theater with four screens, serving a full-meal (and slightly overpriced) menu, beer, and wine.

Coconut Point 16 (239-498-8706), 8021 Cinema Way, Estero.

Gulf Coast Town Center Stadium 16 (230-454-4731; www.gulfcoasttowncenter .com), 10028 Gulf Center Dr., at I-75 and Alico Rd., Fort Myers. Sixteen theaters, including an IMAX.

Island Cinema (239-472-1701; www.islandcinema.com), 535 Tarpon Bay Rd., at Bailey's Shopping Center, Sanibel Island. A two-screen theater showing first-run films.

Marquee Cinema Coralwood Mall (239-458-2543), 2301 Del Prado Blvd., at Coralwood Shopping Center, Cape Coral. Ten screens for first-run films.

Regal Bell Tower 20 (239-590-9696), Daniels Pkwy. and US 41, Fort Myers. A modern megacomplex of theaters in the form of an airport hangar.

DANCE Gulfshore Ballet (239-590-6191; www.gulfshoreballet.org), 2155 Andrea Ln., Suite C 5–6, Fort Myers; mailing address: 1103 Schooner Pl., Sanibel Island 33957. Ballet instruction.

GARDENS ✪ Edison & Ford Winter Estates (239-334-7419; www.efwefla .org), 2350 McGregor Blvd., Fort Myers. Open 9–5:30 daily; guided tours at 11, 1, and 3. Botanical tours at 9 Thursday–Saturday. $20 adults, $11 children ages 6–12; laboratory and museum tour only $12 adults, $5 children. Botanical tours $24 adults, $10 children. A stand of bamboo sold Thomas A. Edison on this piece of property in the late 1800s. He was convinced the plants would be useful in his experiments with lightbulb filament. From there, the inventor expanded his research gardens around his home to include plants he might use in tire-making for friends and fellow Fort Myers winterers Henry Ford and Harvey Firestone. After a 2004 hurricane, estates staff set about restoring the 26-acre property to its original look, including historic landscaping. Mina's Moonlight Garden, named for Edison's wife, is a serene highlight of the lovely riverside grounds, originally designed by a famous landscape architect from New York named Ellen Biddle Shipman, America's foremost landscaper at the time and the first woman landscaper of renown. Rows of stately royal palms, like those Edison had planted along McGregor Boulevard around his home, are eye-catchers along with gushes of flowering foliage such as bougainvillea and angel trumpets. Botanical signs identify the 320 varieties of plants, and special botanical tours further explore the different collections, including cycads, orchids, and exotic fruit trees. The newest gardens include the Heritage Garden, which reflects the estates' original landscape plan, and a propagation garden like the one Edison maintained to start his seedlings.

Fragrance Garden of Lee County (239-432-2034; www.leeparks.org), 7330 Gladiolus Rd., in Lakes Regional Park, Fort Myers. Open daily 7–dusk. Parking: $1 per hour or $5 per day. The garden was designed primarily for the visually and physically impaired, although the general public will also enjoy this one-of-a-kind attraction. For the visually impaired there are pungent herbs and fragrant plants such as frangipani and gardenias. Paved paths with vegetation planted at wheelchair height accommodate the physically challenged. Gazebos were built wide enough for easy wheelchair access, too.

HISTORIC HOMES & SITES Chapel-by-the-Sea (239-472-1646; www.captiva civicassociation.com/html/chapel_by-the-sea.html), 11580 Chapin Ln., Captiva Island. This quaint church is a popular spot for interdenominational Sunday services (during season), weddings, and seaside meditation. Many of the island's early pioneers are laid to rest in its cemetery.

✪ Edison & Ford Winter Estates (239-334-7419; www.efwefla.org), 2350 McGregor Blvd., Fort Myers. Open daily 9–5:30; guided tours at 11, 1, and 3. $20 adults, $11 children ages 6–12; laboratory and museum tour only $12 adults, $5 children. Nowhere in the United States will you find the homes of two such important historical figures sitting side by side. This site is so much more than some preserved houses, however, it's a slice of Floridiana, Americana, and Mr.

Wizard, all rolled into 26 riverside acres. The 75-minute guided or audio self-guided tour begins across the street under the nation's largest banyan tree, a gift from tire mogul Harvey Firestone. The tree, 400 feet around, poses outside a museum that contains many of Edison's 1,093 inventions—including the phonograph, the movie camera, the lightbulb, children's furniture, and cement—as well as the 1907 prototype Model T Ford his friend and wintertime neighbor, Henry Ford, gave him. The newest exhibit, opened in 2009, explores Edison's and Ford's relation to music, movies, and dance. His laboratory, full of old bottles and other ancient gizmos, sits behind the museum. Edison's late-1880s home hides in a tangle of tropical flora with which Edison experimented. (Special garden and in-depth botanical tours are available—see "Gardens.") Actually Edison had two homes, identically built and connected with an arcade. One contained the Edisons' living quarters, the other, guest quarters and the kitchen. A picket fence separates Edison's estate from Ford's. The Mangoes, as it was called in honor of the fruit orchards the car manufacturer so loved, seems humble compared to its neighbor. Its furnishings are true to the era and the Fords' simple tastes. An outbuilding holds three vintage model Fords. In 2006, the estates reopened after a massive, three-year, $9 million overhaul, which included the debut of the Caretaker's House, the oldest building on the property, dating to the 1860s. Improvements are ongoing, including restoration of one of the region's first swimming pools, which is on the property, and a propagation garden designed according to Edison's own, near the banyan tree.

Fishing shacks, Pine Island Sound at Captiva Rocks, east of North Captiva. The last artifacts of the region's early commercial fishing enterprises have braved weather and bureaucracy to strut the shallows along the Intracoastal Waterway. The shack at the mouth of Safety Harbor on North Captiva is the most noticeable. It once served as an icehouse. If you look east, you'll spot several others where fishermen and their families used to live. Privately owned and maintained as weekend fishing homes for local enthusiasts, most are listed in the National Register of Historic Places and serve as picturesque reminders of days gone by.

✪ **Koreshan State Historic Site** (239-992-0311; www.floridastateparks.org/koreshan), 3800 Corkscrew Rd., Estero. Open daily 8 AM–sunset. Narrated tours 10 AM daily, January–March; Saturday and Sunday only the rest of the year. $5 per vehicle with up to eight passengers, $4 per single driver, $2 per cyclist, pedestrian, or extra passenger; tours $2 for adults, $1 for children. Contained within a state park, this site has restored the customs and ways of a turn-of-the-last-century religious cult that settled on the banks of the Estero River. Under the leadership of Cyrus Teed, whose Hebrew name was Koresh, members of Koreshan Unity were well versed in practical Christianity, speculative metaphysics, functional and aesthetic gardening, art, occupational training, and cellular cosmogony. The latter, their most unusual theory, held that the earth lined the inside of a hollow globe and looked down into the solar system. Teed and his followers envisioned an academic and natural utopia of 10,000 followers. They planted their settlement (home for only 250 at its peak) with exotic crops and vegetation. Before losing their momentum upon the death of their charismatic leader in 1908, the Koreshans built a theater, an art hall, a communal mess hall, a store, and various homes and workshops, all of which have been restored or reconstructed to tell their strange story. Demonstrations in season and other special events throughout the year illuminate the times. Camping, hiking, and kayaking count among the recreational activities. Archives are kept at the library of the Koreshan Unity Foundation across the road from the park (239-992-2184).

Mound Key State Archaeological Site (239-992-0311; www.floridastateparks .org/moundkey), 3800 Corkscrew Rd., Estero. The only way to reach this adjunct of the Koreshan State Historic Site (see above), where Calusa Indians and Spanish missionaries have set up camp in eras past, is by boat. Many do it by canoe or kayak from Koreshan, Lovers Key State Park, or Estero River Outfitters. An interpretative trail weaves through the native shell mounds, one of which reaches 32 feet high, qualifying as the county's highest geologic elevation. The 133-acre island was formed from years of shellfish eating as the Calusa piled the discarded shells on a sandbar that grew into the seat of their kingdom. Farmers settled years later, and modern-day explorers can find remnants of the centuries' habitation. It is illegal to take any artifacts from the island, which is under excavation by archaeologists.

Randell Research Center (239-283-2062; www.flmnh.ufl.edu/rrc), 13810 Waterfront Dr., Pineland, on Pine Island. Open daily 10–4; guided tours January–April, Wednesday and Saturday 10 AM. Suggested donation $7 adults, $5 seniors, $4 children. Archaeologists from Gainesville's Florida Museum of Natural History meet here at the time-stilled village of Pineland to discover the lifestyles of the lost Calusa tribes. The center's 3,700-foot Calusa Heritage Trail with modern interpretative signage tells of Pineland's importance as a center of Calusa culture for more than 1,500 years. The short trail climbs to the top of an ancient shell mound. On certain days archaeologists are digging at the site. Volunteers are welcome, but call in advance.

Sanibel Cemetery, off the bike path on Middle Gulf Dr. (not accessible by car). No signs direct you to it. Just follow the path and you'll come across a fenced plot with wooden headstones announcing the names of early settlers—a wonderful, quiet place to ponder times past.

Sanibel Lighthouse, southeast end of Periwinkle Way, Sanibel Island. Built in 1884, the lighthouse was the island's first permanent structure. Once vital to cattle transports from the mainland, it still functions as a beacon of warning and welcome. The lighthouse and Old Florida–style lightkeeper's cottage were renovated in 1991.

KIDS' STUFF ♫ **Broadway Palm Children's Theatre** (239-278-4422; www .broadwaypalm.com), Royal Palm Square, 1380 Colonial Blvd., Fort Myers. Each year, Broadway Palm Dinner Theatre puts on two or three plays geared toward families and served up with kids'-fare lunch.

✪ ♫ **Imaginarium** (239-321-7420; www.imaginariumfortmyers.com), 2000 Cranford Ave., Fort Myers. Open Monday–Saturday 10–5, Sunday noon–5. $12 adults, $10 seniors, $8 for children ages 3–12 (includes 3-D show and a fish food token). I have visited many of the interactive science museums that have hit Florida in the past couple of decades, and I'm happy to say this is among my favorites. It is not overwhelmingly huge, like some, but it is colorfully attractive and varied in its approach to teaching about everything from Florida environment to the world of sports. Emphasis is on weather and water (it occupies a former city water plant). The Hurricane Experience will, as they like to say, "blow you away." You can feel a cloud, tape yourself on location broadcasting a tornado, and walk through a thunderstorm. Aquariums, a touch tank, a swan lagoon, and stingray feedings acquaint visitors with Florida's water creatures. The animal lab exhibits dramatic critters such as tarantulas, an iguana, snakes, and a juvenile alligator. Other displays appeal to all ages with gadgets, toys, and computers; special 3-D movies and hands-on shows are part of the fun.

MUSEUMS ✪ ✿ **Bailey-Matthews Shell Museum** (239-395-2233 or 888-679-6450; www.shellmuseum.org), 3075 Sanibel-Captiva Rd., Sanibel Island. Open daily 10–5. $7 ages 17 and up, $4 children ages 5–16, free for ages 4 and younger. The only one of its kind in the U.S., this museum reinforces Sanibel's reputation as a top shell-collecting destination. It uses nature vignettes and artistically arranged displays to demonstrate the role of shells in ecology, history, art, economics, medicine, religion, and other fields. The centerpiece of the museum is a two-story globe surrounded by shells of the world. Outside is a memorial devoted to the late actor Raymond Burr, who helped establish the museum. The Children's Science Lab provides games and hands-on learning experiences in colorful reef-motif surroundings, but oddly with a touch tank you can't touch. One diorama explores the role of shells in the lives of the Calusa Indians, and a new interactive exhibit scans the menu of edible mollusks. The museum holds about a million specimens in the Great Hall of Shells and scientific collection upstairs, representing a large fraction of the world's 150,000 species of living mollusks.

✿ ✿ **Cape Coral Historical Museum & Rose Gardens** (239-772-7037; www.capecoralhistoricalmuseum.org), 544 Cultural Park Blvd., Cape Coral. Open Wednesday, Thursday, and Sunday 1–4; closed July and August. $2 donation per adult. Exhibits in three buildings include a new Native American Room, a Cracker kitchen model to complement the existing Cracker house model, seashell and model boat collections, a military exhibit, and a replicated burrowing owl nest. A mural depicting Cape Coral's old rose gardens brightens up the spot. Outside, a blossoming garden continues the link between the town and roses, while butterfly, herb, and Florida-friendly yards fill the grounds.

Museum of the Islands (239-283-1525; www.museumoftheislands.com), 5728 Sesame Dr., Pine Island Center on Pine Island; mail: P.O. Box 305, St. James City 33956. Open: November–April, Tuesday–Saturday 11–3, Sunday 1–4; May–October, Tuesday–Thursday and Saturday 11–3. $2 adults, $1 children. Occupying the old Pine Island library at Phillips Park, the museum concentrates on the area's Calusa and fishing heritage. Continue on to the settlement of Pineland to see time standing still on intact Native American mounds.

✿ **Sanibel Historical Museum & Village** (239-472-4648; www.sanibelmuseum.org), 950 Dunlop Rd., near City Hall, Sanibel Island. Open November–April, Wednesday–Saturday 10–4; May–mid-August, Wednesday–Saturday 10–1. $5 adults (ages 18 and older). The village began with a historical Cracker-style abode, once the home of an island pioneer. The museum uses photos and artifacts to focus on Sanibel's ancient and modern history of native Americans, Spanish settlement, commercial fishing, homesteading, citrus farming, steamboating, and tourism. The island's original Bailey's General Store, circa 1927, was moved to the site in 1993 as a kickoff to establishing a pioneer village on the grounds. Since then a 1920s post office, a teahouse, the old one-room schoolhouse for whites, and other vintage buildings have been added. One houses a lens that outfitted the Sanibel Lighthouse in the 1960s.

❧ **Southwest Florida Museum of History** (239-321-7430; www.swflmuseumof history.com), 2031 Jackson St., Fort Myers. Open Tuesday–Saturday 10–5, Sunday noon–5. $9.50 adults, $8.50 seniors, $5 students, free for children under 3. Walking tours of downtown January–April, 10 AM Wednesday and Saturday; $5. The displays in this museum—housed in a handsome Spanish-style railroad depot—take you back to the days of prehistoric mammals and ancient civilizations, and up through the eras of the Calusa Indians, commercial fishing, cattle driving, gladiolus farming, and local World War II training. Well-arranged scale and life-sized models, graphic depictions, videos, changing exhibits, and interactive historical games illuminate the past. Changing traveling and original exhibits have a national and international scope. Outdoors, tours examine a replica of a local Cracker house from the early 1900s and the world's last and longest Pullman private railcar, circa 1930. (Don't miss the Pullman tour; it's truly a highlight if you have a good guide.) Call in advance to participate in the museum's downtown walking tours.

Barbara Sumwalt Historical Museum (239-283-9600; http://useppahs.org), Useppa Island Club, Bokeelia. Open daily 12:15–2 (open until 3 in March). $4 donation requested for visitors over age 18. The wee island of Useppa is stuffed to the gills with history, a fact that calls for a historical museum. This one is exceptionally well presented for such a small place. (It helps that wealth outmeasures square footage on the island.) Dioramas are interpreted via taped presentations that you can listen to on individual players as you tour. They describe the island's Calusa history, its fishing and resort eras, and its role in training revolutionaries for the Cuban Bay of Pigs confrontation in 1960. Its newest exhibits deal with damage the island suffered in 2004's Hurricane Charley. Since the island is owned by a private club, visitors must be island guests or guests aboard the *Lady Chadwick* luncheon cruise to the island (see Captiva Cruises under "Boats & Boating: Sightseeing & Entertainment Cruises" in this chapter).

MUSIC & NIGHTLIFE Downtown Fort Myers is trying to metamorphose into a hot entertainment district featuring jazz bars, bistros, nightclubs, and street festivals, including a first Friday ArtWalk. As for the islands, Fort Myers Beach is definitely the most hopping. On Sanibel and Captiva you'll find a quieter brand of partying; nightlife there is focused on theater and more highbrow forms of music. Friday's *Gulf Coasting* supplement to the *News-Press* covers the region's entertainment scene.

Cape Coral
Jimbob's (239-574-8100), 1431 S.E. 16th Place. Live music on weekends.

La Venezia (239-945-0034), 4646 S.E. 11th Place. Dance every Wednesday from 7 to 10 PM in the fall and winter.

Captiva Island
✪ **Crow's Nest Lounge** (239-472-5161), 'Tween Waters Inn, 15951 Captiva Rd. Live contemporary dance bands Tuesday–Sunday; entertaining crab races on Monday and Thursday. The islands' hottest spot.

Fort Myers
Fort Myers Community Concert Association (239-939-3236), P.O. Box 606, 33902. Highbrow musical entertainment—from brass ensembles to ballet—at the Barbara B. Mann Performing Arts Hall (see "Theater" below).

Neo Lounge (239-878-5995), 1528 Hendry St. Live entertainment includes Friday Latin Night with happy hour specials 8 to 9 PM.

Southwest Florida Symphony (239-418-1500; www.swflso.org), 4560 Via Royale, Suite 2. Performs classical and pops series November–May at the Barbara B. Mann Performing Arts Hall in Fort Myers, BIG ARTS on Sanibel Island, and local churches.

Fort Myers Beach

If you can't find nightlife in Fort Myers Beach, better check your eyes and ears.

The Beached Whale (239-463-5505), 1249 Estero Blvd. Party from the rooftop to live music nightly in the heart of Times Square.

Junkanoo (239-463-6130; www.junkanoo-anthonys.com), 3040 Estero Blvd. You don't have to wait until dark to party in Fort Myers Beach. Here's a popular spot "where the party never ends," and young people headquarter their day at the beach with drinks, food, pool tables, water sports, volleyball, music, and dancing, indoors and out.

Lani Kai Island Resort (239-463-3111 or 800-237-6133; www.lanikaiislandresort.com), 1400 Estero Blvd. *The* premier collegiate party spot on the beach, with live entertainment nightly and during the day on weekends in the rooftop Glider Lounge or the Night Club on the beach.

Ugly's (239-463-8077; www.nervousnellies.net), 1131 First St., at Nervous Nellie's restaurant. Upstairs overlooking the bay, with live music, free boat docking, and all-day happy hour.

Pine Island

Bert's Bar & Grill (239-282-3232; www.bertsbar.com), 4271 Pine Island Rd., Matlacha. Florida funk at its finest, with a salty attitude, good munchies, waterfront stance, and live music in season (see Web site for schedule).

Ragged Ass Saloon (239-282-1131), 3421 Stringfellow Rd., St. James City.

Tarpon Lodge (239-283-3999; www.tarponlodge.com), 13771 Waterfront Dr., Pineland. Midweek music series February–May features live local entertainers from 6:30–9:30 PM on select nights. No cover charge.

Sanibel Island

BIG ARTS (239-395-0900; www.bigarts.org), 900 Dunlop Rd. Hosts classical musical quartets, trios, and orchestras November–April.

Jacaranda (239-472-1771; www.jacarandaonsanibel.com), 1223 Periwinkle Way. The most lively nightlife dancing on Sanibel with top-40 hits, reggae, and island music performed live.

SPECIALTY LIBRARIES For regional reference information by phone, call 239-479-INFO.

(ᵗᵖ⁾ **Sanibel Public Library** (239-472-2483; www.sanlib.org), 770 Dunlop Rd., Sanibel Island. Contains an identification collection of seashells, wireless Internet access, and Internet access computers by reservation. In season, it hosts big-name authors such as Clive Cussler and Jodi Picoult for free talks.

Talking Books Library (239-995-2665; library.lee-county.com), 519 Chiquita Blvd., Cape Coral. This library for the visually and physically impaired has books on tape and other audio formats.

FLORIDA REPERTORY THEATRE PERFORMS PROFESSIONAL PRODUCTIONS IN A HISTORIC MOVIE THEATER.

THEATER **The Arcade Theatre/Florida Repertory Theatre** (239-332-4488 or 877-787-8053; www.floridarep.org), 2267 First St., downtown Fort Myers. The glory of the 1920s, this Victorian playhouse has been restored and advanced to the 21st century. Home to an energetic professional company that brings new life to old boards.

✪ **Barbara B. Mann Performing Arts Hall** (239-481-4849 or 800-440-7469; www.bbmannpah.com), Edison College, 8099 College Pkwy. S.W., Fort Myers. Hosts major Broadway shows, musical performers, and dance troupes. Broadway season runs December–late April.

BARBARA B. MANN PERFORMING ARTS HALL CREATES DRAMA EVEN IN ITS LOBBY SPACES.

Broadway Palm Dinner Theatre (239-278-4422; www.broadwaypalm .com), 1380 Colonial Blvd., at Royal Palm Square, Fort Myers. Lunch and dinner musical performances starring professional actors in a made-over grocery store that seats and serves 448. Each year a few of the shows (and their buffets), such as *The Emperor's New Clothes,* are geared toward families. Its Off-Broadway Palm Theatre presents cabaret-style shows in an adjacent, intimate, 90-seat playhouse.

You can buy tickets for lunch and dinner shows or shows only. Both theaters are closed Monday year-round and Tuesday May–October.

Claiborne & Ned Foulds Theater (239-936-3239; www.artinlee.org), 10091 McGregor Blvd., at Lee County Alliance for the Arts headquarters, Fort Myers. An indoor and outdoor stage for recitals, concerts, and workshops. Theatre Conspiracy and Creative Theatre Workshop troupes present a variety of family and adult shows.

Cultural Park Theatre Company (239-772-5862; www.culturalparktheater.com), 528 Cultural Park Blvd., Cape Coral. A 184-seat facility that hosts community theater. Performances run from mid-September–mid-May. Also, acting classes for kids and adults.

Germain Arena (239-948-7825; www.germainarena.com), 11000 Everblades Pkwy., Estero. Home of the Everblades hockey team, this venue also hosts touring entertainers.

Herb Strauss Schoolhouse Theater (239-472-6862; www.theschoolhousetheater .com), 2200 Periwinkle Way, Sanibel Island. It represents a professional troupe that concentrates on comedies, musicals, and musical revues.

VISUAL ART CENTERS & RESOURCES Flocks of wildlife art and other eclectic galleries make a name for Sanibel Island in cultural circles, while smaller communities support their own offbeat galleries and art associations. On Pine Island, national artists come to hide out and nourish their souls, sparking a growing art colony of sorts that's centered in Matlacha. The following entries introduce you to opportunities for experiencing art as either a viewer or a practicing artist. A listing of commercial galleries is included in the "Shopping" section.

Alliance for the Arts (239-939-2787; www.artinlee.org), 10091 McGregor Blvd., Fort Myers. This not-for-profit center conducts classes and workshops, and operates a public gallery, members' gallery, 150-seat indoor theater, outdoor stage, and Saturday green market. It is home base for the Frizzell Gallery of Fine Art and many local arts and cultural groups.

Art of the Olympians Museum (239-335-5055; www.artoftheolympians.com), 1300 Hendry St., Fort Myers. The vision of the late Al Oerter, a four-time gold medalist, Fort Myers resident, and artist, came to fruition in January 2010, when this beautiful gallery and enrichment center opened on the river downtown. Besides displaying the work of Olympian athletes including Bob Beaman, Florence Griffith-Joyner, and Peggy Fleming, it furthers the Olympic ethic of excellence in all facets of life. This is the only place the U.S. Olympic Committee has allowed the display of the five-ring logo outside of its training centers. Traveling exhibits and learning opportunities make this experience much more than a gallery. Hours are Tuesday–Saturday 10–4. Admission is $2 for adults, free for children under age 12.

BIG ARTS (239-395-0900; www.bigarts.org), 900 Dunlop Rd., Sanibel Island. Home of an energetic multidisciplinary organization that includes the Phillips Gallery. Art shows and classes are scheduled regularly at the facility.

Bob Rauschenberg Gallery (239-489-9313; www.edison.edu/lee/gallery), Edison College, 8099 College Pkwy. S.W., Fort Myers. Hosts exhibits and lectures by nationally and internationally renowned artists.

Cape Coral Arts Studio Rubicond Park (239-574-0802), 4533 Coronado Pkwy.,
Cape Coral. Classes, exhibitions, and sales.

Fort Myers Beach Art Association (239-463-3909; www.fortmyersbeachart
.com), Donora St. and Shell Mound Blvd., Fort Myers Beach. Member and other
exhibits; workshops and classes.

✱ To Do

Shelling, island-hopping, fishing, sailboarding, and warming chilled bones on hos-
pitable beaches: These are a few of the favorite things to do in the Fort
Myers–Sanibel area.

BEACHES The region's 50 miles of local beaches are known for their natural state
and abundance of shells. *Family Fun* magazine recently rated this stretch of beach
the "#1 Beach in the Southeast U.S." In recent years, red algae drift periodically
washes up on the beaches. It is not pretty and is often smelly, but it poses no risk
to your health. Red tide, however, is a different problem, causing dead fish to wash
up on the beach from time to time and people to have allergic reactions to the
algal blooms.

Most beaches charge for parking. Sanibel Island beach stickers, which can be purchased from the police department at City Hall, allow you to park for free at most
accesses. Along the Gulf Drives you'll see signs at beach accesses designating resident sticker–only parking. Cyclists and walk-ins, however, can take advantage of
these accesses without stickers.

Bonita Beach

✍ **Barefoot Beach Preserve County Park** (239-252-4000; www.colliergov.net),
3300 Santa Barbara Blvd., Naples (entrance at Hickory Blvd. and Bonita Beach
Rd., south end of Little Hickory Island). Actually within neighboring Collier County but accessible from Bonita Beach, the 342 acres in this preserve contain a
coastal hammock and 8,200 feet of beach and low dunes. Sea grapes, cabbage
palms, and other native vegetation landscape the grounds. Gopher tortoises often
lumber across the road and footpaths. Rangers give nature walks and shell talks at
the chikee learning center. Facilities: restrooms, showers, nature learning center,
aquatic butterfly garden, snack bar. Parking: $8 per day.

✪ ✍ **Bonita Beach Park** (239-533-7275; www.leeparks.org), 27954 Hickory Blvd.,
south end of Little Hickory Island. The only true public park on Bonita Beach, it
becomes lively during the high season and on weekends. Water sports and volleyball, plus a hamburger joint and bar, create a youthful spirit. Vegetation is sparse;
there's nothing hidden about this beach. Parking fills up early in season and on
weekends year-round. About 10 other accesses with free but limited parking line
Hickory Boulevard to the north, marked by bright signs. Facilities: picnic table
shelters, restrooms, lifeguard, water-sports and beach rentals, volleyball, nearby
restaurants. Parking: $1 per hour.

Cape Coral

✍ **Cape Coral Yacht Club Community Park** (239-574-0806; www.capecoral
.net), 5819 Driftwood Pkwy. The man-made beach on the Caloosahatchee River is
part of a large park that sponsors recreational and other programs, and exudes a
true sense of community. The groomed beach is better for sunning than swim-

ming, for which the pool fills the void. The first Wednesday of every month, the park hosts Sunset Celebration on the Pier with live music and entertainment, food, and arts and crafts. Facilities: restrooms, showers, picnic shelters, barbecue grills, swimming pool, marina, shuffleboard, outdoor racquetball courts, tennis, playgrounds, fishing pier, boat ramps, bait shop, food concession. Swimming pool (239-542-3903) open daily 10–5. Park admission free; pool admission $5.25 ages 18 and up, $4.50 ages 10–17, $3 ages 9 and younger.

Captiva Island

✍ **Alison Hagerup Beach Park,** north end Captiva Rd. Only early arrivals get the parking spots for this prime spread of deep, shelly sand, formerly known as Captiva Beach. It's a good place to watch a sunset, and Travelocity named it the nation's most romantic beach. Facilities: portable restrooms. Open 6 AM–11 PM. Parking: $2 per hour.

Fort Myers

✍ **Lakes Regional Park** (239-432-2034, 239-267-1905 for train; www.leeparks .org), 7330 Gladiolus Dr., Fort Myers. This land of freshwater lakes features a small sand beach and marina, but no swimming. Landscaped with all native vegetation, this is a great place for the family to spend the day. The 279-acre park offers an interactive water playground, kayaking, paddleboating, fishing, nature and bike trails, a miniature train ride (fee), bike rentals, and two fun playgrounds, one with a railroad theme. Facilities: picnic areas, restrooms, showers, playgrounds, climbing wall, fitness trail, bike path, water-sports rentals, snack concession, gardens. Parking: $1 per hour or $5 per day.

A SCULPTURE AT LAKES PARK CAPTURES CHILDHOOD ABANDON.

Fort Myers Beach

Bowditch Point Regional Preserve (239-765-6794 or 239-533-7275; www .leeparks.org), 50 Estero Blvd., at the north end of the island. This pretty, green, 17-acre park fronts Estero Bay and the gulf. It's a nice, quiet beach, unspoiled, and a favorite of boat-ins. Drivers also frequent it, and its 75 parking spaces fill up quickly in season, so you may want to consider taking one of the beach's tram shuttles to get there. Facilities: picnic shelters, restrooms, showers, nature trails, boat docks, food concession. Parking: $1 per hour.

Dog Beach (239-229-0649; www.leeparks.org), 8800 Estero Blvd., south of Lovers Key State Park. A small strip of hard-packed beach makes

ON FLORIDA'S GULF COAST, WHERE SURFING WAVES ARE RARE, SKIM-BOARDING APPEALS TO YOUNG BEACHGOERS.

dogs and their owners happy at New Pass between Lovers Key and Bonita Beach. Plan on crossing some wetland areas to get to the beach, where birds abide despite the running and thrashing of pooches. In season, Dog Beach hosts a monthly kayak-with-your-canine paddle. Lee County's only off-the-leash dog park (most beaches on Sanibel Island allow pets on leash) requires proof of license and immunization. People are allowed no more than two dogs each, and children younger than 15 are not allowed in the off-leash area. Facilities: bag and disposal stations, portable people restrooms, leash-free beach. Free parking.

✤ **Lovers Key State Park** (239-463-4588; www.floridastateparks.org/loverskey), 8700 Estero Blvd., FL 865 between Fort Myers Beach and Bonita Beach. Walk or ride a truck-pulled tram through the natural mangrove environment to South Beach, the park's main beach. To the north, a boardwalk bridge takes you to a beach with no facilities that borders Big Carlos Pass. The area between Estero and Little Hickory Island consists of natural island habitat populated by birds, dolphins, and crabs. On the barrier island of Lovers Key, Australian pines provide shaded picnicking along a narrow, natural stretch of sand. A gazebo provides a picnic shelter and a popular wedding venue. Away from the beach, shaded picnic grounds line estuarine inlets; there is a launch for canoes and kayaks, a playground, and a path that accommodates hikers and cyclists. In 2005 and 2006, Lovers Key was named the most visited and top income-generating Florida state park. Facilities: picnic area, restrooms, showers, boat ramps, fishing, food concession, beach shop. Admission: North Beach, $2 parking; South Beach, $8 per vehicle with up to eight passengers, $4 for single passengers, $2 for extra passengers, bicyclists, and pedestrians.

✪ ✤ **Lynn Hall Memorial Park** (239-765-6794 or 239-533-7275; www.leeparks .org), 950 Estero Blvd., in the Times Square vicinity. Part of the pedestrian Times Square plaza, this park attracts college students in the spring and families the rest of the year. A rocking, rollicking place, it appeals to beach barhoppers, crowd watchers, and those interested in water sports. It features volleyball, a fishing pier, beachwear stores, restaurants, ice cream shops, beachside drinks, parties, parasailing, and jet-skiing. A nightly sunset celebration brings musicians and other performers. For thinner crowds, hit public accesses, marked with banners, on the south end of Estero Boulevard. Facilities: picnic areas, grills, restrooms, showers, playground, fishing pier, water-sports rentals; nearby restaurants, bars, and shops. Parking in lot for $1 per hour. (Warning: Park only in designated areas, or your car will be towed at great expense.)

Sanibel Island

✪ **Bowman's Beach,** Bowman's Beach Rd. off Sanibel-Captiva Rd., Sanibel Island. Bowman's is Sanibel's most natural beach. Long, coved, and edged by an Australian pine forest, it's on an island all its own. It can be reached by footbridges from the parking lot (a rather long walk, so go lightly on the beach paraphernalia). Shells are plentiful here—in some places a foot or more deep along the high-tide mark. Facilities: picnic area, restrooms, fitness trail. Parking: $2 per hour.

Lighthouse Park Beach (239-472-3700), south end of Periwinkle Way, Sanibel Island. Skirting Sanibel Island's historic lighthouse is an arc of natural beach fronting both the gulf and San Carlos Bay. One of Sanibel's most populated beaches, it features a nature trail and a popular fishing pier. Strong currents inhibit swimming off the point. The wide beach, newly replenished in 2010, gives way to sea oats, sea grapes, and Australian pine edging. I like the neighborhood around it, because it is historic and more laid-back than other parts of the island. Facilities: picnic area, restrooms, nature trail, fishing pier, mobile food concession in season. Parking: $2 per hour.

Sanibel Causeway Beach (239-765-6794; www.leeparks.org), Sanibel Causeway Rd. Historically, windsurfers and fishermen favor this packed-sand roadside beach. In 2007, the bridge was reconstructed, which cut down on some of the recreation-

SANIBEL ISLAND'S BEACHES ARE KNOWN NOT ONLY FOR THEIR SEASHELLS BUT ALSO FOR THEIR BIRDING OPPORTUNITIES.

SANIBEL'S LIGHTHOUSE PARK BEACH FEATURES A HISTORIC STRUCTURE, A FISHING PIER, AND BEACHES ON TWO WATERFRONTS.

al use. Beach-lovers in RVs and campers often pull up here to picnic and spend the day in the sun. Facilities: picnic area, restrooms.

⚓ **Tarpon Bay Beach** (239-472-3700), Middle Gulf Dr. at Tarpon Bay Rd., Sanibel Island. Another popular beach, this one is characterized by sugar sand and a nice spread of shells. It's a bit of a hike from the parking lot to the beach, and the area gets congested on busy days. RVs can park here. Great for swimming. Facilities: restrooms. Parking: $2 per hour.

Turner Beach (239-472-3700), south end Captiva Rd., Captiva Island. A pretty beach with wide, powdery sand, Turner tends to get crowded and parking is limited. The entrance is on a blind curve, which can be dangerous. More bad news: Riptides coming through the pass make this taboo for swimming, especially since the pass was reopened in 2009. Park your beach towel far north or south of the pass for calmer, swimmable waters. We like to come here in the evening to watch the sunset and walk the beach. Surfers like the waters to the north in certain weather. It's also a hot spot for fishermen, who line bayside shores and the bridge between Sanibel and Captiva. Facilities: restrooms, foot shower, nearby restaurants, water sports, and store. Parking: $2 per hour.

Upper Islands

✪ **Cayo Costa State Park** (941-964-0375; www.floridastateparks.org/cayocosta), La Costa Island; accessible only by boat. The Lee County coast is blessed with some true getaway beaches, untamed by connection to the mainland. On these, one can actually realize that romantic fantasy common to beach connoisseurs: sands all your own. Cayo Costa stretches for 9 miles and is most secluded at its southern extremes. A larger population of beachgoers congregates at the north end, where docks, a picnic and camping ground, and primitive cabins attract those who seek creature comforts with their sun and sand. A tram transports boaters from docking on the bay side to facilities on the beach side. Or you can walk the short distance on a path that is part of a 5½-mile trail system. Shelling is superb in these parts, particularly at Johnson Shoals, which surfaces at the island's north end during low tide. Facilities: picnic ground, restrooms, showers, nature trails, camping, cabins. Admission: $2 per person.

North Captiva, across Redfish Pass from South Seas Island Resort and Captiva Island; accessible only by boat. Like Cayo Costa, here's a place to go for private beaching. Though it's narrow at the south end, the sand is like gold dust. You'll find no facilities unless you venture across the island to the bay, where restaurants and civilization inhabit the north end.

BICYCLING The bikeways of the Fort Myers–Sanibel region come in two varieties. Bicycle paths, the most common, are separated from traffic by distance and, ideally, a vegetation buffer. Bicycle lanes are a designated part of the roadway. After ranking as the 23rd worst community for pedestrians out of 360 in the U.S. in 2009, Lee County is making a concerted effort to improve walkways and bikeways.

Cyclists also take to the road in rural areas, where no bikeways exist but traffic is light. By law they must abide by the same rules as motor vehicles. Children under age 16 are required to wear helmets.

Best Biking: More than 2 miles of bike trails run through **Lakes Regional Park** (239-533-7275, 239-533-7581), where bike rentals are also available. Long stretches of bike path in **Fort Myers** follow **Daniels Parkway, Metro Parkway, Colonial Boulevard,** and **Summerlin Road.** The **Summerlin path** leads to the Sanibel causeway (cyclists cross for $1) to connect with island paths. **McGregor Boulevard's** sidewalk provides another popular and scenic circuit. Design is under way for **John Yarbrough Linear Park** (239-553-7580), which will follow Ten Mile Canal from downtown Fort Myers to Estero. Far-reaching plans could eventually hook up the system with the West Coast Greenway extending from Tampa to Naples. More than 5 miles of bike paths also wind through **Lovers Key State Park,** and a ranger leads guided bike tours; call 239-463-4588 for a schedule.

Many of **Cape Coral's** city streets designate bike lanes.

✪ **Sanibel's** 23-mile path covers most of the island and occasionally leaves the roadside to plunge you into serene backwoods scenery. Segments along busy Periwinkle Way have recently been widened and moved away from roadside. Cyclists also pedal 4-mile, paved Wildlife Drive through J. N. "Ding" Darling National Wildlife Refuge and its unpaved but hard-packed Indigo Trail.

The 17-mile **Pine Island** bike path, 20 years in the making, was completed in 2007 to stretch along Stringfellow Road from St. James City to Bokeelia.

BMX bikers can use the **Sanctuary Skate Park** (see "Kids' Stuff," below) on Monday evenings. Cape Coral also has a dedicated BMX park.

Rental/Sales: ♪ **Billy's Bikes** (239-472-5248; www.billysrentals.com), 1470 Periwinkle Way, Sanibel Island. Bicycles, surrey bikes, and equipment for family biking. Also scooters and Segway tours. Rentals by the hour, day, or week.

Fun Rentals (239-463-8844; www.funrentals.org), 1901 Estero Blvd., Fort Myers Beach. Rentals start at $12 for two hours. Per-day to per-week rates are available. Scooter and motorcycle rentals, too.

Nature Recreation Management (239-314-0110; www.naturerecreationmanage
ment.com), 8720 Estero Blvd., Fort Myers Beach. Rents bikes at Lovers Key State
Park.

YOLO Watersports (239-472-1296 or 239-472-9656; www.yolo-jims.com), 11534
Andy Rosse Ln., Captiva Island. Rentals by the half day, full day, and 24 hours.
Also, motor scooters, golf carts, and water-sports equipment.

BOATS & BOATING With its procession of unbridged islands and wide bay, the
region begs for outdoor types to explore its waters. Island-hopping constitutes a
favorite pastime of adventurers.

Canoeing & Kayaking: In addition to those outlets listed below, many resorts and
parks rent canoes and kayaks.

✍ **Adventures in Paradise** (239-472-8443 or 239-437-1660; www.adventurein
paradiseinc.com), 14341 Port Comfort Rd., at Port Sanibel Marina, east of Sanibel
causeway toll booth, Fort Myers. Naturalist- or self-guided tours through a marked
mangrove trail. Rentals available. Free pickup from hotels and condos on Sanibel.

Captiva Kayaks & Wildside Adventures (239-395-2925; www.captivakayaks
.com), McCarthy's Marina, 11401 Andy Rosse Ln., Captiva Island. Sea-kayaking
tours for beginning to experienced paddlers focus on natural history and sea life.
Kayak and canoe rentals are available.

Estero River Outfitters (239-992-4050; www.esteroriveroutfitters.com), 20991 S.
Tamiami Trail, opposite Koreshan Historic Site, Estero. Rents and sells quality
kayaks and canoes for a 4-mile adventure down the natural Estero River to Estero
Bay. Guided tours are available.

Fish-Tale Marina (239-463-3600; www.thefishtalemarina.com), 7225 Estero
Blvd., Fort Myers Beach. Rents single, double, and fishing-equipped kayaks.

GAEA Guides (239-694-5513 or 866-256-6388; www.gaeaguides.com). Guides
kayaking tours at Lovers Key State Park, Estero Bay, and up the Caloosahatchee
River for birding. Also teaches kayak clinics on the Orange River and conducts
archaeological kayak tours for Randell Research Center from Pine Island.

✪ **Great Calusa Blueway** (239-461-7400; www.calusablueway.com) This paddling
trail along the island Intracoastal Waters extends more than 190 miles, from Cayo
Costa to Bonita Springs and up the Caloosahatchee River. Using GPS technology,
it takes paddlers to Mound Key, Lovers Key State Park, Bunche Beach, Tarpon
Bay, Cayo Costa, and other dynamic birding, archaeological, and beaching destinations. You can view maps or request a free map at the site or by calling the phone
number listed above.

Gulf Coast Kayak (239-283-1125; www.gulfcoastkayak.com), 4530 Pine Island
Rd., Matlacha, Pine Island. Morning nature and sunset trips in ✪ **Matlacha
Aquatic Preserve** and other local natural areas; full moon and manatee ventures
(Thanksgiving–St. Patrick's Day only for the latter). All guides are naturalists and
kayak instructors. Rentals available for self-guided tours.

Lakes Park (239-839-8656; www.leeparks.org), 7330 Gladiolus Dr., Fort Myers.
Kayak rentals for paddling on a freshwater lake.

✪ **Manatee Park** (239-533-7440 or 239-533-7275; www.leeparks.org), 10901 FL
80, Fort Myers. Paddle among the manatees along the Orange River with a kayak
rental (November–March only). Clinics available.

Nature Recreation Management (239-314-0110; www.naturerecreation management.com), 8720 Estero Blvd., Fort Myers Beach. Rents canoes and kayaks at Lovers Key State Park.

✍ **Tarpon Bay Explorers** (239-472-8900; www.tarponbayexplorers.com), 900 Tarpon Bay Rd., Sanibel Island. Rents canoes and kayaks for use in ✪ **Tarpon Bay** and on the "Ding" Darling refuge's Commodore Creek Canoe Trail. Also guided canoe/kayak tours. *Canoe & Kayak* magazine has rated Tarpon Bay among the top 10 places to paddle in the U.S.

Tropic Star Cruises (239-283-0015; www.tropicstarcruises.com), 7820 Barrancas St., Bokeelia, Pine Island. Rent single and double kayaks for half- and full-day trips from Bokeelia and Cayo Costa.

Dining Cruises: **Big M Casino** (239-765-7529 or 888-373-3521; www.bigmcasino .com), Moss Marine, 450 Harbor Ct., Fort Myers Beach. Gambling cruise with live entertainment and buffet and à la carte dining.

J. C. Cruises (239-334-7474; www.JCCruises.com), 2313 Edwards Dr., Fort Myers Yacht Basin, downtown Fort Myers. Lunch, dinner, Sunday brunch, and sight-seeing cruises up the Caloosahatchee River aboard the *Capt. J.P.*, a three-deck, 600-passenger paddle-wheeler.

Sanibel Harbour Marriott Princess (239-466-2128; www.Sanibel-resort.com), 17260 Harbour Pointe Dr., at Sanibel Harbour Resort off Summerlin Rd. before Sanibel Island causeway, Fort Myers. Sunset dinner buffet and Sunday brunch cruises aboard a sleek, elegant luxury yacht.

Personal Watercraft Rentals/Tours: **Holiday Water Sports** (239-765-4386; www .watersportsrentals.net), Pink Shell Beach Resort, 250 Estero Blvd., Fort Myers Beach; and (239-463-6778), Best Western Beach Resort, 684 Estero Blvd., Fort Myers Beach. WaveRunner rentals and dolphin-spotting tours.

Powerboat Rentals: **Adventures in Paradise** (239-472-8443 or 239-437-1660; www.adventureinparadiseinc.com), 14341 Port Comfort Rd., at Port Sanibel Marina east of Sanibel causeway toll booth, Fort Myers. Rents Grady White bowriders and center consoles or deck boats by half-day, day, and week.

The Boat House (239-472-2531; www.sanibelmarina.com/rentals.html), Sanibel Marina, 634 N. Yachtsman Dr., Sanibel Island. Center consoles and deck boats for trips into intracoastal waters only.

Fish-Tale Marina (239-463-3600; www.thefishtalemarina.com), 7225 Estero Blvd., Fort Myers Beach. Rents Grady Whites, Robalos, pontoons, and skiffs.

Four Winds Marina (239-283-0250; www.fourwindsmarina.com), 16501 Stringfellow Rd., Bokeelia, Pine Island. Rents 20- to 22-foot fishing and deck boats.

Jensen's Marina (239-472-5800; www.gocaptiva.com), 15107 Captiva Dr., Captiva Island. A colorful, locals' corner where fishermen hang out to tell lies. Rent a skiff, center console, or pontoon boat for half- or full-day rates. Water taxi transportation to the upper islands is also available.

Paradise Vacations (239-995-0585; www.paradisevacations.cc), 3444 Marinatown Ln. N., Fort Myers. Rent 37- to 41-foot air-conditioned houseboats for one- to seven-day cruises out of Marinatown. Full galley and fishing gear upon request.

Snook Bight Yacht Club & Marina (239-765-4371; www.snookbightmarina .com), 4765 Estero Blvd., Fort Myers Beach. Quality pontoons (17- to 25-foot), deck, and Aquasport fishing boats by the half-day, day, or week.

Southwest Florida Yachts (239-656-1339 or 800-262-SWFY; www.swfyachts.com or www.flsailandcruiseschool.com), 3444 Marinatown Ln., Suite 19, North Fort Myers. Offers power-yachting lessons and rentals in the 28- to 43-foot range.

Public Boat Ramps: **Bokeelia Boat Ramp** (239-283-0015), 7290 Barrancas Ave. N.W., Bokeelia. Newly renovated, it has two ramps.

Cape Coral Yacht Club (239-574-0806; www.capecoral.net), 5819 Driftwood Pkwy., Cape Coral. Two free public ramps on the Caloosahatchee River, with bait shop, marina, and recreational facilities.

Lovers Key State Park (239-463-4588; www.floridastateparks.org/loverskey), 8700 Estero Blvd., at County Road 865 (CR 865) between Fort Myers Beach and Bonita Beach. Access to Estero Bay and the gulf with picnicking facilities.

Matlacha Park (239-229-7367), 4577 Pine Island Rd. N.W., Matlacha, Pine Island. Playground, fishing pier, and two ramps.

Punta Rassa (239-765-6794), 18500 McGregor Blvd., at Summerlin Rd. before the Sanibel causeway, Fort Myers. Two double ramps, picnic facilities, historic marker, and restrooms.

Sanibel, Causeway Rd. Two ramps at the west end of the Sanibel causeway.

Sailboat Charters: **New Moon** (239-395-1782; www.newmoonsailing.com), 'Tween Waters Inn Marina, 15951 Captiva Dr., Captiva Island. Up to six passengers aboard a 40-foot sloop. Sailing lessons for kids and adults, three-hour cruises, and extended custom sails.

CAPE CORAL YACHT CLUB IS A RECREATIONAL HUB WITH EVERYTHING FROM A MARINA AND FISHING PIER TO A SWIMMING POOL AND RACQUETBALL COURTS.

Sailboat Rentals & Instruction: ✪ **Offshore Sailing School** (239-454-1700 or 888-454-7015; www.offshore-sailing.com), 16731 McGregor Blvd., at South Seas Island Resort Marina on Captiva Island and Pink Shell Beach Resort on Fort Myers Beach. Weeklong and three-day certification (US SAILING) instruction offered, from beginning women's-only and mixed sailing courses to family learning vacations, advanced racing, and coastal navigation. Operated by an Olympic and America's Cup veteran. Course instructors are knowledgeable, experienced, and easygoing ("no yelling" is the rule). Accommodation packages with resorts available.

Southwest Florida Yachts/✪ Florida Sailing & Cruising School (239-656-1339 or 800-262-7939; www.flsailandcruiseschool.com), 3444 Marinatown Ln. N.W., Suite 19, North Fort Myers. American Sailing Association (ASA) certification courses and bareboat charters provide excellent adventures into Charlotte Harbor for live-aboard experiences. Also powerboat courses.

Sight-Seeing & Entertainment Cruises: Look under "Wildlife Tours & Charters" for nature excursions.

✪ ⚓ **Captiva Cruises** (239-472-5300; www.captivacruises.com), P.O. Box 580, Captiva Island 33924, at McCarthy's Marina. It offers a complete menu of upper island sight-seeing, beach, and luncheon trips aboard the finely fitted 150-passenger *Lady Chadwick* and a 48-passenger pontoon; guides share history and lore along the way. These cruises are the only way for nonguests of the inn and club to see private Useppa Island and enjoy lunch at the Collier Inn restaurant.

J. C. Cruises (239-334-7474; http://modernsurf.com/jccruises), P.O. Box 1688, Fort Myers 33902, at Fort Myers Yacht Basin. Sight-seeing river and dining cruises aboard a 600-passenger paddleboat.

⚓ **Nature Recreation Management** (239-314-0110; www.naturerecreation management.com), 8720 Estero Blvd., Fort Myers Beach. Conducts one-hour ecological, shelling, and sunset cruises that depart from Lovers Key State Park.

Sanibel Thriller Cruises (239-472-2328; www.sanibelthriller.com), 634 N.

CAPTIVA CRUISES' *LADY CHADWICK* ANCHORS AT USEPPA ISLAND.

Yachtsman Dr., at Sanibel Marina, Sanibel Island. It offers zippy narrated tours that circle Sanibel and Captiva, and others that take in Boca Grande (see Charlotte Harbor chapter).

Stars & Stripes (239-472-2723; www.sanibelmarina.com/charters.html), 634 N. Yachtsman Dr., at Sanibel Marina, Sanibel Island. Ninety-minute sight-seeing and wildlife tours depart four times daily, plus sunset/cocktail cruises with complimentary beverages according to demand.

Tropic Star Cruises (239-283-0015; www.tropicstarcruises.com), 16499 Porto Bello St., Bokeelia, Pine Island at Knight's Landing. Full-day nature and Boca Grande cruises and ferry service to Cayo Costa (ferry/kayak package available), plus a land-sea Calusa Heritage Trail & Mound Tour at Randell Center.

FISHING Snook and tarpon are the prized catch of local anglers. Snook, which is a game fish and can't be sold commercially, is valued for its sweet taste.

Redfish is another sought-after food fish. More common catches in back bays and waters close to shore include mangrove snapper, spotted sea trout, shark, sheepshead, pompano, and ladyfish. Deeper waters offshore yield grouper, red snapper, amberjack, mackerel, and dolphinfish. Most fish are released in these days of environmental consciousness. Check local regulations for season, size, and catch restrictions.

Nonresidents age 16 and older must obtain a license unless fishing from a vessel or pier covered by its own license. Inexpensive, temporary, nonresident licenses are available at county tax collectors' offices and most Kmarts, marinas, and bait shops.

Deep-Sea Party Boats: **Getaway Deep Sea Fishing** (239-466-3600 or 800-641-3088; www.getawaymarina.com), Getaway Marina, 18400 San Carlos Blvd., Fort Myers Beach. All-day, half-day, and night party boat excursions plus charters.

Fishing Charters/Outfitters: Competent fishing guides work out of the region's major marinas. If it's your first time fishing these waters, I recommend hiring someone with local knowledge.

Captain Mike Fuery (239-466-3649; www.sanibel-online.com/fuery), mailing address: 16341 Vesta Ln., Fort Myers 33908. Located at Captiva Island's 'Tween Waters Inn Marina, he has a good reputation for finding fish.

Captain Pat Hagle Charters (239-283-5991), P.O. Box 245, Pineland 33945. Fish excursions into Pine Island Sound; also nature, history, shelling, beachcombing, and water-taxi cruises.

Sanibel Marina (239-472-2723; www.sanibelmarina.com), 634 N. Yachtsman Dr., Sanibel Island. Several experienced fishing guides operate out of the marina. Captain Dave Case (home phone 239-472-2798) has been at it a long time.

SoulMate Charters (239-851-1242; www.soulmatecharters.com), 17544 Lebanon Rd., Fort Myers. Captain Rob Modys takes you fishing or shelling from Punta Rassa ramp at the east end of the Sanibel Causeway or Fish-Tale Marina (7225 Estero Blvd., Fort Myers Beach). He also specializes in couples getaways.

Fishing Piers: **Cape Coral Yacht Club** (239-574-0815), 5819 Driftwood Pkwy., Cape Coral. The 620-foot lit fishing pier is part of a boating/recreational complex that includes a bait and tackle shop.

ARRIVE EARLY FOR A PRIME SPOT ON SANIBEL'S POPULAR LIGHTHOUSE BEACH PIER.

Centennial Park, Edwards Dr. near Yacht Basin, downtown Fort Myers. Complete park with playgrounds and other facilities.

✪ **Fort Myers Beach Pier,** 1000 Estero Blvd., at Lynn Hall Memorial Park (www.leeparks.org), Fort Myers Beach. The concrete T-pier with wooden railings offers lots of casting room and hungry pelicans. It holds a tin-roofed bait shop, which also rents rods.

Lighthouse Park Beach, southeast end of Periwinkle Way, Sanibel Island. A T-dock into San Carlos Bay.

✪ **Manatee Park** (239-432-2038 or 239-690-5030; www.leeparks.org), 10901 FL 80, Fort Myers. A great place for visitors to learn more about the endangered West Indian manatee that is native to the region. On the Orange River.

Matlacha Park (239-229-7367), 4577 Pine Island Rd. N.W., Matlacha, Pine Island. Playground and boat ramps.

GOLF Home of such golfing greats as Patty Berg and Nolan Henke, the region keeps pace with the growing popularity of golf.

Public Golf Courses: **Alden Pines Golf Club** (239-283-2179), 14261 Clubhouse Dr., Bokeelia, Pine Island. A semiprivate, 18-hole, par 71 course with affordable rates year-round. Snack bar.

Bay Oaks Disc Golf (239-765-4222; www.fortmyersbeachfl.gov), Bay Oaks Recreation Center, 2731 Oak St., Fort Myers Beach. A new twist on golf: an 18-"hole" course you play with Frisbees.

Beachview Golf & Tennis Club (239-472-2626; www.beachviewgolfclub.com), 1100 Parview Dr., Sanibel Island. Public, 18-hole, par 70 course with steakhouse grill, pro shop, rentals, and lessons.

Dunes Golf & Tennis Club (239-472-2535; www.dunesgolfsanibel.com), 949 Sandcastle Rd., Sanibel Island. Semiprivate, 18-hole, par 70 course. Restaurant and bar. Lush, Audubon-preserve links. High rates, especially in season.

✤ **Eastwood Golf Course** (239-321-7487; www.cityftmyers.com/golf), 4600 Bruce Heard Ln., Fort Myers. One of the region's favorites; 18 holes, par 72, located away from traffic. Restaurant and bar.

Fort Myers Beach Golf Club (239-463-2064; www.fmbgolfclub.com), 4200 Bay Beach Ln., off Estero Blvd., Fort Myers Beach. An 18-hole executive course, par 60, surrounded by condo communities yet rife with bird life. Affordable rates.

✤ **Fort Myers Country Club** (239-321-7488; www.cityftmyers.com/golf), 3591 McGregor Blvd., Fort Myers. Fort Myers's oldest, it opened in 1917; 18 holes, par 71. Restaurant and lounge.

HEALTH & FITNESS CLUBS Asylum (239-437-3488; www.asylumfitness club.com), 13211 McGregor Blvd., Fort Myers. Memberships start at one month; fully equipped aerobic and weight studios plus classes.

Gold's Gym (239-549-3354), 1013 Cape Coral Pkwy. E., Cape Coral. Classes in spinning, step aerobics, body flex, yoga, and karate. Personal training.

The Omni Club (239-931-6664; www.theomniclub.com), 1755 Boy Scout Dr., Fort Myers. More than 100 cardio machines, a separate women's-only facility, classes, smoothie-juice bar, a spa-salon next door, and club-style locker rooms with free towel service. Short-term passes and memberships available.

Sanibel Health Club (239-579-0670; www.sanibelhealthclub.com), 975 Rabbit Rd., Sanibel Island. Full cardiovascular and weight-training equipment, yoga and Pilates classes, and personal training. Short-term memberships (day, week, month) available.

Sanibel Recreation Center (239-472-0345; www.mysanibel.com), 3880 Sanibel-Captiva Rd., Sanibel Island. Short-term memberships allow visitors to take advantage of all this complex has to offer: a kids' play pool with fountains and slide, a lap pool, a nicely equipped fitness center, tennis, and aerobic and other classes.

HIKING Cayo Costa State Park (941-964-0375; www.floridastateparks.org /cayocosta), 880 Belcher Rd., at Cayo Costa, Boca Grande. Six miles of trail take you through barrier island ecology, a pioneer cemetery, and remnants of a circa-1904 quarantine station.

Corkscrew Regional Ecosystem Watershed (CREW) Marsh (239-657-2253; www.crewtrust.org), 23998 Corkscrew Rd., Estero, 18 miles east of I-75, exit 123. Five miles of hiking trails through peri-Everglades environment—pine flatwoods, oak and palm hammock, and sawgrass marsh—to a 12-foot observation tower. The Cypress Dome Hiking trailhead is 4 miles west of the Marsh Trails. Free guided tours the second Saturday and the first and third Tuesday of each month, October–May. Full-moon hikes, too.

✿ ✤ ✐ **J. N. "Ding" Darling National Wildlife Refuge** (239-472-1100; www .fws.gov/darling or www.dingdarlingsociety.org), 1 Wildlife Dr., off Sanibel-Captiva Rd., Sanibel Island. Its longest hike, the Indigo Trail, travels for more than 4 miles from the refuge education center, across a boardwalk and along bird-rich ponds. A shorter trail takes you to a protected Calusa shell mound.

CALUSA SHELL MOUND TRAIL AT J. N. "DING" DARLING NATIONAL WILDLIFE REFUGE PROVIDES A QUIET BOARDWALK STROLL INTO A HARDWOOD HAMMOCK.

Estero Bay State Buffer Preserve (239-992-0311; www.floridastateparks.org/esterobay), off W. Broadway in Estero; mailing address: 700-1 Fisherman's Wharf, Fort Myers Beach 33931. Provides about 10 miles of nature trails through scrubland along the Estero River and bay marshes.

☙ **Sanibel-Captiva Conservation Foundation** (239-472-2329; www.sccf.org), 3333 Sanibel-Captiva Rd., Sanibel Island. Nearly 5 miles of trails through natural habitat to an observation tower along the Sanibel River. The majority of wildlife consists of birds, lizards, alligators, and insects.

KIDS' STUFF ☙ **Bounce-N-Glow** (239-226-4569; www.bouncenglowfuncenter.com) 5370 S. Cleveland Ave., Fort Myers. Indoor go-carts, bumper cars, haunted mini-golf, mini-bowling, video arcade, toddler area, and snack center. Admission per activity.

☙ **Eagle Skate Park** (239-573-0206; www.capecoral.net), 315 S.W. Second Ave., Cape Coral. Ramps, half- and quarter-pipes, grind boxes and rails; outfitted for skaters and BMX bikers. Admission $6.

☙ **Fort Myers Beach Pool** (239-463-5759), 2600 Oak St., Fort Myers Beach. Not your ordinary city pool, this one has a two-story slide and the toddler Tad Pool. Admission is $4 for ages 12 and older, $2 for ages 3 to 11, $1 for ages 2 and younger. Closed Tuesday and Thursday in winter.

☙ **Fort Myers Skatium** (239-321-7510; www.cityftmyers.com), 2250 Broadway, Fort Myers. Hours vary for indoor ice skating. Cost for public ice skating sessions is $7 adults, $6 children ages 12 and younger, plus $3 for skate rental.

☙ **Germain Arena** (239-948-7825; www.skateeverblades.com), 11000 Everblades Pkwy., exit 123 off I-75, at Corkscrew Rd., Estero. The public can ice skate at this indoor rink weekdays noon–1:15 PM. Admission is $7 for a regular session. Skate rental is $3. Sunday family skating costs $5 each, including rentals, plus there are special late skate and pizza-and-pop sessions. There are learn-to-skate classes, an ice-hockey league, and a figure-skating club and clinics. A video arcade and snack counter complete the family amenities.

✪ ☙ **Greenwell's Bat-A-Ball and Family Fun Park** (239-574-4386; www.greenwellsfamilyfunpark.com), 35 N.E. Pine Island Rd., Cape Coral. Named after the city's favorite sports son, Red Sox player Mike Greenwell, this facility contains batting cages, a miniature golf course, a small playground, a maze, a video arcade, four go-cart tracks, a paintball field, and snack concessions. Kids really love it here, but be prepared to lay out a lot of money if you spend much time—especially in the arcade room.

🏸 **Periwinkle Park** (239-472-1433; www.sanibelcamping.com), 1119 Periwinkle Way, Sanibel Island. The owner of this trailer park raises and breeds exotic birds and waterfowl. He daddies roughly 400 birds of 90 species, specializing in African and Asian hornbills. Flamingoes, parakeets, cockatiels, cockatoos, and others occupy the park and 15 aviaries. During the off season, visitors can drive through; in season, biking is recommended. A few of the birds raised here can be seen more easily at Jerry's Shopping Center (1700 Periwinkle Way). Take the children in the evening, when the birds are most talkative.

🏸 **Sanctuary Skate Park** (239-321-7558 or 941-337-5297), 2277 Grand Ave., downtown Fort Myers behind the Skatium. Skateboarders and in-line skaters love this city-owned outdoor facility with its cool ramps and half-pipes. Skate and pad rentals are available. Admission is $3 per day. On Monday evenings the park is open for BMX riders.

🏸 **The Shell Factory** (239-995-2141 or 800-282-5805; www.shellfactory.com), 2787 N. Tamiami Trail, N. Fort Myers. A shell shop on steroids, this longtime attraction has grown into a megacomplex. Though still old-fashioned, it now includes restaurants, a fun park, a nature park, a pirate attraction, a money museum, a mining slough, aquariums, video games, a seafood restaurant, and gifts from fine to tacky. Admission to The Shell Factory is free; admission to the nature park is $10 for adults, $8 for seniors, and $6 for children ages 4–12. Bumper boat rides and miniature golf are $5 and water wars $2. Fun park hours are 10–6 daily. Special events such as Gumbo Fest are fun for the whole family and feature live entertainment.

🏸 **Strausser BMX Sports Complex** (239-458-1943; www.capecoralbmx.org), 1410 S.W. Sixth Pl., Cape Coral. A bicycle motocross track is provided for practice and weekly races. Also picnic grounds, a playground, a softball field, and a sand volleyball court.

❂ 🏸 **Sun Splash Family Waterpark** (239-574-0558; www.sunsplashwaterpark .com), 400 Santa Barbara Blvd, Cape Coral. This spot offers wet fun in a dozen varieties and includes pools, slides, flumes, a log roll, cable drops, a river ride, volleyball, food, lockers, and special events. Admission is $16.95 for ages 13 and older, $14.95 for children ages 2–12, and $8.95 for senior citizens (plus tax). Admission prices drop after 2 PM. Parking is $5. The park is open early March–September, but the schedule varies according to time of year and day; it is open daily, mid-June–mid-August.

🏸 **Zuleta's Indoor Batting Cages** (239-362-1819; www.zuletasbattingcages.com), 11495 S. Cleveland Ave., Fort Myers. This new facility enhances Fort Myers's image as "baseball town," home of two major league spring training teams, with four cages that pitch softballs or baseballs from 25 to 85 mph. Rates start at $10 for 10 minutes (94 pitches), plus $1 for bat rental. Clinics and lessons with pro players available.

RACQUET SPORTS Cape Coral Yacht Club Community Park (239-574-0808; www.capecoral.net), 5819 Driftwood Pkwy., Cape Coral. Five lit tennis courts, two outdoor racquetball courts, and a pro shop. Admission.

Fort Myers Racquet Club (239-321-7530; www.cityftmyers.com), 1700 Matthew Dr., Fort Myers. Newly renovated, eight clay courts and two hard courts (eight lit total), lessons, and tournaments. Admission.

Hancock Bridge Community Park (239-565-7748), 2211 Hancock Bridge Pkwy., Cape Coral. The Lee County Community Tennis Association (www.lee countytennis.com) conducts classes and league play on five lit courts.

Rutenberg Community Park (239-432-2154), 6500 S. Pointe Blvd., Fort Myers. Eight lit tennis and two handball courts.

Sanibel Recreation Center (239-472-0345; www.mysanibel.com), 3880 Sanibel-Captiva Rd., Sanibel Island. Four lit courts; admission.

Signal Inn Resort (239-472-4690; www.signalinn.com), 1811 Olde Middle Gulf Dr., Sanibel Island. One racquetball court. Admission fee for nonguests.

STARS Complex (239-321-7545), 2980 Edison Ave., downtown Fort Myers. Two lit tennis courts.

SHELLING Welcome to shelling heaven. Sanibel Island, in particular, is known for its great pickings. Be aware that a state law prohibits the collection of live shells on Sanibel Island, to preclude the possibility of dwindling populations. Collecting live shells is also prohibited in state and national parks. Elsewhere in the county, live collecting is also discouraged. Any shell with a creature still inside is considered a live shell. Shellers who find live shells washed up on the beach—a common occurrence after storms—are urged to gently return (no flinging!) the shell to deep water.

Hot Shelling Spots: **Big Hickory Island,** northwest of Little Hickory Island, accessible only by boat. An unhitched crook of beach favored by local boaters and shellers.

✪ **Bonita Beach,** Little Hickory Island. Look north of the public beach.

✪ **Cayo Costa State Park,** between North Captiva and Boca Grande, accessible only by boat. Because it takes a boat ride to get there, these sands hold caches of shells merely by virtue of their remoteness. North-end Johnson Shoals provides a thin strip of sandbar for good low-tide pickings.

Sanibel Island. Known as the Shelling Capital of the Western Hemisphere, the island even has its own name for the peculiar, shell-bent stance of the beach collector: the Sanibel Stoop. Unlike the other Gulf Coast barrier islands, Sanibel takes an east-west heading. Its perpendicular position and lack of offshore reefs allow it to intercept shells that arrive from southern seas. Its fame as a world-class shelling area has made Sanibel a prime destination for shell collectors for decades. With shell-named streets, store shelves awash in shells and shell crafts, an annual shell fair, and a shell museum, one risks suffering shell shock just by visiting there. Best gulfside shelling spot: Bowman's Beach, midisland, away from the paths leading to the parking lot.

Shelling Charters: **Adventures in Paradise** (239-472-8443 or 239-437-1660; www.adventureinparadiseinc.com), 14341 Port Comfort Rd., at Port Sanibel Marina, east of Sanibel toll booth, Fort Myers. Shelling and lunch excursions to Cayo Costa and North Captiva Island aboard power catamarans.

Captain Mike Fuery's Shelling Charters (239-466-3649; www.sanibel-online .com/fuery), P.O. Box 1302, Captiva Island 33924. A local shelling expert takes small groups to Cayo Costa, Johnson Shoals, and other shelling hot spots.

Captiva Cruises (239-472-5300; www.captivacruises.com), P.O. Box 580, Captiva Island 33924, at McCarthy's Marina. Full- and half-day shelling trips, with experienced instruction, to Cayo Costa or North Captiva Island.

SPAS Aquagene (239-463-6181; www.pinkshell.com), Pink Shell Resort, 275 Estero Blvd., Fort Myers Beach. The area's newest resort spa takes its cues from the sea in design and spa treatments, which include a red algae marine wrap, Sea of Life facial, and Dead Sea Salt Glow. Seashells and waves set the motif for its fashionable locker and waiting areas.

Esterra Spa & Salon (239-765-4772; www.esterraspa.com), 6231 Estero Blvd., Fort Myers Beach. A day spa but affiliated with the three Sunstream Resorts (DiamondHead, Gull Wing, and Pointe Estero) on Fort Myers Beach; complete services including hydrotherapy.

Sanibel Day Spa (239-395-2220 or 877-695-1588; www.sanibeldayspa.com), 2075 Periwinkle Way #24, upstairs at Periwinkle Place, Sanibel Island. Long-established and well-reputed place of pampering offers extensive à la carte and spa package services, including hair care, manicures, pedicures, men's treatments, facials, oxygen therapy, ayurvedic wellness treatments, scrubs, and massages.

Sanibel Harbour Marriott Resort & Spa (239-466-4000 or 800-767-7777; www.sanibel-resort.com), 17260 Harbour Pointe Dr., directly before the Sanibel causeway, Fort Myers. Sanibel Harbour was a spa before it became a resort (see "Lodging"). Guests, members, and day visitors can take advantage of the swimming pool, whirlpools, training room, aerobics and tai chi classes, saunas, steam rooms, and racquetball courts. The spa offers special services including interactive couples treatments, herbal wraps, aromatherapy massage, personal training, facials, and the unique BETAR musical and sound relaxation system.

Spada (239-482-1858; www.spadasalonanddayspa.com), 13161 McGregor Blvd., Fort Myers. Full line of classic and creative body and skin care treatments, including prenatal and couples massages, chocolate massage, acupuncture, salt glows, facials, cranberry spa manicure, and microdermabrasion.

THE BOSTON RED SOX COME OUT SWINGING EACH SPRING IN FORT MYERS.
Boston Red Sox

Touch Spa Salon (239-454-9933; www.touch-spa-salon.com), 13499 S. Cleveland Ave., Fort Myers. Facials are its strong suit and come in flavors of European, pumpkin chiffon, pearl and ginseng, and more. Also massage and hair and nail services.

SPECTATOR SPORTS

Crab Races: ✪ ✎ **'Tween Waters Inn Crow's Nest** (239-472-5161; www.tween-waters.com), 15951 Captiva Dr., Captiva Island. Participate or watch at 6 and 9 every Monday and Thursday night. The early session is geared toward families.

Pro Baseball: **City of Palms Park** (239-334-4700 or 877-RED-SOX9;

http://boston.redsox.mlb.com), 2201 Edison Ave., Fort Myers). Home of the Boston Red Sox's spring exhibition games, starting in March and played into April. In 2012, the training facility will move to a new location on Daniels Parkway, east of I-75.

Hammond Stadium (239-768-4225), 14400 Six Mile Cypress Rd., Fort Myers. Hosts the Minnesota Twins (239-768-4270 or 800-279-4444; http://minnesota.twins .mlb.com) for spring training in March. From April–August, the Miracle Professional Baseball team (239-768-4210; www.miraclebaseball.com), a member of the Florida State League, competes here.

Pro Hockey: **Florida Everblades** (239-948-7825; www.floridaeverblades.com), Germain Arena, 11000 Everblades Pkwy., Estero, exit 123 off I-75. Southwest Florida's professional ice hockey team plays its October–April season at Germain Arena. The public can skate at the rink daily (times vary) for a fee. (See "Kids' Stuff," above.)

Waterskiing: ❧ **Southern Extreme Waterski Show Team** (239-494-2774; www .southernextreme.com) Puts on a free show every Sunday at 4 during the season at Miromar Outlets (see "Shopping").

WATER SPORTS

Dive Shops & Charters: **Underwater Explorers** (239-481-4733; www .underwaterexplorers.net), 12600 McGregor Blvd., Fort Myers. National Association of Underwater Instructors (NAUI) certification courses and equipment, plus dive trips out of the region. This operation has been around for years. Others come and go throughout the region, but this is the most dependable.

Parasailing & Waterskiing: **Holiday Water Sports** (239-765-4FUN; www.holiday watersportsfmb.com), 250 Estero Blvd., at Pink Shell Beach Resort; and (239-463-6778), 684 Estero Blvd., at Best Western Beach Resort, Fort Myers Beach. Hobie Cat, kayak, aquacycle, parasailing, and WaveRunner rentals available.

GIRL-WATCHING IS ANOTHER POPULAR ISLAND COAST SPORT.

Ranalli Parasail (239-565-5700; www.ranalliparasail.com), 2000 Estero Blvd., Fort Myers Beach. Rides along Fort Myers Beach and WaveRunner rentals.

YOLO Watersports (239-472-9656 or 239-472-1296; www.yolowatersports.com), 11534 Andy Rosse Ln., Captiva Island. Parasailing rides from 600 to 800 feet high with dips, plus water-sport rentals.

Sailboarding & Surfing: Winter and summer storms bring the sort of waves that surfers crave, but in general, gulf waves are too wimpy for serious wave riders. Strong winds, however, provide excellent conditions for sailboarders at several locations throughout the region. Sanibel Causeway is the most popular windsurfing spot. The latest board-sport craze involves a stand-up board that you paddle.

Ace Performer (239-489-3513; www.aceperformer.com), 16842 McGregor Blvd., Fort Myers. Rents equipment and gives lessons for windsurfing, kite boards, and kayaks (including a four-person kayak). Free delivery to the Sanibel causeway.

YOLO Watersports (239-472-9656; www.yolowatersports.com), 11534 Andy Rosse Ln., Captiva. Rents surfboards, skim boards, body boards, and stand-up paddle boards.

Snorkeling & Scuba: Florida's west coast has no natural reefs, but several have been built to provide homes for marine life and make divers and fishermen happy. Nearly 20 of these artificial reefs lie along the Sanibel Island–area coast. The Edison Reef, one of the largest, was created from the sinking of a former Fort Myers bridge in 42 feet of water 15 nautical miles off the Sanibel Lighthouse. The Belton Johnson Reef, constructed of concrete culvert, lies about 5 nautical miles off Bowman's Beach on Sanibel. Other popular sites include the Redfish Pass Barge, lying in 25 feet of water less than a nautical mile from Redfish Pass between Captiva and North Captiva, and the Doc Kline Reef, a popular tarpon hole less than 8 nautical miles from the Sanibel Lighthouse. Cayo Costa State Island Preserve offers snorkelers nice ledges in 2 to 5 feet of water alive with fish, sponges, and shells.

WILDERNESS CAMPING Cayo Costa State Park (941-964-0375; www .floridastateparks.org/cayocosta), 880 Belcher Rd., Boca Grande, La Costa Island) You'll need boat transportation to reach this unbridged island (see Tropic Star Cruises under "Boats & Boating: Sight-seeing & Entertainment Cruises"), which is home to wild pigs and myriad birds. Bring your own fresh drinking water and lots of bug spray. And don't expect to plug in the laptop. There are showers, picnic grounds, boat docks, nature trails, a tram that runs cross-island, tent sites, and some very primitive cabins to rent. Call ahead to reserve the latter. Camping was once allowed anywhere on the 2,225-acre island, but today it's restricted to a specific area.

Koreshan State Historic Site (239-992-0311; www.floridastateparks.org /koreshan), P.O. Box 7, Estero 33928. Koreshan's 60 campsites circle a volleyball court and are built fairly close together; a few face the Estero River. The park contains a nature trail, canoe trail, boat ramp, and 11 buildings in the historic compound. For reservations call 800-326-3521 or visit www.reserveamerica.com.

WILDLIFE SPOTTING Loggerhead turtles lumber up on local beaches each summer to lay their cache of eggs. (Only vigilant night owls actually see them, but you can find their tracks in the morning light and see their nests, which patrols stake off.) Brown pelicans swarm fishing piers for handouts. Black skimmers nest on uninhabited sandy islands, while hundreds of other birds visit or stay in local habitats. The Fort Myers–Sanibel area is a vital area for wildlife, and many opportunities exist to spy on animals in their natural setting.

Alligators: Once endangered, the alligator population sprang back in recent decades, only to be decimated in past years by fear gone overboard. Thanks to organizations and laws that fought to protect the prehistoric reptiles, the jawsome creatures have been taken off endangered lists. Sanibel Island paved the way by pioneering a no-feeding regulation that later became state law. (Hand-fed alligators lose their fear of people.) Then, in 2004, after a couple of deadly attacks on Sanibel, the city began open harvesting of the creatures; when a gator trapper is called, he is allowed to take as many gators as he wishes at that outing. Now the alligator, once a common sight, especially at J. N. "Ding" Darling National Wildlife Refuge, is rarely seen. Concerned citizens and naturalists continue to cry for reform, but for now the slaughter continues.

Innate homebodies, alligators usually leave their home ponds only during spring and summer mating. That's when you're most likely to spot them. You will hear the bellow of the bull gator in the night and sometimes see both males and females roaming from pond to pond in search of a midsummer night's romance. They can do serious damage to a car, so be alert. And never approach one on foot.

When it's cold, alligators stay submerged to keep warm. When they're in the water, you first spot their snouts, then their prickly, tire-tread profiles. Once your eye becomes trained to distinguish them from logs and background, you'll notice them more readily. On sunny days throughout the year you may spot them soaking up rays on the banks of freshwater rivers and streams.

Birds: Roseate spoonbills are the stars of the J. N. "Ding" Darling National Wildlife Refuge, but hundreds of other species live among the sanctuary's wiry mangrove limbs and shallow estuarine waters, including ibises, brown and white pelicans, tricolor herons, red-shouldered hawks, snowy egrets, anhingas, and ospreys. In 2002 *Birder's World* magazine listed "Ding" Darling as third among its Top 15 Birding Hot Spots.

Dolphins: Playful bottle-nosed dolphins cruise the sea, performing impromptu acrobatic shows that it's hard to believe aren't staged. When the next performance will be is anybody's guess, but if you learn their feeding schedules you have a better chance of catching their act. They often like to leap out of the wake of large boats. Out in the gulf I've been surrounded by their antics to the point where I suffered minor whiplash from spinning around to keep track of them all. Don't expect them to get too close—take some binoculars—and forget seeing them in captivity around here. Locals once staged a protest in Pine Island Sound when collectors tried to take some of their dolphins. And when a swim-with-the-dolphins facility was proposed near Sanibel Island, citizens again rose up in arms against animal exploitation.

Manatees: In east Fort Myers—where warm waters discharged from the Florida Power & Light Company have always attracted the warm-blooded manatees to so-called Yankee Canal in the winter months—✪ ✿ **Manatee Park** (see "Nature Preserves & Eco-Attractions") has opened to provide a manatee viewing area, exhibits, and other recreational and educational assets on the wild and natural Orange River.

Pine Island's backwaters offer a good venue for manatee spotting. Check out the bay behind Island Decor & More, a popular sea-watch site, just before the Matlacha Bridge. If you're around South Seas Island Resort on Captiva Island, watch the marina waters for surfacing manatees.

Nature Preserves & Eco-Attractions: ♂ ♫ **Butterfly Estates** (239-690-2359 or 877-690-2359; http://thebutterflyestates.com), 1815 Fowler St., Fort Myers. Open daily 9–5 in season, 9–3 in summer. $15 for ages 17 and older, $9 for ages 3–16. A recent addition to downtown's cultural scene, this greenhouse structure gives wing to thousands of butterflies, moths, and the imagination. Lush plants and trickling waterfalls add to the beauty of the small but lively butterfly house. A gift shop, café, and ice cream and candy shop occupy charming, renovated, historic cottages at the estates.

♫ **Calusa Nature Center & Planetarium** (239-275-3435; www.calusanature .org), 3450 Ortiz Ave., Fort Myers. Open Monday–Saturday 9–5, Sunday 11–5. Call for astronomy and laser show times. Museum, trails, and planetarium $9 adults, $6 children ages 3–12, children under 3 free. This multifaceted environmental center offers three wildlife trails with a butterfly aviary, a native plant garden, a caged bobcat and foxes, a touch tank, and an injured-bird aviary. Join a guided walk of the Cypress Swamp Boardwalk every Tuesday and Friday at 9:30 AM. Indoors you can see more live animal exhibits—snakes, tarantulas, alligators, turtles—and demonstrations. The new Insectarium opened in 2009 with live bugs and interactive fun such as dressing up like an insect. Daily programs allow visitors to get up close and personal with some of the fascinating creatures of Southwest Florida, plus the center hosts special nature programs for children and adults every month. Snake feedings take place every Sunday at 11:15 AM. The planetarium uses telescopes, laser lights, and astronomy lessons in its presentations.

Cayo Costa State Park (941-964-0375; www.floridastateparks.org/cayocosta), 880 Belcher Rd., Boca Grande. Located on Cayo Costa Island; accessible only by boat. $2 per person. A wildlife refuge occupies about 90 percent of this 2,225-acre island. Cayo Costa preserves the Florida that the Native Americans tried to protect against European invasion. Besides the occasional feral hog that survives on the island, egrets, white pelicans, raccoons, ospreys, and black skimmers frequent the area. The path across the island's northern end features a side trip to a pioneer cemetery. Blooming cacti and other flora festoon the walk, which is sometimes a run when the weather turns warm and uncontrolled mosquito populations remind us of the hardships of eras gone by. Campsites and cabins accommodate overnighters.

♫ **C.R.O.W.** (239-472-3644; www.crowclinic.org), 3883 Sanibel-Captiva Rd., Sanibel Island. Open May–October, Tuesday–Sunday 10–4; closed Sunday the rest of the year. $5 adults, $3 ages 13–19, free for children 12 and younger, $15 family rate. C.R.O.W. is the acronym for 40-year-old Clinic for the Rehabilitation of Wildlife. It opened the impressive Healing Winds Visitor Education Center in January 2009 to great acclaim. Among its state-of-the-art hands-on exhibits, visitors can watch recovering patients via critter-cam, and can learn what it takes to be a wildlife vet from exhibits such as "Peek at a Pelican" and "Radiographs." The hospital tends to sick and injured wildlife: more than 4,000 birds, bobcats, raccoons, rabbits, and otters.

✪ ❦ ✐ **J. N. "Ding" Darling National Wildlife Refuge** (239-472-1100; www
.fws.gov/dingdarling or www.dingdarlingsociety.org), 1 Wildlife Dr., off Sanibel-
Captiva Rd., Sanibel Island. Refuge open sunrise to sunset (closed Friday); education center open January–April 9–5, May–December 9–4. Refuge parking $5 per
car, $1 per cyclist or pedestrian. More than 6,300 acres of pristine wetlands and
wildlife are protected by the federal government, thanks to the efforts of Pulitzer
Prize–winning cartoonist and politically active conservationist J. N. "Ding" Darling,
a regular Captiva visitor in the 1930s. A 4-mile drive takes you through the refuge,
once a satellite of the original Everglades National Wildlife Refuge. To really experience "Ding," get out of the car. At the very least follow the easy trails into mangrove, bird, and alligator territory. Look for roseate spoonbills, yellow-crowned
night herons, white pelicans, painted buntings, and dozens of other life-list prizes.
Narrated tram and guided canoe tours are available (239-472-8900). The new education center holds hands-on wildlife displays, realistic habitat vignettes, bird
sculptures, a birders' room, and a peek into the world of the refuge's namesake.
Naturalist programs take place throughout the week in season.

Four Mile Cove Ecological Preserve (239-549-4606), at the end of S.E. 23rd
Terrace, north of Midpoint Memorial Bridge in Cape Coral (follow the signs off
Del Prado Blvd. north of Coralwood Mall at S.E. 21st Ln). Open daily 8–sunset.
An urban preserve runs parallel to the bridge and allows exploration of 365 acres
of wetlands along a 1.5-mile nature trail that takes you away from the bustle of
traffic. Interpretative center and restrooms (open 8–3:30), picnicking, guided
nature walks, and kayak rentals are available on the weekends (October–May only).
The kayak trail into Alligator and Deerfly Creeks becomes shallow and narrow at
times, sometimes requiring portage.

❦ ✐ **Lakes Regional Park** (239-432-2034; www.leeparks.org), 7330 Gladiolus
Dr., Fort Myers. Open: daily 7–dusk; train village open Monday–Friday 10–1:45,
Saturday 10–3:45, Sunday noon–3:45 (last rides a half-hour before closing). Park-

J. N. "DING" DARLING NATIONAL WILDLIFE REFUGE, THE NATION'S SECOND-MOST-VISITED
REFUGE, DRAWS BIRDERS FROM AROUND THE WORLD.

ing $1 per hour, $5 per day; mini train rides $4 for ages 6 and older, $1 for ages 1–5 (includes admission to the railroad museum). Having made a grand comeback from severe hurricane damage in 2004, Lakes Regional Park has reinvented itself not only as a family picnic-and-play park, but also as a prime birding spot. For the family, there's a sand beach on the lake (a former quarry), a water fountain park, playgrounds with a climbing wall, a miniature train and railroad museum, a fragrance garden, butterfly house, walking and biking trails, and rentals for pedal boats, hydrobikes, and kayaks. The park's concession also sells ice cream and rents bikes for its more than 2 miles of trails that reach across the lake.

✦ ✎ ✪ **Manatee Park** (239-690-5030; www.leeparks.org), 10901 FL 80 (Palm Beach Blvd.), Fort Myers. Open daily 8–sunset. Parking $1 per hour, $5 per day. A well-kept, 17-acre recreational park feeds our fascination with the lovable manatee, teddy bear of the water world. In addition to a manatee viewing area, it provides polarized filters for peeping underwater, habitat exhibits, a nature boardwalk, a canoe and kayak launch (and rentals and clinics in winter), nature programs (in winter), wildlife habitat areas (including a butterfly garden), an information center, and picnic facilities. The park also serves as a rescue and release site for injured and rehabilitated manatees. For manatee viewing updates, call 239-690-7275.

Matanzas Pass Preserve (239-432-2127; www.leeparks.org), 199 Bay Rd., Fort Myers Beach. Open daily dawn to dusk. A quiet respite from vacationland action, this 56-acre preserve provides 1.25 miles of wooded hiking on two loop trails and boardwalks through mangroves and the island's last maritime oak hammock. The Historic Cottage at the trailhead is open free to the public every Wednesday and Saturday 10–noon.

✎ **Ostego Bay Foundation's Marine Science Center** (239-765-8101; www .ostegobay.org), 718 Fisherman Wharf, Fort Myers Beach. Open Wednesday– Friday 10–4; Saturday 10–1 in season. Suggested donation $5 per adult, $2 per child ages 6–12. Primarily a marine-science education and research facility, Ostego Bay maintains a showroom of local sea life for visitors to tour. Aquariums hold local species in various habitats, such as sea grass, estuarine, and gulf. Call to ask about feeding times, when reclusive creatures come out of hiding for optimal viewing. Manatee, loggerhead, and other kiosks explain the plight of endangered species and the workings of the local shrimping industry. Interactive displays include a touch table, microscopes, and a touchable shark skin and blue marlin's bill. The foundation has built a boardwalk along the bay where the shrimp boats dock off Main Street. Here you can learn still more about shrimping, estuaries, and local maritime heritage. The

VISIT MANATEE PARK NOVEMBER THROUGH APRIL TO SEE ITS EPONYMOUS, LOVABLE, BLUBBERY SEA MAMMALS LIVE.

three-hour Wednesday working waterfront tour takes you along the boardwalk beginning at 9 AM October–May; the cost is $15 per person.

✦ **Sanibel–Captiva Conservation Foundation Center** (239-472-2329; www .sccf.org), 3333 Sanibel-Captiva Rd., Sanibel Island. Open during summer, Monday–Friday 8:30–3; October–May, Monday–Friday 8:30–4; also open Saturday 10–3, December–April. Nature Center admission is $3 for visitors ages 17 and older. This research and preservation facility's main campus encompasses more than 1,800 acres. A guided or self-guided tour introduces you to indigenous flora and natural bird habitats and leads to an observation tower. Indoor displays and dioramas further educate and include a touch tank. Guest lecturers, seminars, and workshops address environmental issues during winter. The weekly beach walk is fun and informative. A native plant nursery and butterfly house are also on the premises.

Six Mile Cypress Slough Preserve (239-533-7555; www.leeparks.org/sixmile), 7751 Penzance Blvd., on Six Mile Cypress Pkwy., Fort Myers. Trails open daily dawn to dusk; interpretive center November–April, Tuesday–Friday 10–4, Saturday–Sunday 10–2; Tuesday–Sunday 10–2 the rest of the year. Parking $1 per hour. Egrets, herons, ibises, bald eagles, and belted kingfishers come to feed at this shallow waterway, its cypress forest, and ponds. Alligators also take up residence. Take a guided or self-guided tour around the more than 1-mile-long boardwalk through cypress stands and wetlands. Guided 90-minute walks start at 9:30 daily. A new interpretative center opened in 2008, most remarkable for its green construction, maintenance, and sustainability. The display room holds engaging interactive displays and short video clips that explain relevant topics such as cypress knees, bird migration, and flora and fauna. The center also hosts special monthly events such as nature photography classes, wet walks into the slough, and full moon hikes.

Wildlife Tours & Charters: ✦ **Adventures in Paradise** (239-472-8443 or 239-437-1660; www.adventureinparadiseinc.com), 14341 Port Comfort Rd., at Port Sanibel Marina off Summerlin Rd., before the Sanibel causeway, Fort Myers. Sea-life-encounter excursions led by a marine biologist who throws a seine net from a 40-foot power catamaran. Also shelling and dolphin quests.

Canoe Adventures (239-472-5218), Sanibel Island. Guided tours with a noted island naturalist in J. N. "Ding" Darling National Wildlife Refuge, on the Sanibel River, and in other natural areas.

Manatee World (239-693-1434), 5605 Palm Beach Blvd., on FL 80 at I-75 exit 141, Coastal Marine Mart, East Fort Myers. Specializes in one-hour tours at 11 AM up the Orange River to spot manatees. Educational video viewing. Closed mid-April–October.

Sanibel-Captiva Conservation Foundation Center (239-472-2329; www.sccf .org), 3333 Sanibel-Captiva Rd., Sanibel Island. Hosts guided nature trail, beach walk, and island boat tours.

✦ **Tarpon Bay Explorers** (239-472-8900; www.tarponbayexplorers.com), 900 Tarpon Bay Rd., Sanibel Island. Naturalist-guided kayak, pontoon boat, and tram tours through J. N. "Ding" Darling National Wildlife Refuge and ✪ **Tarpon Bay.** Also canoe and kayak rentals, bike and boat rentals, and free lunchtime wildlife talks.

✳ Lodging

Maine may boast its bed & breakfasts, Vermont its historic inns, and Colorado its ski lodges. But when vacationers envision Florida, it's the beachside resorts that flash first through the mental slide projector. The Fort Myers/Sanibel coast has perfected this image of sun-and-sand abandon. Megaresorts are designed to keep guests (and their disposable income) on property. Not only can you eat lunch, rent a bike, and get a tennis lesson, you can hire a masseuse, charter a boat for a sunset sail, play golf, and enroll your child in Sandcastle Building 101. These destination resorts are in business to fulfill fantasies, and they spare no effort to achieve that goal.

Side by side with the resorts, you'll also find homey little cottages that have held their ground against buyouts and takeovers. Existing between the two extremes is a wide variety of high-rise condos, funky hotels, retirement resorts, mom-and-pop motels, fishing lodges, and inns. The recent economic downturn has had its effect on the destination, but island resort communities seem to withstand the pressure more so than many other parts of the state. The good news: It has frozen ever-rising lodging rates; some even have gone down a notch. Privately owned second homes and condominiums provide another source of upscale accommodations along the coast. For families and other groups, these can often be a better value than hotel rooms. Timeshare rental was practically invented on Sanibel Island, and you'll find plenty of these options still around. Vacation brokers who match visitors with such properties are listed under "Home & Condo Rentals" at the end of this section.

The highlights of Lee County hospitality listed here—alphabetically by town—include the best and freshest in the local industry. While spanning the range of endless possibilities, this list concentrates on those properties that break out of the skyscraping, wicker-and-floral mold. Toll-free 800, 888, or 877 reservation numbers, where available, are listed after local numbers.

Pricing codes are explained below. They are normally per unit/double occupancy. The range spans low- and high-season rates and standard to deluxe accommodations. Many resorts offer off-season packages at special rates and free lodging for children. Pricing does not include the 6 percent Florida sales tax. Some large resorts add service gratuities or maid charges, and Lee County imposes a 5 percent bed tax as well, which goes toward beach and environmental maintenance.

Rate Categories

Inexpensive	Up to $100
Moderate	$100 to $200
Expensive	$200 to $200
Very Expensive	$300 and up

An asterisk (°) after the pricing designation indicates that the rate includes at least a continental breakfast in the cost of lodging and occasionally other meals as described in the listing.

Note that under the Americans with Disabilities Act (ADA), accommodations built after January 26, 1993, and containing more than five rooms must be useable by people with disabilities. I have indicated only those small places that do not make such allowances.

ACCOMMODATIONS

Cabbage Key

✪ **Cabbage Key Inn** (239-283-2278; www.cabbagekey.com), P.O. Box 200, Pineland 33945. Cabbage Key appeals to vacationers seeking an authentic Old Florida experience. Built on an unbridged island atop an ancient shell mound, the inn and its guest accommodations are reminiscent of the 1930s, when novelist Mary Roberts Rinehart commissioned a home for her son and his bride made from native cypress and pine. Six cypress-paneled guest rooms in the inn and six cottages (two of them historic) accommodate overnighters. Four of the cottages have kitchens, and four have their own private docks. A couple of the cottages date back to the Rinehart era; the others are modern homes. The restaurant and its currency-papered bar attract boaters and water tours for lunch, but the island shuts down to a whisper come sundown. The inn can give you a list of boat charters from Captiva or Pine Island for transportation to and from the island. Boat rentals are available for day use. Moderate to Expensive (two-night minimum stay required).

Cape Coral

(((ŗ))) **Casa Loma Motel** (239-549-6000 or 877-227-2566; www.casalomamotel .com), 3608 Del Prado Blvd., 33904. If you're looking for a place to stay while enjoying the town's family attractions or somewhere less costly than the beaches, this tidy little property has its own charm—and canal-front views and docks in the bargain. Its 49 efficiencies are each stocked with a kitchenette containing a microwave, mini fridge, and stove top. Reclining chairs in some rooms and stylish motel furnishings provide comfort. Some porches and balconies overlook the canal and paved sundeck. Nicely landscaped grounds complement the Spanish villa architecture, with its red roof and arched balcony openings. A canalside pool and waterside tables and loungers on a tiki-covered deck offer scenic places to relax. Inexpensive to Moderate.

♂ ♪ (((ŗ))) **The Resort at Marina Village** (239-463-0559 or 888-372-9256; www.marinavillageresort.com), 5951 Silver King Blvd., 33914. In November 2009, Marina Village opened its sliding glass doors onto a stunning lobby with a magical, tubular waterfall and marble passage to the view of yachts, mangroves, and blue water of Tarpon Point Marina. Cape Coral's first luxury resort rises 19 stories high at the edge of mangrove estuary in the southwest part of town. Its inventory of 263 units includes studio accommodations and condos from one to three bedrooms. They showcase the finest furnishings in neutral tones, smart lamps and other decor accessories, stainless kitchen appliances, tile and marble bathrooms, and spacious comfort—up to 2,225 square feet inside. Built to green lodging standards, the resort's room key system turns on lights and air conditioning. The studios come with mini fridges and have access to communal laundry facilities. The condos have their own washer and dryer (full-size in the two- and three-bedroom units) in addition to a full kitchen and dining area. Adjoining condos and studio formats are also available. Sweeping balconies, many with views of the water, extend the living space. Although one could feel content just getting comfy and gazing at the panorama, the resort offers plenty of enticement to go out and enjoy its amenities. Perhaps its best idea was to offer a complimentary 40-passenger shuttle aboard the *Silver King* to Fort Myers Beach. The trip from mangrove to beach takes less than an hour. On campus, trendy Marker 92 Bar & Bistro, its flagship restaurant, serves breakfast, lunch, and dinner in a spacious bistro setting that spills out onto the harborside terrace and bar known as the Nauti Mermaid Dockside Bar & Grill. Expensive to Very Expensive.

Captiva Island

✪ **Jensen's Twin Palm Cottages & Marina** (239-472-5800; www.gocaptiva .com), 1507 Captiva Dr., 33924. One of Captiva's most affordable lodging options is also one of its homier places. You get an immediate sense of neighborliness on the grounds. Perhaps it has to do with its partiality to fisherfolk, demonstrated by its bayside docks, fishing charters, boat rentals, and bait supplies. I expected to find the accommodations in that same vein, where what's out in the water matters more than what's indoors. The 14 units look plain enough from the outside: white stucco cottages with tin roofs and a splash of blue trim. Each screened-in porch holds a plain picnic table. Inside, the one- and two-bedroom cottages are entirely cheery, with immaculate white board-and-bead walls, perky curtains, and simple, sturdy wooden furniture. The full kitchens are modern and spotless—nothing fishy about 'em. Just charming old-island style dressed up comfortably. Owners David, John, and Jimmy Jensen are known to make some music and entertain the local fishermen in the evenings. Moderate to Expensive.

✪ ♂ ✐ **South Seas Island Resort** (239-472-5111 or 800-965-7772; www .southseas.com), 5400 Plantation Rd., 33924. South Seas is historically one of the great destination resorts of Florida, where you can enter through the security gates and leave one week later without ever having gone off property. In 2006, it reopened after a two-year makeover following the 2004 hurricane season with added panache, but still a sea-oriented, islandy style. Celebrities have always craved its privacy and discretion. South Seas offers any type of getaway dwelling you could imagine, from tennis villas to beach cottages to harborside hotel rooms—nine different types of accommodations in all. Rooms are furnished with stylish, high-quality pieces, 32-inch LCD televisions, pillow-top beds, and other luxury appointments. The property monopolizes a third of the island with about 550 guest units—mostly privately owned—six poolside eateries; formal lounges; shops; a gorgeous gulfside, nine-hole golf course; a fitness center and spa; a yacht harbor; 19 swimming pools, including a mini waterpark with two slides; 18 tennis courts; boating; fishing; water-sports equipment rentals and lessons; excursion cruises; a recreation program and nature center for children; and 2.5 miles of beach. A free trolley takes guests around the 330-acre property, which is embraced on three sides by water. Very Expensive.

♂ ✐ (ᵞ) **'Tween Waters Inn** (239-472-5161 or 800-223-5865; www .tween-waters.com), 15941 Captiva Rd., 33924. 'Tween Waters spans the gap between beach cottage lodging and modern super resort. Built early in the 1930s, when wildlife patron Jay N. "Ding" Darling kept a cottage there, the property shows glints of Old Florida architecture (some of it rather unglamorous) and easygoing attitudes. Compact but complete, it holds 149 rooms, restored historic cottages, efficiencies, and apartments as well as restaurants, a bustling marina, tennis courts, a fitness center, and a swimming pool. Named for its location between two shores at Captiva's narrowest span, the inn lies across the road from a length of beach that is usually lightly populated because it lacks nearby public parking. Its marina, one of its best features, is the island's top water-sports center, with charters, tours, boat and canoe rentals, and the Canoe & Kayak Club. The Crow's Nest lounge provides the island's best nightlife. Continental breakfast is included in the rates. Expensive to Very Expensive.°

Fort Myers
(ᵞ) **Crowne Plaza Fort Myers** (239-482-2900 or 877-227-6963; www

myers.com), 13051 Bell Tower Dr., 33907. Close to the airport, shopping, dining, and movie theaters, one of this property's best features is the relaxation factor of the rooms, which provide sleep masks, lavender spray, nightlights, and massage showerheads. As part of the bustling Bell Tower entertainment area, Shoeless Joe's, the hotel's sports bar/restaurant, draws a lively crowd to its outdoor porch area and indoor pool-table scene off the spacious marble-floored lobby. Abstract metal and glass sculptures, a baby grand piano, and black-and-white checkered marble and granite flooring add touches of highbrow elegance to the entryway. Priority Club guests enjoy complimentary continental breakfasts, evening appetizers, cookies and milk at night, and drink specials in the fifth-floor concierge lounge. All 226 rooms have mini fridges. Airport transportation is free to all guests. Free high-speed wireless Internet access, a waterfall outdoor pool, and a small cardio fitness center are available. Moderate.

✪ ♂ ♪ (ᵠ) **Sanibel Harbour Marriott Resort & Spa** (239-466-4000 or 800-767-7777; www.sanibel-resort .com), 17260 Harbour Pointe Dr., 33908. Stunningly beautiful for a property its size, the Sanibel Harbour Resort, which came under Marriott management in 2009, capitalizes on Florida style and a spectacular location. Not actually on Sanibel Island as the name suggests, the resort's near 400 rooms, suites, and condos are located on a chin of land across San Carlos Bay from the island, on an inlet known as Sanibel Harbour. Half the units have water views of either the bay or nearby estuaries. The concierge-style Captiva Tower holds 107 of the rooms and suites, which are decorated in European style and shiny brass, and are more intimate and away from the bustle than the Sanibel Tower accommodations. Suites feature heavy four-poster beds and oversized bathtubs. The property encompasses four restaurants, a coffee bar–bistro, a buffet–dining yacht, three outdoor swimming pools, five lit Har-Tru tennis

SANIBEL HARBOUR MARRIOTT RESORT & SPA MAKES AN ELEGANT WATERFRONT STATEMENT.

courts, a complete spa, and a small bayside beach. Charley's Cabana Bar has a 280-degree view of the sea and a lovely, breezy cocktail patio. Dining runs the gamut from a coffee and pastry stand to a steakhouse and an intimate fine-dining venue. The fitness center, canoe/kayak trail, and watersports charters and rentals provide guests with a well-rounded menu of fitness and recreation options. Kid's Klub takes youngsters out for weekend activities. Moderate to Very Expensive.

Fort Myers Beach

(ɯ) **Harbour House** (239-463-0700 or 866-998-9250; www.harbourhouseattheinn.com), 450 Old San Carlos Blvd., 33931. This new kid on the block opened in January 2010 with surprisingly affordable prices for attentively decorated condos a short walk from the beach. All of its 34 studios and one- and two-bedroom condos are individually owned, but decorated with basically the same starfish-and-rattan motif. Their most outstanding feature is their paint job, mixing many bright colors within one unit behind hot pink doorways. All have kitchen facilities (some without ovens), flat-screen TVs, Wi-Fi access, and balconies or lanais. The views are not equal in all, but not great in any. With only three floors, you can't see the gulf, but some give glimpses of Matanzas Pass or the second-floor swimming pool and Jacuzzi. A community room with a full kitchen at the pool gives guests a cozy place to pour a cup of coffee, read the paper, get out of the sun, read e-mail, and hold gatherings. Two restaurants are across the street, with more en route to the beach. Moderate to Expensive.

✍ **The Outrigger Beach Resort** (239-463-3131 or 800-657-5659; www.outriggerfmb.com), 6200 Estero Blvd., 33931. The Outrigger Beach Resort occupies the quiet south end of Fort Myers Beach, where the sand flares wide and gorgeous and is protected by a sandbar that's a bird hangout. The 30-year-old, 144-room resort boasts a casual, unstructured vacationing style that works well for families. Activity centers around its white-fenced pool and tiki bar deck area, where guests can sun and mingle. Or you can rent water-sports equipment through the front desk. Rooms are compact, modern, and furnished simply. Five types of accommodations range from the traditional to efficiencies with full kitchens. Prices also depend on whether they're on the first or second floor and the quality of the view. Beach volleyball, a little café, a full-service restaurant across the street, and live entertainment keep the place vivacious. Moderate to Very Expensive.

✍ (ɯ) **Pink Shell Beach Resort & Spa** (239-463-6181 or 888-222-7465; www.pinkshell.com), 275 Estero Blvd., 33931. Set between bay waters and 1,500 feet of beach, the 12-acre property encompasses high-rise accommodation towers, an Octopool fantasy water feature with an underwater theme, and a world-class spa. Older Sanibel View Villas holds 60 gulfside kitchenette suites and Beach Villas 28 two-bedroom condos. Newer White Sand Villas has 92 one- and two-bedroom units with floor-to-ceiling gulf-facing windows and a central reception area with a mammoth stylized banyan tree "growing" through it. Captiva Villas, the fourth and newest building, contains another 43 units. All accommodations are privately owned and decorated in tasteful tropical style with a view of the wide, powdery beach and gulf. Three restaurants, a coffee shop/deli, three pools, boat docking, a kids' program, and a slew of watersports rentals and tours complete Pink Shell's reputation as a destination resort at the northern tip of Fort Myers Beach, away from the bustle of the Times Square area. Moderate to Very Expensive.

☙ **Silver Sands Villas** (239-463-2755 or 800-603-0501; www.silver sands-villas.com), 1207 Estero Blvd., 33931. In Fort Myers Beach, not much can be found that one could describe as charming, but here's a notable exception. Its assemblage of 20 one- and two-bedroom, circa-1935 cottages with pale yellow paint jobs and tin roofs make a strong personality statement. Inside they are simple in character, with white wainscoting and yellow walls, full kitchens in all but three units (all of which have refrigerators; two also have microwaves), and Old Florida–style porches. The compact, pet-friendly property, bordered by a canal and within walking distance of the beach, holds complimentary docking for guests, a small pool, a fountain courtyard, a huge shady banyan tree, canal-front views, outdoor tables, gas grills, and laundry facilities—all behind a picket fence and hibiscus hedge right on the happening strip of Estero Boulevard, from where you hardly notice it. It's very congenial and convenient while feeling deliciously hidden away. Inexpensive to Expensive.

Pine Island

☙ **Bridge Water Inn** (239-283-2423 or 800-378-7666; www.bridgewaterinn .com), 4331 Pine Island Rd., Matlacha 33909. In fish-frenzied Pine Island, Matlacha has its share of fishing cottages where what matters is what's biting. Fishing types will also like this tropically bright, nine-unit roadside lodge because its wraparound covered deck hangs over the water. Rooms and efficiencies, decorated with distinct style and comfort, open up onto the deck, so you can step right out the door and cast. Suites 2 and 3 have the best

views. With leather furniture and eye-catching colors (check out the hanging tropical bird planters made in Colombia from recycled tires), Bridge Water is a step up from other Matlacha accommodations. Restaurants, fish markets, shops, and galleries are within walking distance. Moderate to Expensive.

Sanibel Island

✪ ♨ (ᵗ) **Gulf Breeze Cottages and Motel** (239-472-1626 or 800-388-2842; www.gbreeze.com), 1081 Shell Basket Ln., 33957. The address is Shell Basket Lane, and this place is just that delightful and seashell oriented. A dozen classic cottages, efficiencies, and duplexes make for the ideal barefoot beach vacation. Shuffleboard, a picnic pavilion with barbecue grills, and a station where you can clean your shells and fish provide outdoor-time amenities. Sandi and Charley Hutchings, the grandma and grandpa who have owned Gulf Breeze for more than 30 years, love children and treat their guests like family. This property blends old island with new, holding its ground amid low-rise, concrete neighbors. Sea grapes, bougainvillea, Bahama shades, carved balustrades, lattice, and fish-scale siding add a fairy-tale quality. Moderate to Very Expensive (for up to six people).

✪ (ᵗ) **Island Inn** (239-472-1561 or 800-851-5088; www.islandinnsanibel .com), 3111 W. Gulf Dr., 33957. Sanibel's only historic lodging—more than 100 years old—displays all the refinement of Florida's great old inns and hotels but without the snobbery. It has the same congenial and relaxed atmosphere that Granny Matthews, a Sanibel matriarch of renown, created at the turn of the 20th century when she entertained the whole island (including guests from other resorts) at Saturday night barbecues. She also initiated the Sanibel Shell Fair as a way to keep guests busy; she hosted it in the lobby, where white wicker, French doors, a windowed dining room, a fireplace, and shell displays now give an immediate impression of immaculate spaciousness and island graciousness. During the winter season (mid-December– mid-April), a breakfast buffet is available free to guests. In summer, rates include continental breakfast. Lodging includes 54 rooms and nine cottages, which have one to three bedrooms. Rooms have either full kitchens or refrigerators only and can be combined into suites. The resort doesn't pretend to furnish extravagantly; all is done in uncontrived old-island style. That does not translate into shoddiness, however. The Island Inn is owned by shareholders who reinvest profits for constant upgrading. Decor is cheerful, comfortable, and impeccably maintained. Outside lodge room doors sits a wooden table where guests display their shell finds for others to peruse and admire. It's an Island Inn tradition. The atmosphere is saturated with conviviality. Dinner at Traditions (closed some months during the off-season) is announced by the blowing of a conch shell. Outdoors, native vegetation landscapes tin-roofed structures. A butterfly garden frames a croquet court, a swimming pool sits squarely on the beach, and volleyball, tennis, and shuffleboard provide recreation. As a recent nod to technology, the inn now provides free Internet access throughout the property. Moderate to Expensive° (minimum stay for cottages).

((ɪ)) **Sanibel's Seaside Inn** (239-472-1400 or 866-565-5092; www.seasideinn .com), 541 E. Gulf Dr., 33957. I recommend this place to visitors looking for intimacy on the beach without great extravagance. A measure of Key West—banana yellow tints, tin roofs, and gingerbread-trimmed balconies— creates Seaside Inn's old-island charm.

ISLAND INN WEARS ITS 100-PLUS YEARS GRACIOUSLY.

It's the kind of place where you kick off your shoes the first day and don't find them again until you're packing to leave. Kitchen facilities and DVDs come in every studio, beach cottage, and one-, two-, and three-bedroom suite, of which there are 32 in all. A swimming pool, brick-paved deck, complimentary continental breakfast (delivered to your door if you so desire), video- and book-lending library, complimentary bike use, and tropical appointments complete the picture of seaside coziness. Use of facilities and amenities at Seaside Inn's sister resorts, including Sundial Beach Resort and Sanibel Inn, is available free of charge to guests. An inter-resort trolley provides transportation. Expensive to Very Expensive.*

✪ 🖉 ((ψ)) **Sundial Beach Resort** (239-472-4151 or 866-565-5093; www.sundialresort.com), 1451 Middle Gulf Dr., 33957. Sundial promises the perfection of a worry-free vacation. Sanibel's fine shelling beach is the focus of the 20-acre resort, which takes its name from a species of shell. In the stunning lobby, a sundial shell mosaic is inset in a marble floor. The resort provides extensive recreation, with 12 tennis courts, five heated swimming pools, bike and beach rental concessions, a fitness center, game room, recreation programs, and an eco-center complete with touch tank. The lavish main building houses one of two bar-and-grills; the second is located poolside. Less stylish, low-rise condo buildings are camouflaged by well-maintained vegetation and hold 270 fully equipped one- and two-bedroom units. Decorated in tropical array and natural rattan, the units take advantage of gulf or garden views. Given its high level of service, the Sundial is one of the area's least pretentious and most comfortable properties, especially for families. Expensive to Very Expensive.

((ψ)) **West Wind Inn** (239-472-1541 or 800-824-0476; http://westwindinn.com), 3345 W. Gulf Dr., 33957. "Friendliness and cleanliness" is its motto—old-fashioned values for a Sanibel resort that started in the late 1960s. But this casual favorite looks anything but worn-out. The four lodging buildings of the two-story low-rise cluster beachside, and most of its 103 rooms have at least a glimpse of the gulf. Many overlook the pool and its fun-time pool bar, which, like the rest of the buildings, shows a bit of Mediterranean flair with tile embellishments and a red barrel–tile roof. The pool bar serves lunch, or guests can get out of the weather and dine in the Normandie restaurant for breakfast, lunch, and, on in-season weekends, dinner. Rooms, decorated demurely in plantation prints, come with a kitchenette or small refrigerator and microwave oven. All rooms have DVD players and free access to wireless Internet service. For recreational purposes, there are two tennis courts, free use of balls and racquets, a fish- and shell-cleaning tiki hut, a lovely butterfly garden, and 500 feet of gorgeous beach. Expensive to Very Expensive.

Useppa Island

✪ **Collier Inn & Cottages** (239-283-1061; www.useppa.com), P.O. Box 640, Bokeelia 33922. Used to be that only club members could enjoy the delicious privacy and historic elitism of Useppa Island. Once an escape for turn-of-the-20th-century celebrities, the island remains exclusive and aloof from the world. Now, if you can afford the price, you can be admitted onto the carefully guarded island by checking into the Collier Inn. The 100-year-old building, the original circa-1900 home of Barron Collier's Izaak Walton Club, holds seven elegant rooms and suites individually designed for classic mood and comfort; historic cottages and the marina reception building add another four units. Plus, there are privately owned two- and three-bedroom cottages with kitchens available. Guests have access to the Useppa Island Club's full-service marina, Har-Tru tennis courts, swimming pool, man-made beach, croquet, outdoor chess, and fitness center. The pink-paved walkway around the island takes you past historic cottages, bounteous gardens, an ancient shell mound, and the 100-acre island's intriguing historical museum. Collier Inn Restaurant serves daily meals; a continental breakfast buffet is included for accommodations without kitchen facilities. Price: Expensive to Very Expensive* (minimum stay for cottages and homes; for all accommodations on weekends and holidays).

HOME & CONDO RENTALS

Leisure American Vacation Rentals (239-463-3178 or 800-741-5694; www.leisureamerican.com), 2450 Estero Blvd., Fort Myers Beach 33931. Condos, cottages, and homes in Fort Myers and Fort Myers Beach.

Sanibel & Captiva Accommodations (239-472-3191 or 800-237-6004; www.sanibelaccom.com), 2341 Palm Ridge Rd., Sanibel 33957. Has a catalog of condo and home rentals on Sanibel and Captiva Islands available online.

RV RESORTS Fort Myers–Pine

Island KOA (239-283-2415 or 800-562-8505; www.pineislandkoa.com), 5120 Stringfellow Rd., St. James City 33956. Resort has 371 sites, cabins, a pool, saunas, hot tub, exercise room, tennis court, shuffleboard, horseshoes, lake fishing, and free bus to the beach a couple times a week.

Red Coconut RV Resort (239-463-7200 or 888-262-6226; www.redcoconut.com), 3001 Estero Blvd., Fort Myers Beach 33931. Right on the beach but packed in a bit tightly; 250 full hook-up sites, on-site trailer rentals, laundry, shuffleboard, and cable TV. Call for reservations.

✳ Where to Eat

The Island Coast is home to two of the nation's shellfish capitals. Shrimp—that monarch of edible crustaceans—reigns in Fort Myers Beach, where a fleet of shrimp boats is headquartered and an annual festival pays homage to America's favorite seafood. The sweet, pink gulf shrimp is the trademark culinary delight of the town and its environs.

THE COLLIER INN HAS BEEN WELCOMING BY-BOAT TRAVELERS SINCE THE EARLY 20TH CENTURY.

The fish markets of Pine Island, an important commercial fishing and transshipment center, sell all sorts of fresh seafood—oysters, shrimp, scallops, snapper, catfish, mullet—but the signature seafood is the blue crab and stone crab that come from local waters.

The following listings cover the variety of Island Coast feasting in these price categories:

Inexpensive	Up to $15
Moderate	$15 to $25
Expensive	$25 to $35
Very Expensive	$35 or more

Cost categories are based on the range of dinner entrée prices, or, if dinner is not served, on lunch entrées. Those restaurants listed with "Healthy Selections" usually mark such on their menu.

Note: Florida law forbids smoking inside all restaurants and bars serving food. Smoking is permitted only in restaurants with outdoor seating.

Cabbage Key

✪ **Cabbage Key Inn** (239-283-2278; www.cabbagekey.com), P.O. Box 200, Pineland 33945. Accessible only by boat and still funky after all these years, Cabbage Key has a reputation among boaters as a safe haven for a beer, a cheeseburger, and all-around friendliness. Everyone's in a good mood at Cabbage Key, particularly the bartender and wait staff (despite their sassy T-shirts that answer all the questions they get asked daily). Lunch—the most popular meal—consists of shrimp, salads, stone crab in season, burgers, sandwiches, and key lime pie. Tour boats bring in crowds, so it can get crazy, and waits for a table are often a beer-sodden affair. (If you're driving the boat, you may wish to opt for a walk around the nature trail instead.) Dinner is much quieter, and

the local fish couldn't get any fresher. I recently had grouper with a chipotle sauce drizzle and nearly swooned; it ruined me for grouper anywhere else. The shrimp scampi on pasta is another good bet. So are the Bloody Marys. Moderate to Expensive. No handicap access. Reservations required for dinner.

Cape Coral

🦎 ᴛ **Iguana Mia** (239-945-7755; www.iguanamia.com), 1027 E. Cape Coral Pkwy. This, the original Iguana Mia, spawned others in Fort Myers and Bonita Springs, but we like this one best, even if it means we have to cross the bridge to Cape Coral and pay a toll to get there. It's the most down-to-earth of the three. Sure, it's just as flashy, with its electric-green exterior paint job and nicely rendered interior Mexican frescos, but it retains some of the unpretentious lunchroom ambiance it started out with. Stacked cases of Mexican beer still count as decor elements. And most importantly, the food is flat-out better. Things seem more rushed at the newer places; here it's mañana paced. My husband invariably orders the sour cream chicken chimichanga, a specialty. I—usually already half full from shoveling in huge gobs of the salsa I can't resist with warm, crunchy tortilla chips—like the veggie burrito, nachos, quesadilla, or Pedro's tamales. You're bound to find something you like on the menu—it's huge and lets you do some of your own meal engineering. Inexpensive. No reservations. Closed Sunday and Monday in summer.

Rumrunners (239-542-0200; www.capeharbourdining.com), 5848 Cape Harbour Dr., at the Cape Harbour Marina. Operated by the people who wow us at Bistro 41 in Fort Myers, it has its own imaginative style and overlooks a mangrove waterway in the midst of recent upmarket development. Even better: Prices are surprisingly affordable for such specialties as seafood potpie—chock-full of shrimp, scallops, and crab with a creamy lobster sauce and a flaky pastry sitting atop it. We've sampled a wide variety of starters, main courses, and desserts besides the potpie and have had no complaints except that the calamari could be crispier. In the "loved it" category: chicken quesadilla with blackened tomato "jam," salsa fresca, and cumin-scented crème fraîche; Buffalo chicken tossed with Gorgonzola crema; spinach and blue cheese salad; vodka penne; angel hair pasta generously decorated with shrimp, scallops, mussels, and torn basil; and warm chocolate bread pudding (did I detect a splash of rum in there?). Pasta dishes are available in full and half portions. The building at first seems cold and oversized, but once you're sitting in the glassed room or on the deck overlooking the water, you immediately warm to the location. Inexpensive to Moderate. No handicap access. Reservations accepted.

❂ ♿ **Siam Hut** (239-945-4247), 4521 Del Prado Blvd. A long-standing favorite in Cape Coral, Siam Hut's affordability is matched by its versatility and authentic goodness. You basically can design your own meal from the noodles, stir-fried, curry, and fried rice sections. For instance, I've tried the pad kee mao, a stir-fried rice-noodle dish of basil, colorful and crunchy veggies, and chili paste. I had a choice of tofu, beef, pork, chicken, shrimp, or squid to centerpiece that, and I chose the last—tender, tasty rings set afire by the seasonings. (You also get to pick your degree of spiciness.) The coconut milk green curry also turned out to make a flavorful, filling, and bargain lunch with the inclusion of the day's soup and a small romaine and carrot salad dressed in a tasty peanut vinaigrette. Dinners, which do not come with soup and salad, include specialties such as fried-crispy frog legs with garlic and black pepper, fried whole tilapia in a variety of preparations, and Thai entrée salads. Go traditional and sit at a floor table on pillows that support your back, or choose one of the more plentiful booths or standard

RUMRUNNERS CATERS TO BOAT- AND DRIVE-IN GUESTS LOOKING FOR CREATIVE CUISINE AND FINE VIEWS.

tables and chairs. Inexpensive. No reservations. Closed Sunday and lunch Saturday. Minimum $10 charge for credit cards.

Captiva Island

In recent years, one owner has bought up the majority of restaurants in downtown Captiva, resulting in lack of competition and growing mediocrity. Luckily a few individually owned and resort restaurants remain that reach further.

✄ **The Bubble Room** (239-472-5558; www.bubbleroomrestaurant.com), 15001 Captiva Dr. OK, so this too is tourist food, but the Bubble Room is so Captiva—something you have to experience once. It's especially fun to take kids there. The quirkiness begins outside, where bubbles bedeck the kitsch-cottage structure and lawn gnomes greet you. Inside, the tables are glass-topped showcases filled with jacks, Monopoly money, comic books, dominoes, and assorted toys from the past. A Christmas elves scene, circus plaques, Betty Boop, celebrity photos, a plaster hippo's mouth, and other nostalgic memorabilia fill every wall, phone booth, bathroom door, nook, and cranny. A toy train runs under the ceiling in one of its five rooms, and servers—Bubble Scouts—wear goofy hats. So that's the atmosphere—and you've gotta see it for yourself. The menu continues the frivolity. At lunch, Mae West's is a grilled chicken breast sandwich. The Piggly Wiggly barbecued pork sandwich I ordered was delicious, from the sweet bun to the coleslaw heaped on the messy meat. Dinner's Duck Ellington is a tasty rendition of roasted duck with orange and banana sauce. Other snappily titled dishes include Beignet Goodman (crispy light grouper fingers), Smoke Gets in Your Eyes (grilled or blackened fresh catch), and Eddie Fisher-

man (grouper topped with Ritz cracker crumbs and pecans, then steamed in a bag). The service is exceptional, considering the tight quarters and volume of business. Other things for which the Bubble Room is known are its basket of bubble bread (yum! cream cheesy), its sticky buns with dinner, and its fabulous desserts. You must leave room for a huge slab of moist and delicious red-velvet cake, the rich almond-studded orange crunch cake, or any of the other many tempting selections. Moderate to Expensive. Limited handicap access. No reservations.

✄ **Mucky Duck** (239-472-3434; www.muckyduck.com), 11546 Andy Rosse Ln. A Captiva dining landmark since 1976, its name is a parody of English pubs, and the goofy attitude and gags don't end there. Despite its name, there's little British influence other than fish 'n' chips. Barbecue shrimp with bacon is a signature dish for lunch and dinner, demonstrating the importance of seafood at this popular beachside spot. At lunchtime, it's wise to plan on spending some beach time while you wait for your name to be called. The fried grouper sandwich is huge, and the grilled meat loaf sandwich a tasty alternative to fish. At dinner, come early for sunset and expect an hour or so wait in season. If the name makes you crave duck, there is a roasted duckling l'orange dish on the dinner menu, along with some other landlubber options. Seafood-lovers should go for the crabcakes, mahimahi with dill cream sauce, scallops au gratin, or shrimp sampler. The key lime pie comes frozen, which is especially refreshing in the summer. The bar does serve vodka drinks, made with 40-proof liquor. Inexpensive to Moderate. Handicap access difficult; some steps to negotiate, and tight quarters. No reservations. Closed Sunday.

Estero

⊕ ✦ **Blue Water Bistro** (239-949-2583; www.gr8food.net), 23151 Village Shops Way, Suite 109, at Coconut Point Center. Successful Naples restaurateur Skip Quillen (Chops City Grill, Bistro 821) opened Blue Water Bistro with an old concept, but one new for him: seafood. He has put his thumbprint on it by using sauces and products with zing. A global novelty of fish selections, burgers, and steaks offers enough diversity to satisfy the whims of the restaurant's large indoor and outdoor capacity. Begin with the long, tall drink menu, filled with the expected to the unexpected in beers, wines, tequilas, martinis, shots, and other fun quaffs. The bar dominates the modern, semicircular space, so it's no surprise that drinking is as much a priority here as dining—everything from a bubble gum martini to a passion fruit mojito. Start off with a sushi roll or "morning after" mussels steamed Bloody Mary style (the alcohol infusion doesn't end with the drink menu here). House specialties include king crab Alfredo, lobster-crab cakes, chipotle BBQ baby back ribs, and miso-glazed sea bass with wasabi crumb crust. The blackened salmon with bourbon and brown sugar glaze sounded sweet, but I was pleasantly surprised at the subtleness of the flavors, particularly when combined with the buttery jalapeño-pecan sauce. For those who prefer less fussy seafood and meat, the day's catches and four chops (including a "chicken chop") come simply grilled. Early dining and all-night bar menus are available and affordable. Inexpensive to Expensive. Reservations accepted.

⊕ ✦ **Blu Sushi** (239-334-2583; www.blusushi.com), 10045 Gulf Center Dr., at Gulf Coast Town Center. Started in Fort Myers, Blu Sushi has spun off into a location in Estero, where it has become even more popular than its original location. The restaurant is as blue and cutting edge as its name. Outdoor seating, great people-watching, and fun martinis (in blue-stemmed glasses, of course), sakes, and saketinis are part of the adventure. Try the mango X-rated martini or the Asian pear saketini for something exotic. Appealing to even the less-than-enthusiastic sushi fan, the specialty rolls fuse Japanese and American favorites for the tastiest, most creative sushi this town has ever seen. The clear winner, LoyalTV.com, stuffs chopped tuna, chunks of avocado, cucumber, and flying fish roe into a thick rice wrapping. Other recommendations from the 22 varieties of specialty rolls: Lava Drops (chopped crab and spicy mayo with cream cheese deep-fried and brushed with eel sauce), the Bahama (spicy conch, cucumber, and smelt roe), and Fire Dragon (spicy tuna inside out with tilapia and avocado on top). The seaweed salad is tasty and proportioned to share as an appetizer; the king miso soup adds crabmeat to the traditional. Or try the tuna tataki, carpaccio-thin slices of lightly seared top-quality tuna wading in a pool of ponzu sauce. Dessert comes liquid and spiked only, and includes such offerings as Iced Mocha Chai T-latte (green tea vodka, chai liqueur, and more), Dreadlock Holiday (vanilla rum, mint Irish cream, chocolate liqueur, and coffee), and Butterfly Kisses and Bites (chocolate vodka, butterscotch, and toffee liqueur). Inexpensive. No reservations.

Fort Myers

✦ **Bistro 41** (239-466-4141; www.bistro41.com), 13499 S. Cleveland Ave. #143, at Bell Tower Mall. Whether you choose a sidewalk table looking out at Saks Fifth Avenue or an indoor booth between brightly painted walls, Bistro 41 feels festive and chic.

The regular dinner menu highlights oak-grilled specialties such as signature rosemary-marinated rotisserie chicken and filet mignon with a Gorgonzola pesto crust and sun-dried cherry demiglace. Other eclectic offerings include mussels simmered with sambal and harissa paste, berry and goat cheese salad, herbed potato-crusted salmon, and shrimp and scallop risotto. To further complicate decision-making, a separate menu presents a tableau of specials from which we typically order and are always pleasantly surprised. For lunch, ready-to-drop shoppers renourish on the grilled lobster melt half-sandwich with tomato-Parmesan soup, smoked salmon croissant sandwich with Boursin and bacon, pulled chicken pizzetta, and crabcakes with red caramelized onions. This is a favorite of ours both for dinner *à deux* and girls' gatherings. Moderate to Expensive. Reservations accepted.

&. **Chile Ranchero** (239-275-0505), 11751 S. Cleveland Ave. #18, in Family Thrift Center. A refreshing departure from Tex-Mex chains, Chile Ranchero serves home-cooked, fresh-tasting, affordable specialties designed for the local Hispanic population. Tongue or liver taco, anyone? That aside, most dishes are suited also to less adventurous gringo palates: homemade nachos with a tongue-tingling peppery salsa, bean soup, huge burritos, sautéed sirloin with tomatillo sauce, grilled chicken with guacamole and roasted tomato sauce, fried tilapia, shrimp à la diabla, and flan. Try the nacho de ceviche, topped with slices of avocado, for a change of pace and taste. Wash it down with a Modelo Especial or Pacifico beer. Mexican music plays in the background, and Spanish-speaking staff efficiently attend at the spacious, pleasant café with its red-and-white checked oilcloth and painted cement floor. Mariachi bands perform on weekends. Inexpensive. No reservations.

&. **El Patio Restaurant** (239-278-3303), 4444 Cleveland Ave., at Regency Square. This strip-mall place packs 'em in—Peruvians, gringos, families alike—for an exotic taste of Peruvian cuisine, known for the invention of ceviche, its great variety of corn, and its Asian influence. El Patio's extensive menu sweeps the country's specialties, starting with exotic soups such as hen broth with noodles, potatoes, and eggs, and a green rice and seafood soup. Appetizers include tamales, avocado stuffed with chicken or seafood, giant white corn with cheese, and mashed potatoes stuffed with seafood. Ceviche—seafood marinated in lime juice, which causes a chemical reaction that seems to cook the fish—comes as an entrée instead of an appetizer, as we are increasingly seeing it in mainstream restaurants. Varieties include fish, mussels, shrimp, and combinations thereof. I chose the fish and, when given a choice by our charming Peruvian waiter, asked for it hot (as in spicy; the dish itself is always served chilled). It came with two cold, yamlike vegetables and a lettuce leaf filled with corn fries—roasted and salted large-kernel corn, somewhat akin to corn nuts but starchier and not as hard. They're a favorite bar snack in Peruvian eateries. The ceviche, garnished simply with red onion slices, was outstanding. Another of my favorite dishes, hearty *tacu tacu*, has a fried rice base that you can customize with choice of beans and meat or seafood. I did lentils with beef, which came served with toppings of sautéed onions and chunks of tomatoes. Other entrées span seafood and beef realms, and include a specialty marinated fish dish with spicy cream sauce, stir-fried rice with beans and steak, paella, and Peruvian-style spaghetti with beef. For dessert, there are Peruvian versions of doughnuts, flan, and more. Inexpensive. No reservations.

❧ **Nomiki's Plakka** (239-433-5659), 12901-3 McGregor Blvd. The food and atmosphere here are genuine Greek—straight out of *My Big Fat Greek Wedding*. Walls match the color of Mediterranean skies, with murals and pictures of Greece and her islands to prove it. Greek art and black lace under glass top the tables lined up around the kitchen window and a small market of Greek food products. Greek knickknacks, lattice, and faux grapevines add to that inimitable Greek-American style. With a few nods to American palates, most of the menu describes Greek specialties such as *spanakopita* (baked spinach and feta pie), Greek and *souvlaki* salads, *gyros*, *pastisio*, *moussake*, *dolmathes*, roast leg of lamb, pan-fried smelt, octopus, and shrimp sautéed in tomato-ouzo sauce with melted feta. Desserts sound Greek to me—except for the *baklava* and rice pudding: *yalaktobouriko*, *kataif*, *melfr*. They look yummy. There's even a *baklava* sundae. Beer and wine also come from Greece, along with American selections. Inexpensive to Moderate. Restaurant has handicap access; restrooms do not. No reservations.

⚓ **Saigon Paris Bistro** (239-936-2233; www.frenchroastcafe.net), 12995 S. Cleveland Ave., Suite 118, at Pinebrook Park Plaza. The fine French food here is delightfully affordable, but the best deal is the lunchtime Vietnamese specials. I favor the grilled beef wrapped in grape leaves (exquisitely seasoned with garlic, ginger, and lemongrass) over rice vermicelli—one of 23 selections. For $8.95, I also get delicate spring rolls with a light sweet-sour dip and all that the menu promised in flying flavors. The rest of the

lunch menu offers a typical and full complement of salads, sandwiches, and burgers. Crêpes are available for breakfast and lunch; I can recommend the turkey Dijon with Swiss cheese. Dinner in this cozy, elegant setting of fireplace, arches, and columns offers Vietnamese and classic French dishes such as tableside-flamed steak Diane, snapper provençal, breast of duck Chambord, and crêpes à la Grand Marnier (made tableside). Despite its mundane elevated view of a parking lot, this place achieves romance and excels at all it prepares. Moderate to Expensive. Reservations accepted. Closed for breakfast Monday and Wednesday–Saturday.

✪ ⚓ ♿ **The Veranda** (239-332-2065; www.verandarestaurant.com), 2122 Second St. My husband and I had our first "big" dinner date at The Veranda, so it will always be one of my favorites—but not solely for sentimental reasons. Victorian trappings and Southern charm create an atmosphere of romance in a historic-home setting. Occupying two early 20th-century houses, the Veranda is a place for business lunches and special-occasion dinners. The dining room huddles around a two-sided redbrick fireplace and looks out on a cobblestone garden courtyard, separated from traffic by showy greenery and a white fence. Historic Fort Myers photos and well-stocked wine cases line the dark-wood bar. Start with something unusual from The Veranda's appetizer board—perhaps the superb blue crabcakes, artichoke fritters stuffed with blue crab and topped with béarnaise sauce, or Southern grit cakes with pepper jack cheese and grilled andouille sausage. Entrées are traditional but exceed the ordinary. Tender medallions of filet are dressed Southern-style in a rich, smoky, sour-mash whiskey sauce. Rosemary merlot sauce complements the

THE VERANDA INFUSES CREATIVITY INTO SOUTHERN CUISINE.

rack of New Zealand lamb. Tender crawfish top pan-seared yellowtail snapper. Daily specials typically include fresh seafood catches, and the menu changes to reflect the seasons. Lunches span the spectrum from specialties such as chicken picatta or pasta to a grilled portobello sandwich or soup and salad. Desserts wilt willpower with such temptations as chocolate pâté on raspberry coulis, peanut-butter-fudge pie, and Baileys cheesecake. Expensive to Very Expensive. Reservations recommended. Closed for Saturday lunch, Sunday lunch and dinner.

& **Vino de Notte** (239-322-1800), 1520 Broadway, downtown at Hotel Indigo. Its name means "night of wine," but you don't have to wait 'til dinner to try its intriguing list of Italian vintages, most offered by the glass, including some sparkling varieties. Pair up with some antipasti (veal and ricotta meatballs with tomato cream or olive tapenade and white bean purée with crostini, for instance), salad such as the tasty roasted golden beets with goat cheese or shaved fennel with olives and lemon vinaigrette, or panini (the smoked turkey with portobello is a good choice). Other options include pizza (fennel sausage and broccoli rabe, perhaps?), pasta from spaghetti Bolognaise to proscuitto- and Gorgonzola-stuffed ravioli, and entrées such as oven-roasted striped bass with blood orange and citrus butter, olive oil poached salmon over asparagus risotto, or veal chop saltimbocca. For dessert, there's ricotta cheesecake with grappa-soaked berries, gelato, and more. If you choose the gooey rich chocolate cake and ice cream, make sure you have someone with which to share it. Bright with windows looking onto the street and a historic arcade, Vino de Notte is part of the Hotel Indigo complex. Moderate. Reservations accepted.

Fort Myers Beach

Locals go to Fort Myers Beach expecting fresh seafood and reasonable prices. It's known more for fun dining and waterfront views than for culinary innovation, and menus are fairly predictable.

& **Bayfront Bistro** (239-463-3663; www.bayfrontbistro.com), 4761 Estero Blvd., at Snook Bight Marina behind Publix. To break away from Fort Myers Beach's typical fried shrimp mold, this one takes you to a higher level of culinary daring. Literally, the new waterside restaurant sits elevated at the second level overlooking the marina's boats and unadulterated mangroves across the bay. Opt for patio seating or air-conditioning. Inside, staggered levels give everyone an eyeful around a commanding bar with a striking snook sculpture that ties in with the location. An upscale marina calls for an upscale restaurant, and the clientele here is as attractive as the wood and leather setting with cobalt blue accents. The menu lives up to the location, specializing in such seafood creations as pan-seared grouper with sage caper brown butter, and crispy yellowtail snapper and pancetta lardoons. The lunch and dinner menus do have an annoying habit of often being vague about the type of fish you're getting—the ceviche starter, for instance. When I asked what the "local fish" was in the fish tacos, my waiter told me either cod or haddock, neither of which is local. That aside, steaks, chops, ribs, and Gorgonzola tortellini round out the menu for non-seafood-lovers. Moderate to Expensive. Reservations accepted.

& ∅ & **JoJo's at the Beach** (239-463-6181 or 888-847-8939; www.pinkshell .com), 275 Estero Blvd., at Pink Shell Beach Resort. Sort of a well-kept secret, the restaurant at Pink Shell has everything going for it: On a crazy busy day in high season, I found a poolside table without any problem; the food shows more character than most Fort Myers Beach restaurants; it was much more affordable than I expected; and you can't beat the atmosphere of this quirky Octopool setting and funky Bongo's bar. I was delighted to find

unusual options that made my decision-making difficult, but was more than happy with the Asian club at lunch—a pressed baguette holding shredded pork, ham, sweet ginger carrots, spicy pickled cucumbers, and wasabi mayo. It provided just the right combination of fire, sweet, and crunch. Other lunch items include a jerk chicken sandwich with pepper jack cheese, and Mediterranean chopped salad with sundried tomatoes, artichoke hearts, and kalamata olives. Appetizers on both lunch and dinner menus kick off the meal in style: microbrew onion rings, grilled lemongrass chicken sticks, black bean cakes, and rum barbecue chicken quesadilla, for instance. Dinner specialties include lemongrass-marinated chicken breast, seafood Cobb salad, and a four-cheese (asiago, bleu, and two types of cheddar) mac 'n' cheese with shrimp, scallops, and crab. Wait! Don't fill up yet! There's warm banana chocolate chip bread pudding and crème brûlée cheesecake you'll want to try. If you prefer not to sit poolside, climb the stairs to the surfboard-themed, open-walled dining room above. Inexpensive to Moderate. No reservations.

& ∅ & **Matanzas Inn** (239-463-3838; www.matanzasrestaurant.com), 416 Crescent St. When I think of Fort Myers Beach, I think of three things: shrimp, boats, and water. Matanzas Inn embodies the laid-back, free-spirited soul of the "the Beach" with its ramshackle look and landmark position in the shadow of the high bridge, where boat traffic, dolphin antics, and aerial bird shows provide entertainment whether you're sitting inside or out. I invariably order fried shrimp when I sit down to a meal here, despite the fact that the menu comprehensively stretches beyond Fort Myers Beach's trademark dish. I can depend on its crunch and freshness. It appears on both the lunch and dinner menu.

Other worthy considerations: the steamer platter, grouper stuffed with seafood and provolone, crunchy grouper (coated with cornflakes), barbeque shrimp, and baby back ribs. The key lime pie is well worth the calories—creamy, and, like Fort Myers Beach, just tart enough. Inexpensive to Moderate. No reservations.

Pine Island

🐾 ♿ **Red's Fresh Seafood House & Tavern** (239-283-4412; www.reds freshseafoodhouse.com), 10880 Stringfellow Rd., Bokeelia. This barn red, red-hot Pine Island sensation gives you page after page of options, highlighting seafood but covering all bases from a chipotle chicken sandwich and burritos to Tuscan rib eye (marinated in rosemary, garlic, and olive oil), seafood pasta dishes, steamer platters, and filet mignon. If you doubt that any one restaurant can do justice to more than 100 entrées, not counting salads and sandwiches, you haven't seen the nightly mobs at Red's. Locals crowd around the L-shaped bar and fill tables and booths that are all dressed in red (natch). Begin with an unusual martini off the extensive drink and wine list—something in root beer or strawberry cheesecake, perhaps? Two pages of starters include steamed shellfish, baked oysters, tuna carpaccio, and popular finger foods such as nachos, fried cheese, and ribs. Dinners come the old-fashioned way—with a choice of two salads or sides. The house salad with the ginger scallion vinaigrette and mashed butter pecan sweet potatoes are clear winners. For an entrée, I can highly recommend the linguine with shrimp and spinach-Gorgonzola sauce or the Mediterranean grouper en papillote. Everything tastes fresh and properly cooked, and the atmosphere bubbles with happy customers and servers. Inexpensive to Moderate. No reservations.

♿ **Tarpon Lodge Restaurant** (239-283-2517; www.tarponlodge.com), 13771 Waterfront Dr., Pineland. Before there was Tarpon Lodge, Pine Island dining projected an Old-Florida-meets-the-Midwest image. Since then, there's a creative, gifted force to reckon with. Set in a 1926 fishing lodge, banked with vintage wavy-glass windows looking out on the water, the restaurant brings on the freshness in every sense of the word. For lunch, the marinated portobello mushroom and goat-cheese sandwich, quesadilla, crab-cake sandwich, or shrimp and crab fettuccini gratify. Imaginative dressings and sides make the dishes; for example, a tasty garlic mayonnaise, potato salad, and coleslaw accompanied the crabcake sandwich, which was slightly heavy on breading but nicely seasoned. Try the hearty and fresh-tasting crab and roasted corn chowder for lunch or dinner. The succinct menu's dozen dinner entrées include vegetarian pasta, veal piccata, and beef tenderloin medallions wrapped in bacon and finished with demi-glace, plus the day's fresh catch and nightly specials. Here in this seafood kingdom, with its steep fishing heritage, you can't go wrong ordering the catch, or—thanks to the chef's savvy—anything else, for that matter. Moderate to Expensive. Reservations suggested.

Sanibel Island

✪ ♿ **Gramma Dot's Seaside Saloon** (239-472-8138), 634 N. Yachtsman, at Sanibel Marina. I have finally found it: the island's (perhaps all of Lee County's) best key lime pie. Flecks of lime zest give this creamy version its pucker power, and now I'm afraid I'm addicted. That's not all that makes this place popular among locals, boaters, and other visitors. Take in the view of luxury yachts in the harbor and savor the freshness of the seafood dishes to get the full picture. The curried lobster salad and fried grouper sandwich are top choices on the lunch menu, which is available until the little screened-porch eatery closes at 7:30 PM. (After 5 PM, lunch items go up $1 in price.) Salad-lovers can choose from a variety of different Caesars—fried oyster, grouper, shrimp, and popcorn shrimp. Winning entrées include the mesquite grouper, coconut shrimp, bacon-wrapped shrimp with BBQ sauce, and fried oysters. Portions are generous and accompanied by a tasty potato croquette, the house tartar sauce, fresh sautéed veggies, and fruit served in a chocolate cup molded in the shape of a scallop shell. Inexpensive to Expensive. No reservations.

&. **The Jacaranda** (239-472-1771; www.jacarandaonsanibel.com), 1223 Periwinkle Way. Restaurants come, go, and change formats quickly on Sanibel Island, but "the Jac" has remained constant and consistently fine for more than 20 years. Its menu—a modernized version of Continental with a strong lean toward seafood—gets tweaked to abide with the times, but the quality of execution puts this long-timer at the top of the island restaurant list. Islanders and visitors alike first get to know its bar, which is famous for its live music and dance floor. In the restaurant, the extensive drink and martini menu successfully segues from the bar scene to the artistry one finds from the kitchen. The Sanibel Rain martini kicked off our recent soiree with refreshing Rain Vodka and Cointreau. We led off with the SanCap Shrimp appetizer, a delightful threesome wallowing in spiced rum, coconut cream, and orange juice. From the dinner menu, divided between pasta (shrimp Alfredo, linguine DiMare, and so on), seafood specialties, and meat (such as cowboy steak, veal Rockefeller, and roast duckling)—we like the crabcakes

with honey mustard and plum sauces, and sesame crusted yellowfin tuna, done perfectly rare to my specifications and sided with wakame salad. Everything was fresh, flavorful, and just how it was supposed to be. The service was professional while entertaining, and all in all we enjoyed one of our most pleasurable meals in a very long time out on Sanibel. Expensive. Reservations accepted.

🦐 🎣 **Lazy Flamingo** (239-472-5353; www.lazyflamingo.com), 6520-C Pine Ave., at Blind Pass. This is the original Lazy Flamingo, which has spawned another on Sanibel's southeast end and others in the region. Look for a Pepto Bismol–pink building at Blind Pass, just before the bridge to Captiva. Neighborhood and nautical are the concepts behind this first Flamingo, where you order and pick up your own food at the counter, eat off plastic plates in the shape of scallop shells, and wipe your hands with paper towels from a roll at the table. The menu and ambiance have an essence of the Florida Keys, including the popular ring-and-hook game that originated in a bar down there. Conch fritters, clam pot, mesquite-grilled grouper, wings, prime-rib sandwich, and Caesar salad are some of the most popular menu items. Avoid the Dead Parrot Wings; they are inedibly searing to all but the most callused, but the regular chicken wings rank highest on the island. Most of the meals come with fries, but you can substitute a small Caesar salad, which is usually crisp and tasty. The place is small: about a dozen counter seats and a few booths plus some outdoor tables. For the same food but more room, shrimp-boat decor, and table service, try the Lazy Flamingo at 1036 Periwinkle Way (239-472-6939). Inexpensive to Moderate. No handicap access. No reservations.

&. **Timbers Restaurant & Fish Market** (239-472-3128; www.prawnbroker .com), 703 Tarpon Bay Rd. Glancing at the restaurant's regular daily menu might not convince you there's something special going on here. But take a look at the nightly specials; that's undoubtedly where you want to be. Regular specialties include crunchy grouper, broiled Florida lobster tail, scallops broiled or fried, steak, peel-and-eat steamed shrimp, and the triple shrimp platter with scampi, baked and stuffed with seafood, and crunchy style. The crunchy style is best, so you may want to skip the other tasters and sink your teeth into some of the finest, crispiest fried shrimp around. Daily specials showcase what's fresh in the market with your choice of preparation and sauce. The sesame tuna and yellowtail snapper with citrus beurre blanc are winners, when available. Dinners come with a choice of soup or salad (the Manhattan clam chowder rocks, add crab bisque for $1) and a starch. Desserts are homemade at a Fort Myers bakery. The key lime pie is just the right amount of tart, and the moist coconut cake? Plan to share or take half of it home. Inexpensive to Moderate. No reservations.

&. **Traders Store & Café** (239-472-7242), 1551 Periwinkle Way. This is the equivalent of performance art, where you become a part of the store. You sit among wooden tribal masks on imported chairs at the café, which occupies the front section of this unusual store. Over the years, it has become *the* place for islanders to meet for lunch, with its succinct menu of sandwiches, pastas, and small plates. The soup of the day is usually a good bet, the white gazpacho legendary, and the seafood gumbo, fortified with rice, could be a meal. I also

can recommend the sesame-seared tuna with Asian slaw and wasabi vinaigrette and the passion berry iced tea for lunch. The dinner menu describes such complex masterworks as macadamia-crusted grouper with Thai peanut sauce, bourbon-glazed lollipop pork chops, panko-crusted salmon with lemon-caper dill vinaigrette and avocado salsa, and horseradish salmon with roasted red pepper sauce and black bean salsa. Nightly specials—such as the pan-seared grouper with lobster ravioli and sauce we recently enjoyed—dazzle. Cutting edge aside, Traders is also known for its burgers and barbecue baby back ribs. Moderate to Expensive. Reservations accepted. Closed Sunday and month of September.

&. **Twilight Café** (239-472-8818; www.twilightcafesanibel.com), 2761 W. Gulf Dr. It gets the prize for most creative use of a grill. Vegetarians and just plain veggie-lovers will appreciate dishes such as grilled zucchini and squash on red pepper linguine, grilled eggplant, and grilled portobello. But veggies aren't all that get fired up on the grill—pork chops, spicy shrimp, chicken breast, blackened salmon, burger, and steaks also succumb to the flame. The menu is extensive, but in our experience, all is equally well-executed, especially at dinnertime. Oddly enough, grilled broccoli is a star in the evening. The restaurant's Web site keeps count of how many helpings of the side dish have been consumed. Don't know what they marinade it in, but it's addicting. The chef, a longtime island fixture, has some other tricks up his culinary sleeve, such as the tasty Thai peanut sauce that he applies to the shrimp, or the goat cheese and basil mashed potatoes with the filet. Or his famous roasted corn and crawfish mashed potato served with the juicy grilled veal chop. You can also order it along with other starch, sauce, and protein choices from the Create Your Own Entrée portion of the menu. Breakfast and lunch dawn equally bright with a fulfilling Florentine Benedict (order the yummy potato casserole rather than grits) and a turkey and spinach omelet with cream cheese and hollandaise for breakfast. Lunch favorites include chicken and sausage gumbo with shrimp, Southwest seafood salad, grouper Reuben, and chicken and pineapple stir fry. The setting is bright but simple, and the service usually spot-on. It's worthwhile to leave Sanibel's main drag of restaurants to search this one out. Moderate to Expensive. Reservations accepted.

BAKERIES European American Baking Co. (239-694-7964 or 800-200-BAKE; www.eabake.com), 12450 Metro Pkwy., Fort Myers. Wholesale, retail, and café operation with the most tempting international treats: éclairs, scones, strudel, Italian butter cookies, cheesecake, napoleons, tarts, turnovers, and artisan breads. Also specialty coffees and deli foods.

Mason's Bakery (239-334-4525; www.masonsbakery.com), 4224 Cleveland #7, Fort Myers. It lures sweet-tooth types with coffee, yummy cakes, cookies, breads, bagels, Danishes, cinnamon rolls, and more. Also prepares box lunches.

BREAKFAST ❧ ✪ Crave (239-466-4663), 12901 McGregor Blvd., at the Bridge Plaza, Fort Myers. Highly acclaimed for its creative comfort food breakfast, lunch, and dinner, its early morning menu (available until 4 PM) describes incredible omelets such as one with seafood, asparagus, shiitake mushrooms, broiled tomato, and hol-

landaise. Other unusual offerings include salmon and eggs with creamed horseradish, shrimp and grits, hash eggs Benedict, and specials such as bourbon-glazed filet and bleu cheese omelet.

Over Easy Café (239-472-2625; www.overeasycafesanibel.com), 630–1 Tarpon Bay Rd., Sanibel Island. Islanders are happy to have an alternative (and a better one at that!) to breakfast at Lighthouse Café, a tourist favorite long touted for its breakfasts. Over Easy's menu does standard along with unusual dishes such as my favorites: egg Reuben sandwich, vegetarian Benedict (ask for extra hollandaise on the side because it tends to run off), and portobello and spinach omelet. Also lunch.

CANDIES & ICE CREAM Chocolate Expressions (239-472-3837; http://chocolate-expressions -sanibel.com), 2075 Periwinkle Way #37, at Periwinkle Place, Sanibel Island. Homemade chocolates (including sugar-free varieties), hand-scooped Love Boat ice cream, homemade fudge, chocolate-dipped strawberries, and other treats.

❧ Love Boat Ice Cream (239-466-7707), 16229 San Carlos Blvd., Fort Myers. Homemade ice cream at a longtime favorite at the crossroads leading to Fort Myers Beach and Sanibel Island.

Norman Love Confections (239-561-7215 or 866-515-2121; www .normanloveconfections.com), 11380 Lindbergh Ave., Fort Myers. Treat yourself or a loved one to chocolates and pastries that have won kudos and awards throughout the country. Love's specialties are locally flavored truffles such as passion fruit, coconut, and key lime.

⚓ **Pinocchio's Ice Cream** (239-472-6566; www.pinocchiosicecream.com), 362 Periwinkle Way, Sanibel Island. Homemade Italian ice cream and sundaes. Try the Dirty Sand Dollar–caramel ice cream with malted milk balls and chocolate flakes.

🍴 (ᵰ) **Poco Loco** (239-395-0290; www.pocolocosanibel.com), 1700 Periwinkle Way #9, Jerry's Shopping Center, Sanibel Island. It owns exclusive county rights to sell 600 flavors of Palazzolo's Gelato—from mascarpone caramel pistachio to seasonal pink champagne with rose petals. Also gourmet coffee, smoothies, and European pastries.

COFFEE (ᵰ) **Blackhawk Fine Coffee & Provisions** (239-433-7770), 13499 S. Cleveland Ave. #137, at Bell Tower Shops, Fort Myers. An inviting setting of easy chairs, coffee tables, and backgammon boards, where you can enjoy coffee, lattes, desserts, flavored ice tea, and other goodies. Wireless Internet access available.

Café Matisse (239-362-1831), 2236 First St., Fort Myers. Indoor and sidewalk operation that will hopefully give nearby Starbucks a run. It sells espresso shots, organic and seasonal coffee, Cuban coffee, lattes, frappés, smoothies, and a menu of meals made with local ingredients.

Latté Da (239-472-0234; www.captivaislandinn.com), 11508 Andy Rosse Ln., Captiva Island. Sells Seattle's Best brand coffees and espresso, plus locally homemade Queenie's Real Ice Cream.

(ᵰ) **Origins Coffee Roasterie & Café** (239-542-6080), 1021-A Cape Coral Pkwy. E., Cape Coral. Have a seat at a sidewalk table for specialty coffees, a pastry, hot breakfast, lunch, and a Wi-Fi connection. Also 30 different types of coffee beans from around the world.

(ᵰ) **Poco Loco** (239-395-0290; www.pocolocosanibel.com), 1700 Periwinkle Way #9, Jerry's Shopping Center, Sanibel Island. Especially known for its Sanibel Blend coffee and exclusive black-white-black tea. Also gourmet gelato, smoothies, and artisanal pastries.

(ᵰ) **Sanibel Bean Island Coffees** (239-395-1919; www.sanibelbean.com), 2240-B Periwinkle Way, Sanibel Island; also at Southwest Florida International Airport. Sanibel's popular buzz shop, it serves the usual espresso, cappuccino, and latte selections, plus fresh-squeezed juice, smoothies, ice cream, bagels, breakfast, sandwiches, and salads.

DELI & SPECIALTY FOODS
Cheese Nook (239-472-2666; www.cheesenook.com), 2075 Periwinkle Way #20, Periwinkle Place, Sanibel Island. A longtime favorite of locals for not only cheese but also wine and gourmet hot sauces, preserves, and soups.

European Food Market (239-332-7200), 12901 McGregor Blvd., at Bridge Plaza, Fort Myers. Eastern European specialties from Poland, Romania, and the Slavic countries including pierogies, fresh and smoked kielbasa and other meats and sausages, beers, bread, and jarred salads and pickled vegetables.

Francesco's Italian Deli and Pizzeria (239-463-5634), 7205 Estero Blvd., at Santini Marina Plaza, Fort Myers Beach. Homemade breads, calzones, deli sandwiches, pizza whole or by the slice, Italian dishes for reheating, homemade Royal Scoop ice cream, and gourmet cheeses and groceries.

India Bazaar (239-939-0797), 5228 Bank St., Fort Myers. A shop filled with exotic smells, foods, and gifts from India, Thailand, the Middle East, and Britain. Fresh, packaged, and frozen ethnic ingredients plus premade meals.

Kim Orient Mart (239-275-8812), 1910 Boy Scout Dr., Fort Myers. Adjacent to a Chinese restaurant, this Oriental market sells fresh, packaged, frozen, and canned goods in bulk or small packages—everything from soy sauce to dried fungus.

✪ **Mario's Italian Meat Market & Deli** (239-936-7275; www.marios meatmarket.com), 12326 Cleveland Ave., Fort Myers. Fresh homemade sausage, braciola, and other meats; delicious homemade Italian cheeses, sauces, pastas, soups, and sandwiches; and hot and frozen prepared Italian specialties. Limited seating.

Mediterranean Middle Eastern Food (239-939-3090), 1916 Boy Scout Dr., Fort Myers. Stop here for feta cheese, flat breads, gyros, and unusual processed items such as rose jam, stuffed eggplant, and exotic candies.

✪ **Sandy Butler Gourmet Market** (239-482-6765; www.sandybutler.com), 17650 San Carlos Blvd., Fort Myers Beach. A spacious culinary dream filled with wonderful cheeses, wines, bakery goods, prepared dishes, fresh produce, and gourmet products.

(((•))) **Sanibel Deli & Coffee Factory** (239-472-2555; www.sanibeldeli.com), 2330 Palm Ridge Rd., Sanibel. Breakfast sandwiches, pastries, salad, pizza, sandwiches; free Wi-Fi access; free "earth-friendly" delivery.

FRUIT & VEGETABLE STANDS

For the freshest produce, visit the plentiful roadside stands along the coast. Some feature U-Pick options, especially for tomatoes and strawberries.

Downtown Farmer's Market (239-332-6813), under the bridge near Centennial Park, Fort Myers. Look for fresh fruit, vegetables, flowers, herbs, live plants, and arts and crafts every Thursday, 7–2, at this traditional market.

GreenMarket (239-939-2787; www .artinlee.org), Alliance for the Arts, 10091 McGregor Blvd., Fort Myers. More than 30 food and arts vendors congregate every Saturday from 9 AM to 1 PM. Live entertainment and kids activities.

Oakes Brothers Produce (239-466-4464 or 800-413-6881), 16758 McGregor Blvd., Fort Myers. My personal favorite for locally grown tomatoes, citrus, and other fresh fruit, vegetables, and preserves. They also ship fruit.

Sun Harvest Citrus (239-768-2686 or 800-743-1480; www.sunharvestcitrus .com), 14810 Metro Pkwy. S., at Six Mile Cypress, Fort Myers. Part tourist attraction, part citrus stand, Sun Harvest offers free samples, tours, demonstrations, a playground, and a gift shop.

NATURAL FOODS **Chef Brooke's Natural Café** (239-332-2433), 1850 Boy Scout Dr. #A106, Fort Myers. Organic smoothies and juices; breakfast, lunch, and dinner hot and cold entrées; health-food products; cooking classes.

Island Nutrition Center (239-472-4499; www.islandnutritioncenter.com), 2330 Palm Ridge Rd. #9, Sanibel Island. Small but well stocked with refrigerated and packaged organic, low-fat, low-carb, and low-sodium products.

Pizza Fusion (239-337-7979; www .pizzafusion.com), 12901-5 McGregor Blvd., at Bridge Plaza, Fort Myers. Everything from the pizza to the wine and the art on the wall is sustainability-oriented. Besides pizza, there's creative salads, sandwiches, and desserts. Signature pizzas include organic eggplant and fresh mozzarella, and Philly steak.

PIZZA & TAKE-OUT **El Mambo Cuban Restaurant** (239-542-9995), 4716 Del Prado Blvd. S., Cape Coral.

FRUITFUL ISLANDS

For those in the know, Pine Island is synonymous with exotic fruit. Guavas once grew wild throughout the island, brought to this subtropical land from the tropical Caribbean. Later, mangoes flourished. The only other place in Florida where tropical fruits grow in such abundance is Homestead, on the east coast, at a latitude some 90 miles south of Pine Island.

What makes Pine Island so nearly tropical? The warm waters of Charlotte Harbor run wide at the island's north end, around Bokeelia. They insulate the land, warming cold air before it reaches fragile fruit groves. Longans, sapodillas, carambolas, lychees, and other rare treats thrive as a result of this pocket of climate. Fructose freaks from miles around make a pilgrimage to roadside stands along Pine Island and Stringfellow roads throughout the summer and fall. To celebrate its fruity reputation, Pine Island throws MangoMania each summer.

Serving Cape Coral's Hispanic population and those who love the food, it sells Cuban bread, desserts, fresh fruit juices, Cuban sandwiches, and other sandwiches and Cuban specialties.

Little Lilly's Island Deli (239-282-9264; www.littlelillysislanddeli.com), 10700 Stringfellow Rd., Bokeelia. Locals rave about the homemade soup du jour, plus there is crabcake croissant, tropical chicken sandwich, sausage and peppers sub, and build-your-own options.

Mad Take-Out (239-693-TOGO), 12995 S. Cleveland Ave. #112, at Pinebrook Plaza, Fort Myers. Not-your-typical take-out includes a lamb burger with feta, Thai chicken salad, rib-eye steak, mushroom ragout pizza, and sushi.

Plaka I on the Beach (239-463-4707), 1001 Estero Blvd., Fort Myers Beach. Gyros, spinach pie, moussaka, and baklava to go or eat in a screened-in dining room near the beach.

Starz Restaurant & Pizzeria (239-482-7827; www.starzpizzeria.com), 16740 McGregor Blvd., Fort Myers. Close to the islands, its pizzas, cal-zones, subs, and Italian specialties have a faithful following.

Taste of New York Pizzeria (239-432-0990), 13499 S. Cleveland Ave., at Bell Tower Shops, Fort Myers. Declared to be among the best take-out or eat-in for regular or gourmet pizza—white, vegetarian, tropical, pesto, garlic—and other New York–Italian specialties. Delivery $1.

Tropical Beach Grill (239-454-0319), 17260 San Carlos Blvd., Fort Myers Beach. Better-than-average drive-up take-out for burgers, chicken sandwiches, and more.

SEAFOOD Beach Seafood (239-463-8777 or 800-771-5050), 1100 Shrimp Boat Ln., on San Carlos Island, Fort Myers Beach. Fresh seafood at its source, specializing in shrimp—fresh, frozen, steamed, and dinners. This is a locals' hot spot for lunch, by the way.

Skip One Seafood (239-482-0433), 15820 S. Tamiami Trail, Fort Myers. Fresh and fairly priced wild shrimp, stone crab (in season), lobster tails, clams, and fish. Join the crowds who have discovered the quality and value of its food for lunch and dinner. Shipping service available.

Timbers Fish Market (239-472-3128), 703 Tarpon Bay Rd., Sanibel. Located inside a popular seafood restaurant, Timbers has the best selection, prices, and freshness on the island for all types of seafood—fresh, steamed, and smoked.

✱ Selective Shopping

SHOPPING CENTERS & MALLS

Two new mega shopping-entertainment malls have opened in recent years in the fast-growing Estero–San Carlos Park area south of Fort Myers, near Florida Gulf Coast University. They are Coconut Point, a residential-retail development, and Gulf Coast Town Center, which includes a Bass Pro Shops Outdoor World attraction.

Bell Tower Shops (239-489-1221; www.thebelltowershops.com), 13499 S. Cleveland Ave., Fort Myers. Saks Fifth Avenue anchors this alfresco, Mediterranean-style plaza of one-of-a-kind shops, upscale chains (Victoria's Secret, Brookstone, Williams-Sonoma), terrific restaurants, and movie theaters. Newly renovated in 2009.

Captiva Island. Like Captiva in general, the shopping scene here is quirky and beach oriented.

Coconut Point (239-992-9966; www.simon.com), 23106 Fashion Dr., Tamiami Trail and Coconut Point Rd., Estero. New in 2007, the fashionable mall within a planned community includes major chains such as Victoria's Secret, Brookstone, and Johnny Rockets along with some local venues, including Blue Water Bistro.

Coralwood Shopping Center, 2301 Del Prado Blvd., Cape Coral. An outdoor mall of restaurants and chain stores, including Bealls Department Store, Sears, and JCPenney.

Downtown Fort Myers, First Street. Downtown is slowly looking up as a three-year redevelopment project puts utility lines underground and paves streets and sidewalks with recycled brick. More business- and government-minded than commercial, it does harbor some interesting book and cigar stores and unusual antique and what-not shops. Urban renewal emphasis is on entertainment and dining, so most shops are utilitarian.

Edison Mall (239-939-5464; www.simon.com), 4125 Cleveland Ave., Fort Myers. An entirely commercial, enclosed, and air-conditioned mall with major department stores such as Macy's, Dillard's, JCPenney, and Sears, plus about 150 smaller clothing and gift shops and a food court.

Fort Myers Beach. Shop in your bikini, if you wish, at Times Square, a hub of ultracasual island activity. You'll find a profusion of swimsuit boutiques, surf shops, and food outlets at this open-air pedestrian mall. At the island's south end, Santini Marina Plaza has some interesting shops and food stops.

⟨⟨ɲ⟩⟩ Gulf Coast Town Center (230-267-0783; www.gulfcoasttowncenter.com), 9903 Gulf Coast Main St., at I-75 and Alico Rd., Fort Myers. Opened in 2007, its Market Plaza serves as a family entertainment hub (there's live music every Friday and Saturday), and its University Plaza caters to university students with free wireless Internet access. Among its 120-plus stores and restaurants is a Bass Pro Shops outlet (239-461-7800; www.basspro.com).

Matlacha, Pine Island. Sagging old fish houses, cracker-box shops, quirky art galleries, and fishing motels heavily salt the flavor of this island village. Knickknack historic structures painted in candy-store colors give the town an artistic, Hansel-and-Gretel feel.

Sea-themed gifts, art, and jewelry make up the majority of merchandise.

McGregor Antiques District, Fort Myers. A nucleus of several shops in small strip centers at College Parkway.

Sanibel Island. Periwinkle Way and Palm Ridge Road constitute the shopper's routes on Sanibel, which is known for its galleries (specializing in wildlife art), shell shops, and resort-wear stores. These are clustered in tastefully landscaped, nature-compatible outdoor centers, the largest being Periwinkle Place (www.periwinkleplace.com) on Periwinkle Way.

ANTIQUES & COLLECTIBLES

Albert Meadow Antiques (239-472-8442), 15000 Captiva Dr., Captiva Island. High-quality, turn-of-the-20th-century decorative arts by Tiffany and Gallé, plus antique jewelry, lamps, silver, Navajo weavings, and art deco and art nouveau pieces. Closed mid-April–mid-December.

Fancy Flamingo Antiques (239-334-1133), 2259 Widman Way, Fort Myers. It nicely displays a wide variety of clothing, housewares, dolls, toys, and knickknacks between vintage red brick interior walls.

Flying Fish Trading Company (239-463-9900; www.flyingfishtrading.com), 2471 Estero Blvd., Fort Myers Beach. Specializing in nautical antiques—dive helmets, spyglasses, anchors, etc.—it's also famous for its custom-made, tropical-style Adirondack chairs and other nautically themed furniture and gifts.

Judy's Antiques (239-481-9600), 12710-3 McGregor Blvd., Fort Myers. One of the oldest in the McGregor Antiques District, this establishment is well organized and sells quality sterling, porcelain, and crystal, specializing in estate jewelry.

McGregor Antique Mall (239-433-0200), 12720 McGregor Blvd., Fort Myers. In the same neighborhood as Judy's but more folksy and nostalgic in its considerable offerings—household goods, books, toys, country-style furnishings, and more.

The Swap Shop (239-432-0906; www.swapshopantiques.com), 17851 Pine Ridge Rd., Fort Myers Beach. Stop at this big red barn for affordable housewares, fine ceramics, '50s furnishings and decor, and carved tiki statues.

Vamped Up Vintage (239-936-4888), 11601 S. Cleveland Ave, Suite #5, Fort Myers. This off-the-beaten-path shop is fun any time of the year, but especially when prepping for Halloween or June weddings. It deals entirely in vintage clothing, carrying everything from tuxes and wedding gowns to gaudy bell-bottom jumpsuits and fur-trimmed hats.

BOOKS Beach Book Nook (239-463-3999), 7205 Estero Blvd., at Santini Marina Plaza, Fort Myers Beach. New and used paperback exchange; a nice selection of new local guides, adult books, and kids' books.

MacIntosh Books & Paper (239-472-1447; http://macintoshbooks.com), 2407 Periwinkle Way, Sanibel Island. A tiny shop packed full of books of local and general interest; a small selection of cards earns it the "Paper" in its name.

CLOTHING Brown Bag (239-472-1171), 2075 Periwinkle Way, at Periwinkle Place, Sanibel Island. Tropical shirts, T-shirts, and other casual menswear.

Francesca's Collections (239-267-5050), 13499 Cleveland Ave., at Bell Tower Shops, Fort Myers. Young, fun, affordable women's fashions, accessories, and gifts.

Giggles (239-395-0700), Plantation Rd., Captiva Island. Cute and whimsical Florida-appropriate clothing for kids, particularly little girls.

H20 Outfitters and Footloose of Captiva (239-472-8890), 2075 Periwinkle Way, at Jerry's Shopping Center, Sanibel Island. Name-brand men's and women's beach and marina fashions, shoes, and quality souvenir T-shirts and sweatshirts.

Jos. A. Banks Clothiers (239-454-3543), 13499 Cleveland Ave., at Bell Tower Shops, Fort Myers. Fine sporting, casual-tropical, and formal wear for men.

Lucky Dog of Sanibel (239-395-3733), 2359 Periwinkle Way, Sanibel Island. Select, pricey threads for trendsetters.

Mr. Pants and Michelle's Resortwear (239-463-1515), 7205 Estero Blvd. #712, at Santini Marina Village, Fort Myers Beach. Fine casual, Florida-fit fashions for men and women.

Peach Republic (239-472-8444; www.peachrepublic.com), 2075 Periwinkle Way #16, at Periwinkle Place, Sanibel Island. Stylish cotton and other tropical resort wear for women, plus shoes and jewelry.

Pier Peddler (239-765-0660), 1000 Estero Blvd., Fort Myers Beach. At the base of the Fort Myers Beach Fishing Pier, it carries beach and tropical fashions for men and women.

Trader Rick's (239-489-2240), 13499 U.S. 41 #217, at Bell Tower Shops, Fort Myers; and (239-472-9194), 2075 Periwinkle Way #38, at Periwinkle Place, Sanibel. Creative-casual Florida wear for women plus unusual and handmade jewelry, toiletries, and other accessories.

CONSIGNMENT Buying secondhand on the Island Coast is not the embarrassment it is in some places. Because of the wealthy and transient nature of its residents, the area offers the possibility of great discoveries in its consignment shops.

Classy Exchange (239-278-1123), 12791 Kenwood Ln. #B1, Fort Myers. Designer women's fashions and housewares.

Elite Repeat (239-437-1222), 12995 Cleveland Ave. #156, at Pinebrook Park, Fort Myers. Formal, career, and casual wear, including shoes and jewelry, for women.

Once Again Boutique (239-482-5445), 12721 McGregor Blvd., Fort Myers. Nicely arranged women's clothing and shoes with brand names, including a rack of Chico's.

Periwinkle Way Consignments (239-472-5222; www.sanibelbrights.com), 2431 Periwinkle Way, Sanibel Island. Collectibles, nostalgia, seashells, art, and other decorative items.

Second Hand Rose (239-574-6919), 1532 S.E. 14th St., at Del Prado Mall, Cape Coral. Extensive selection of fashion, jewelry, household items, furniture, and collectibles.

FACTORY OUTLET CENTERS

Miromar Outlets (239-948-3766; www.miromaroutlets.com), 10801 Corkscrew Rd. #199, at exit 123 off I-75, Estero. An above-average assortment of more than 140 factory shops, designer outlets, and eateries, including Adidas, Nike, Reebok, Nautica, Coach, and Restoration Hardware. Watch the Southern Extreme Waterski Show Team (239-571-4957; www.southernextreme.com) on Sunday in season, take the kids to Playland, or replenish (so you don't drop) at one of several restaurants.

Tanger Outlets Fort Myers (239-454-1974 or 888-471-3939; www.tanger outlet.com/fortmyers), 20350 Summerlin Rd., at McGregor Blvd., Fort Myers. Sitting at Sanibel's doorstep are more than 45 outlets for Samsonite, Maidenform, Gap, Reebok, OshKosh, Polo Ralph Lauren, Bass Shoes, and more.

FLEA MARKETS & BAZAARS

Fleamasters Fleamarket (239-334-7001; www.fleamall.com), 4135 Dr. Martin Luther King Jr. Blvd., Fort Myers. Some 400,000 indoor square feet of produce, souvenirs, and novelties in more than 900 shops and eateries; open Friday–Sunday. A new amphitheater hosts live country and doo-wop concerts and dances.

McGregor Boulevard Garage Sales, Fort Myers. Drive the boulevard early—the earlier you go, the better the pickings—every Friday and Saturday morning and watch for garage sale signs directing you to private sales.

Ortiz Avenue Flea Market (239-694-5019; www.ortizavenuefleamarket .com), 1501 Ortiz Ave., Fort Myers. Smaller than Fleamasters, this market convenes every Friday and Saturday 7–4 and Sunday 6–4.

GALLERIES In season, hit Pine Island's Matlacha, a thriving artists' community, for Art Night the second Friday of the month. Besides gallery tours, visitors get entertainment, food, and Pine Island's special brand of fun.

Arts for ACT Gallery (239-337-5050; www.artsforactgallery.com), 2265 First St., Fort Myers. Local artists and traveling exhibits to benefit abused women. Prices range from one to four figures for original paintings, jewelry,

pottery, painted furniture, artistic clothing, and more.

BIG ARTS on Periwinkle (239-472-9700; www.bigarts.org), 2244 Periwinkle Way, behind the Sanibel Bean, Sanibel. The area's most talented artists sell their paintings, glass, jewelry, baskets, and fabrics here.

Crossed Palms Gallery (239-283-2283), 8315 Main St., Bokeelia, Pine Island. A delightful gallery facing the sea, it occupies two restored 1950s fishermen's cottages built around a cistern, which has become part of the gallery. Its rooms are filled with original fine art, glasswork, pottery, and jewelry by local and national artists.

Howl Gallery/Tattoo (239-332-0161; www.howlgallery.com), 1514 Broadway #101, Fort Myers. Whether you want to wear your art or hang it in your home, Howl's got you covered. Unusual gallery with changing exhibits.

Jungle Drums (239-395-2266; www .jungledrumsgallery.com), 11532 Andy Rosse Ln., Captiva Island. On the outside, dolphins and birds are carved into the stair rail and floor studs. Inside, local and national artists depict wildlife themes in various media, much of it whimsical, all of it delightfully creative.

Lovegrove Gallery & Gardens (239-282-1244; www.leomalovegrove .com), 4637 Pine Island Rd., Matlacha. Spend some time with the irrepressible, energetic Leoma Lovegrove, whose art has gotten her into the White House and beyond. Her colorful, lively art spans many media into the realm of performance art. She may be most famous for her Beatles art and painted coconuts, which has started a Florida trend.

Portfolio (239-489-4333), 13499 S. Cleveland Ave., at Bell Tower Shops, Fort Myers. Affordable original art, prints, and posters, framed or unframed.

Space 39 Gallery (239-690-0004; www.spacethirtynine.com), 39 Patio de Leon, Fort Myers. One of downtown's leading galleries for national traveling exhibitions, it has a colorful Byzantine storefront.

Tower Gallery (239-472-4557; www.towergallery-sanibel.com), 751 Tarpon Bay Rd., Sanibel Island. In its charming Caribbean-motif old-beach-house digs, this cooperative specializes in fine tropical art by 23 area artists: masterful black-and-white photography by Charles McCullough, Sanibel scenes, pottery, and glass.

WildChild Gallery (239-283-6006, www.wildchildartgallery.com), 4625 Pine Island Rd. N.W., Matlacha. Part of Pine Island's quirky art scene, it has wares ranging from jewelry and pottery to original oils and sculptures by local artists. On weekends, you can sometimes find artists at work or demonstrating.

GENERAL STORES Bailey's General Store (239-472-1516), 2477 Periwinkle Way, at Bailey's Shopping Center, Sanibel Island. An island fixture for ages, it stocks mostly hardware and fishing and kitchen supplies. It also has an attached grocery, bakery, coffee counter, and deli.

Island Store (239-472-2374), 11500 Andy Rosse Ln., Captiva Island. Here's where you can buy those necessities you forgot, including deli products and liquor. But try not to forget too much, because the prices reflect the location, here at the end of the earth. A seafood wagon pulls up to sell its wares most days.

GIFTS Bubble Room Emporium (239-472-6545; www.bubbleroom restaurant.com/gift.html), 15001 Captiva Dr., Captiva. Find some of the same zany buttons and hats that the Bubble Room servers wear (see "Where to Eat"), plus toys and baubles for you and your home.

Cheshire Cat Toys (239-482-8697), 13499 S. Cleveland Ave., at Bell Tower Shops, Fort Myers. Brio, Playmobil, stuffed animals, puppets, fine dolls, books, arts and crafts, and learning toys.

Discovery Bay (239-463-4715), 7205 Estero Blvd., at Santini Marina Plaza,

LOVEGROVE GALLERY & GARDENS CREATES ITS OWN MICROCOSM OF FANTASY.

Fort Myers Beach. Whimsical, tasteful nautical and tropical gifts and home accessories, plus crystal.

Island Girl (239-765-4475), 7205 Estero Blvd., at Santini Marina Plaza, Fort Myers Beach. Everything from fine art to fun and artsy apparel to entertaining accessories for the island lifestyle.

Local Color (239-463-9199), 1021 Estero Blvd., at Times Square, Fort Myers Beach. This tiny shop packs in a little of everything—clothing, jewelry, tableware, toiletries, cards, and more—all with an artistic flair.

Needful Things (239-472-5400), 1995 Periwinkle Way, at Tahitian Gardens, Sanibel. Kids especially love this place, although the novelties, toys, and cards also appeal to the teens' and adults' sense of fun and budgets.

Pandora's Box (239-472-6263), 2075 Periwinkle Way #1, at Periwinkle Place, Sanibel Island. Delightful decorative items, creative jewelry, potpourri, specialty children's gifts, soaps, yard art, and the best selection of greeting cards on the island.

Sanibel Surf Shop (239-472-8185), 1700 Periwinkle Way, at Jerry's Shopping Center, Sanibel Island. Collections of T-shirts, beach toys, jewelry, and shells all under one roof, selling affordable mementos of the island. Formerly Jerry's Bazaar.

A Swedish Affair (239-275-8004 or 888-867-9567; www.swedensfinest .com), 1400 Colonial Blvd., at Royal Palm Square, Fort Myers. Scandinavian gifts from funny to fine: amusing cards, old-fashioned toys, lingonberry preserves, folk art, candles, glassware, Christmas ornaments, and fine pewter serving pieces.

Toys Ahoy (239-472-4800), 2075 Periwinkle Way, at Periwinkle Place, Sanibel Island. Old-fashioned and learning-focused toys, puppets, books, stuffed toys, and more.

JEWELRY ✪ **Congress Jewelers** (239-472-4177 or 800-882-6624; www .congressjewelers.com), 2075 Periwinkle Way #35, at Periwinkle Place, Sanibel Island. Dolphin, mermaid, bird, sandals, sand bucket, and shell pendants, plus other fine jewelry.

Enjewel (239-415-4023), 2218 First St., Fort Myers. Artistic sterling silver pieces, turquoise and glass jewelry, sparkly bags and shoes.

Mayors (239-590-6166), 13499 S. Cleveland Ave., at Bell Tower Shops, Fort Myers. Swiss watches and pens, rings, bar- and tableware, and elegant baubles of all sorts in a spacious setting.

Sanibel Diamond (239-472-1454 or 800-850-6605; www.sanibeldiamond .com), 1700 Periwinkle Way #1, in Jerry's Shopping Center, Sanibel. Specializes in diamonds; home of the ultra-brilliant "Sanibel Diamond."

Scruples (239-463-0500), 7205 Estero Blvd. #730, at Santini Marina Plaza, Fort Myers Beach. I like this shop for its interesting heirloom-style and fused glass pieces and other affordable jewelry.

KITCHENWARE & HOME DÉCOR
Cheese Nook (239-472-2666; www .cheesenook.com), 2075 Periwinkle Way #20, at Periwinkle Place, Sanibel Island. Fun and tropical place mats, towels, and dishware; also gourmet food items, including a wide selection of hot sauces and select wines.

Island Decor & More (239-283-8080), 4206 Pine Island Rd., Matlacha. Affordable decorative home art and accessories with an islandy appeal.

Island Style (239-472-6657; www .islandstylegalleries.com), 2075 Periwinkle Way #6 and #10, at Periwinkle Place, Sanibel Island. Whimsical, artistic, and one-of-a-kind decorative elements with a Sun Belt motif: hand-painted chairs, carved wooden mobiles and stabiles, brightly colored dishware, and Caribbean-inspired pieces.

Miromar Design Center (239-390-5111; www.miromardesigncenter.com), 10800 Corkscrew Rd., Suite 382, at I-75 across from Miromar Outlets, Estero. This ultrasophisticated facility gathers high-end furniture stores, tile and fixtures merchants, flooring, rugs, and art galleries under one elegant roof. Valet parking and one complimentary hour of designer-on-call service.

Sanibel Home Furnishings (239-472-5552; www.sanibelhomefurnishings.com), 1618 Periwinkle Way, Sanibel. Sophisticated and tasteful island-style furnishings and decoration ideas.

Traders (239-395-3151; www.traders storeandcafe.com), 1551 Periwinkle Way, Sanibel Island. This restaurant-and-store combo excels at both (see "Where to Eat"). Warehouse-sized, the shop brims with objets d'art, candles, hats, scarves, and imported gifts.

Wilford & Lee (239-395-9295), 2009 Periwinkle Way, at Tahitian Gardens, Sanibel. Affordable (for Sanibel) and distinctive home decorations, including lamps, marine-life wall sculptures, and tableware.

SHELL SHOPS Island Decor & More (239-283-8080), 4206 Pine Island Road, Matlacha. The focus at this longtime shell shop has changed to home decor (see above), but it still carries an aisle of specimen shells. Bonus: a good location for spotting dolphins and manatees.

✿ **Sanibel Seashell Industries** (239-472-1603; www.seashells.com), 905

Fitzhugh St., just off Periwinkle Way, Sanibel. Serious shell junkies and shell artisans should head here for the best specimens at the best prices. The same family has opened a smaller, more gifty shop in front of the warehouselike outlet at 1544 Periwinkle Way.

The Shell Factory (239-995-2141 or 800-282-5805; www.shellfactory.com), 2787 N. Tamiami Tr., North Fort Myers. A palace of Florida souvenirs, tacky to fine, The Shell Factory is built like a bazaar. In addition to shells, it sells jewelry, art, clothes, Christmas decorations, and knickknacks. More than 350 taxidermy animals from all over the world reside inside the Quonset hut that makes up the original core of the attraction. Also at the complex (can't miss it; look for the giant conch shell on the sign) are restaurants, an arcade, a kids' entertainment center, and a nature park with wild animals and a petting zoo.

She Sells Seashells (239-472-6991), 1157 Periwinkle Way, Sanibel; and (239-472-8080), 2422 Periwinkle Way, Sanibel. The island's oldest shell dealer has everything you need for shell crafts and displays.

Showcase Shells (239-472-1971), 1614 Periwinkle Way, at Heart of the Islands Center, Sanibel Island. As elegant as a jewelry store, this boutique adds a touch of class to sifting through specimen shells by putting them under glass and into artistic displays.

✴ **Special Events**

January: **Caloosahatchee Celtic Festival** (239-321-7530), Centennial Park, downtown Fort Myers. One day at the end of the month devoted to Irish and Scottish music, dance, and food. **Cape Coral Festival of the Arts** (239-945-1988; www.capecoral festival.com), Cape Coral Pkwy., Cape Coral. This main thoroughfare closes down for a street festival the second weekend of the month. **Jazz on the Green** (239-477-4683; www.jazzonthe green.com), Florida Gulf Coast University, Fort Myers. A weekend of soothing alfresco jazz by well-known artists. Admission.

February: ✪ ♪ **Edison Festival of Light** (239-334-2999; www.edison festival.org), Fort Myers. Commemorates the birthday of Thomas Edison and culminates in a spectacular lighted night parade. Two weeks early in the month.

March: ♪ **Fort Myers Beach Lions Club Shrimp Festival** (239-463-6986; www.fortmyersbeachshrimpfestival.com), Lynn Hall Memorial Park, Fort Myers Beach. Kids' run, 5K run, parade, and shrimp boil. One weekend midmonth. **Greek Fest** (239-481-2099; www.greekfestfortmyers.com), Greek Orthodox Church, 8210 Cypress Lake Dr., Fort Myers. Ethnic food and music. Three days early in the month. Admission. **Sanibel Music Festival** (239-336-7999; www.sanibelmusic festival.org), Sanibel Island. Features concerts by classical artists from across the nation. Most events held at Sanibel Congregational Church, 2050 Periwinkle Way. Monthlong. **Sanibel Shell Fair and Show** (239-472-2155; www .sanibelcommunityhouse.net), Sanibel Community House, 2173 Periwinkle Way, Sanibel Island. Showcases sea life, specimen shells, and shell art. Three days in early March. In 2012, the event observes its 75th anniversary with a weeklong Shellabration. Admission fee for show. **Southwest Florida Reading Festival** (239-479-4636; www.lee-county.com/library/reading festivalhome.htm), Centennial Park, downtown Fort Myers. One day midmonth to celebrate literacy; features prominent authors and related activities.

April: **Earth Day** (239-472-1100), J. N. "Ding" Darling National Wildlife Refuge, 1 Wildlife Dr., Sanibel Island. Green giveaways, nature arts and crafts, lectures, and free admission to Wildlife Drive for cyclists and pedestrians. **River & Blues Festival** (239-229-9825; www.riverandbluesfestival .com), Centennial Park, Fort Myers. One day midmonth of live music, local food, and activities for kids. Admission.

June: **Caloosa Catch & Release Fishing Tournament** (239-671-9347; www.caloosacatchandrelease.com), Pink Shell Beach Resort, Fort Myers. Four-day event that kicks off a three-event fishing series throughout the summer.

July: ✪ **MangoMania Tropical Fruit Fair** (239-283-4842; www.floridas creativecoast.com), German-American Social Club, 2101 S.W. Pine Island Road, Cape Coral. Celebrates Pine Island's favorite fruit with music and

GRANNY MATTHEWS STARTED THE SANIBEL SHELL FAIR TRADITION 70 YEARS AGO.

Island Inn

stands selling mangos, mango trees, mango drinks, mango cookies, and other local delicacies. Good, honest community fun. One weekend in mid-July. Admission.

September: **Summer Slam** (239-671-9347; www.caloosacatchandrelease .com), Pink Shell Beach Resort, Fort Myers Beach. Three days of slam-bang fishing competition awarding more than $20,000 in cash and prizes; this is the second leg of the Caloosa Tournament Series.

October: **The Calusa Blueway Paddling Festival** (239-433-3855; www .calusabluewaypaddlingfestival.com), Pine Island. Ten days, late October into November, for paddling the Great Calusa Blueway trail and learning about kayaking, fishing, and more. ❧ ✐ **"Ding" Darling Days** (239-472-1100), J. N. "Ding" Darling National Wildlife Refuge, Sanibel Island. One week in mid-October is devoted to birding, exploring the refuge, and celebrating conservation art. ✐ **Friendly Forest** (239-275-3435; www.calusa nature.org), Calusa Nature Center, 3450 Ortiz Ave., Fort Myers. Two weekends of family-friendly trick-or-treating on the nature trails. **Oktoberfest** (239-281-1400; www.gasc-cape coral.com), German-American Social Club, Cape Coral. Cape Coral celebrates its strong German heritage with Oktoberfest music, food, and activities. Two weekends. Admission. ✐ **Pirate Festival** (239-454-7500 or 866-553-

1441; www.beachpiratefestival.com), Old San Carlos Blvd., Fort Myers Beach. Treasure hunts, a walking pub crawl, and pirate look-alike contests. One weekend early in the month.

November: **American Sandsculpting Contest** (239-454-7500 or 866-916-SAND; www.sandfestival.com), Gull-Wing and Holiday Inn resorts, Fort Myers Beach. Amateur and masters divisions, entertainment, and workshops. One weekend in mid-November. ✐ **Cape Coral Coconut Festival** (239-573-3125), Sun Splash Family Water Park, Cape Coral. Tropical food, live music, and a carnival. One weekend midmonth. Admission.

December: **Cape Coral Boat-a-Long** (239-573-3123; www.capecoral.net), Four Freedoms Park, Cape Coral. Decorated boat parade with live entertainment, Santa, Christmas crafts, food, and more. **Christmas Luminary Trail** (239-472-1080), Sanibel and Captiva Islands. More than 3 miles of luminary candles line the main roads of Sanibel's and Captiva's commercial areas, where businesses stay open and dole out free drinks and food. One weekend early in the month. ✐ **Holiday Nights** (239-334-7419; www .efwefla.org), Edison & Ford Winter Estates, 2350 McGregor Blvd., Fort Myers. Period and seasonal exhibits and miles of light strings draw crowds to this popular monthlong attraction. Admission.

Naples & the South Coast 4

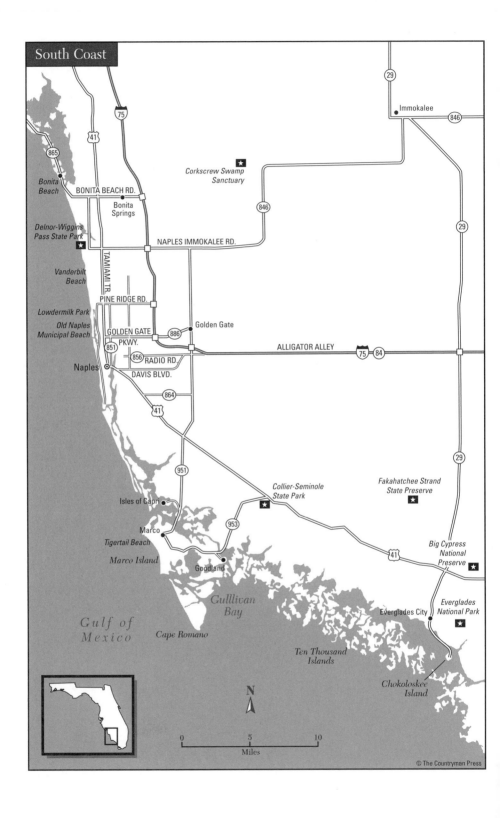

South Coast

NAPLES & THE SOUTH COAST

PRECIOUS COMMODITIES

Perched on alabaster sands at the edge of Florida's Everglades, meticulous Naples transcends its wild setting like a diamond in the rough. Settled by land developers late in its life, this cultural oasis historically has appealed to the rich and the sporting. Today the state's final frontier is known for its million-dollar homes, great golfing, art galleries, posh resorts, world-class shopping, and fine dining. In the spirit of its Italian namesake, Naples underwent a sort of renaissance in the 1990s that included a highly successful urban renewal project on Fifth Avenue South and various cultural venues, including Sugden Community Theatre, von Liebig Art Center, and the world-class Naples Museum of Art. In 2010, the developing Naples Botanical Garden opened a major new phase, and a children's museum is planned to open in fall 2010.

In its northern reaches the city spreads into the quiet residential district of **North Naples,** seaside **Vanderbilt Beach,** and the town of **Bonita Springs,** and it continues to grow now eastward, where the new Catholic college community of **Ave Maria** has popped up.

Bonita Springs still adheres to an early agricultural heritage with its reputation for tomatoes, citrus, and other cash crops. Citrus freeze-outs farther north, plus the town's navigable Imperial River, created the community, first called Survey, in 1893. Here Henry Ford maintained a hunting lodge to which he and his Fort Myers friends, including Thomas Edison, traveled by horseback. Today, where the tomato fields end, upscale golfing communities begin, all surrounding a neighborly little town left frozen in time by dint of the Tamiami Trail's rerouting. These days Bonita Springs starts to blend in with north Naples, both physically and in its character. New residential, hotel, and shopping developments boost it upward like an overachieving tomato vine climbing above its stake.

At the South Coast's southern and eastern extremes, the civility is balanced with swamp-buggy mud races, agriculture, Native American villages, fishing lodges, Florida panthers, and the unvarnished wilderness of the Everglades.

Neighboring **Marco Island** introduces the labyrinthine, mysterious land of Ten Thousand Islands. It was once an important center of the ancient Calusa culture, and the carved Key Marco Cat archaeological find (now exhibited at the Smithsonian Institution) has become an island icon. Tempered in a rough-and-tumble history, the island also boasts contemporary upscale resorts and good manners. Ancient Indian mounds, clam canneries, and pineapple plantations color the past of its three communities: **Isles of Capri, Marco,** and ✪ **Goodland.** First settled by the clan of William Collier (no relation to Barron Collier) in 1871, Marco Island has done most of its growing in modern times. Between 1960, when plans for a modern bridge were being formed, and 1980, the population increased by 755 percent. Goodland, so named because its land provided fertile soil for avocado farming, purposely kept itself behind the times—giddily stuck in a good-time, catch-fish mode—for most of its life. But these days signs of upscaling appear on the laid-back horizon.

✪ **Everglades City**—the county seat until Naples took over—languishes in its wilderness setting at the doorstep to Big Cypress Swamp and Ten Thousand Islands. Its settlers have always kept a step ahead of the law, doing what they must to survive, whether it was fishing, alligator poaching, or pot smuggling. Today, with a population of about 500, commercial fishing restrictions have channeled the town's orientation toward stone crabbing and tourism. Across a long, narrow causeway, **Chokoloskee Island** remains relatively untouched by change. It's a haven for RV campers and fishermen.

✴ To See

The affluent residents of Naples—many of them transplanted CEOs and captains of industry from lands to the north—share their county with impoverished migrants who work in Immokalee, the nearby agricultural center. The influences of Haitian, Puerto Rican, Jamaican, and other Caribbean cultures are finding their way into the mainstream, while flashes of Southern spirit and Cracker charm surface in Goodland, Everglades City, and Chokoloskee.

EVERGLADES CITY'S RIVERFRONT— FESTOONED WITH CRAB TRAPS, NETS, AND BUOYS—STILL REFLECTS ITS FISHING ROOTS.

The Miccosukee and Seminole Indians inhabit reservations in the Everglades. They celebrate their culture each year at the Green Corn Ceremony during the first new moon in June. They contribute the South Coast's only authentic, indigenous art: colorful weaving, stitching, jewelry, dolls, and other age-old handicrafts.

Highbrow art has become a trademark of Naples and its long roll of galleries and performance spaces. For information on cultural events, contact the United Arts Council of Collier County at 239-263-8242 or visit www.collier arts.com.

ARCHITECTURE In Naples, commercial architecture is marked by style and panache, not to mention the architectural beauty of homes and resorts.

THE ARCHITECTURE OF THE VILLAGE ON VENETIAN BAY SHOPPING DISTRICT CONTRIBUTES TO THE ITALIAN FLAVOR OF AMERICA'S NAPLES.

Banks and insurance companies seem to compete for virtuosity. It's truly a land of visual allure. Pelican Bay developments provide examples of a new residential style and provide a contrast with old-money Port Royal.

Old Naples, that neighborhood in the vicinity of the pier and Fifth Avenue South, has held on to some real treasures, including the tabby-mortar **Palm Cottage,** the old **Mercantile,** and the **Old Naples building** at Broad and Third. In the same neighborhood, on **Gordon Drive,** pay attention to the charming board-and-batten Cracker survivors.

In **Everglades City** and **Chokoloskee Island,** recreational vehicles and cement-block boxes typify the fishing-oriented community's traditional style, though that is changing with a trend toward gentrification. The **Rod & Gun Club,** built in 1850, stands out and dresses the town in Southern flair. The style of thatch housing, perfected by the Indians and known as chikee (pronounced *chi-KEY*), prevails in the Everglades and serves as a trendy beach-bar motif at the ritziest resorts throughout the coastal region.

CINEMA **Marco Movies** (239-642-1111; www.marcomovies.com), 599 S. Collier Blvd., at Marco Walk, Marco Island. Four screens with first-run movies, food, beer, and wine service.

Pavilion Cinema (239-596-0008), Vanderbilt Beach Rd., at Pavilion shopping center, Naples. Ten theaters.

Regal Hollywood Cinema 20 Cinemas (239-597-9494), 6006 Airport Pulling Rd., at Pine Ridge Rd., Naples.

Silverspot at Mercato (www.silverspotcinema.com), 9259 Mercato Way, Tamiami Trail at Vanderbilt Rd., Naples. The first in a line of luxury cinemas, it opened in

2009 and features oversized leather seats, reserved seating, a lounge, and gourmet restaurant. Two to three of its 11 screens show indie films.

GARDENS Naples Botanical Garden (239-643-7275 or 877-433-1874; www .naplesgarden.org), 4820 Bayshore Dr., Naples. Open daily 9–5. $9.95 adults, $4.95 children ages 4–14. Developing its 170 acres of subtropical and tropical gardens with plants from many warm lands in phases, it currently has three acres open to the public, including a butterfly house and a 1-mile loop trail that explores uplands habitat, including cypress swamp, wetlands, and oak scrub. In November 2009, the gardens reopened with the addition of a Children's, Brazilian, and Caribbean Garden plus 90 acres of preserved Everglades habitat. Plans to add Florida and Asian gardens are in the works.

✒ **Naples Zoo at Caribbean Gardens** (239-262-5409; www.napleszoo.com), 1590 Goodlette-Frank Rd., Naples. Open daily 9–5 (last ticket sold at 4). $19.95 adults, $18.95 seniors, $11.95 children ages 3–12. These tropical gardens, today the setting for a nicely proportioned zoo (see "Kids' Stuff" in this section), were planted in 1919 by Dr. Henry Nehrling, a botanist who brought his private collection to Naples. After he died, Julius Fleischmann, a developer, restored and expanded the doctor's 3,000-plus specimens and opened the gardens to the public in 1954. Besides native vegetation, exotics such as magnificent creeping figs, birds of paradise, and monkey-puzzle, calabash, mango, and kapok trees flourish in wetlands and on hammocks.

Palm Cottage's Norris Gardens (239-261-8164; www.napleshistoricalsociety .org), 137 12th Ave. S., Naples. Open November–April, Tuesday–Saturday 1–4; May–October, Wednesday and Saturday 1–4. Donation of $8 for garden and cottage tour; $5 for children under age 12. The Norris Gardens, which opened in 2007, encircle a green oval lawn next to the historic Palm Cottage. Circular residential-scale theme gardens grow at the quadrangle's corners to reflect horticulture at the turn of last century. They include the Pioneer Garden, Edible Garden, Palm Garden, Water Garden, Garden of the Senses, and Shade Garden. A genuine Seminole pole-and-thatch chikee structure provides space for community programs at the gardens. Self-guided garden tours are included with the cost of admission to Palm Cottage. Docents conduct one-hour tours of the gardens at 10 AM the first and third Thursday of the month. A self-guided tour of Palm Cottage is included in the fee.

HISTORIC HOMES & SITES Indian Hill, Indian Hill Dr. off Scott Dr., Goodland. Marco Island is rich in natural and historic heritage, but hides it well among 20th-century trappings. Witness Indian Hill. On your own you'll have to search to find it, and when you do, you'll know it only by the way the road peaks, leaving you unable to see what's on the other side. (Or take a trolley tour—**Marco Island Trolley,** 239-394-1600—to get there.) Southwest Florida's highest elevation at 58 feet above sea level, built up by ancient Calusa Indian shell mounds, it now holds a ritzy neighborhood called the Heights, which feels the tiniest bit like San Francisco.

Otter Mound Preserve (239-642-4043), 1831 Addison Ct., Marco Island. This Calusa archaeological site and its short interpretive trail along a mulch pathway tell the story of the Indians who once inhabited this area. The land's later owner,

SCULPTURES AND AN AUTHENTIC SEMINOLE CHIKEE HUT ADD INTEREST TO THE GARDENS AT PALM COTTAGE.

Ernest Otter, used the hundreds of whelk shells they left behind, evidence of their shellfish diet, to line terraces around the property starting in the 1940s. Plenty of the ancient whelks still lie strewn alongside the path.

Palm Cottage (239-261-8164; www.napleshistoricalsociety.org), 137 12th Ave. S., Naples. Open November–April, Tuesday–Saturday 1–4; May–October, Wednesday and Saturday 1–4. Donation of $8 for garden and cottage tour; $5 for children under age 12. Land was selling for $10 a lot in 1895 when Naples founder Walter N. Haldeman built a winter home for fellow worker Henry Watterson. Haldeman, publisher of *The (Louisville) Courier-Journal,* had discovered the exotic beaches and forests of Naples in 1887 and proceeded to buy up land and sing its praises. His enthusiasm persuaded winter escapees from Kentucky and Ohio, including Watterson, his star editor, to visit. The cottage Haldeman built for his friend was made of Florida pine, tidewater cypress, and a certain type of tabby mortar made by burning seashells over a buttonwood fire. It was one of the first permanent buildings in southwest Florida to be constructed of local materials and is Naples's oldest house. Before reaching its current museum status, the cottage—rather spartan by modern standards—knew many lives. If the walls could talk at Palm Cottage, as it eventually came to be known, they would tell of wild parties with the likes of Gary Cooper and Hedy Lamarr in attendance. In 2010, a theater opened that shows oral history films telling more stories about Naples. The renovated cottage is the headquarters of the Collier County Historical Society, which conducts guided tours. In the cottage's adjacent historic garden (see "Gardens" above), visitors can view vegetation early settlers used and planted. Every Wednesday from November–April, 90-minute walking tours of Naples's historic district depart from Palm Cottage at 10 AM (arrive by 9:45); cost is $15 per person. From May–October, the walking tours take place the first Wednesday of the month only at 9 AM (arrive at 8:55).

Smallwood Store (239-695-2989; www.florida-everglades.com/chokol/smallw .htm), 360 Mamie St., south of Everglades City, Chokoloskee Island. Open December 1–May 1, daily 10–5; May 2–November 30, Friday–Tuesday 10–4. $3 adults, $2.50 seniors, children under age 12 free. A historic throwback to frontier days in the 'Glades, this museum preserves a Native American trading post of the early 1900s. Splintery shelves hold ointment containers, FlyDed insect killer, live-stock spray, a sausage-making machine, Seminole cloth work, and hordes of memo-rabilia. A post office and bedroom recall life in the pioneer days and look pretty much the same as they did at that time. One of the best features is the view from the back porch. This was the site of a Jesse James–era murder immortalized in Peter Matthiessen's novel, *Killing Mr. Watson.*

KIDS' STUFF ✿ **C'MON** (239-514-0084; www.cmon.org), North Collier Region-al Park, Livingston Road, Naples. The Golisano Children's Museum of Naples, opening in summer 2011, will be an inspiring environment where children and their families play, learn, and dream together. Under construction at North Collier Regional Park in Naples, the 30,000-square-foot facility will feature 10 spectacular-ly designed, child-scaled exhibits to invite sensory and intellectual exploration. Children's museum specialist Mary Sinker and acclaimed exhibit designer Jack Rouse Associates conceived each exhibit as a model of three interrelated princi-ples: an appreciation of children's play behavior, knowledge of how an environment can influence play and learning, and an understanding of children's develop-mental milestones. These three core beliefs enabled them to transform the learning landscape so that serious learning looks like play . . . for those who know how to look.

KIDS WILL ENJOY THE RE-CREATED SEMINOLE WAR FORT AT COLLIER COUNTY MUSEUM.

✿ **Naples Zoo** (239-262-5409; www .napleszoo.com), 1590 Goodlette-Frank Rd., Naples. Open daily 9–5 (last ticket sold at 4). $19.95 adults, $18.95 sen-iors, $11.95 children ages 3–12. Pri-mates, big cats, and other carnivores are specialties of this small, neighbor-hood zoo. Among its newest exhibits are Black Bear Hammock, the largest such accredited exhibit east of the Mis-sissippi; fossas from Madagascar; a ven-omous snakes exhibit; and Leopard Rock. Multimedia shows educate and advance a conservation mission. A boat ride takes a close-up look at the zoo's monkey and lemur population, which is sequestered on nine islands. Play areas amuse toddlers. Shaded, meandering, chirp-orchestrated paths take you past other fenced animals. The 52-acre grounds are attractively maintained with the lush vegetation of the zoo's once-called Caribbean Gardens (see "Gardens" in this section). To take in all the sights and shows requires about four hours.

MUSEUMS ✪ 🐾 ✎ **Collier County Museum** (239-774-8476; www.collier museums.com), 3301 Tamiami Trail E., Naples. Open Monday–Friday 9–5, Saturday 9–4. Donations accepted. The unique aspects of this village of history include typical Seminole chikee huts, a vintage swamp buggy that kids can climb into, the skeleton of an Ice Age giant ground sloth, a working archaeological lab, a replicated Seminole war fort, and a 1910 steam locomotive from the county's cypress-logging era. State-of-the-art exhibits of prehistoric fossils, vignettes, and artifacts up to the 1960s include a video of a Gary Cooper movie filmed in the area. New to the grounds: the original restored circa-1935 *Kokomis* ferry, once used at the old offshore Keewaydin Island Club.

Holocaust Museum of Southwest Florida (239-263-9200; www.hmswfl.org), 4760 Tamiami Trail N., Suite 7, at Sandalwood Square, Naples. Open Tuesday–Sunday 1–4. $8 per person. This museum began as a student project, and today its photos, written materials, and artifacts take visitors chronologically through the Jewish experience from pre–World War II through post-Nazi liberation. In 2007, the museum acquired an authentic, 10-ton, World War II-era railway boxcar as a mobile educational tool. The facility also hosts exhibits related to war and the Holocaust.

Marco Island Historical Museum (239-389-6447; www.themihs.org), 180 Heathwood Dr., Marco Island. Open Monday–Friday 9–4. Through photographs, artifacts, replicas, and memorabilia, this fledgling museum depicts the island's past in three rooms: the Calusa Room, Pioneer Room, and Modern Marco Room. The Calusa Room displays a life-size diorama, Calusa shell tools, masks, wood carvings, and other artifacts unearthed in the 1895 archaeological expedition that established Marco as an important center of the Calusa kingdom. The dig's most important find, the Calusa Cat, has become an island icon and is replicated here. The original resides at the Smithsonian Institution. The Collier Room tells the story of early settler Bill Collier and the island's clam canneries. The island's modern-day development starts with the Mackle brothers in the final room. In 2010, the historical society that operates the museum completed a new building nearby and anticipates its exhibits' completion by 2012.

🐾 **Museum of the Everglades** (239-695-0008; www.colliermuseums.com), 105 W. Broadway, Everglades City. Open Tuesday–Friday 10–5, Saturday 9–4. $2 suggested donation. This facility occupies a renovated historic laundry started by developer Barron Collier to serve the community of road builders during the construction of the Tamiami Trail in the 1920s. The museum concentrates on the tremendous feat of blazing a trail through the swampy, buggy Everglades, and on the region's Calusa Indian and fishing heritage. It also hosts special changing exhibits.

✎ **Naples Depot Museum & Lionel Train Museum** (239-252-8476 for museum, 239-262-1776 for Lionel; www.colliermuseums.com), 1051 Fifth Ave. S., corner Tamiami Trail and 10th St. S., Naples. Museum open Monday–Friday 9–5, Saturday 9–4; Lionel open Thursday–Saturday 10–2. Admission free for Depot Museum; $5 for adults, $3 for children for Lionel. Gary Cooper, Hedy Lamarr, and other illuminati of yore once arrived at this circa-1927 depot. Recently, Collier

County initiated a new museum here, devoted to the history of the railroad and transportation in the region—from dugout canoes to mule wagons to swamp buggies. Three authentic rail cars sit alongside the depot. Lionel has set up an elaborate display of eight operating model trains and a small railroad outside for kiddie rides.

MUSIC AND NIGHTLIFE ✪ Famous Fish (239-394-7111), 657 S. Collier Blvd., Marco Island. A lively resort-scene, indoor/outdoor venue for live dance music—pop, jazz, reggae, and Motown—nightly. Serves a full food menu until midnight.

Little Bar (239-394-5663; www.littlebarrestaurant.com), 205 Harbor Dr., Goodland. Hosts live music Thursday–Sunday nights. Site of the annual summertime Spammy Jammy, where participants in pajamas bring their crazy Spam sculptures and creations.

✪ **McCabe's Irish Pub** (239-403-8777; www.mccabesirishpub.com), 699 Fifth Ave. S., Naples, Authentic Irish music and food along with rowdy camaraderie in an authentic Dublin-built pub.

Naples Concert Band (239-263-9521; www.naplesconcertband.org), Naples. For more than 38 years its 90 volunteer musicians have been performing free Sunday concerts once a month, October–April, at Cambier Park in Old Naples.

Off the Hook Comedy Club (239-389-6900; www.offthehookcomedy.com), 599 S. Collier Blvd., at Captain Brien's Seafood & Raw Bar, Marco Island. Nationally known comedians perform Thursday–Sunday; special shows other nights of the week, too.

Snook Inn (239-394-3313), 1215 Bald Eagle Dr., Marco Island. Live local bands, contemporary and island music.

Stan's Idle Hour (239-394-3041 or 877-387-2582; www.stansidlehour.net), 221 Goodland Dr. W., Goodland. Live music, often of a comical nature, happens throughout the day. Sunday celebrations are packed with drinkers and dancers doing the trademark Buzzard Lope. Entertainment often includes the colorful owner himself, Stan Gober.

Tommy Bahama's Tropical Café (239-643-6889), 1220 Third St. S., Naples. Lively island music in the evenings, with outdoor seating.

THEATER Gulfshore Playhouse (239-261-7529 or 866-811-4111; www .gulfshoreplayhouse.org), Norris Center Theater, 755 Eighth Ave. S., Naples. Naples's newest professional company performs January–Easter.

Marco Players (239-642-7270; www.themarcoplayers.com), 1083 N. Collier Blvd., at Marco Town Center Mall, Marco Island. Nonprofit community theater that produces comedies and musicals November–April.

✪ **Philharmonic Center for the Arts** (239-597-1900 or 800-597-1900; www .thephil.org), 5833 Pelican Bay Blvd., Naples. "The Phil," as locals call it, is home to the 85-piece Naples Philharmonic and the Miami City Ballet (miamicityballet .org). It hosts audiences of up to 1,425 for Broadway shows, touring orchestras, opera, comedians, modern dance, and more than 400 events yearly. It also has a 200-seat black-box theater and four art galleries.

THRILL TO "THE PHIL"—NAPLES'S PREMIER SHOWPLACE.

Sugden Community Theatre (239-263-7990), 701 Fifth Ave. S., Naples. The home of the Naples Players (www.naplesplayers.org), a community theater troupe that has been entertaining October–May for more than 50 years. The complex features a main stage, plus a more experimental black-box theater, and plays host to the Naples Jazz Society, ballet, opera, and other performance art. Every Sunday–Tuesday at 6 PM, a local band gathers outside for a 20-minute "Naples Patriotic Moment" featuring the national anthem and "Taps" in honor of those serving in the military.

TheatreZone (888-966-3352; www.theatrezone-florida.com), G&L Theatre at Community School of Naples, 13275 Livingston Rd., Naples. Dramas, comedies, and musical revues late December–mid-June.

VISUAL ART CENTERS & RESOURCES Like its Italian namesake, Naples serves as the region's aesthetic pacesetter. Gallery-lined streets host artists of local, national, and international stature. The following entries introduce you to opportunities for experiencing art as either a viewer or a practicing artist. A listing for commercial galleries is included in the "Shopping" section.

Art League of Bonita Springs Center for the Arts (239-495-8989; www.art centerbonita.org), 26100 Old 41 Rd., Bonita Springs. An impressive 10-acre complex of galleries, a gift shop with art supplies and works, and photography, pottery, sculpture, and other studios. It hosts classes, children's programs, lectures, dance performances, exhibitions, and national art festivals in January and March (see "Special Events").

Art League of Marco Island (239-394-4221; www.marcoislandart.com), 1010 Winterberry Dr., Marco Island. Workshops, lectures, two galleries with monthly changing exhibits, and a gift shop. It also sponsors an annual arts and crafts festival in January and other cultural events.

✪ **Patty & Jay Baker Naples Museum of Art** (239-597-1900 or 800-597-1900; www.thephil.org), Philharmonic Center for the Arts, 5833 Pelican Bay Blvd., Naples. Open October–June, Tuesday–Saturday 10–4, Sunday noon–4; closed July–September. Complimentary guided tours available at 11 and 2. $12 adults, $6 students (late January–early May); $8 adults, $4 students (early May– late June and October– late January), free for children under age 5. Permanent exhibits include a collection of modern American masters from 1900 to 1955, including Alexander Calder, Jackson Pollock, and Hugh Breckenridge. The museum holds the Pollak Collection of Modern Art and a miniatures collection. World-renowned glass sculptor Dale Chihuly created one of his famous ceilings and two magnificent chandeliers for the museum: one that hangs from its dome glass conservatory and another suspended in the three-story stairwell. The museum's 15 galleries elegantly showcase world-class traveling exhibitions.

United Arts Council (239-263-8242; www.uaccollier.com), 2335 Tamiami Trail N., Suite 504, Naples. A central clearinghouse for culture, music, dance, theater, and visual arts in the Naples area.

✪ **The von Liebig Art Center** (239-262-6517; www.naplesartcenter.org), 585 Park St., Naples. Home of the Naples Art Association, the center holds classes, workshops, and showings for children and its members, and presents other special exhibitions. The skylit library contains arts information.

✷ To Do

The Ten Thousand Islands are the meat of the South Coast's recreational banquet. Here, the old-fashioned sports—fishing, canoeing, hiking—are most in style. The beaches of Naples and Marco Island serve up the newer, exhilarating side dishes, everything from parasailing to jet-skiing.

BEACHES In 2003, a poll conducted by Yahoo! Travel Web site and *National Geographic Traveler* magazine ranked Naples as number 10 for "Top Sands" in the nation.

Parking fees are levied at most beaches; county residents can purchase stickers that allow them to park for free. For information on county beaches, contact Collier County Parks and Recreation Department (239-353-0404; www.collierparks .com), 15000 Livingston Rd., Naples 34109.

✒ **Clam Pass Park** (239-252-4000; www.collierparks.com), 410 Seagate Dr., at Naples Grande Resort & Club, Naples. This beach, used by guests of Naples Grande Resort & Club but open to the public, is reached by a tram that follows a nearly 1-mile boardwalk over a tidal bay and through mangroves. Boat and cabana rentals are available at this county facility. The sand is fine and fluffy and, once past the resort crowd, leads to preserve lands. You can kayak or sail into the sea or paddle along a trail among the mangroves, which are frequented by ospreys, hawks, and a variety of other feathered creatures. Facilities: restrooms, showers, food and beach concessions. Parking: $8 per day.

✔ **Delnor-Wiggins Pass State Park** (239-597-6196; www.floridastateparks.org
/delnorwiggins), 11135 Gulf Shore Dr. N., at CR 846, Vanderbilt Beach, Naples.
This highly natural, low-key beach, named among America's 40 Certified Healthy
Beaches, extends for a mile south from the mouth of the Cocohatchee River. The
lush white sands are protected during loggerhead turtle nesting season (summer)
and support stands of natural maritime vegetation, such as cactus, sea grape,
nickerbean, and yucca. A nature trail leads to an observation tower at the beach's
north end. This is a popular park, but you can usually find parking in one of the
many lots. Restrict your swimming to south of the pass's fast-moving waters, which
are a boon to fishermen. Facilities: picnic areas, grills, pavilion, restrooms, showers, boat ramp, volleyball, lifeguard. Admission: $6 per car, up to eight passengers;
$4 for singles; $2 for pedestrians, cyclists, or extra passengers.

✪ ✔ **Lowdermilk Park** (239-213-3029), 257 Banyan Blvd. at Gulf Shore Blvd.,
Naples. Beach headquarters for the South Coast: There are lots of special activities
at this gulfside party spot and its 1,000 feet of sandy beach. Families love its little
duck pond. Across the street, a deli and restaurant fuel your beach day. Facilities:
picnic area, restrooms, showers, volleyball, playground, concessions, special handicap access, wheeled surf chairs. Parking: metered, 25 cents per 10 minutes.

Naples Municipal Beaches (239-213-3062), Gulf Shore Blvd. south of Doctors
Pass, Naples. The historic pier on 12th Avenue South, where facilities and a parking lot are located, anchors stretches of natural beach. Smaller lots lie to the north
and south. Facilities: restrooms, showers, concessions, fishing pier. Parking:
metered, 25 cents per 10 minutes.

South Marco Beach (239-252-4000;
www.collierparks.com), S. Collier Blvd.
at Swallow Ave., south end of Marco
Island. Parking is on the other side of
Collier Blvd., half a block away. A
paved brick path beneath palm trees
leads to this patch of public beach
between giant high rises. No facilities,
but there's a restaurant next door.
Parking: $8 per vehicle.

✔ **Sugden Regional Park** (239-252-
4000; www.collierparks.com), 4284
Avalon Dr., Naples. On the east side of
town, it is most famous for the waterskiing shows it hosts Saturdays or Sundays (check www.gulfcoastskimmers
.com for schedule) on its freshwater
lake. A sand beach edges it on the side
opposite the bleacher stands, and here
you can rent a canoe or kayak, or swim
in a guarded, roped-off area. A bike
path loops the lake, plus there are cool
playgrounds, picnic areas, and a fishing
pier. Parking is free.

DELNOR-WIGGINS PASS STATE PARK: A
HAVEN FOR BIRDS, BEACHERS, SHELLERS,
SEA TURTLES, AND FISHERMEN ALIKE.

⚓ **Tigertail Beach** (239-252-4000; www.collierparks.com), Hernando Dr., north end of Marco Island. This county-owned beach is a good place for shelling and sunning. In season, arrive early to find a parking spot. Wooden ramps cross dunes to 31 acres of wide, marvelous beach. The south end fronts high rises, but the north end stretches into wilderness. The fun playground is divided for two different age groups. Tidal pools separate the main beach and a fronting sandbar known as Sand Dollar Island, which attracts shellers and feeding and nesting birds. Facilities: picnic area, restrooms, showers, water-sports rentals, restaurant, playground, volleyball. Parking: $8 per vehicle.

Vanderbilt Beach (239-252-4000), 280 Vanderbilt Dr., north of Naples, Vanderbilt Beach. This recently refurbished stretch of sand runs alongside resorts and is well suited to those who like sharing the beach with a lot of people, as well as bar- and restaurant-hopping along the beach. Facilities: restrooms, showers, food; water-sports rentals available at nearby resorts. Parking: $8 per vehicle at nearby parking ramp on Vanderbilt Dr.; metered on the street.

BICYCLING City and country biking paths are available to those who prefer this slow, intimate mode of exploration. Sidewalks, bike paths (marked with white diamonds), and roadsides accommodate cyclists. By state law, cyclists must conduct themselves as pedestrians when using sidewalks. Avoid cycling on crowded downtown walks. Where they share the road with other vehicles, cyclists must follow all the rules of the road. Children under age 16 must wear helmets.

Best Biking: Naples has laid out a sporadic system of metropolitan bike paths. A favorite route of local cyclists loops through 10 miles of pathway in the north-end Pelican Bay development. Within it, a 580-acre nature preserve provides a change of scenery from upscale suburbia.

A bike path runs the length of **Bonita Beach,** nearly 3 miles long. At its south end it connects to another, which leads to **Vanderbilt Beach.**

Naples Bicycle Tours (239-455-4611; www.naplesbicycletours.com) conducts half- and full-day excursions, with transportation, in Naples and to the Everglades.

Marco Island's bike paths parallel main drives such as Collier Boulevard and Barfield Drive.

Bike paths traverse **Everglades City** and cross the causeway to **Chokoloskee Island.** Back-road bikers take to the 12-mile (one-way) ✪ **W. J. Janes Memorial Scenic Drive** through Fakahatchee Strand Preserve State Park, off CR 29 north of Everglades City. Royal palms, cypress trees, and air plants provide pristine scenery and bird habitat (10 miles in you'll find a popular bird feeding pond). Morning or sunset riders may spot wild turkeys, alligators, raccoons, snakes, otters, bobcats, and deer. Rangers at **Everglades National Park** (239-695-2591 or 866-628-2591; www.nps.gov/ever) lead two-hour bike tours every Thursday in season (mid-December–Easter). A 3.5-mile mountain bike trail at ✪ **Collier-Seminole State Park** travels through cabbage palm hammock.

Rentals/Sales: Many resorts rent bikes or provide bike use to guests.

Bonita Bike & Baby (239-947-6377; www.bonitabikeandbaby.com) It delivers a variety of bikes, including kids' bikes, trailers for kids, and beach and jogging strollers.

Island Bike Shop (239-394-8400; www.islandbikeshops.com), 1095 Bald Eagle Dr., Marco Island. Rents scooters and bikes in various sizes and styles; also offers bike tours. Rates by the hour, day, and week. Delivery available.

Naples Cyclery (239-566-0600; www.naplescyclery.com), 813 Vanderbilt Beach Rd., at Pavilion Shopping Center, Naples; and (239-949-0026), 27820 S. Tamiami Trail, Bonita Springs. Rents a wide variety of speed bikes, recumbent bikes, surreys, and equipment for kids.

BOATS & BOATING Naples, Marco Island, and Everglades City are lousy with marinas. These are headquarters for boat rentals, tours, and charters to serve every interest, from shelling and fishing to gaping at mansions.

Canoeing & Kayaking: The ultimate paddling experience, Everglades National Park has marked a 99-mile ✪ **Wilderness Waterway** trail that extends from Everglades City to Flamingo, the park's main eastern access. Platform campsites accommodate overnighters. There are also good canoeing trails near the Oasis Visitors Center in ✪ **Big Cypress National Preserve.** Outfitters in Everglades City provide rentals, supplies, tours, and shuttle service. In addition to the outlets listed below, many resorts and parks rent canoes and kayaks.

Collier County is working on developing the ✪ **Paradise Coast Blueway** (www .paradisecoastblueway.com), a system of paddling trails throughout the county that will provide GPS-marked trail routes. Phase I, the Ten Thousand Islands section, was completed in 2009. Seventy-three miles long, it includes one long trail from Everglades City to Goodland and six shorter day-trip trails. Phases II and III will extend to north Naples and Bonita Springs. The **Paradise Coast Paddling Club** (www.paradisecoastpaddlers.com) is a good resource for kayaking in Collier County.

Cocohatchee Nature Center (239-592-1200; www.cocohatchee.org), 12345 Tamiami Trail N., Naples. Rents kayaks and canoes for self-guided or guided tours into the estuary wilderness of the Cocohatchee River, which empties into the gulf.

✪ **Collier-Seminole State Park** (239-394-3397; www.floridastateparks.org /collierseminole), 20200 E. Tamiami Trail, between Naples and Everglades City. Rents canoes for use on the park's 13.6-mile canoe trail into mangrove wilderness preserve. Guided tours available some Sundays in season by reservation.

Conservancy of Southwest Florida (239-262-0304; www.conservancy.org), 1450 Merrihue Dr., Naples; and (239-775-8569), 401 Shell Island Rd., Naples. Kayaks are available to rent for use in the nature center's waterways.

Everglades Area Tours (239-695-3633; www.evergladesareatours.com), 238 Mamie St., Chokoloskee Island. Knowledgeable naturalists take you on paddling adventures deep into the Everglades by transporting you and your kayak via a "mother" powerboat. Some excursions involve camping, fishing, biking, and hiking.

⚓ **Everglades National Park Boat Tours** (239-695-2591 or 866-628-2591; www .nps.gov/ever), Everglades Ranger Station, 815 Oyster Bar Ln., Everglades City. Free ranger-led canoe trips in season (mid-December–Easter) every Wednesday, Saturday, and Sunday 10–2, and Thursday and Friday 2–4. You must bring or rent a canoe or kayak. Rentals and launch also available for self-guided tours.

North American Canoe Tours (239-695-4666; www.evergladesadventures.com), 107 Camellia St., Everglades City. Rents 17-foot aluminum canoes, high-quality kayaks, and equipment with complete outfitting and shuttle service. Guided excursions into the Everglades range from one day to skiff-assisted trips of six nights.

⚓ **Rookery Bay National Estuarine Research Reserve** (239-417-6310, ext. 401; www.rookerybay.org), 300 Tower Rd., Naples. Naturalist-led kayak tours of the mangroves in Henderson Creek and Rookery Bay every Wednesday (also Friday, October–April) for ages 12 and older.

Saltwater Sports (239-262-6149; www.saltwatersportsflorida.com), 11369 Tamiami Trail E., Naples. Rentals, nature tours, and sales from five locations throughout Collier County. Delivery and pickup available to some areas. *Sea Kayaker* magazine's Readers Choice Awards voted it Best Sea Kayak Outfitter, Southeast/Gulf Coast and Best Tour Operator, Southeast/Gulf Coast for 2008–2010.

Dining Cruises: **Marco Island Princess** (239-642-5415; sunshinetoursmarcoisland .com), 951 Bald Eagle Dr., at Rose Marco River Marina, Marco Island. Daily narrated sight-seeing cruises, lunch and dinner cruises, and sunset hors d'oeuvres excursions.

Naples Princess (239-649-2275; www.naplesprincesscruises.com), Port-O-Call Marina, 550 Port-O-Call Way, on US 41 across the river from Tin City, Naples. Excursions include a sight-seeing cruise, buffet lunch, sunset hors d'oeuvres, and sunset buffet dinner. Full-service cash bar.

Personal Watercraft Rentals/Tours: **Marco Island Water Sports** (239-642-2359; www.marcoislandwatersports.com), 400 S. Collier Blvd., at Marco Island Marriott Beach Resort, Golf Club & Spa, Marco Island. Rents WaveRunners and conducts WaveRunner excursions into Ten Thousand Islands. Also parasailing.

Powerboat Rentals: **Big Hickory Fishing Nook Marina** (239-992-3945), 26107 Hickory Blvd., Bonita Beach. Rents deck boats and pontoons by the half or full day. Kayaks, too.

Cedar Bay Marina (239-642-6717 or 800-906-2628; www.cedarbayrentals.com), 705 E. Elkcam Circle, Marco Island. Top-of-the-line, fully equipped fishing and pleasure boats.

Naples Watersports (239-774-0479; naples-boatrentals.com), Port-O-Call Marina, 550 Port-O-Call Way, off US 41 E., Naples. Rents deck boats and powerboats 19 to 22 feet in length to accommodate four to 10 people.

Walker's Coon Cay Marina (239-394-2797), 604 E. Palm Ave., Goodland. Rents 19-foot center consoles with VHF radios.

Public Boat Ramps: **Caxambas Park** (239-642-0004; www.collierparks.com), 909 Collier Ct., Marco Island. Restrooms, bait, fuel, and access to Roberts Bay. Launch fee.

Cocohatchee River Park (239-591-8596; www.collierparks.com), 13531 Vanderbilt Dr., at Vanderbilt Beach, Naples. Park with three ramps onto the river (which runs to the gulf), restrooms, picnic tables, and boat rentals. Launch fee.

Delnor-Wiggins Pass State Park (239-597-6196; www.floridastateparks.org/delnorwiggins), 11135 Gulf Shore Dr. N., Naples. The boat ramp allows access to the back bays, the Cocohatchee River, and the Gulf of Mexico, providing visitors with excellent fishing opportunities. Admission.

Marco Island approach, 1 mile before the bridge on CR 951.

Naples Landing (239-213-3070), 1101 Ninth St. S., Naples. One ramp.

Sailboat Charters: **Sail Marco** (239-272-0939; www.sail-marco.com), Rose Marco River Marina, 951 Bald Eagle Dr., Marco Island; mailing address: 821A Palm St., Marco Island 34145. Take a powered or sailing boat to unbridged barrier islands for shelling.

Sweet Liberty (239-793-3525; www.sweetliberty.com), 880 12th Ave. S., at the City Dock, Naples. Daily shelling/beach, sight-seeing, dolphin-spotting, and sunset trips aboard a 53-foot catamaran.

Sight-Seeing & Entertainment Cruises: Look under "Wildlife Tours & Charters" for nature excursions.

Speedy Johnson's Airboat Tours (239-695-4448 or 800-998-4448; www.florida -everglades.com/speedy), 621 Begonia St., Everglades City. You'll find any number of airboat tour operators in and around Everglades City. Many, contrary to good environmental practice, feed wildlife to attract it to the boat. This one is better than others for its accessibility to grasslands and its elevated seats.

FISHING Many visiting sports folk arrive at the South Coast eager to fight the big fish and brave the deep waters of the Gulf of Mexico. They come equipped with their 50-pound test line, heavy tackle, and tall fish tales. Yet closer to home, in the back bays and shallow waters of Ten Thousand Islands, experienced fishermen find what's best about the region. Sea trout, snook, redfish, sheepshead, mangrove snapper, and pompano abound in the brackish creeks, grass flats, and channels.

Nonresidents age 16 and older must obtain a license unless fishing from a vessel or pier covered by its own license. You can buy inexpensive, temporary, nonresident licenses at county tax collectors' offices and most Kmarts and bait shops. Check local regulations for season, size, and catch restrictions.

Fishing Charters/Outfitters: Check the large marinas for fishing guides. Experienced guides can take the intimidation and guesswork out of open-water fishing.

Captain Paul 34 (239-263-4949), 1200 Fifth Ave. S., Naples. Half-day bay fishing trips aboard a 34-foot pontoon boat offered twice daily.

Captains Lee and Larry Quick (239-695-0006 or 888-657-0006; www.florida -southwest.com/quick/guide.htm), 905 Copeland Ave., Everglades City. Fly and light-tackle fishing in Ten Thousand Islands and the Everglades.

Chokoloskee Island Outfitters (239-695-2286; www.cyberangler.com/guides/ prickett), P.O. Box 172, Chokoloskee Island, 34138. Captain Dave Prickett takes you out for half and full days.

Hickory Bay Charters (239-947-3851), 26107 Hickory Blvd., at Big Hickory Fishing Nook Marina, Bonita Springs. Board the *Ramble On III,* a 30-foot pontoon, for four-hour trips into the backcountry. Can combine fishing excursions with sightseeing, birding, and shelling.

Lady Brett 45 (239-263-4949; www.tincityboats.com), 1200 Fifth Ave. S., at Tin City, Naples. Half-day offshore trips aboard a 45-foot powerboat with head on board.

Mangrove Outfitters (239-793-3370 or 888-319-9848; www.mangrove-outfitters .com), 4111 E. Tamiami Trail, Naples. Guide charters and, in season, teaches classes on fly-tying.

SNOOK: A PRIZED CATCH ON THE NAPLES PIER.

Peg Leg Charters (239-642-4333 or 239-250-0625; www.peglegcharters .com), at Stan's Idle Hour Restaurant, Goodland. Captain Ron Kennedy takes anglers offshore for half- and full-day trips.

Sunshine Tours (239-642-5415; www .sunshinetoursmarcoisland.com), 951 Bald Eagle Dr., at Rose Marco River Marina, Marco Island. Takes small parties aboard a 32-foot boat with head for offshore excursions, half to full day. Also does backcountry fishing trips.

Tide Teaser Native Charter Guide (239-992-2857, cell 239-248-1058), at Big Hickory Fishing Nook Marina, 26107 Hickory Blvd., Bonita Beach. Captain Brad Hurd says, "No Fish— No Pay" on his back-bay and offshore fishing excursions. He specializes in light tackle and offers night shark and tarpon excursions in season.

Fishing Piers: ✪ **Naples Fishing Pier** (239-213-3062), 25 12th Ave. S., Naples. Extends 1,000 feet into the gulf and has a bait shop, snack bar, restrooms, and showers.

GOLF Naples earns its title as Golf Capital of the World with more golf holes per capita than any other statistically tracked metropolitan area.

Public Golf Courses: **Bonita Fairways Country Club** (239-947-9100; www.bonita fairways.com), 9751 W. Terry St., Bonita Springs. Play 18 newly renovated holes at a reasonable price. Restaurant.

Lely Resort Flamingo Island Club (239-793-2223 or 866-392-2100; www.lely -resort.net), 8004 Lely Resort Blvd., off CR 951 east of Naples. Two public courses designed by Robert Trent Jones Sr. and Lee Trevino. Offers 36 holes, par 72, and a golf school called Naples Golf Authority (239-821-0279).

The Links of Naples (239-417-1313), 16161 E. Tamiami Trail, Naples. Lit 18-hole course with driving range, PGA lessons, rentals.

Naples Beach Golf Club (239-435-2443; www.naplesbeachhotel.com), 851 Gulf Shore Blvd. N., Naples. An 18-hole, par 72 resort course that hosts many pro and amateur tournaments. Restaurant and lounge.

Pelican's Nest Golf Club (239-947-2282; www.nestgolf.com), 4450 Pelican's Nest Dr., Bonita Springs. A 36-hole course, par 72.

Tiburón Golf Club (239-594-2040; www.wcigolf.com), 2600 Tiburón Dr., at the Ritz-Carlton Golf Resort, Naples. One of Naples's most exclusive golfing venues; semiprivate with two 18-hole courses—the Black and the Gold—and a golf academy.

Golf Centers: **David Leadbetter Golf Academy** (239-592-1444 or 888-633-5323; www.davidleadbetter.com), at LaPlaya Beach & Golf Resort, 333 Palm River Blvd.,

Naples. Offers golf school at LaPlaya Golf Course. Lessons, classes, and golf retreats can last anywhere from one hour to three days.

Naples Golf Academy (239-732-9944; www.learninggolf.com), 5375 Hibiscus Dr., at Hibiscus Golf Club, Naples. Half- to two-day courses, private lessons, weekly clinic.

The Rick Smith Golf Academy (239-594-2040; www.wcigolf.com), 2600 Tiburón Dr., at the Ritz-Carlton Golf Resort, Naples. Features individualized instruction, computerized swing analysis, private video viewing rooms.

Golf Shops: **World of Golf** (239-263-4999 or 800-505-9998; www.worldofgolf .com), 4500 N. Tamiami Trail, Naples. From tees to clubs, this shop carries all name-brand equipment and apparel.

HEALTH & FITNESS CLUBS The following offer daily or weekly rates for visitors.

Fitness Quest (239-643-7546), 6800 Golden Gate, Naples. Complete fitness center, aerobics, karate, heart-healthy café, nursery.

Golden Gate Fitness Center (239-353-7128; www.collierparks.com), at Golden Gate Community Park, 3300 Santa Barbara Blvd., Naples. Full range of Cybex and Keiser equipment, cardio machines, and free weights. Personal training and assessment available.

⊘ **Greater Marco YMCA** (239-394-3144; www.marcoislandymca.org), 101 Sandhill St., Marco Island. Full-service gym with personal training and fitness assessment programs, swimming lessons, massage, tennis, and a wide variety of aerobic classes.

Marco Fitness Club (239-394-3705), 871 E. Elkcam Circle, Marco Island. Top-of-the-line cardiovascular and weight machines, free weights, personal trainers, massage therapist.

Naples Fitness Center (239-262-1112; www.naplesfitnesscenter.com), 1048 Castello Dr., a block off the Tamiami Trail, Naples. A modern, three-tiered workout club with racquetball and handball courts, a heated swimming pool and Jacuzzi, fitness classes, and a smoothie bar.

HIKING ✪ **Big Cypress National Preserve** (239-695-1201; www.nps.gov/bicy), HCR 61, Ochopee. East of FL 29, short hiking trails lead off Route 839; longer trails begin about 15 miles away at the Oasis Visitor Center and join up with the Florida Trail (www.floridatrail.org), a national scenic trail that traverses the state's length. A boardwalk trail at the Oasis lets visitors look down at dozens of big alligators. Another good boardwalk for gator-gazing is at H. P. Williams Roadside Park, west of the Oasis.

✪ **Collier-Seminole State Park** (239-394-3397; www.floridastateparks.org/ collierseminole), 20200 E. Tamiami Trail, Naples. A 7-mile trail winds through pine flatwoods and cypress swamp with a primitive campsite. A self-guided trip along a boardwalk leads into a salt marsh.

Conservancy of Southwest Florida (239-262-0304; www.conservancy.org), 1450 Merrihue Dr., Naples. Guided and unguided nature hikes through a subtropical hammock. Also hosts day-trip safaris that involve hiking.

✪ **Fakahatchee Strand Preserve State Park** (239-695-4593; www.floridastate parks.org/fakahatcheestrand), W. J. Janes Memorial Scenic Dr., FL 29, north of US 41, Copeland. Several trails—actually, old logging tramways—traverse the strand off 12-mile (one-way) Janes Drive from the gates on either side of the road. They range in length from 1 to 2 miles. Summer flooding can make your hike a slosh. Park volunteers lead *swamp* walks November– February, when you can spot many different varieties of wild orchids. Adjacent **Picayune Strand State Forest** (at the end of Janes Drive) introduces access to 3.2-mile Sabal Palm Hiking Trail, which winds through cypress forest, habitat for a variety of birds.

HUNTING The Everglades provides some of Florida's best shots at hunting. You must obtain a state license and a Wildlife Management Area stamp. Permits are required for early-season and special types of hunting. For information on seasons and bag limits, request a copy of the *Interactive Hunting Regulations Handbook and Florida Hunting Seasons* when you buy your license. (You can also download the publications at www.myfwc.com/hunting.) Skeet and clay shooting is available at **Port of the Islands Gun Club** (239-642-8999; www.poigunclub.com), 12425 Union Rd., between Naples and Everglades City.

KIDS' STUFF ✐ **Bonita Springs B3 Skate Park** (239-992-2556; www.bonita springsrecreation.org), 26740 Pine Ave., at Bonita Springs Recreation Center, Bonita Springs. New, small facility.

✐ **Coral Cay Adventure Golf** (239-793-4999; www.funspotrentals.com), 2205 E. Tamiami Trail, Naples. Two 18-hole miniature golf courses with a tropical island theme. Admission.

✐ **Edge Skate Park** (239-213-2037; www.naplesgov.com), 1600 Fleischmann Blvd., Naples. Newly renovated, it welcomes skaters and BMX bikers.

✐ **Golden Gate Community Center** (239-353-7128; www.collierparks.com), Golden Gate Community Park, 3300 Santa Barbara Blvd., Naples. Swimming fun for all ages, with water slides, wading pool and fountain, and competition pool with

---

STEALING A PEEK AT ORCHIDS

Susan Orleans's true account of orchid lust, *The Orchid Thief,* inspired the outlandish 2003 movie adaptation starring Nicholas Cage, Chris Cooper, and Meryl Streep. The setting: Florida's steamy corners—specifically, Faka-hatchee Strand Preserve State Park.

Here Orleans sloshed through the swamps with her unlikely hero searching for the coveted ghost orchid. You can, too, through ranger slough walk programs held in season. The waterway—approximately 20 miles long and 3 to 5 miles wide—has enjoyed a surge in popularity since the book and movie. As the orchid capital of the U.S., it harbors nearly 40 species of native wild orchids listed as threatened or endangered, among them the ghost orchid. In fact, biologist Mike Owen reports spotting six specimens on a recent trip.

low and high dives. Also a BMX track and skate park at 4701 Golden Gate Pkwy. (239-252-4180). Admission.

✒ **Golf Safari** (239-947-1377; golfsafariminigolf.com), 3775 Bonita Beach Rd., Bonita Springs. Jungle-themed miniature golf. Go online for coupons.

✒ **King Richard's Family Fun Park** (239-598-2042; www.kingrichardspark.net), 6780 N. Airport Rd., Naples. Merlin's Moat interactive water attraction (bring your swimsuit), kiddie rides, bumper boats, batting cages, a castle full of video games, laser tag, go-carts, a rock-climbing wall, and an 18-hole miniature golf course. You can buy tickets per attraction or for unlimited rides. Age restrictions apply for some of the rides.

✪ ✒ **Sun-n-Fun Lagoon** (239-252-4021; www.collierparks.com), 15000 Livingston Rd., at North Collier Regional Park, Naples. Naples's newest recreational addition, it has slides, a lazy river, and sandy beaches. A concession operation sells food, ice cream, sunscreen, swim diapers, and more. In late 2010, watch for a state-of-the-art children's museum to open at the same park. Admission.

✒ **Velocity Skate Park** (239-793-4414; www.collierparks.com), 3500 Thomasson Dr., Naples. Formerly East Naples Skate Park, it contains a full array of pipes, drops, ramps, and rails for skaters and BMX bikers. Admission.

RACQUET SPORTS Arthur L. Allen Tennis Center at Cambier Park (239-213-3060; www.allentenniscenter.com), between Eighth and Park Streets, Naples. Twelve lit Hydro-grid tennis courts. Fee.

Collier County Racquet Center (239-394-5454), 1275 San Marco Rd., Marco Island. County facility with two clay and four regular courts, two racquetball courts, pro shop, and lessons.

Fleischmann Park (239-213-3020; www.naplesgov.com), 1600 Fleischmann Blvd., Naples. Four lit racquetball courts.

TUBULAR FUN AT NAPLES'S SUN-N-FUN LAGOON.

Golden Gate Community Park (239-353-0404; www.collierparks.com), 3300 Santa Barbara Blvd., Naples. Four lit tennis and racquetball courts.

Mary C. Watkins Tennis Center (239-435-4351; www.naplesbeachhotel.com), at the Naples Beach Hotel & Golf Club, 851 Gulf Shore Blvd. N., Naples. Its six Har-Tru courts are open to the public for a fee; lessons and clinics available.

Naples Park Elementary, 111th Ave. N., Naples. Two lit courts.

Pelican Bay Community Park (239-598-3025), 764 Vanderbilt Rd., Naples. Eight lit tennis and four lit racquetball courts.

Tommie Barfield Elementary, 101 Kirkwood St., Goodland, Marco Island. Two lit courts.

SHELLING It is illegal to collect live shells in state and national parks. Collier County also discourages the collection of live shells.

Hot Shelling Spots: **Coconut Island,** north of Marco Island. A destination for most Marco Island shelling expeditions.

✪ **Key Island,** south of Naples, accessible only by boat. A partly private, partly state-owned unbridged island, Key holds a great many shell prizes that are not as picked over as on beaches that are accessible by car.

Ten Thousand Islands, Shell Island, Kingston Key, and Mormon Key provide lots of empty shells to collect.

Shelling Charters: **Marco Island Water Sports** (239-642-2359; www.marcoisland watersports.com), 400 S. Collier Blvd., at Marco Island Marriot Beach Resort, Golf Club & Spa and other nearby resorts, Marco Island. Shelling and other boat tours aboard *Calusa Spirit*, a 45-foot power catamaran with canopy shade.

Sail Marco (239-272-0939; www.sail-marco.com), Rose Marco River Marina, 951 Bald Eagle Dr., Marco Island; mailing address: 821A Palm St., Marco Island 34145. Shelling excursions via powered or sailing boat.

SPAS Everglades Spa (239-695-1006; www.spa-fari.com), 201 W. Broadway, at Everglades Spa & Lodge, Everglades City. Holistic treatments including colon hydrotherapy, ear candling, magnetic clay baths, intense pulse light therapy, and acupuncture in addition to more traditional massage, wraps, and skin care.

Naples Beach Hotel & Golf Club (239-261-2222 or 800-237-7600; www.naples beachhotel.com/spa/spa.html), 851 Gulf Shore Blvd. N., Naples. This vital component to a landmark Naples hotel brings full-service spa facilities, from extensive massage services (including aromatherapy, Reiki, shiatsu, neuromuscular massages) to body treatments (wraps, scrubs) and facials. A hair salon and fitness center enhance the wellness experience here.

The Ritz-Carlton Spa (239-514-6100; www.ritzcarlton.com), 280 Vanderbilt Beach Rd., Naples. A divine respite from the world, it offers a full menu of massages and body treatments, hydrotherapies, and wellness evaluations and training. Signature treatments include sleep therapy and Green Your Body Eco—salt and sugar scrubs, a scalp mud experience, and a body wrap using organic products. H20+ Café sells yummy smoothies and healthy snacks and lunches seasonally.

SeaSide Day Spa (239-393-2288 or 888-393-4SPA), 651 S. Collier Blvd., Marco Island. This spa administers a full line of massage, body, and skin treatments, with a focus on facials and face treatments.

Spa 41 (239-263-1664; www.spa41.net), 4910 Tamiami Trail N., Suite 200, at Tanglewood Marketplace, Naples. Offers therapeutic massage and other spa treatments, plus tanning beds.

Spa on Fifth (239-280-2777; www.spaonfifth.com), at Inn on Fifth, 699 Fifth Ave. S., Naples. Full line of facials, massages, and body scrubs and wraps.

Viva La Difference Day Spa (239-948-1733), 9124 Bonita Beach Rd., in Sunshine Plaza, Bonita Springs. Facials come in yummy flavors such as mint julep and pumpkin chiffon. Besides facials, its specialty, the spa offers massages, wraps, waxing, and nail services.

SPECTATOR SPORTS *Greyhound Racing:* **Naples-Fort Myers Greyhound Track** (239-992-2411; www.naplesfortmyersdogs.com), 10601 Bonita Beach Rd. S.E., Bonita Springs. Matinees, afternoon and night races, horse race simulcasting, poker room, and trackside dining. Admission.

Waterskiing: ✿ **Gulf Coast Skimmers** (239-732-0570; www.gulfcoastskimmers .com), Lake Avalon at Sugden Regional Park, Outer Drive, Naples; mailing address: 4002 Cindy Ave., Naples 34112. This group stages live shows October–April, Sunday at 3; and May–December, Saturday at 6:30.

WATER SPORTS *Extreme Water Sports:* **Florida Water Sports** (239-825-4866; www.floridaparasail.com), 500 S. Collier Blvd., at Marco Beach Ocean Resort, Marco Island. Twelve- to 15-minute parasail rides of 600 or 1,200 feet high.

Marco Island Water Sports (239-642-2359; www.marcoislandwatersports.com), 400 S. Collier Blvd., at Marco Island Marriot Beach Resort, Golf Club & Spa and other nearby resorts, Marco Island. Parasailing and WaveRunner and other waterbound tours.

Snorkeling & Scuba: Murky waters here send most divers to Florida's east coast and the Keys, although some charters take you out into deep local waters.

SCUBAdventures (239-434-7477; www.scubadventureslc.com), 971 Creech Rd., Naples. Supplies, instruction, and diving arrangements.

WILDERNESS CAMPING ✪ **Big Cypress National Preserve** (239-695-1200; www.nps.gov/bicy), HCR 61, Ochopee. Four primitive campgrounds and two others with limited facilities (cold showers) lie along the Tamiami Trail and Loop Road, about 18 miles east of FL 29 in Big Cypress National Preserve, a 729,000-acre sanctuary adjacent to Everglades National Park. Two campgrounds close seasonally; some require an off-road vehicle permit.

✪ ✿ **Collier-Seminole State Park** (239-394-3397; www.floridastateparks.org /collierseminole), 20200 E. Tamiami Trail, 17 miles south of Naples. This 6,470-acre park straddles Big Cypress Swamp and Ten Thousand Islands National Wildlife Refuge, and provides the least primitive camping in Everglades Country. There are RV hook-ups and tent sites; the first loop is more conducive to tenters, while the second has sites close together, a laundry, dump station, and recreational facilities for RVers. The park is full of possibilities for exploring nature and history, but no swimming is allowed.

✪ **Everglades National Park** (239-695-2591; www.nps.gov/ever) Backcountry camping along the Everglades canoe trails requires a permit, available from the Everglades City Ranger Station. Most sites provide platforms (some with shelters) on pilings with chemical toilets. Take mosquito repellent—gallons in summer.

Trail Lakes Campground (239-695-2275), 40904 US 41 E., 5 miles east of FL 29, Ochopee. Tent or RV camping. Also the site of Skunk-Ape Research Headquarters and a "real" animal park. Look for the supersized statue of a Florida panther, and you know you've reached funky Old Florida.

WILDLIFE SPOTTING The Florida Everglades, Big Cypress National Preserve, and Ten Thousand Islands and Florida Panther National Wildlife Refuges are home to the reclusive golden Florida panther, along with bobcats, manatees, wood storks, brown pelicans, black skimmers, roseate spoonbills, and ibises. Some creatures, such as the panther and bobcat, are rarely seen out of captivity. Others, especially the brown pelican, live side by side with residents. I've driven along FL 29 between the interstate and Tamiami Trail and spotted flocks of ibises and clumps of white-tailed deer. Deep in the 'Glades birds flock like a blizzard. So do mosquitoes in summer. Optimum wildlife viewing is December–March, when birds migrate and dry weather concentrates them in diminished ponds and other waterways, and insects are not quite so ferocious.

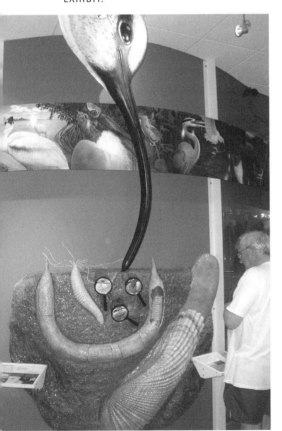

A SUPERSIZED WHIMBREL POKES FOR FOOD BENEATH THE RE-CREATED SANDS OF A ROOKERY BAY EDUCATION CENTER EXHIBIT.

Alligators: The Everglades is the New York City of Florida's alligator population. They thrive in the freshwater ponds and brackish creeks of the River of Grass. When the sun is shining along Alligator Alley (I-75) and the Tamiami Trail, you can see hundreds of these prehistoric reptiles on the banks sunning themselves. Crocodiles also live in the 'Glades, but they are rare on this side.

Birds: The South Coast is a birdwatcher's haven—especially in winter, when migrating species add to the vast variety of the coast's residential avifauna. Rare visitors and locals include roseate spoonbills, black skimmers, yellow-crowned night herons, wood storks, white pelicans, limpkins, and bald eagles. More commonly seen are frigates, ospreys, little blue herons, great blue herons, ibises, snowy egrets, brown pelicans, anhingas, cormorants, terns, seagulls, plovers, pileated woodpeckers, belted kingfishers, purple gallinules, owls, and hawks.

In its October 2002 issue, *Birder's World* magazine named two of the South Coast's sanctuaries among its

Top 15 Birding Hot Spots. For the best bird-watching, try ✪ **Everglades National Park** (rated #4); Naples's ✪ **Corkscrew Swamp Sanctuary** (rated #5), home to the largest nesting colony of wood storks in the U.S.; ✪ **Rookery Bay National Estuarine Reserve** near Marco Island; and Ten Thousand Islands National Wildlife Refuge, a haven for waterbirds. Marco Island is a proclaimed sanctuary for bald eagles. Barfield Bay in Goodland is one of their favorite locales. At the beach, the threatened piping plover gets support and protection from local environmentalists.

The **South Florida Birding Trail,** the last leg of the Great Florida Birding Trail, maps the region's best spotting venues. Corkscrew Swamp Sanctuary serves as the trail's regional gateway. For a map and more information, visit www.floridabirding trail.com.

Nature Preserves & Eco-Attractions: ✪ **Big Cypress National Preserve** (239-695-2000; www.nps.gov/bicy), HCR 61, adjacent to Everglades National Park, Ochopee. New welcome center less than 5 miles east of FL 29 at 33000 Tamiami Trail E., Ochopee; Oasis Visitors Center about 23 miles east of FL 29. Welcome center and visitor center open daily 9–4:30. This 729,000-acre preserve abuts Everglades National Park to the north and Fakahatchee Strand Preserve State Park to the east. The new, state-of-the-art welcome center opened in March 2010 with interpretative exhibits devoted to wetlands and their creatures. From the Oasis Visitor Center you can depart on wilderness hikes to sample its Everglades environment. In summer the trails—which connect to the Florida National Scenic Trail—can be very wet. You'll see the grasslands and bald cypress stands for which Big Cypress is known, as well as profuse birds and an alligator nursery. The preserve boasts the state's major population of the reclusive, endangered Florida panther. A small museum at the Oasis Visitors Center contains Indian artifacts and wildlife exhibits. A new Big Cypress Swamp Welcome Center with a wildlife observation platform and information opened in early 2010. Rangers lead swamp walks, bike and canoe trips, and campfire programs from both centers in season. A 26-mile scenic loop road is open to vehicles when road conditions allow. Closer to Everglades City, Birdon Road (CR 841) takes a 17-mile trip through sawgrass prairie habitat. It connects to CR 837 and then CR 839, which leads to two 2.5-mile hiking trails, one to the north and the other to the south of the intersection.

✪ ✿ **Collier-Seminole State Park** (239-394-3397; www.floridastateparks.org /collierseminole), 20200 E. Tamiami Trail, Naples. Open daily, 8–sundown; visitors center open 8–5. $5 per car, up to eight passengers; $4 per car, single occupant; $2 cyclists or pedestrians. Here, Naples meets the Everglades. One of the region's prettiest state parks, its 7,271 acres encompass manicured lawns to contrast with its jungle wilderness. Besides its historic attractions—a garden memorial to developer Barron Collier, the only remaining dredge used to build the Tamiami Trail across the Everglades, and a replicated Civil War blockhouse—it harbors a wealth of birds, otters, cats, manatees, and other critters who seek shelter in the outlying Everglades. Learn about them at the little visitors center in the blockhouse, then take to the nature, bike, and canoe trails. Ranger activities will provide biological background. Camping available.

✪ ✿ **Conservancy Nature Center** (239-262-0304; www.conservancy.org), 1450 Merrihue Dr., one block east of Goodlette Rd., Naples. Open November–April,

Monday–Saturday 9–4:30, Sunday noon–4. Admission: nature center, $7.50 adults and $2 children ages 3–12; nature trails and wildlife rehabilitation facility are free. This tucked-away nature complex on the Gordon River was built by the Conservancy of Southwest Florida to educate the public about the environment. Within its 21 acres, it encompasses a nature store; trail walks; boat tours of the river (free with paid admission); a rehabilitation center for birds, deer, turtles, and other injured animals (a new wildlife clinic is expected to be completed by mid-2011); and a nature discovery center with live Florida snakes, an offshore marine life tank (where you'll often find a loggerhead turtle swimming), fascinating touch tables, interactive games, and habitat vignettes where you can see and hear local fauna. Friendly and chattily informative guides conduct special programs throughout the day as they feed their live critters. The conservancy also hosts interpretative nature field trips; seasonal, guided paddle trips around Isles of Capri; and pontoon cruises into Rookery Bay. Kayak rentals are available for use on the Gordon River.

✪ ✿ **Corkscrew Swamp Sanctuary** (239-348-9151; www.corkscrew.audubon.org), 375 Sanctuary Rd., off Naples-Immokalee Rd., 21 miles east of N. Tamiami Trail, Naples. Open April 11–September, daily 7–7:30; October–April 10, daily 7–5:30 (no admission less than one hour before closing). $10 adults, $6 college students, $4 children ages 6–18. This 13,000-acre sanctuary, operated by the National Audubon Society, protects one of the largest stands of mature bald cypress trees in the country. Some of the towering specimens date back nearly 500 years. The threatened wood stork once came to nest here in great numbers. Diminished populations still do, at which time the nesting area is roped off to protect them. About 200 other species come and go or reside permanently at this keystone stop along the Great Florida Birding Trail. A 2.25-mile-long boardwalk takes you over swampland inhabited by rich plant and marine life. You can usually spot an alligator or two. The state-of-the-art Blair Audubon Center occupies a "stealth" building that blends with the pristine environment. Its Swamp Theater dramatically re-creates seasons and times of day on the boardwalk, plus there are hands-on opportunities for kids.

THE BOARDWALK THROUGH CORKSCREW SWAMP SANCTUARY EXPLORES A VARIETY OF ECOSYSTEMS.

✿ **Delnor-Wiggins Pass State Park** (239-597-6196; www.floridastateparks .org/delnorwiggins), 11135 Gulf Shore

Dr. N., at Vanderbilt Beach, Naples. Open sunrise to sunset. $6 per car, up to eight passengers; $4 per car, single occupant; $2 cyclists or pedestrians. Prehistoric loggerhead turtles lumber ashore to lay and bury their eggs every summer, away from the lights and crowds of other area beaches. Fifty-six days later, the baby turtles emerge and scurry to the sea—hopefully before birds can snatch them up. Beach turtle talks are available during the loggerhead season. Year-round, fishing, beaching, and climbing the observation tower are popular activities.

 Dolphin Explorer (239-642-6899 or 800-979-3370; www.dolphin-explorer .com), 951 Bald Eagle Dr., at Rose Marco River Marina, Marco Island. $61 for adults, $51 for seniors, $29 for children ages 3–16. Lead by dolphin researchers, this excursion takes passengers on a participatory excursion with Ten Thousand Islands Dolphin Project, a five-year scientific research study to identify and track the movement of resident dolphins in the Marco Island and Naples areas. Children may complete tasks on-board that earn them entry into the Dolphin Explorer's Club, with a survey patch, newsletter, and follow-up activities after they return home from vacation. Two survey trips depart daily, one in the morning at 9, another at 1. Advance reservations highly recommended.

 Everglades National Park/Gulf Coast Visitor Center (239-695-3311; www.nps.gov/ever), 815 Oyster Bar Ln., Everglades City. Tamiami Trail south of Naples; ranger station and visitors center on FL 29, before the Chokoloskee Causeway in Everglades City. Visitor center open mid-November–March, daily 8:30–4:30; April–mid-November, daily 9–4:30; concessions open daily 8:30–5. This massive wetland—home to the endangered Florida panther and other rare animals—covers 2,200 square miles and shelters more than 600 types of fish and 347 bird species. It stretches from here to the Florida Keys on the east coast. Along with Ten Thousand Islands, it also contains the largest mangrove forest in the world. So what's the best way to see this seemingly overwhelming expanse of wildlife? Take your pick. From this end, you really can't drive through it, but you can from the eastern access, two hours away. US 41 skirts the edge of the park and Big Cypress National Preserve, which is part of the same ecosystem. Closest access to Naples is FL 29 and Everglades City. Canoe trips from 8 to 99 miles long put you in closer range of birds, manatees, dolphins, and alligators. There's also a variety of other options. The park offers boat tours, and other private sight-seeing cruises exist. During the winter, ranger programs and kayak tours from the Gulf Coast Visitor Center teach about the unique environment. You can rent a pontoon boat or hire a charter captain in Everglades City for sightseeing and fishing. Get advice at the visitors center, or see "Wildlife Tours & Charters," below. The visitors center holds hands-on Calusa Indian, bird, sea turtle, manatee, and other exhibits. Outdoors, tables and a chikee hut accommodate picnickers.

Fakahatchee Strand Preserve State Park (239-695-4593; www.floridastate parks.org/fakahatcheestrand), W. J. Janes Memorial Scenic Dr. (FL 29) north of US 41, Copeland. Preserve administration office open weekdays 9–4. Donations accepted. Knowledgeable volunteers lead swamp walks the third Saturday of the month, November–February. You can also hike drier paths on your own. Park at the gates on either side of the road and follow the short pathways into the strand. In summer the trails are often muddy and submerged. You can also access the strand (a linear swamp forest that snakes along ancient slough valleys) via the 2,000-foot Big Cypress Bend boardwalk, west of Everglades City on US 41.

The ecosystem is known for its wild orchids, including 47 varieties of threatened and endangered species, 14 native varieties of bromeliads, and stately stands of native royal palm. Florida panthers, black bears, mangrove fox squirrels, and Everglades minks have all been documented along the 20-mile-long strand. You're more likely to spot alligators, white-tailed deer, ospreys, ibises, egrets, and snakes (keep an eye out for the deadly cottonmouth). Next to the boardwalk you'll find an Indian village with a gift shop. A ranger office on W. J. Janes Memorial Scenic Drive, past the old fire tower, has displays and information on the preserve.

The Naples Preserve (239-261-4290; www.naplesgov.com), 1690 Tamiami Trail N., Naples. Open daily, dawn–dusk; eco-center open Tuesday, Thursday, and Saturday 10–4. This 9.5-acre patch of ancient ecology along the inner-city highway was recently cleaned up and fitted with a 0.4-mile boardwalk that crosses scrub oak, grassy meadow, and pine-flatwoods communities. Gopher tortoises, deer, bobcat, and birds occupy the habitat. An eco-center houses a diorama plus rotating exhibits depicting the preserve's fauna and flora and interactive programs.

✪ ✍ **Rookery Bay Environmental Learning Center** (239-417-6310; www .rookerybay.org), 300 Tower Rd., off FL 951 (Collier Blvd.) toward Marco Island. Open Monday–Saturday 9–4; closed Sunday year-round and Saturday in summer. $5 for adults, $3 for children ages 6–12. The Gulf Coast's largest and most pristine wildlife sanctuary west of the Everglades occupies more than 110,000 acres at the gateway to Ten Thousand Islands. It's "Ding" Darling without the crowds (or ease of accessibility), and a favorite for fishermen and birdwatchers. Rare creatures such as the American crocodile, manatee, Atlantic green and Ridley sea turtles, bald eagle, and roseate spoonbill inhabit its backwaters and shores. For an introduction to this vast, largely inaccessible land, stop at this Department of Environmental Protection laboratory and education facility. The mangrove estuary is the star of high-tech, interactive exhibits. The centerpiece, a 2,000-gallon aquarium, has a 15-foot-tall mangrove "growing" out of it and spaces into which kids can crawl and get to know the crucial habitat. Forming a backdrop to the aquarium, a curved wall holds various habitat dioramas, three-dimensional tactile displays of local creatures, local wildlife-artist murals, a touch tank, Mosquito Landing, and other fun and original learning tools. An audio self-tour is available for a $2 fee. The unusual polka dot batfish is the center's mascot and has been replicated in huge proportion. Kids can climb aboard a replicated research boat to do the sea turtle dance, hear bird sounds, and watch glass-bottom boat video. The second floor holds exhibits exploring the area's and reserve's timeline, a replica of an Old Florida homestead, and recorded stories from the different eras. A new bridge opened in 2009 that leads from the second floor to a 1-mile nature trail on the other side of Henderson Creek. Guided tours and kayak excursions are available.

Wildlife Tours & Charters: ✍ **Cocohatchee Nature Center** (239-592-1200; www.cocohatchee.org), 12345 Tamiami Trail N., Naples. Four times daily, nature and sunset boat tours dip into the pristine, bird-rich waters of the Cocohatchee River and onto the gulf, where passengers often spot dolphins.

✍ **Conservancy of Southwest Florida** (239-262-0304; www.conservancy.org), 1450 Merrihue Dr., one block east of Goodlette Rd., Naples. Boat tours of the mangrove waterway are included in admission. It also hosts wildlife cruises of Rookery Bay National Estuarine Research Reserve aboard the pontoon boat *Good Fortune.*

Double Sunshine (239-263-4949; www.tincityboats.com), 1200 Fifth Ave. S., at Tin City on US 41, Naples. Departs five times daily for 1.5-hour narrated nature/dolphin-sighting and sunset cruises.

Everglades National Park Boat Tours (239-695-2591 or 866-628-7275; www.nps.gov/ever), Gulf Coast Visitor Center, 815 Oyster Bar Ln., Everglades City. Naturalist-narrated tours wind through the maze of Ten Thousand Islands and its teeming bird and water life; other tours take you up the mangrove-lined Turner River.

✔ **Manatee Sightseeing Eco-Adventure** (239-642-8818 or 800-379-7440; www.see-manatees.com), 24988 Tamiami Trail E., at Port of the Islands Resort and Marina, Naples. Captains Barry and Carol take up to six passengers on a 90-minute sight-seeing charter into a manatee sanctuary by appointment. If you don't see a manatee, you don't pay.

Power Boat Birding & Eco Tours (239-695-3633; evergladesareatours.com/power_boat_tours.htm), Calusa Island Marina, Goodland. An experienced naturalist leads this journey into Ten Thousand Islands and Rookery Bay to point out birds and other wildlife. Ninety-minute tours depart four times daily, including a sunset excursion.

✳ Lodging

The South Coast was once a place for roughing it and low-key vacationing. The old wooden Naples Hotel, built in the 1880s by town developers, was as posh as it got. In 1946 Naples became a forerunner in the golf resort game when the Naples Hotel was bought and converted. In 1985, the Ritz-Carlton came to town and set a new tone. Naples changed forever. Naples Grande and other smaller luxury hotels followed the Ritz, including the Ritz-Carlton Golf Resort. Downtown, new properties continue to rise and tend toward intimacy and European style, giving Naples a well-rounded menu of options, from cottages and inns to golf meccas and grandes dames. Bonita Springs, to the north, is growing into its own as a destination with fine lodging, including a Hyatt Regency that opened in fall 2001. Nearby Marco Island lines up high-rise after high-rise resort and condo community along its coveted beaches. Privately owned second homes and condominiums provide another source of upscale accommodations along the South Coast. (Vacation brokers who match visitors with such properties are listed under "Home & Condo Rentals" at the end of this section.) Away from the metropolitan airs of Naples and Marco Island, lodging options reflect the simple, primitive nature of the Florida Everglades.

The highlights of South Coast hospitality listed here include the best and freshest in the local industry. Toll-free 800, 877, 866, or 888 reservation numbers, where available, are listed after local numbers.

Pricing codes are explained below. They are normally per unit/double occupancy. The range spans low- and high-season rates and standard to deluxe accommodations. Many resorts offer packages at special rates. Prices do not include the 6 percent Florida sales tax, and some large resorts add service gratuities or maid charges. Collier County imposes a 4 percent tourist bed tax as well, proceeds from which are applied to beach and environmental maintenance.

Rate Categories

Inexpensive	Up to $100
Moderate	$100 to $200
Expensive	$200 to $300
Very Expensive	$300 and up

An asterisk (°) after the pricing designation indicates that at least a continental breakfast is included in the lodging rate.

Note that under the Americans with Disabilities Act (ADA), accommodations built after January 26, 1993, and containing more than five rooms must be useable by people with disabilities. I have indicated only those small places that do not make such allowances.

ACCOMMODATIONS

Bonita Springs

✪ ♂ ♪ **Hyatt Regency Coconut Point Resort & Spa** (239-444-1234 or 800-55-HYATT; www.coconutpoint .hyatt.com), 5001 Coconut Rd., 34134. This tower of luxury makes a glamour statement on the shores of pristine estuary. Despite its high-rise contrast to the surrounding low-key landscape, the resort strives to blend with its Florida setting wherever possible. The elegant Italian marble and mahogany lobby is localized with Florida-look terrazzo, and the colors of the public spaces and 454 rooms and suites reflect the sea, sand, and verdure. All rooms and suites are outfitted with mini fridges, CD and DVD players, robes, safes, and coffeemakers. The Tarpon Bay restaurant resembles old fish-shack architecture and serves local seafood. To make up for the lack of readily available beach (guests must take a boat shuttle to a private island for sand), Hyatt's signature water features fill in with a waterslide kiddie pool, a lazy river, a toddler's pool, adult pools, stunning fountains, and a reflecting pool. Many guests are more interested in golfing, anyway, and the Hyatt pleases them with 18 top-notch holes. A kids' camp, a spa with one of Florida's few Watsu (water + shiatsu) pools, tennis, and a medley of bars and casual eateries make this a full destination resort for those who don't mind being a short drive away from the beach, shopping, and nightlife that's getting the Bonita-Naples area noticed. Moderate to Very Expensive.

✪ **Trianon Bonita Bay** (239-948-4400 or 800-859-3939; www.trianon.com), 3401 Bay Commons Dr., 34134. The name implies "a special place" in the spirit of the Grand Trianon and Petit Trianon on the grounds of Versailles near Paris. Heavy on European influence, the hotel's lobby displays both elegance and intimacy, with an inviting fireplace, polished marble, and high-arched ceilings. The dramatic entryway segues into a cozy lounge/breakfast nook, where there is a fireplace and baby grand piano and where tropical iced tea and fruit are on hand to refresh guests. Attention to detail is a hallmark of Trianon, which is a spin-off of a Naples Fifth Avenue South prototype. In its 100 spacious guest rooms and suites you'll find the same refinement previewed in the lobby: dark-wood armoires, sliding French doors to a balcony, gourmet European coffee service, roomy all-white baths, and space enough to dance. Continental breakfast, served in the lounge, is included in the rates. A small pool lies in the backyard of the four-story, chateaulike structure, and the new Lake House Bar & Grill overlooks the pool and a pond. Shoppers will like Trianon's walking-distance proximity to the fine stores and restaurants of Promenade. Moderate to Expensive.°

Everglades City

🦐 ((ᵩ)) **The Ivey House** (239-695-3299 or 877-567-0679; www.iveyhouse.com),

107 Camellia St., 34139. The family-run Ivey House is tailor-made for outdoor enthusiasts. The original Ivey House Lodge, a born-again boarding-house from the 1920s, offers 11 simple B&B rooms. The 17-room Ivey House Inn opened in 2001, plus there's the Ivey House Cottage (two-night minimum stay), which has two small bedrooms. In the original B&B, men's and women's bathrooms are separate, dorm style, from the simple, wood-paneled rooms. The new inn's rooms, which encircle the courtyard swimming pool, have private baths and offer added style and comforts, including TVs, phones, and free Wi-Fi. Breakfast (hot buffet in winter, cold buffet in summer) is included in all room rates. Ivey's main attraction is its proximity to Everglades waterways and its partnership with North American Canoe Tours. In fact, you could call this a BB&B: bed, breakfast, and backcountry. North American Canoe Tours leads tours into the Ten Thousand Islands by canoe, kayak, or boat; rents equipment; and provides shuttle service to launching and landing sites. Inexpensive to Moderate.°

♦ **Rod & Gun Club** (239-695-2101; www.evergladesrodandgun.com), 200 Broadway, 34139. Steeped in both history and outdoorsmanship, this circa-1864 lodge crowns a modest town that serves as the South Coast's gateway to the Everglades. The club's main building was built as luxury pioneer-era housing; the Old South–style mansion came under the ownership of the county's developer and namesake, Barron Collier, who turned it into a fishermen's and hunters' haven during the 1920s. A sportsman's lodge in the finest sense, it has cypress walls that are still decorated with mounted fish and animal heads, a gator hide, and tools of the fishing trade. Seventeen freshly renovated rooms in tin-roofed cottages scatter around the white-clapboard lodge, which has a wrap-around veranda and yellow-striped awnings. The rooms are furnished for function rather than pampering—TV, paddle fan, fridge, and air-conditioning are the extent of luxury. The club's restaurant, which has a screened porch facing the river, specializes in local delicacies and will cook your catch for a nominal fee. Banana trees, lattice, and rock waterfalls decorate the swimming pool deck off the dining room. Inexpensive to Moderate. No credit cards. No handicap access.

Marco Island

♦ ☀ (ᵯᵖ) **The Boat House Motel** (239-642-2400 or 800-528-6345; www.theboathousemotel.com), 1180 Edington Place, 34145. Marco Island's north end, known as Olde Marco, reflects more strikingly the island's nautically nice personality. If you're seeking something less upscale and expensive than Marco's trademark resort scene, drive past the new Olde Marco Island Inn and turn the corner to this waterfront secret. Twenty rooms, studios, condos, and the two-bedroom gazebo house (Moderate to Expensive) run perpendicular to the boat docks and a small pool in a two-story strip. The rooms are nicely appointed, outfitted with kitchen appliances, and designed for easy, breezy waterfront living. The two end rooms have the best view and largest porch/balcony. Wireless Internet access is available throughout the resort, which is within walking distance to several restaurants. Inexpensive to Moderate.

○ ♂ (ᵯᵖ) **Marco Beach Ocean Resort** (239-393-1400 or 800-260-5089; www.marcoresort.com), 480 S. Collier Blvd., 34145. If you want the same wide beach but wish to knock it up a cha-ching from the Marriott, try this exclusive enclave just a couple of doors south. Compared to the Marriott, it is more compact, more intimate (though still 12 stories with sheltered parking, 83 one- and 15 two-bedroom suites), and more elegant. Its greatest asset may be Sale e Pepe, its Tuscan-style restaurant overlooking the beach. The sumptuous rooms, newly redecorated in 2010, all face the gulf. The swimming pool and its pool bar are elevated to a fifth-floor rooftop. Guests have club privileges at a nearby golf and tennis facility. Moderate to Very Expensive.

🖈 **Marco Island Lakeside Inn** (239-394-1161 or 800-729-0216; www .marcoislandlakeside.com), 155 First Ave., 34145. Escape from the madhouse traffic and high rises along the beach to this Superior Small Lodging gem on Marco Lake. The 17-year-old property's perky attitude is enhanced by its Italian steakhouse and in-house art gallery. Its 10 suites offer either lakeside views from screened porches (or, on the second floor, balconies) or poolside ground-level accommodations with a shared patio. The lakeview rooms have full kitchens and one or two bedrooms (Moderate to Expensive for the two-bedroom accommodations), while those around the pool have kitchenettes and no separate sleeping quarters. In all, deluxe amenities such as pillow-top chiropractic mattresses, French doors, and white spic-and-span tiled bathrooms lend a boutique feel. A small sand beach that edges the lake and nicely maintained landscaping have raised the once motel-like structure into something soothing and special. Inexpensive to Moderate.

✪ ♂ ✍ (((ɯ))) **Marco Island Marriott Resort, Golf Club & Spa** (239-394-2511 or 800-438-4373; www.marco islandmarriott.com), 400 S. Collier Blvd., 34145. In 2007, the Marriott completed a three-year renovation that brought to the long-stretching beachfront property a magnificent new spa with an outdoor Watsu therapy pool, a pool with slides, and an infinity pool overlooking the Gulf of Mexico. It remains a sprawling complex on the beach—an extra-wide, shell-cluttered, sandbar-sheltered beach—and still provides a fantasy playground for vacationers of all ages. Families enjoy water-sports rentals, a pizza parlor, a game room with table tennis, and a remarkable kids' program. Adults can shop in the marble-floored arcade, golf at an off-site Marriott course, dine grandly or beach style, and act like a kid when the mood strikes. The 664 rooms and 63 suites—with a palm/plantation look—each provide a mini fridge, coffeemaker, hair dryer, and mini bar. Historic photography and beach sculptures adorn the walls; blond-wood furniture in the guest rooms is decorated with carvings of palm fronds. In the spa building, a state-of-the-art fitness center extracts a fee from guests; or they can use the original fitness room for free. There's a charge for Wi-Fi use in the room, but it is complimentary in the lobby bar area. Expensive to Very Expensive.

Naples

✪ ♂ **Bellasera Hotel** (239-649-7333 or 888-612-1115; www.bellaseranaples .com), 221 Ninth Street S., 34102. Feel the warmth of Tuscany as you splash in the tiled fountain pool and sup on Italian specialties from Zizi, the poolside restaurant. Inside the lobby, a sweeping staircase and rich Tuscan tones introduce a motif that carries through in the hotel's 100 studios and one- to three-bedroom suites. In the studios, plantation shutters in the bathroom open onto the living area so you can watch TV from the jetted tub. The spacious suites include all the comforts and modern conveniences of home, plus full kitchens and porches and balconies overlooking the beautifully landscaped courtyard and grounds. A small fitness center fits into a room near the pool. Locationwise, the hotel sits steps away from the action and smart social scene of downtown Naples, but is tucked away enough to ensure peace and romance. A free shuttle whisks you off to the beach, minutes away. Expensive to Very Expensive.

Cove Inn (239-262-7161 or 800-255-4365; www.coveinnnaples.com), 900 Broad Ave. S., 34102. Back before the Ritz-Carlton and Naples Grande, Naples was about water, boating, and fishing. Cove Inn persists in the old tradition by focusing on the harbor that it edges at Naples's original, circa-1915 settlement of fishermen and builders of Tamiami Trail. Accommodations range from hotel rooms to efficiencies to one- and two-bedroom units with separate living/dining areas. The 85 balconied units are individually owned and decorated; most have a view of the harbor, and even the hotel rooms come equipped with a refrigerator, coffeemaker, microwave, ironing board, and iron. An old-fashioned coffeehouse serves breakfast and lunch, and the marinaside chikee bar slaps down cold ones for sunbathers around the pool. Part of the Crayton Cove and City Dock communities, Cove Inn is close to casual-to-fine waterfront restaurants, shops, and marina services. Moderate to Expensive.

♂ ♪ ((ŋ)) **The Edgewater Beach Hotel** (239-403-2000 or 800-821-0196; www.edgewaternaples.com), 1901 Gulf Shore Blvd. N., 34102. The Edgewater hints at New Orleans style with lacy, white-iron balustrades on two of its three buildings, all of which face the gulf-lapped beach. You can't stay much

closer to the sand than at this appropriately named hotel. Its 124 one- and two-bedroom suites are spacious, convenient, and handsomely appointed with clay tiles, designer furnishings, and thick bedspreads. The floor plan of each includes a full kitchen with microwave, living/dining area, and private patio or balcony. Guests can dine in the chic lobby restaurant, Coast, or poolside under stylish market umbrellas. There's an on-site exercise room, spa services, and opportunities for other recreation nearby, including golf at the Naples Grande Golf Club. Guests also have privileges at the Naples Grande sister resort. Expensive to Very Expensive.

((ŋ)) **Lemon Tree Inn** (239-262-1414 or 888-800-LEMON; www.lemontree inn.com), 250 Ninth St. S., 34102. Despite its lemon-pulp-yellow paint job and free lemonade in the lobby, this property, recently converted to a condo-hotel operation, is anything but a lemon. At the edge of downtown's fashionable drags, it retains a humble charm, dressed in white tin roofs and flowering plants. The 34 rooms with porches (most are screened) are named Periwinkle, Plumosa, Poinciana, and such, after local flowers. Spacious, simple, and cottage style in decor, they are individually decorated and outfitted with tiled kitchens containing a microwave, toaster, coffeemaker, and mini fridge. Around the pool and a gazebo in the courtyard, thick foliage, a butterfly garden, and stylish globe streetlamps create character. At the poolside breakfast nook you can help yourself to continental goodies. Shopping is steps away, and the beach is a short drive. Moderate to Expensive.*

♂ ♪ ((ŋ)) **Naples Beach Hotel & Golf Club** (239-261-2222 or 800-237-7600; www.naplesbeachhotel.com), 851

Gulf Shore Blvd. N., 34102. The doyenne of Naples resorts, this combines the best of the area—its beaches and its golf—into a three-generation tradition in the heart of town. The 18-hole golf course hosts the Florida State PGA Seniors Open and other major golf tournaments. Its stand-alone spa-and-clubhouse complex overlooks the greens. The spacious facility also holds meeting rooms, a fitness center, and Broadwell's, an elegant dining room. Har-Tru tennis courts, a heated pool, the Beach Klub 4 Kids, and watersports equipment rentals vie for off-the-course recreational hours. The hotel's spacious lobby and Everglades Room, where a breakfast buffet is served, communicate Old Florida vacationing ease. Its 329 guest rooms, efficiencies, and suites are done in Florida decor and display some lingering classic trademarks of yesteryear. Accommodations overlook the wide, palm-studded beach or the lush golf course. Golf, tennis, and other packages are available. Expensive to Very Expensive.

○ ♂ ♪ (ᵢ) **Naples Grande Resort & Club** (239-597-3232 or 800-247-9810; www.naplesgrande.com), 475 Seagate Dr., 34103. Formerly The Registry, Naples Grande recently came under new management and benefited from a major face-lift, which included the addition of a stand-alone Golden Door Spa and upscale Strip House steak restaurant. The resort's distinctive red-capped tower, villas, and 15 Har-Tru tennis courts dominate north Naples's pristine, mangrove-fringed estuaries. Luxurious but with beach casualness, the resort's style impresses from the moment you walk through the front door into the newly redesigned, sleek, chic lobby with its smart bar and Aura restaurant. Outside, the family pool, one of three, has a Flintstones feel with a 100-foot on-the-rocks waterslide

and private cabanas. Also for families is a fine kids' program. Tram service along the boardwalk traverses estuaries to Clam Pass Park, a 3-mile stretch of plush sands with all manner of watersports rentals. Fifty luxury bungalows recently redesigned with an Asian flair edge the tennis courts; another 395 rooms and 29 suites overlook the gulf. All of these are spacious and furnished with a dry bar, walk-in shower, soaking tub, and class. Naples Grande owns a nearby 18-hole golf course and provides a golf concierge. Five restaurants range from poolside casual to Aura's fashion-forward breakfast, lunch, and dinner. Covered parking and fitness room use is included in a resort fee. Very Expensive.

♪ (ᵢ) **Park Shore Resort** (238-263-2222 or 800-548-2077; www.parkshore fl.com), 600 Neapolitan Way, 34103. Its 156 one- and two-bedroom condos stack up a couple stories high in buildings that encircle a fountained lake. A tropically landscaped island in the middle of the lake, accessible by several wooden footbridges, holds a swimming pool with a craggy waterfall backdrop. The pool complex includes a whirlpool, barbecue and sunning decks, and a poolside pub serving fun martinis, frozen drinks, and Caribbean-inspired dishes. Paver stone paths encircle the pool complex and lead to racquetball, volleyball, tennis, and basketball courts. Free shuttles are available to the beach, which is only minutes away. Tucked into one of Naples's exclusive neighborhoods, the resort is also convenient to shopping and dining. On property, guests enjoy free Internet access, laundry facilities, and a friendly atmosphere and homelike accommodations, complete with fully equipped kitchens. Expensive to Very Expensive.

♂ ♪ (ᵢ) **The Ritz-Carlton Golf Resort** (239-593-2000 or 800-241-

grill, cigar bar, room service, and other lounges help fill the dining-entertainment bill. The golf resort also has an on-property fitness center, four lit tennis courts, and a pool. Kids from both resorts learn golf and golf etiquette at the newer resort. Overlooking the greens with private balconies, 295 rooms and suites have it all, from cuddly robes and oversized marble bathrooms to high-speed wireless Internet access and safes large enough to hold laptop computers. Very Expensive.

✪ ♂ ✎ ((ɣ)) **The Ritz-Carlton Naples** (239-598-3300 or 800-241-3333; www .ritzcarlton.com/resorts/naples), 280 Vanderbilt Beach Rd., 34108. The gold standard for regal accommodations, the Ritz-Carlton melds Old World elegance with Old Florida environment. The hotel's facade looms majestically classic. Inside, oversized vases of fresh flowers, massive chandeliers, cabinets filled with priceless china, 19th-century oil paintings, vaulted ceilings, and crystal lamps detail Ritz extravagance. Each of the 460 units in the U-shaped configuration faces the gulf. Guest rooms and suites are dressed in fine furniture, plush carpeting, and marble bath areas. Accommodations include an honor bar, bathrobes, hypoallergenic pillows, telephones in the bathroom, clothes steamers, and private balconies overlooking the hotel's backyard, where wilderness and civility meet. In the courtyard, fountains and groomed gardens exude European character. Classic arches, stone balustrades, and majestic palm-lined stairways lead to a boardwalk that takes you through mangroves. At the end of the boardwalk lie golden sands, where Gumbo Limbo restaurant serves daytime fare and water-sports rentals are available. Two new features in 2009 expanded family leisure activities: Nature's Sanctuary, a new interactive aquarium and touch-tank element; and

PARK SHORE RESORT BOASTS ITS OWN ISLAND IN A LUXURIANT GREEN SETTING.

3333; www.ritzcarlton.com/resorts /naples_golf_resort), 2600 Tiburón Dr., 34109. The golf resort operates amid 27 holes of lush, Greg Norman –designed greens. The Rick Smith Golf Academy, a putting course and practice area, and a clubhouse with pro shop make this a complete golf resort. Its sybaritic relationship with its elder sister out on the beach gives both properties the most complete menu of leisure activities possible. Guests at the golf resort have access via shuttle to the beach resort's spa, beach, kids' program, and fine restaurants. Its own Lemonia restaurant gives guests a reason to stay right on property for a fabulous Tuscan feast overlooking the links. A gourmet pastry shop, pool the vue (Virtual User Experience with interactive games) lounge. Other amenities and services that earn the Ritz its five stars include a formal dining room, afternoon tea service, a fine steak grill, a sushi bar, a gourmet coffee shop, an elegant stand-alone spa, a lap pool and free-form family pool, a lounge, a ballroom, tennis courts, sister-property golf facilities (see above), a fitness center, a beauty salon, children's programs, a nature walk, bicycle rentals, shops, transportation services, and twice-daily maid service. Poolside cabanas are equipped with all relaxation necessities—from high-speed Internet and a flat-panel TV with DVD player to fresh fruit and a cabana butler. Very Expensive.

Vanderbilt Beach

✪ ⚘ ❦ **LaPlaya Beach & Golf Resort** (239-597-3123 or 800-237-6883; www.laplayaresort.com), 9891 Gulf Shore Dr., 34108. LaPlaya's gracious, Southern-style lobby, Thai spa, exercise room, rocky waterfall pool, pool bar, and trendy restaurant menu (see Baleen under "Where to Eat") put it on par with Miami Beach's boutique hotels. Rooms show a meticulous attention to detail; some sport Jacuzzis with sea views, and all are luxurious with four-poster beds, Frette linens, goose-down pillows, private balconies, and marble baths. Of its 189 units, 141 are beachfront with private balconies. The "golf" part of the name refers to privileges on a course 15 minutes away. The "beach" part is obvious—a delicious slice of sands that gives way to the property's lush tropical garden and Colonial-style public areas. Moderate to Very Expensive.

❦ ((ᵽ)) **Vanderbilt Beach Resort** (239-597-3144 or 800-243-9076; www.vanderbiltbeachresort.com), 9225 Gulf Shore Dr. N., 34108. This longtime fixture on the barefoot-casual Vanderbilt Beach scene comes in two parts: a two-story, Old Florida beach motel with a small swimming pool in the shadow of next door's towering high rise and, across the street, a four-story bayside condo building. The efficiencies and apartments in the older beach building have an easygoing feel, while the condos sport a bit more elegance. All 34 units come with fully equipped kitchens, but plan on at least one dinner at the inimitable and highly hailed Turtle Club restaurant. It serves lunch and dinner inside or outside on the patio or in the sand. A private fishing dock and a tennis court add to the convenience of the compact property. Moderate to Expensive.

HOME & CONDO RENTALS

Waterstone Resorts (239-992-6620; www.waterstoneresorts.com), 26201 Hickory Blvd., Bonita Springs 34134. Rentals from Captiva Island to Naples.

RV RESORTS **Chokoloskee Island Park** (239-695-2414; www.chokoloskee .com), 1140 Hamilton Way, Chokoloskee 34138. Rustic fishing paradise with easy access to the Everglades and the gulf. Full-service marina, tackle shop, guide service, ramps, and docks. Overnight or seasonal tent and RV sites with complete hook-ups; efficiency and mobile home rentals.

Outdoor Resorts of Chokoloskee Island (239-695-3788; www.outdoor -resorts.com/ci), 150 Smallwood Dr., Chokoloskee 34138. Marina, boat rentals, a bait-and-tackle shop, and guide service for fishing and touring. Pull into one of 283 full-service sites or stay in the motel. Either way you can take advantage of the resort's three pools, health club, lit tennis and shuffleboard courts, and marina.

((ᵽ)) **Rock Creek RV Resort** (239-643-3100; www.rockcreekrv.com), 3100 North Rd. at Airport Rd., Naples 34104. Full hook-ups for more than

230 RVs, pool, laundry, Wi-Fi hot spots, and shade trees. Limited pet area.

✳ Where to Eat

Everglades City considers itself a fishing and stone-crab capital, so figure you can expect some highly fresh seafood in these parts. Stone crab, in fact, was discovered as a food source in the Everglades—at least that's the way some of the old-timers tell it. Before a couple of locals began trapping stone crabs and selling them to a Miami restaurant, the delicate, meaty flavor of these crustaceans went unappreciated. Along with stone crab, alligator, frog legs, blue crab, and other local delicacies make up the substance of Everglades cookery.

Marco Island, too, is known as a good market for buying stone crab, which gets quite expensive farther from the source. With more than 100 restaurants on the island, Marco covers every genre of cuisine. Its trademark is its Old Florida style of no-nonsense, trend-resistant seafood preparation, particularly in Goodland.

Naples's dining reputation is staked on hauteur and imagination. Even the old fish houses dress up their catches in the latest fashion, which ranges from redesigned home cooking and continental nouvelle to Floribbean, Pacific Rim, and fusion styles. Naples is a dining-out kind of place. Downtown's Fifth Avenue South brings its restaurants out into the street for what has been termed Naples's "café society."

The following listings sample all the variety of South Coast feasting in these price categories:

Inexpensive	Up to $15
Moderate	$15 to $25
Expensive	$25 to $35
Very Expensive	$35 or more

Cost categories are based on the range of dinner entrée prices, or, if dinner is not served, on lunch entrées.

Note: Florida law forbids smoking inside all restaurants and bars serving food. Smoking is permitted only in restaurants with outdoor seating.

Bonita Beach

& **Big Hickory Seafood Grille** (239-992-0991; www.bighickory grille.com), 26107 Hickory Blvd. A masterful blend of fish-shack chic and contemporary tropical Florida style makes this longtime marinaside favorite a sure keeper. Its all-day menu adheres to its roots, with fresh seafood prepared in both traditional and creative modes. One entrées section devotes itself to Old Florida–style deep-fried seafood baskets of oysters, grouper fingers, shrimp, and clam strips. The other, along with the weekly changing special menu, goes gourmet to a Caribbean beat. The Cubana Grouper is a catch in all senses of the word—a generous supply of pan-seared, banana-crusted fish swimming in a creamy banana-liqueur sauce with the fresh veggie of the day, which is usually nice and garlicky. Salads, paninis, and other sandwiches are available all day. Nightly specials such as Dijon scallops or sesame-crusted mahi with miso ginger get creative. Inexpensive to Expensive. No reservations. Closed Monday in summer.

🦞 🌿 & **Doc's Beach House** (239-992-6444; www.docsbeach house.com), 27980 Hickory Blvd. This is the kind of place where Gidget and Moondoggie would hang out (if there were surfable waves, that is). It's all about being on the beach—Bonita's colorful, action-packed beach. If you can't bear leaving the sands, you can just grab a quick burger or dog and get back to it. If you need a break from the sun, duck inside. Downstairs is open and barefoot casual. Upstairs is blessedly air-conditioned and has huge picture windows so you won't miss any of the beach action. Both levels have bars and sports TVs. The menu makes no pretense of fine dining, but the food is solidly good. Grab-and-go items include Sand Dollar Burgers, Chicago-style pizza (after 4 PM), tacos, chili, and sandwiches of all sorts. For dinner or a heartier lunch, add a choice of grilled seafood, strip steak, and a fried seafood combo basket. Parking is by valet. Inexpensive. No reservations. No credit cards (ATM available).

Bonita Springs

✪ ♿ **Chops City Grill** (239-992-4677; www.chopsbonita.com), 8200 Health Center Blvd., US 41 and Coconut Rd., at Brooks Grand Plaza. A spin-off from its original downtown Naples success, Chops's name is a double entendre for the food it does unerringly well: steaks and Pacific Rim–style dishes. Seriously fashionable, with a burnished copper bar and modern kitchen-theater dining room, Chops's ambience sets a tone of nouvelle sophistication that the food follows. The menu rhapsodized my pan-seared grouper's sauce, for instance, as "screaming hot rock shrimp with tomatoes, garlic, and white wine." The "screaming hot" was overstated, but certainly not the garlic, which was apparent in crunchy slices throughout the sauce and the gooey-good wild-mushroom risotto. We discovered a clear penchant for garlic here, for in my husband's mound of arugula whipped potatoes, the chef had buried treasures of whole roasted garlic cloves. Creative sushi rolls and other Asian and eclectic inspirations (beef satay, baked oysters topped with andouille sausage and garlic-vodka cream sauce, shrimp and beef spring

rolls) start the meal out right. Meat-lovers can order the unadulterated finest in steaks, while more adventurous palates will choose from the day's specials and a selection of imaginative entrées such as mango-chili-glazed tuna with wasabi mashed potatoes, teriyaki-yuzu-glazed sea bass with coconut sticky rice, or panko-crusted pork porterhouse with sun-dried cherry and port wine demi-glace. Moderate to Expensive. Reservations accepted.

❀ ♿ **The Fish House** (239-495-5770), 4685 Bonita Beach Rd. This place is almost too darn cute to be real. Outside, a humble, canal front facade greets you and an archway invites you to Paradise. Upon entering Paradise, you reach the restaurant's open-air patio and screened porch seating on the water. Inside, where summer's humidity forced me, corrugated tin and painted buoys decorate the bar,

ENTER A PARADISE OF WATERFRONT DINING AND SEAFOOD NOSHING AT THE FISH HOUSE.

around which a handful of Caribbean-color wood booths with hand-painted tables huddle. The menu covers are colored by children, whose artwork also decorates the walls. There's a lot of sensory input before the food even arrives, so you're happy to find familiar seafood dishes prepared from fresh ingredients on the all-day menu. I can recommend the conch chowder for a starter. Entrées range from sandwiches and salads to fried seafood baskets and house specialties such as coconut shrimp, shrimp and lobster in lobster cream sauce over pasta, bacon-wrapped scallops, grouper tacos, and combo dinners including surf and turf. The Fish House runs specials such as the $3 daily cocktail and the weekday $6.99 choice of five luncheon sand-wiches with fries. Happy hour runs 3–6 weekdays, all day on weekends. Karaoke happens Tuesday evenings. Inexpensive to Moderate. No reserva-tions.

&. **Tarpon Bay Restaurant** (239-444-1234; www.coconutpoint.hyatt.com), 5001 Coconut Rd., at the Hyatt Regency Coconut Point Resort & Spa. White-clapboard fish houses were once the architectural icon of this just-lately developed area. The Hyatt Regency designed its restaurant to pay homage to the Old Florida it replaced. Consid-erably more well dressed than the real thing, the ambiance nonetheless feels cottage comfortable. (Outdoor seating overlooks a pond containing a fountain and a floating golf hole, which can pro-vide its share of entertainment during the still-light hours.) Local and import-ed seafood get a tropical zing. My favorite reason for dining here is the ceviche raw bar. Besides the typical shellfish, you can sample one of eight types of raw seafood "cooked" in vari-ous citric marinades. Can't make up your mind? Try the sampler for $28. Oyster-lovers have a choice of a dozen

or so varieties from around the coun-try. From the menu's entrée selections, crispy fried red snapper is a visual and gastronomic masterpiece. Unusual ingredients and exquisite freshness make the meal: banana leaf-wrapped mahi with ginger-lime pesto, brown butter–basted scallops with saffron vegetable risotto (highly recommend-ed), warm honey-ginger pork tender-loin, and herb-crusted chicken with roasted garlic polenta are just some examples. You can also design your own dish from a selection of about 15 fresh catches. Choose the preparation and up to three sauces. I, for instance, ordered pan-seared wahoo with yellow tomato emulsion, ponzu, and spicy Vietnamese sauces. Two deeply deca-dent passion fruit truffles from Nor-man Love (see "Candy & Ice Cream" in the Island Coast section) finished a great meal on the sweetest of notes. Expensive. Reservations accepted.

&. **Wylds Café** (239-947-0408; www .wyldscafe.com), 4271 Bonita Beach Rd., at Lighthouse Square. If I were to describe Wylds in a word, it would be "buttery." So leave the diet at home and prepare to be slathered. It began with the buttery, garlicky, herby spread between the crusty bread, and ended with cinnamon bread pudding crusted with pecan praline and sauced with warm caramel and crème anglaise. Wow! In between, we sampled an appetizer of pan-seared scallops, cooked to perfection and majestically throned upon bread, maple creamed spinach, and toasted prosciutto. The Enigma Salad was a romaine-based creation with avocado, shiitakes, shred-ded duck, capers, and a rich, creamy Parmesan-peppercorn dressing. The Parmesan-crusted walleye wore a shawl of impeccable tomato-basil beurre blanc and came with a gooey side of roasted shallot risotto. An orange beurre blanc accompanied my husband's grilled swordfish. Mango-pineapple chutney supplied an added flavor boost (and, hey, even a measure of health!). Both entrées came with young unshelled peas that were so flavorful we guessed butter and meat broth, if not bacon fat, must have been an accomplice in the sautéing process. Other starters range from chicken tortilla soup and an interesting cheese plate to calamari tossed with cremini mushrooms and roasted red peppers in a scampi soy broth. Entrées are seafood heavy with some intriguing concessions to meat-lovers (duck and foie gras sausage with roasted duck over pasta in a sage butter sauce, braised cranberry barbecue boneless short ribs, and grilled heirloom pork chop) and vegetarians (pasta pomodoro and vegetable manicotti). In a simple setting of linen and russet-textured walls and with service that was right on, the Wylds experience is as soothing as it is rich. Moderate to Expensive. Reservations accepted. Closed September.

Chokoloskee

✪ 🦪 & **Havana Café** (239-695-2214), 191 Smallwood Dr., Chokoloskee Mall, Chokoloskee. I love Everglades food—frog legs, 'gator tail, and all that. But when I'm looking for a refreshing change in the Everglades City area, this is my first choice. The menu looks deceptively simple, with eggs or biscuits and gravy for breakfast, sandwiches and plates for lunch, but the Cuban accent gives everything an exotic twist. The egg sandwich is pressed on Cuban bread and the café con leche strong and sweet. The lunch-dinner menu ranges from grilled cheese sandwich and Cuban and medianoche sandwiches to grouper or steak plates with rice and beans and yucca. The Cuban, with pulled pork rather than sliced the way it's more typically pre-

pared, was the best we've tasted—and we've tasted plenty. We also sampled one of the day's specials, picadilla, a flavorful ground beef ragu with kalamata olives and bell peppers served with black beans and rice. Our server recommended the cook's special chicken wing appetizer, flavored with cilantro, garlic, and other Cuban spices, but we were saving a piece of our appetite for a slice of key lime pie. We were happy we did: It was fluffy with a nice crumb crust and the right amount of tart. On a nice day, choose a tile-inset cement table outside or otherwise dine among brightly painted walls at the counter or one of the floral-tableclothed tables. Inexpensive. No credit cards. No reservations. Closed for dinner Sunday–Thursday.

Everglades City

& **City Seafood** (239-695-4700), 702 Begonia St. A dozen or so picnic tables on the dock outside the fresh seafood market afford guests the freshest of catches and views. Some of the tables are one-sided at deck's edge for the optimal overlook of the river and its working waterfront. Stone crab is the main currency here, in season October 15–May 15. Any time of year order up a soft-shell crab sandwich, blue crab-cake sandwich , oyster po' boy, grilled shrimp salad, grouper wrap, fried mullet, or basket of cracked conch, frog legs, or fried 'gator. For dessert, there's key lime pie and an ice cream shop that sells locally made flavors. Moderate to Expensive. No reservations.

& **Joanie's Blue Crab Café** (239-695-2682), 39395 US 41, just east of the US 41–County Route 29 (CR 29) intersection, Ochopee. Now you KNOW you're in the Everglades: a shack made out of corrugated aluminum painted red, coconut heads hanging from the ceiling, a porch peering over the River of Grass, catfish

TRUE EVERGLADES FLAVOR AT JOANIE'S BLUE CRAB CAFE, A LONGTIME HONKY-TONK FAVORITE.

sandwiches, frog legs, hush puppies, and what Joanie claims to be the "best 'gator in town." I have to agree. The tender little nuggets are floured and seasoned with ginger and cilantro before panfrying and serving atop Indian fry bread, a flatbread that is staple for local Indian tribes. The side of salsa contained fresh chopped tomatoes, onions, summer squash, and bell pepper in a sweet-sour bath. Joanie is also known for her homemade soups, particularly the she-crab, and her black beans and rice, fried green tomatoes, and soft-shell crab salad. Walk on in, grab your drink from the cooler (or wait and order a fresh mango or strawberry fruit shake), find a seat at a wood table in or out, and prepare yourself for a true swamp experience. Inexpensive to Moderate. No reservations. Closed Monday and Tuesday.

Goodland

& **Little Bar Restaurant** (239-394-5663; www.littlebarrestaurant.com), 205 Harbor Pl. This place is as much about the personality as the food. Let me just mention that every year in July it throws Spammy Jammy, where people dress in pajamas and make stuff out of Spam—like sculptures and dips. That said, the rest of the year Little Bar reflects the slightly akilter personality of Goodland with unusual decor—salvaged wood from a historic boat, pieces of pipe organ, stained glass, and various pieces with a past. As for the food, like other Goodland restaurants, it tastes of the Everglades and the sea, but climbs a bit above typical frog legs fare. Yes you'll find them on the menu—Buffalo frog legs, no less—but also an eclectic variety of conch chowder (served with a cruet of sherry), marinated herring, smoked amberjack spread, fried seafood baskets, kielbasa and kraut, blue crabs with lobster cream sauce, Cajun prime rib, soft-shell crab, and blackened shrimp. Most days, there's a fight for the outdoor tables on the boat docks with a view of crab trap stacks and fishing boats across the canal. You get the same view from a screened porch and the dining rooms. I'd like to recommend the peach berry tart, but it was a sellout on my last visit. The Absolut Bloody Mary, however, earns my deepest respect. Moderate.

Isles of Capri

♂ ♿ **Capri Fish House** (239-389-5555; www.caprifishhouse.com), 203 Capri Blvd. Hidden Isles of Capri has but one beach, a natural patch of sands behind this circa-1968 fish house where folks gather on Sunday for family dining, kayaking, and beaching. You can opt for an indoor air-conditioned setting in a renovated, sparkling clean setting, but most want the waterfront, open-air chikee bar even when it's warm. Paddle fans and breezes off the water cool it down. Menus offer extensive choices. For lunch, there are burgers and wraps, including Maine lobster salad, plus pasta and salads. Dinner may start out with alligator nuggets or mussels marinara and work into the signature Seafood Capri (lobster, shrimp, scallops, mussels, and clams with pasta and a cream sauce), Continental choices such as duck a l'orange or veal piccata, and seafood specialties with a tropical flair—coconut shrimp, Florida lobster tail, grouper baked with tomato and artichoke hearts, and seafood kabob—flesh out the menu. Expensive. No reservations.

Marco Island (see also Goodland and Isles of Capri)

♿ **Bistro Soleil** (239-389-0981; www.bistrosoleil.net), 100 Palm St., at the Olde Marco Inn. Since the 1870s and pioneer Bill Collier, this location has fed and boarded pilgrims to this part of the world. Back in Collier's day, he advertised rooms for $1 a night, bring your own meat. Through the decades, the inn's dining room has evolved into a gracious Victorian setting with a cranberry glass chandelier and Audubon prints. Bistro Soleil, with its delightful Continental interpretations, sheds new light on a culinary tradition that had grown tired. For starters, the sun-dried tomato and basil veloute gratinee with Swiss and blue cheese, or Prince Edward Island mussels steamed

BISTRO SOLEIL SLANTS A RAY OF CULINARY SUNSHINE UPON A 19TH-CENTURY LODGE.

with herbs and white wine immerse you in Chef Denis Meurgue's irresistible style. Reasonably priced follow-up courses continue to tantalize with offerings such as roasted black grouper topped with blue crabmeat, lemon butter caper sauce, and wild mushroom risotto with truffle oil and char-grilled chorizo; slow-roasted crispy Long Island duck a l'orange; cassolette seafood, vegetables, and mushrooms in saffron cream sauce; tilapia topped with crab and capers with lemon butter sauce; fresh beignets with chantilly; and homemade warm apple tarte tatin with vanilla ice cream and balsamic vinegar reduction. Moderate. Closed Sunday and Monday in off-season. Reservations accepted.

✪ ♂ ♿ **Sale E Pepe** (239-393-1600; www.sale-e-pepe.com), 480 S. Collier Blvd., at Marco Beach Ocean Resort. Whether it's your fantasy to dine under the Tuscan sun or the Florida moon, Sale e Pepe brings it to reality in a replicated, palace-proportioned, Italian-villa setting with an outdoor terrace. Perched on the second floor, it affords an elevated perspective of sand and sea. Inside, you can choose a formal frescoed dining setting or a more casual lounge setting. All serve the same finely crafted, award-winning, Tuscan-based creations. Everything's made fresh, from the crusty olive and rustic herb breads to the pasta, soup, sausage, and tiramisu. The menu adapts to the seasons, always paying tribute to the main Tuscan food groups: antipasto, fish, meat, and pasta. You may find a chestnut, roasted shrimp, and Italian bacon soup in winter, for example. In the pasta department I can recommend the addicting agnolotti stuffed with spinach and ricotta cheese and topped with silky mascarpone and Parmesan cream or the Maine lobster over fettucine—entire meaty tail and claw sections atop

a subtly spicy tomato sauce, flavor-bolstered by strips of dried tomato. I've also raved about the seared yellowfin tuna, masterfully complemented with a tangle of caramelized onions and grained mustard sauce. The formal dining room also offers a four- or five-course tasting menu for about $55 (or $85, including wine pairings). Lunch (in season only) and breakfast on the terrace and in the lounge are prepared by a different operation and not as impressive. Stop in the huge gaslit bar, a shrine to artist Toulouse-Lautrec, for an after-dinner drink. Or take the staircase down to the beach to walk off the dinner in which you've most likely overindulged. Moderate to Expensive. Reservations accepted.

♪ ♿ **Snook Inn** (239-394-3313; www.snookinn.com), 1215 Bald Eagle Dr. Snook Inn's tiki bar packs them in despite the less-than-stellar talent of its musicians. The view of the Marco River and the feeling of Margaritaville ARE stellar, however. And the food? Dependably tasty and just enough old-fashioned to ensure its longevity. Inside, where some retreat in summer's swelter, the salad bar, with its huge barrel of dill pickle chunks, is signature. It comes with every sandwich or entrée lunch and dinner. For lunch, I recommend the Marco River grilled cheese—brie, a thick slice of turkey, and thinly sliced Granny Smith apple are melted together between sourdough bread. For the ultimate decadence, order Shrimp Denny—stuffed with scallops, wrapped in bacon, deep-fried (wait it's not over yet), and topped with hollandaise! The dinner menu does seafood and meat with equal confidence: fried grouper, char-broiled mahi, Caribbean barbecued ribs, and surf and turf. If you can fit it in, there's fried banana cheesecake to further wreak havoc on your diet. Inexpensive to Moderate. No reservations.

Naples

✪ ♿ **Bha! Bha!** (239-594-5557; www
.bhabhapersianbistro.com), 847 Vanderbilt Rd., at Pavilion Shopping Center. A merger of creativities results in a
sleek, bright, and sunny setting of
ocher and key lime green walls, veils,
throw pillows, a fountain, and Turkish
tapestries. They call it a Persian bistro.
In an Iranian dialect the name means
"Yum! Yum!" And that's where Chef
Michael Mir comes in. He fuses his
native background with his experience
in fine American kitchens to present
an intriguing menu that maintains the
authenticity and boldness of Middle
Eastern cuisine while employing a few
tricks of classic Continental and experimental new American styles. Prepare
your palate for a magic carpet ride.
Aash, a peasant-style herbed bean and
noodle soup, starts out simple but, as
you nibble into the center garnish of
yogurt and onions, becomes more and
more complex and extraordinary. In
the appetizer of eggplant and artichoke, we could discern an orchestra
of flavors: distinctive Bulgarian feta,
dill, and a hint of sweetness in the
mustard sauce, and the peanut oil in
which the eggplant was sautéed. Yum,
yum. From the lunch menu, the marinated portobello mushroom stuffed
with grilled vegetables and feta is
divine. The dinner menu is divided
between classic and innovative Persian
cuisine and *khoreshes* (specialties). I
recommend the spicy kermani beef, its
dark saffron sauce enlivened by pep-
peroncini and cucumber yogurt; char-
broiled lamb (incredibly beautiful and
tasty); garlic eggplant chicken (wonderful!); and duck fesenjune, braised in
orange saffron stock and served with
pomegranate walnut sauce (a bit heavy
sweet). Turkish coffee comes served in
a delicate espresso service with an
ornamental wooden box full of rock
candy and sugar. Try the seasonal sorbet such as pomegranate-strawberry
with rosewater or gooey baklava for
dessert. Moderate to Expensive.
Reservations accepted for dinner.
Closed Monday in off-season.

♿ **Bistro 821** (239-261-5821; www
.bistro821.com), 821 Fifth Ave. S.
Bistro 821, the maverick of Fifth
Avenue South and trendsetter in the
local bistro craze, still leads today
despite a swell of competition in its
wake. The menu benefits from an
injection of fearless creativity. Small
plates range from the familiar escargot,
oysters Rockefeller, and fried calamari
to the inventive shrimp and spiced
beef chile relleno and grilled prawn on
a sugarcane skewer. Salads come in
appetizer and full portions (be sure to
indicate "appetizer" even if you order
it as a first course). One menu section
is devoted to pasta and risotto, also as
appetizer and full options, with such
tempters as shrimp-and-prosciutto
macaroni and seafood risotto. Entrées,
too, wax from such traditional bistro
fare as chicken potpie and pot roast to
house specialties: honey
mustard–glazed roasted duck, filet
mignon with walnut-Gorgonzola and
pesto crust, seafood paella, and miso-
sake roasted sea bass. The coconut,
ginger, and lemongrass–encrusted
snapper with coconut-ginger jasmine
rice and coconut butter sauce will dazzle any sweet tooth. The restaurant
began serving lunch in summer 2009,
offering some of dinner's faves plus
sandwiches and an interesting lineup
of salads. A robust wine list, handsome
indoor-outdoor dining space, and
intriguing dessert menu round out the
reasons Bistro 821 will always remain
at the Fifth Avenue forefront. Moderate to Expensive. No reservations.
Closed Sunday for lunch.

♿ **Cilantro Tamales** (239-597-5855;
www.cilantrotamales.com), 10823

Tamiami Trail N. Cilantro Tamales touts "modern Mexican food" in a bright bistro setting. With a slab of clay tile for a place mat and two bottles of chili sauce on the table, you're ready to dip into a Mexican dining experience that's as authentic as it is creative. I knew this the minute the cursory presentation of chips and salsa hit the table. An earthenware throne held two types of sauces: a fresh pico de gallo and a spicier, garlicky red tomatillo sauce. Full of flavor, its heat played backup to the first mouth burst. This is how Mexican food is supposed to be: zest, then zing. We ordered a side of guacamole—my barometer for truth in Mexican—and a cup of sopa de tortilla to get things rolling. The guac passed the litmus test with flying colors, neither puréed nor mashed and dressed lightly in a garlic-seasoned tomato sauce. We ended up eating it out of its flowerpot dish with a spoon. The tortilla soup also carried off that homemade flavor, full of the goodness of chicken and cilantro. For entrées try the house specialty: cilantro tamales, what else? The smoked Gouda cheese stuffing lends an unusual, worldly quality to the bell pepper and onions inside. Tamales also come in pork and chicken varieties, plus the menu carries many other Tex-Mex standards and a few surprises, such as the Mexican rice bowl and Mexican chicken wings. Inexpensive. No reservations. Closed Monday in summer.

✪ 🐾 🖊 ♿ **The Dock at Crayton Cove** (239-263-9940; www.dock craytoncove.com), 845 12th Ave. S. The Dock remembers what Naples is about—clear down to its roots—while keeping up with what Naples has become. The roots part is reflected in the fun, casual, waterlogged atmosphere exuded from its breeze-through setup and location along Naples's original, circa-1915 fishing harbor. Opened in 1976, the fish-house-style eatery has kept abreast of Naples's sophistication with remakes and menu upgrades. Once a purveyor of typical fried seafood fare, today it takes a serious stance among the town's tough culinary standards. Seafood still reigns in traditions such as grouper and chips, Ipswich clams, and Maine smelts, but island and Cajun influences have washed in to give us such offerings as Red Stripe baby back ribs with guava sauce, key lime grouper, and pineapple-glazed sea bass. Chefs execute the creative offerings with complexity. Crafty salads, sandwiches, and specials complete the luncheon offerings, plus the all-day menu offers nine fresh catches grilled and brushed with key lime butter. Inexpensive to Moderate. No reservations.

♿ **Escargot 41** (239-793-5000; www .escargot41.com), 4339 N. Tamiami Trail, at Park Shore Shopping Center. Who would have thought: near-perfect French cuisine with only a dozen tables in the corner of a shopping center next to Kmart? The wine list, nearly as big in size as the restaurant itself, came as the first surprise. Our white Bordeaux, Chateau Peyruchet 2002, started out light but opened up marvelously to meet the rich creaminess of our appetizers, which followed a charming amuse-bouche of puréed eggplant and goat cheese. We felt we must try escargot, and so opted for the night's special appetizer in cognac cream. They were as divine as our mussels appetizer in their soup of wine, tomato and red pepper coulis, basil, and a touch of cream. If you're on a splurge and visiting in winter, you might want to go for the black truffle and foie gras appetizer with proscuitto, morels, and spinach in phyllo dough for $95. Otherwise, smoked salmon, foie gras, onion soup, lobster bisque, and Caesar salad kick off the meal.

The *fruits de mer aux morilles* delightfully surprised us next by sheer non-stingy volume of the morel strips tucked among shrimp, scallops, and mushrooms—all luxuriously napped in a champagne cream sauce with a subtle thyme undertone. The yellowtail snapper was fresh, lightly pan-fried, and served in a shallot–white wine cream sauce flecked with fresh tomatoes and marjoram. Other entrées wander into meat categories: tournedos sautéed with anchovy butter, duck in plum port wine sauce, and veal scaloppini in Calvados cream sauce. For dessert, the vanilla crème brûlée came heavily caramel crusted in a heart-shaped dish. The velvety smooth underlie was a creamy counterpoint, and we toasted it with a small glass of port and bubbly kir royale. It was the perfect wrap to a perfect dining experience. Moderate to Expensive. Reservations required. Closed Sunday.

✪ ♿ **Handsome Harry's Third Street Bistro** (239-434-6400; www .handsomeharrys.com), 1205 Third St. S. Every detail about Handsome Harry's Third Street Bistro lives up to its name. But don't let the attention to the cover sway your opinion about the book. Beauty goes much deeper than the chic black-and-white floor, booths, and tables accented by rich tones. The food is as smart as the place is pretty. Both the ambiance and menu take their cue from classic steakhouses and contemporary bistros. Starting with the drink menu, Harry's creative spirit and eye for quality shows in a selection of above-average wines and fun martinis blended with top-shelf spirits. Lunch prices put it into the special-occasion category, but it's well worth it. Starters on both lunch and dinner menus include the extraordinary: lemon cream of lobster bisque, a chunky lump crabcake, and grilled filet mignon tips. At lunchtime, the Maine lobster salad is a winner—loaded with sweet, tender claw and tail chunks tossed lightly with citrus aioli and bedded upon mixed greens with avocado, tomato, and splotches of two types of dressing. At dinner, meat and pasta receive top billing: fine grilled meats, bourbon and chipotle barbecued pork spare ribs, wood-grilled pork chop with portobello sauce, grouper saltimbocca, gulf prawns and pasta. For dessert, choose the incredibly moist and large serving of carrot cake or Blackout Chocolate. Expensive to Very Expensive. Reservations accepted.

♿ **Naples Tomato** (239-598-9800; www .naplestomato.com), 14700 Tamiami Trail N. The dining room offsets black exposed ductwork with grand glass bowl and wrought-iron chandeliers. Black granite tabletops are free of cloths or place mats. Everything is pared down to basics because the food is what Naples Tomato is about. Like its name, it takes the fundamentals of fine cuisine and turns them ripe and juicy. Wine is a huge focus and calls for experimentation, which its ground-breaking enomatic wine system allows. Using a debit card, guests can try samples of one, three, or six ounces. With a nice red in hand, start with the tomato bisque, unusual in its texture—chunky yet silky with only the lightest application of cream—and made with imported Italian tomatoes for utmost flavor. The crabcake—all lump crab with only egg to bind and panko crumbs to crust—is another triumphant appetizer. Groups may do the mozzarella bar for starters; you can actually make a meal of it for lunch. You have a choice of five different cow- and buffalo-milk mozzarellas made daily, plus various antipasti condiments such as red wine fig chutney. Homemade pasta dominates the menu in expected and unexpected ways. The lasagna is classic and wonderful. Hard to decide between it or surprises such as truffle raviolini Bolognese or butternut squash ravioli with duck leg confit. Pasta accompanies most meat and seafood dishes such as the wonderfully complex alder plank tilapia, veal saltimbocca, and chicken and eggplant Parmesan. For dessert, you'll be equally happy with the traditional tiramisu as the custardy key lime pie. Moderate to Expensive. Reservations accepted.

& **Ridgway Bar & Grill** (239-262-5500; www.ridgwaybarandgrill.com), 1300 Third St. The name has changed a few times since Chef's Garden set a new standard for Naples dining in the 1970s. But its ownership and wicker-and-linen ambiance have remained constant—now Ridgway, named for constant chef-owner Tony Ridgway. With Tommy Bahama drawing the casual crowd down the street, Tony has kept true to a higher-reaching cuisine with such nice turns as crabcakes with corn and sweet red pepper cream, pork schnitzel with herb demi-glace, rack of lamb with couscous and tzatziki, and fennel pollen–seared grouper with braised orange fennel. For lunch, try the prime burger, goat cheese tart with ratatouille, chicken potpie, spinach salad with roasted pears, or fettuccine pomodoro. The luscious desserts, another constant hallmark, come from next door at Tony's Off Third. Pastries are the highlight of well-executed meals with, unfortunately, typically lax service. Inexpensive to Expensive. Reservations recommended.

& **Sea Salt** (239-434-7258; www.sea saltnaples.com), 1186 Third St. S. With 70 or more different types of sea salt in-house on any given day, salt-tasting becomes central to this dining experience. Then there's also Chef Aielli's Venetian birthright and obvious pen-chant for Asian flavors, a whole organic and hormone-free commitment, wines from everywhere, and Norman Love Chocolates. First came a flight of salt with lovely bread and olive oil. We tasted the sulfur undertones of a Hawaiian volcanic salt, smoked Washington state salt, and French gris. It was so much fun—even for a salt eschewer such as myself—that I ordered the salt and raspberry sherbet for dessert. In between, we sampled the thoroughly enjoyable Parma ham and Taleggio cheese served with fig jam and pistachios in honey from the Carpaccio, Crudo & Charcuterie menu. Our server made a convincing case for the Kona Kampachi fish off the Simple Grill menu. I would have preferred this a little rarer, but the

TONY RIDGWAY, NAPLES'S GODFATHER OF CUISINE, CONDUCTS COOKING CLASSES AT HIS EPONYMOUS RESTAURANT.

presentation with shiitake mushrooms was elegant. Other seafood specialties include broiled bourbon salmon and crispy oysters with jalapeño lime tequila. For landlubbers, kobe or wagyu beef, which the menu uses interchangeably, suits the most discriminating of palates—appearing in everything from a rigatoni ragu and tenderloin with foie gras sauce at dinner to burgers and quesadillas for lunch. Meat connoisseurs will also appreciate the korobuta, the "kobe" of the pork world. Desserts come bite-sized. In addition to Love truffles, unusual sherbets and gelato and other confections vie for attention. We relished a square of chocolate passion fruit and the raspberry-orange lava black salt sorbet with a frothy cup of cappuccino to bring this adventure in dining to a sweet ending. In 2009, *Esquire* magazine listed this dramatically designed restaurant among the 20 best new restaurants in the United States. Moderate to Very Expensive. Reservations accepted.

Vanderbilt Beach

& **Baleen** (239-598-5707; www.laplaya resort.com), 9891 Gulf Shore Dr., at LaPlaya Beach & Golf Resort, Naples. Monkeys have become the motif of fashion these days in Florida, and here you see their likeness hanging from chandeliers and poking their noses out of the earthy tropical decor. The round crusty loaf of bread is even called "monkey bread"—why, I'm not sure. (I'm also a bit confused by the whale reference in the restaurant's name.) Outdoors, heavy teak tables and chairs provide a front-row seat to the sunset and percussion of the surf. The menu allows you to order your seafood simple—roasted, grilled, or sautéed—or dressed in all the trappings of creative New World cuisine. The grouper, for instance, comes with red wine risotto

and green peppercorn sauce. The yellowfin tuna gets a Moroccan spice rub and comes with a saffron and pistachio couscous. A couple of meat dishes round out the menu, and the Roquefort-crusted filet mignon we sampled demonstrated the kitchen's expert handling in that department. It was done to the perfect degree of wellness as ordered. For lunch try the BLT salad or lobster roll. Moderate to Very Expensive. Reservations accepted.

BAKERIES Bakeries today are often combined with delis, grocery stores, and even wine shops.

Tony's Off Third (239-262-7999; www.tonysoffthird.com), 1300 Third Ave. S., Naples. Dessert bakery featuring legendary cakes, pastries, and tarts and a well-respected selection of wine and coffee, plus deli and take-out items and sandwiches.

BREAKFAST ✪ **Breakfast Plus** (239-642-6900), 1035 N. Collier Blvd. #302, at Marco Town Center, Marco Island. The best and most unusual selection of breakfast items around: apple dumplings, peach-stuffed French toast, scrambled eggs and chicken livers, berry crêpes, latkes, and more. The New Orleans-style Benedict, egg Hussarde, is phenomenal. Serves breakfast until 2:30 (1:30 in summer), lunch starting at 11.

Hoot's (239-394-4644), 563 E. Elkcam Circle, Marco Island; and (239-304-4644), 12676 Tamiami Trail E., Shops at Eagle Creek, Naples. Breakfast served all day; known for its bread baked fresh daily. Also lunch.

Old 41 Restaurant (239-948-4123), 25091 Bernwood Dr., at Old 41, Bonita Springs. Both breakfast and lunch are served 7–3. The kitchen grinds its own Colombian coffee and makes everything from scratch, with a Philly nod: Taylor pork roll, scrapple, corned beef hash homemade from Boar's Head meat, killer Texas-style French toast with homemade caramel sauce and pecans, Carbon's malted Belgian waffles, omelets, Benedicts, and more.

○ **Skillets Café** (239-262-3788; www .goodbreakfast.com), 4170 Tamiami Trail N., Naples; (239-566-1999), 5461 Airport Rd., Naples; and (239-992-9333), 9174 Bonita Beach Rd., Bonita Springs. A cheery way to wake up, it offers a menuful of Belgian waffles, pancake platters, Irish oats, Benedicts, frittatas, and healthy options. Don't skip the Skillets potatoes—hash browns baked with sour cream and scallions. Also serves lunch.

CANDY & ICE CREAM *The Chocolate Strawberry* (239-394-5999; www.chocstraw.com), 937 N. Collier Blvd., Marco Island. The specialty is strawberries hand-dipped in various types of chocolate; also offers seahorse-shaped lollipops, Italian gelato, smoothies, coffee, and chocolates in the shape of turtles, shells, dolphins, and other local critters.

Everglades Scoop (239-695-0375), 203 S. Copeland, Everglades City. Cheerful, bright ice cream parlor serving 16 flavors of hand-dipped ice cream, plus shakes, sundaes, homemade key lime pie, and sandwiches.

Olde Naples Chocolate (239-262-3975; www.oldenapleschocolate.com), 1305 Third St. S., Naples. An old-fashioned chocolate and ice cream fantasy with sidewalk tables.

Regina's Ice Cream (239-434-8181), 824 Fifth Ave. S., Naples. An old-fashioned soda fountain with modern frozen yogurts, sorbets, and sugar-free and name-brand ice cream.

Royal Scoop (239-992-2000; www .royalscoop.com), 15 Eighth St., Bonita

Springs. Close enough to the beach to cool down, this local tradition feels retro and hosts community events including tours of their homemade ice cream–making operation. Recommended flavors: royal turtle and cookie dough.

The Serious Cookie Company at Tin City Sweets (239-263-3382 or 877-263-3383), 1200 Fifth Ave. S., at Tin City, Naples. Just try to pass this place without succumbing. Besides their trademark half-pound cookies, they make brownies, saltwater taffy, chocolates, turtles, chocolate pretzels, cordial creams, and other irresistible goodies.

Sweet Annie's Ice Cream & Candy (239-642-7180), 692 Bald Eagle Dr., Marco Island. Old-fashioned-style parlor with black-and-white tiled floor, counter, and chrome-legged stools. It serves 45 flavors of ice cream, including sugar free, frozen yogurt, gelato, and frozen custard. Its video arcade holds 20 games.

COFFEE (( )) C Grape Coffee and Wine Bar (239-221-7388; http: //cgrape.com), 4450 Bonita Beach Rd. #1, Bonita Springs. Hot and iced espresso, smoothies, breakfast and lunch/dinner sandwiches, desserts, live entertainment, and wine events.

(( )) **Fifth Avenue Coffee Company** (239-261-5757), 599 Fifth Ave. S., Naples. Hot and iced coffee and tea, cappuccino, cafe latte, macchata, bakery goods. Seating indoors and out with high-speed wireless Internet connections.

The Villaggio Café (239-643-0004), 4350 Gulf Shore Blvd. N., at the Village on Venetian Bay, Naples. Coffee, cappuccino, espresso, chai latte, iced coffee and tea, milk shakes, frozen daiquiris, sandwiches.

DELI & SPECIALTY FOODS Artichoke & Co. (239-263-6979), 4370 Gulf Shore Blvd. N., at the Village on Venetian Bay, Naples. Gourmet takeout, soups, breads, cheeses, pastries, salads, coffee, and wines. Serves breakfast and lunch.

Irish Pub (239-642-6206), 591 S. Collier Blvd., Marco Island. Deli sandwiches.

Pepper's Fine Food (239-643-2008), 4165 Corporate Square, Naples. Butcher shop with every kind of sausage, plus fresh sauerkraut, potato salad, and other German products.

Ródes Fresh & Fancy (239-992-4040 or 800-786-0450; www.rodesfreshandfancy.com), 3756 Bonita Beach Rd., Bonita Beach. Fresh produce and local seafood market. Also sells fresh breads and gourmet groceries.

Tony's Off Third (239-262-7999; www.tonysoffthird.com), 1300 Third St. S., Naples. Sandwiches, prepackaged deli salads, and a selection of entrées for quick warm-ups at home.

Wynn's (239-261-7157; www.wynnsonline.com), 141 Ninth St. N., Naples. Since 1948 the Wynn family has operated this landmark, most famous for its fine selection of wine, seafood, fresh bakery goodies, desserts, and hot-and-cold prepared deli foods.

FRUIT & VEGETABLE STANDS
Bonita Springs Farmer's Market (239-949-6262), Old 41 Rd. and Pennsylvania, Riverside Park, Bonita Springs. Fresh fruits and vegetables and baked goods every Wednesday 8–1.

Third Street South Farmer's Market (www.thirdstreetsouth.com/Third-Markets.html), parking lot at Third St. S. and 13th Ave., Old Naples. Every Saturday 7:30–11:30 A.M. year-round.

NATURAL FOODS Food & Thought Organic Market & Restaurant (239-213-2222; www.foodandthought.com), 2132 Tamiami Trail N., at Gateway Plaza, Naples. Smoothies and juice bar; fresh, prepared, and preserved organic food; indoor and outdoor seating.

For Goodness Sake (239-992-5838; www.forgoodnesssake123.com), 9118 Bonita Beach Rd. E., at Sunshine Plaza, Bonita Springs; and (239-597-0120), 2464 Vanderbilt Beach Rd., at Naples Walk, Naples. Full line of health groceries, including local honey, fresh produce, frozen products, and a menu of salads, sandwiches, and fruit or protein smoothies.

Summer Day Market and Café (239-394-8361), 1027½ N. Collier Blvd., in Marco Town Center, Marco Island. Inviting market with full line of fresh, frozen, bulk, and processed organic and low-carb products, including baby food. Sandwich and smoothie-juice bar with outdoor tables.

PIZZA & TAKE-OUT 5 Brothers Pizza (239-394-5100), 1089 N. Collier Blvd. #439., Marco Island. New York–style pizza, subs, and Italian dinners delivered all day.

Aurelio's (239-403-8882; www.aureliospizza.com), 590 N. Tamiami Trail, Naples. Since 1959, this Chicago-born chain has served pizza, pasta, and other Italian specialties to eat in or to go.

Cilantro Tamales (239-597-5855; www.cilantrotamales.com), 10823 Tamiami Trail, Naples; and (239-949-9955), 25301 Tamiami Trail, Bonita Springs. Modern Mexican food for take-out and delivery.

Kitchen 845 (239-593-6966; www.kitchen845.com), 845 Vanderbilt Beach Road, at Pavilion Shopping

Center, Naples. Tomato dill bisque, Caesar wrap, coconut tilapia, and other such delights to go.

SEAFOOD Capri Fisheries (239-394-8616), 417 Papaya Dr., Goodland. Right on the fish docks, with crab traps piled around it, selling wholesale and retail.

Captain Jerry's Seafood (239-262-7337), 141 Ninth St. N., inside Wynn's Market, Naples. Shrimp, stone crab, fish, and live Maine lobster.

City Seafood (239-695-4700), 702 Begonia St., Everglades City. Find all that's fresh and special about Everglades cuisine: stone crab in season, alligator tail, frog legs, lobster, grouper, and key lime pie. Serves lunch and early dinner dockside.

Lee Be Fish Company (239-389-0580), 350 Royal Palm Dr., Old Marco Shops, Marco Island. Everything local and beyond—from shrimp, stone crab claws, and grouper to oysters, clams, and Maine lobster.

✪ **Randy's Paradise Shrimp** (239-949-6001 or 866-949-6005; www .paradiseshrimpcompany.com), 24851 Tamiami Trail S. #5, Bonita Springs. The pick of local gourmet cooks, it sells seafood fresh, frozen, and prepped to heat and eat, along with bottled and boxed products to complement. Randy's key lime pie is some of the best you'll find in this part of Florida.

Ródes Fresh & Fancy (239-992-4040 or 800-786-0450; rodesfreshandfancy .com), 3756 Bonita Beach Rd., Bonita Springs. Fresh produce and local seafood market.

✴ Selective Shopping

Custom-designed jewelry, exclusive top-designer fashion lines, original masterpiece art, and the world's first street concierge make the experience of browsing, buying, and window-yearning in Naples entirely unique. Naples ranks with Palm Beach's Worth Avenue and Sarasota's St. Armands Circle among Florida's most chic arenas for spending. Downtown's renaissance concentrates the shopping frenzy in the Old Naples districts of Fifth Avenue South and Third Street Plaza, but a number of other fashionable shopping centers are found throughout town. Downtown shops are known for their individually owned and one-of-a-kind galleries and designer outlets.

SHOPPING CENTERS & MALLS
Coastland Center (239-262-2323; www.coastlandcenter.com), Tamiami Trail N. and Golden Gate Pkwy., Naples. Naples's largest and only enclosed, climate-controlled shopping center has 150 stores and eateries, including a full array of shopping options, from major department stores to small specialty shops. Chain names include Macy's, Sears, Old Navy, Victoria's Secret, Bath & Body Works, and Starbucks.

✪ **Fifth Avenue South** (www.fifth avenuesouth.com), Naples. Once upon an eon, members of the Seminole Indian tribe sold their crafts from a stand on Fifth Avenue. Today it's one of Naples's most fashionable addresses. In 1996 a movement started to update the historic district, which had begun to look run-down. Famed Florida planner Andre Duany was hired to breathe new life into the district. Besides making cosmetic improvements, he brought a new bustle to the street. Tony hotels, shops, and 20-plus restaurants and sidewalk cafés attract Naples's "café society." Live entertainment and special events are regularly scheduled, including Evening on Fifth the second Thursday of each month.

Marco Town Center Mall (www .marcotowncentermall.com), Collier Blvd. and Bald Eagle Dr., Marco Island. A popular cluster of more than 10 distinctive eateries and 40 shops. There's live entertainment January–April on Wednesday evenings from 6–8.

Mercato (239-594-9400 or 877-797-9400; www.mercatonaples.com), 9259 Mercato Way, Tamiami Trail at Vanderbilt Rd., Naples. Naples's newest marketplace community is still developing, but its Whole Foods anchor already draws them in, along with its fine restaurants and cinemas.

The Promenade (239-261-6100; www .promenadeshops.com), at Bonita Bay on US 41. This fashionable plaza takes cues from neighbor Naples and includes Mediterranean-style fine restaurants, galleries, and name shops. A lot of storefronts are sitting empty at

ART AND GREENERY MAKE WINDOW-SHOPPING ALONG NAPLES'S THIRD STREET SOUTH A MULTIDIMENSIONAL EXPERIENCE.

the moment, but its restaurants and entertainment continue to draw. January–April, the center hosts Friday Jazz Jams the last Friday of the month from 1–4, and a fresh market on Saturdays from 7 AM–noon.

Shops of Marco, San Marco Rd. and Barfield Dr., Marco Island. One-of-a-kind clothing and gift shops.

Third Street South Plaza and the Avenues (239-434-6533; www.third streetsouth.com), Naples. Visit this upscale shopping quarter in Old Naples, the heart of the arts scene. This is window-shopping (on my budget, anyway) at its best—exquisite clothes, art, jewelry, and home decorations and furnishings. Saturdays in season, a farmer's market convenes in the main parking lot. There's music and other entertainment every Thursday evening in season; the third Thursday in the off-season.

✿ **Tin City** (239-262-4200; www .tin-city.com), 1200 Fifth Ave. S., US 41 at Goodlette Rd., Naples. I love the structure of this mall, which resurrected old tin-roofed docks. Its 30 shops in two buildings tend to be touristy, selling mainly nautical gifts and resort wear. But it also offers enjoyable waterfront restaurants, and it's a good place to catch a fishing or sight-seeing tour.

❂ **The Village on Venetian Bay** (239-261-6100; www.venetianvillage .com), 4200 Gulf Shore Blvd., at Park Shore Dr., Naples. Upscale, Mediterranean-style domain of fashion, jewelry, and art. Located on the waterfront. The complex throws a party with live entertainment the first Thursday of each month.

Waterside Shops at Pelican Bay (239-598-1605; www.watersideshops .com), 5415 Tamiami Trail #320, Naples. This shopping enclave features Saks Fifth Avenue, Nordstrom,

WELCOME TO TIN CITY—NAUTICAL KITSCH AT ITS BEST.

Williams-Sonoma, Ann Taylor, other high-end chains, and some fun dining options—all located in a setting of contemporary stainless steel, cascading waters, and lush foliage. Valet parking available.

ANTIQUES & COLLECTIBLES
Ashley Adams Arts & Antiques (239-435-7273; www.ashadams.com), 795 Fifth Ave. S., Naples. Literally packed with large European, Oriental, and American bronze, silver, and porcelain sculptures, plus clocks, furniture, and more, both new and old.

The Englishman (239-649-8088; www.theenglishmanusa.com), 1170 Third St. S., at The Plaza on Third Street, Naples. For top-shelf European furniture, oil paintings, and sculpture from the 19th and 20th centuries, browse the fine treasures here.

Shirley Street Antique Mall (239-643-1881; www.shirleystreet.com), 50 Goodlette Rd. S., Naples. One of Naples's largest antique malls, containing 40 sellers and antiques of every kind from vintage clothing to Victorian furnishings.

BOOKS Sunshine Book Sellers (239-393-0353; http://sunshinebook sellers.com), 677 S. Collier Blvd., Marco Island; and (239-394-5343), 1000 N. Collier Blvd., Marco Island. Large, modern stores with a complete line of books.

CLOTHING Cottontails (239-594-9005), 7935 Airport Pulling Rd. #114, Naples. A wide variety of children's clothing in a large range of sizes.

Island Woman (239-642-6116), 1 Harbor Pl., Goodland. Goodland's answer to a department store: hand-painted silk fashions, gemstone jewelry, T-shirts, sarongs, tropical art, crafts, wild wigs, and other crazy stuff.

Kay's on the Beach (239-394-1033), 1089 Bald Eagle Dr., Marco Island. A distinctive blend of suits and gorgeous formal wear for mature women.

Marco Island Clothing Co. (239-642-7277; www.marcoislandclothing .com), 117 S. Barfield Dr., at Shops of Marco, Marco Island. Stylish name-brand women's swimsuits, shoes, tropical resort fashions, and accessories.

Marissa Collections (239-263-4333; www.marissacollections.com), 1167 Third St. S., Naples. Carries prestige designer labels such as Versace, Jil Sander, and Oscar de la Renta.

Mondo Uomo (239-434-9484), 4200 Gulf Shore Blvd., at the Village on Venetian Bay, Naples; and (239-947-3312), 26841 South Bay Dr. #106, at The Promenade, Bonita Springs. Fine, tasteful fashion and European styles for men: tropical wool, German cotton, sweaters, and distinctive casual and dress wear for Gulf Coast climes. The Promenade store is called Mondo Uomo & Donna, and also carries stylish name-brand women's wear.

Outback T's (239-261-7869), 1200 Fifth Ave. S., Tin City at US 41 E. and Goodlette Rd., Naples. The best in souvenir T-shirts, with wildlife and local themes.

Simply Natural (239-643-5571), 4330 Gulf Shore Blvd. N., Suite 302, at The Village on Venetian Bay, Naples. High-end youthful women's fashions in lace, denim, and other contemporary fabrics and styles.

Weekends (239-949-4163), 26841 South Bay Dr. #156, at The Promenade, Bonita Springs. Sporty casual threads for Florida men and women, including women's footwear.

Wildflower (239-643-6776), 4222 Gulf Shore Blvd. N., at The Village on Venetian Bay, Naples. Distinctive fun and formal women's wear with Florida flair and style.

Zazou (239-436-3927; www.zazou naples.com), 1170 Third St. S., Naples; and (239-261-2882), 2950 Ninth St. N., at Hibiscus Center, Naples, plus two other Naples/Bonita Springs locations. Expressive women's clothing and home accessorizing products.

CONSIGNMENT Naples is a second-hand shopper's paradise. In many of the clothing consignment shops you can find designer fashions with the price tags still attached. Oh, the joys of hunting down the castoffs of the well-to-do!

Encore Shop (239-775-0032; www .davidlawrencecenter.org/encore.php), 3105 Davis Blvd., Naples. Designer furniture, paintings, decorative items, and collectibles.

New to You Consignments (239-262-6869), 933 Creech Rd., Naples. Women's designer clothing, furniture, and decorative items.

FACTORY OUTLET CENTERS
Naples Prime Outlets (239-775-8083 or 888-545-7196; www.primeoutlets .com), 6060 Collier Blvd. #121, Naples. Factory outlet discounts of up to 65 percent off for Harry and David gourmet foods, Coach bags, Bass shoes, and Liz Claiborne and Izod clothing, among other name brands.

FLEA MARKETS & BAZAARS
Flamingo Island Flea Market (239-948-7799; www.flamingoisland.com), 11902 Bonita Beach Rd., Bonita Springs. Open Friday–Sunday 8–4, with up to 600 vendors.

Naples Twin Drive-In Flea Market (239-774-2900), Immokalee Rd. and 39th Ave., Naples. Open Saturday and Sunday.

GALLERIES Naples has earned a reputation as a mecca for fine art. Gallery Row, along Broad Avenue South at Third Street South, is a good place to begin your art quest. Galleries line the street and sell a wide spectrum of art. Several more lie in the immediate vicinity. Fifth Avenue South is another area, although the galleries there are more spread out.

Art Modern Gallery (239-659-2787; www.artmoderngallery.com), 824 Fifth Ave. S., Naples. Delightful works by artists Natalie Guess and Phil Fisher, plus other locals.

The Blue Mangrove Gallery (239-393-2405; www.bluemangrovegallery .com), 1089 N. Collier Blvd. #417, at Marco Town Center, Marco Island. Exhibits the paintings, glass, jewelry, and photography of more than 150 local and national artists.

The Darvish Collection (239-261-7581; www.artnet.com/darvish.html), 1199 Third St. S., Naples. Features the work of North American and European masters within its seven wood-lined, clublike galleries. Most works in the four- to six-figure range.

Gallery Matisse (239-285-1415; www .gallerymatisse.com), 1170 Third St. S., Suite C106, Naples. Picasso and Chagall pieces, fine oils, art jewelry, and a bit of whimsy.

Gallery One (239-263-0835; www .galleryonenaples.com), 1301 Third St. S., Naples. My favorite Naples gallery, it has a large showroom that exhibits mostly three-dimensional art, including a preponderance of glass. Paintings include the work of popular local artist Paul Arsenault.

Native Visions Gallery (239-643-3785; www.callofafrica.com), 737 Fifth Ave. S., Naples. Remarkable works themed around Africa, the sea, and the environment.

New River Fine Art (239-435-4515; www.newriverfineart.com), 600 Fifth Ave. S., Naples. Truly fine art, pieces here range from contemporary paintings to the etchings of Salvador Dalí and exquisite glass sculptures by Frederick Hart.

Riverside Park (239-297-7227), Old US 41 Rd. and Pennsylvania, downtown Bonita Springs. When the park renovated in 2005, city officials saved a row of historic fish shacks from demolition by renovating them and turning them into a string of six art galleries. You'll find the most activity the second Friday of each month, when "Evening in the Park" takes place during season, and Thursdays from 10–4 when visitors can meet the artists.

Silver Eagle (239-403-3033; www .silvereaglegallery.com), 651 Fifth Ave. S., Naples. Decorative Native American drums, blankets, and candles; paintings and beautiful silver and turquoise jewelry.

Sweet Art (239-597-2110; www.the sweetartgallery.com), 2054 Trade Center Way, Naples. Affordable tropical decorative art and home accessories.

GIFTS Some of Naples's best souvenirs are found in the gift shops at the town's visitor attractions.

Holiday House Gifts (239-642-7113), 133 S. Barfield Dr., at Shops of Marco, Marco Island. Candles, country- and tropical-style items, Christmas ornaments and decorations.

Regatta (239-262-3929), 760 Fifth Ave. S., Naples. Its subtitle describes it best: "fun things for fun people." Clothes, toys, and things for the home, all in a fine and whimsical tone.

Sweet Pea (239-389-0165), 330 Royal Palm Dr., Olde Marco Shops, Marco Island. An oddball assortment of fur-trimmed can coolers, scented bubbles, beach towels, candles, and other beach paraphernalia and gifts.

JEWELRY Cleopatra's Barge (239-261-7952 or 800-678-7934; www.cleopatrasbarge.com), 1197 Third St. S., Naples. Home of "Naples Medallion" jewelry and other fine and estate pieces. Certified jewelers and diamond setters.

DuFrane Jewelers (239-495-9005 or 888-DUFRANE; www.dufranejewelers.com), 26841 S. Bay Dr. #152; at The Promenade, Bonita Springs. Besides gorgeous jewelry and watches, this large outlet sells fine china and crystal and other elegant table- and barware.

✪ **Port Royal Jewelers** (239-263-3071), 623 Fifth Ave. S., Naples. This place is like a museum: It includes 18th-century royal jewels and antique pieces in art deco, Edwardian, Georgian, and Victorian styles, as well as custom-designed and estate jewelry. It's so exclusive you have to ring a doorbell to get in, and there's a special vault containing the real treasures.

Schilling Fine Jewelers (239-642-3001), 1845 San Marco Dr., at Shops of Marco, Marco Island. Custom design and manufacturing; cloisonné turtles and fish jewelry; extraordinary sea-themed pieces.

Thalheimers Fine Jewelers (239-261-8422 or 800-998-8423; www.thalheimers.com), 3200 Tamiami Trail N. #100, Naples. The most respected name in jewelers, carrying quality watches, diamond jewelry, gems, crystal, and porcelain. Watchmaker, designer, and appraiser on premises.

✪ **Wm. Phelps, Custom Jeweler** (239-434-2233; www.phelpsjewelers.com), 4380 Gulf Shore Blvd., at The Village on Venetian Bay, Naples. Fine-crafted pendants, rings, earrings, and pins on display, including its signature nature collection of gorgeous birds and shells, plus colored stones and diamonds for customizing.

Yamron Jewelers (239-592-7707), 5415 Tamiami Trail N., at Waterside Shops, Naples. A select stock of exquisite jewelry and Swiss watches.

KITCHENWARE & HOME DÉCOR
El Condor Imports (239-732-5855; www.elcondornaplesfl.com), 6060 Collier Blvd. #123, at Prime Outlets, Naples. Rustic pine furniture, pottery, and decorative crafts from Mexico.

Fabec-Young & Company (239-649-5501), 4360 Gulf Shore Blvd., Suite 604, at The Village on Venetian Bay, Naples. Unusual table settings, including napkins, candles, glassware, silver, and ceramics.

Gattle's (239-262-4791 or 800-344-4552; www.gattles.com), 1250 Third St. S., Naples. Fine linens for bed, bath, and table; home accessories and art.

A Horse of a Different Color (239-261-1252), 4226 Gulf Shore Blvd. N., at The Village on Venetian Bay, Naples. Pricey, one-of-a-kind, highly contemporary gifts, tableware, and home accents.

Lady from Haiti (239-649-8607; www.theladyfromhaiti.com), 515 Park St., Naples. Steel-drum sculptures, hand-painted wooden items, fine Haitian art. Enjoy the sand on the floor and Caribbean music while you shop.

SHELL SHOPS Marco Craft & Shell Company (239-394-7020; www.marcocraftandshellcompany.com), 1089 N. Collier Blvd. #424, at Marco Town Center Mall, Marco Island. Craft and specimen shells, locally handcrafted gifts, craft classes.

Sea Shell Co. (239-390-1815), 4461 Bonita Beach Rd., Bonita Springs. Pristine as an art gallery, its manager, Scott Ritchie, displays fine specimen shells along with jewelry and other gifts.

Shells by Emily (239-394-5575; www
.shellsbyemily.com), 651 S. Collier
Blvd. 2C, Marco Island. Walk up or
take the elevator to the second floor to
find this award-winning shell crafter,
who sells specimen shells and crafting
supplies.

✴ Special Events

January: **Bonita Springs National
Art Festival** (239-495-8989; www
.artinusa.com/Bonita), The Promenade, Bonita Springs. A top-rated, two-
day show midmonth featuring fine
artists from around the world. Also in
March. **Marco National Fine Arts &
Fine Crafts Festival** (239-394-4221;
www.marcoislandart.com), 1010 Winterberry Dr., at the Art League of
Marco Island grounds, Marco Island.
Two days midmonth for an outdoor art
fling. **Mullet Festival** (239-394-3041
or 877-387-2582; www.stansidlehour
.com), Stan's Idle Hour restaurant,
Goodland. Celebrating Goodland's
fishing heritage with an extravaganza
of music and tomfoolery, including the
Buzzard Queen contest. Three days
late in the month. **Naples Winter
Wine Festival** (239-514-2239 or 888-
837-4919; www.napleswinefestival
.com), 6200 Shirley St. #206, Naples.
Held throughout Naples in late May, it
benefits local children with a high-
yielding live auction and pricey vintner
dinners in private homes. **Southwest
Florida Nature Festival** (239-417-
6310, ext. 401), Rookery Bay National
Estuarine Research Reserve, Naples.
Weekend midmonth; live animals, family activities, guided field trips, children's programs. **Swamp Buggy
Races** (239-774-2701 or 800-897-2701;
www.swampbuggy.com), Florida Sports
Park, CR 951, East Naples. Nationally
televised event; the Everglades equivalent of tractor pulls or monster truck
racing.

February: **Bluegrass Festival** (239-
394-3397; www.floridastateparks.org
/collierseminole), Collier-Seminole
State Park. Second weekend of the
month. ♪ **Collier County Fair** (239-
455-1444; www.colliercountyfair.com),
Collier County Fairgrounds,
Immokalee Rd., Naples. A good old-
fashioned fair with rides and exhibits.
Early February for 11 days. ❂ **Everglades Seafood Festival** (239-695-
4100; www.evergladesseafoodfestival
.com), Everglades City. Three days of
music, arts and crafts, carnival rides,
and fresh seafood. Early in the month.
Greek Festival (239-591-3430), St.
Katherine's Greek Orthodox Church,
7100 Airport Rd., Naples. Greek food
specialties, music, costumed dancers,
and exhibits. First weekend. **Marjory
Stoneman Douglas Festival** (239-
695-0008; www.colliermuseums.com
/events.php), Museum of the Everglades, Everglades City. Pays tribute to
author Douglas's groundbreaking work
in preserving the Everglades with four
days of boat tours, guided walks, and
canoe trips. Late month. **Naples
National Art Festival** (239-262-6517;
www.naplesart.org), Cambier Park,
downtown Naples. This prime art festival event takes place over two days late
in the month. Donation suggested.

March: **Bonita Springs National Art
Festival** (239-495-8989; www.artinusa
.com/Bonita), The Promenade, Bonita
Springs. Two days midmonth featuring
fine artists from around the world.
Also in January. **Kayak Festival** (239-
262-6149; www.paradisecoastpaddlers
.com), Capri Fish House, Isles of
Capri. Late month Sunday devoted to
kayaking demonstrations, clinics, and
guided tours. **Marco Island Seafood
Festival** (www.marcoislandseafood
festival.com), Veterans Park, 403
Elkam Circle, Marco Island. Seafood,
music, and good times. One weekend
late in the month. **Naples St.**

Patrick's Day Parade (239-436-0050) Celebrate in true Irish spirit as this parade makes its way through Fifth Avenue South and Third Street South one day mid-March. **Swamp Buggy Races** (239-774-2701 or 800-897-2701; www.swampbuggy.com), Florida Sports Park, CR 951, East Naples. See above, under January.

May: **A Taste of Collier** (239-272-1907; www.tasteofcollier.com), Fifth Ave. S., Naples. Naples's renowned restaurants serve samples of their culinary specialties. Live music. One weekend day early in the month. **Great Dock Canoe Race** (239-261-4191; www.greatdockcanoerace.com), The Dock at Crayton Cove restaurant, 12th Ave. S., Naples. More than 200 teams, many in festive costumes, paddle across Naples Bay in good-spirited competition that kicks off with a parade. One Saturday.

June: **Spammy Jammy** (239-394-5663; www.littlebarrestaurant.com), The Little Bar, Goodland. A wacky celebration befitting Goodland, featuring Spam creations, nighttime apparel, and a good bit of drinking. End of month. **SummerJazz** (239-261-2222), Naples Beach Hotel & Golf Club, Naples. A series of sunset concerts under the stars one Saturday every month, June–September.

October: **South Florida PGA Open** (239-261-2222), Naples Beach Hotel & Golf Club, 851 Gulf Shore Blvd. N., Naples. Golf enthusiasts can qualify to play side by side with PGA pros in the four-day competition midmonth. **Swamp Buggy Races.** See above, under January. The October races kick off the season with a parade. Late month.

November: ✑ **Old Florida Festival** (239-252-8476; www.colliermuseums.com), Collier County Museum, Naples. Living history from the Stone Age to World War II, with food, crafts, games, demonstrations, and re-enactments. First weekend of the month.

December: **Christmas Walk and Avenue of Lights** (239-435-3742; www.fifthavenuesouth.com), Fifth Avenue South, Naples. Holiday street- and tree-lighting festivities, open houses at shops and other merchants. Early December. Mid-December brings "A Tuba Christmas" with Christmas songs and competition for a best-dressed tuba award. **New Year's Eve Downtown Art Festival** (239-435-3742; www.fifthavenuesouth.com), Fifth Ave. S., Naples. Fine artisans fill the street the weekend after Christmas.

INFORMATION

✳ Practical Matters

We hope that you never need a hospital or a police officer, but in case you should, we offer that information here, as well as information on other topics:

HEED THIS WARNING SIGN AT PINE ISLAND'S "WORLD'S FISHINGEST BRIDGE."

AMBULANCE/FIRE/POLICE All five southwest coast counties have adopted the 911 emergency phone number system. Dial it for ambulance, fire, sheriff, and police. The Poison Control number is 800-222-1222. Listed below are nonemergency numbers for individual communities.

PUNTA GORDA'S HISTORIC CITY HALL.

Town	Ambulance	Fire	Police/Sheriff
FOR EMERGENCY	911	911	911
Anywhere in the region	Florida Highway Patrol 800-342-3557		

CHARLOTTE COUNTY

Boca Grande	941-964-2908		
Punta Gorda	941-575-5529	941-639-4111	
Charlotte County	941-743-0811	941-474-3233	
Florida Highway Patrol			
(Venice)			941-483-5911

COLLIER COUNTY

Everglades City	239-695-2902	239-695-3341	
Isles of Capri	239-394-8770		
Naples		239-213-4844	
Collier County Sheriff		239-774-4434	
Florida Highway Patrol			
(Naples)			239-354-2377

Town	Ambulance	Fire	Police/Sheriff
LEE COUNTY			
Bonita Springs	239-949-6200		
Cape Coral	239-574-0501	239-574-3223	
Captiva	239-472-0344		
Fort Myers	239-334-6222	239-334-4155	
Fort Myers Beach	239-463-6163	239-765-2300	

Pine Island (Matlacha)	239-283-0030	
Sanibel	239-472-5525	239-472-3111
Lee County Sheriff		239-477-1000
Florida Highway Patrol		
(Fort Myers)		239-278-7100

SARASOTA/BRADENTON COUNTIES

Anna Maria	941-741-3900	941-708-8899
Bradenton	941-708-6233	941-932-9300
Bradenton Beach	941-741-3900	941-778-6311
Holmes Beach	941-741-3900	941-708-5804
Longboat	941-316-1944	941-316-1977
Sarasota	941-951-4211	941-316-1201
Venice	941-480-3030	
Manatee County Sheriff		941-747-3011
Sarasota County	941-951-4211	941-927-4190
Florida Highway Patrol		
(Bradenton)		941-751-7647

AREA CODES/TOWN GOVERNMENT *Area Codes:* The area code for the Sarasota Bay area and the Charlotte Harbor Coast is 941. The 239 code covers the entire Island Coast and South Coast.

Town Government: All incorporated cities within the region are self-governing and have councilpersons, commissioners, mayors, and city managers in various roles. The unincorporated towns and communities are county ruled.

The incorporated cities of the Sarasota Bay coast include Bradenton, Anna Maria, Holmes Beach, Bradenton Beach, Sarasota, Longboat Key, North Port, and Venice. Bradenton is the county seat for Manatee County; Sarasota is county seat for Sarasota County. On the Charlotte Harbor Coast, Punta Gorda (county seat) is incorporated. Bonita Springs, Cape Coral, Fort Myers (county seat), Fort Myers Beach, and Sanibel make up Lee County's incorporated cities. Naples is Collier County's seat; Naples, Marco Island, and Everglades City are incorporated.

BANKS Several old and established banks have branches located throughout Florida's Gulf Coast. Some are listed below with toll-free information numbers.

Bank	Number
Bank of America	800-299-2265
Regents	800-267-6884
SunTrust	800-732-9487
Wachovia	800-922-4684

CLIMATE, SEASONS, AND WHAT TO WEAR

The tropics brush the Mangrove Coast but do not overwhelm it.

—*Karl Bickel, The Mangrove Coast, 1942*

Florida's nickname, the Sunshine State, was once as fresh as it was apt. Although overuse has tended to cloud the once-perfect image, Florida still remains the ultimate state of sunshine through the sheer power of statistics. The sun beams down on the Gulf Coast for nearly 75 percent of all daylight hours and constitutes the one asset on which locals can bank.

To residents, the sun's smile can seem more like a sneer as they await fall's begrudging permission to turn off air conditioners and open windows. They suffer their own brand of cabin fever during the summer months, which often seem to linger as long as a Canadian winter. Although visitors revel in the warmth and sunlight, they often wonder how residents endure the monotony of seasonal sameness.

The seasons *do* change along the southern Gulf Coast, although more subtly than "up north." Weather patterns vary within the region. The Sarasota Bay and Charlotte Harbor areas often get more rain. However, weather can be very localized—it may rain on the southern end of 12-mile-long Sanibel Island while the north end remains dry. Islands generally stay cooler than the mainland in summer and warmer in winter, thanks to their insulating jacket of gulf water. This is especially true where Charlotte Harbor runs wide and deep, creating a small pocket of tropical climate.

Winter is everyone's favorite time of year weatherwise. Temperatures along the coast reach generally into the 70s during the day and drop into the low 50s and upper 40s at night. Visitors find green, balmy relief from snow blindness and frostbite. Floridians enjoy the relative coolness that brings with it a reprieve from sweltering days, steamy nights, and bloodthirsty insects. The fragrance of oranges, grapefruits, and key limes fills the air. It's a time for activity; one can safely schedule a tee time past noon. Resort areas fill up, and migratory houseguests from the north arrive.

Spring comes on tiptoe to the coast. No thaw-and-puddle barometer alerts us; the sense of spring giddiness affects only longtime residents. Floridians emerge from hibernation raring to leap and frolic—and perhaps do a little mischief. Gardenias, Hong Kong orchids, and jasmine bloom, and everything that already looks green and alive bursts forth with an extra reserve of color. It's a time to celebrate the end of another tourist season and to greedily enjoy the domain that's been shared with visitors during the winter months.

Summers used to be reserved for die-hard Floridians. All but the most devoted residents boarded up their homes and businesses and headed somewhere—*anywhere*—cooler. Now there's a summer trade, composed of Floridians, Europeans, and northern families—enough to keep the resort communities alive through temperatures that inch up to 100 degrees. Although technically classified as subtropical, the region, starting in June, feels the bristles of a tropical brush. The pace of life slows, and late-afternoon rains suddenly and unpredictably revolt against the sun's constancy. Mangoes and guavas blush sweet temptation. Moonlit nights bring magic to the cereus vine and its white starburst blooms the size of Frisbees.

Fall appears in October as a sharpening of vision after a blur of humidity. Residents don't exactly go out and buy wool plaids, but they do break out sweatshirts. Many build fires in hearths that have held dried floral arrangements for eight months. The leathery leaves of the sea grape tree turn as red as the northern oak, and the deciduous gumbo-limbo coaxes out rakes. The best part about a Gulf Coast fall, for those residents who once endured northern winters, is that it doesn't forebode snow boots and long underwear.

Winter temperatures dip, albeit rarely, into the freezing range, so be prepared for just about any weather between December and February. Fortunately swimsuits take up little room, so pack more than one. (Florida's high humidity often prevents anything from ever really drying out.) Loose-fitting togs and cotton work best in any season. Long sleeves are welcome in the evenings during winter. Summer showers require rain gear, especially if you plan on boating or playing outdoors.

Don't worry about dress codes in most restaurants. Ties and pantyhose are strictly for the office and (possibly) the theater. Worry more about comfort, particularly if your skin burns easily. Pack hats and lots of sunscreen. Bring insect repellent, too, especially if you plan on venturing into the jungle—or simply watching an island sunset, for that matter. Counties do spray for mosquitoes, but spraying has little effect on the tiny but prolific no-see-um (sandfly). The best protection against both pests is sitting under a ceiling fan—practically standard equipment in homes and hotels.

On the cloudier side, Florida weather includes a high incidence of lightning, summer squalls, tornadoes, waterspouts, and the dreaded H-word. Hurricane season begins in June, but activity concentrates toward season's end in October and November. Watches and warnings alert you in plenty of time to head inland or north; to be safest, do so at first mention, especially if you are staying on an island.

Florida's celebrated sunshine is at its best on the Gulf Coast. Ol' Sol visits practically every day, and it's also where he slips into bed. Gulf Coast Florida boasts the most spectacular sunsets in the continental United States. (OK, so I'm a little biased.)

HOSPITALS & CLINICS

Charlotte Harbor Coast
Charlotte Regional Medical Center (941-639-3131; www.charlotteregional.com), 809 E. Marion Ave., Punta Gorda. Emergency room open 24 hours.

Englewood Community Hospital (941-475-6571; www.englewoodcommhospital.com), 700 Medical Blvd., Englewood. Emergency room open 24 hours. For 24-hour Consult-a-Nurse line, call 941-473-3919 or 888-685-1598.

Fawcett Memorial Hospital (941-629-1181; www.fawcetthospital.com), 21298 Olean Blvd., Port Charlotte. Emergency room open 24 hours.

Peace River Regional Medical Center (941-766-4122; www.peaceriverregional.com), 2500 Harbor Blvd., Port Charlotte. Emergency room open 24 hours.

AVERAGE GULF COAST AIR TEMPERATURES

Month	Avg. Max.	Avg. Min.
Jan.	72.8°	52.8°
Feb.	73.8°	53.8°
Mar.	78.3°	57.8°
Apr.	82.5°	61.6°
May	87.7°	67.1°
June	89.7°	72.1°
July	90.5°	73.7°
Aug.	90.9°	73.8°
Sept.	89.1°	72.7°
Oct.	84.9°	66.8°
Nov.	77.9°	59.4°
Dec.	74.1°	53.8°

Gulf Coast Water Temperatures

Annual average	77.5°
Fall/winter average	70.8°
Spring/summer average	84.1°
Winter low	66.0°
Summer high	87.0°

Island Coast

Cape Coral Hospital (239-574-2323; www.leememorial.org), 636 Del Prado Blvd., Cape Coral. Emergency room open 24 hours.

Gulf Coast Medical Center (239-768-5000; www.leememorial.org), 13681 Doctor's Way, Fort Myers. Emergency room open 24 hours.

HealthPark Medical Center (239-433-7799; www.leememorial.org), 9981 S. HealthPark Dr., Fort Myers. Home of Children's Hospital of Southwest Florida. Emergency room open 24 hours; 24-hour medical information via HealthLine, 800-936-5321.

Lee Memorial Hospital (239-332-1111; www.leememorial.org), 2776 Cleveland Ave., Fort Myers. Emergency room open 24 hours.

Sarasota Bay Coast

Doctors Hospital of Sarasota (941-342-1100; www.doctorsofsarasota.com), 5731 Bee Ridge Rd., Sarasota. Emergency room open 24 hours.

HCA L. W. Blake Medical Center (941-792-6611; www.blakemedicalcenter .com), 2020 59th St. W., Bradenton. Emergency room open 24 hours.

Lakewood Ranch Medical Center (941-782-2100; www.lakewoodranchmedical center.com), 8330 Lakewood Ranch Blvd., Bradenton. Emergency room open 24 hours.

Manatee Memorial Hospital (941-746-5111 or 941-745-7466 for emergencies; www.manateememorial.com), 206 Second St. E., Bradenton. Emergency room open 24 hours.

Sarasota Memorial Hospital (941-917-9000 or 800-917-8255; www.smh.com), 1700 S. Tamiami Trail, Sarasota. Emergency room open 24 hours.

Venice Regional Medical Center (941-485-7711; www.veniceregional.net), 540 The Rialto, Venice. Emergency room open 24 hours.

South Coast

Marco Healthcare Center (239-394-8234; www.nchmd.org), 40 Heathwood Dr., Marco Island. Medical care and rehab on an outpatient basis.

Naples Downtown Hospital (239-436-5000; www.nchmd.org), 350 Seventh St. N., Naples. Heart and cancer institutes; emergency room open 24 hours.

North Naples Hospital (239-552-7000; www.nchmd.org), 11190 Health Park Blvd., off Immokalee Rd., Naples. Emergency room open 24 hours.

MEDIA Media flood the Gulf Coast like high tide. Many publications are directed toward tourists, and some are only as permanent as the shoreline during a tidal surge. Magazines come and go, and radio stations often shift formats.

Four daily newspapers stand out for their endurance and dependability: the *Bradenton Herald,* the *Sarasota Herald-Tribune, The News-Press,* and the *Naples Daily News.* Weeklies are also firmly established in their respective communities, primarily because many are owned collectively by one corporation. Specialty tabloids address seniors, shoppers, fishermen, women, and other groups.

Magazines show the most fluctuation. Traditionally they were created to appeal to the region's upscale, mature population, which is concentrated in Sarasota and Naples. *Sarasota Magazine, Times of the Islands, Naples Illustrated,* and *Gulfshore*

Life have been the stalwarts of regional lifestyle glossies, but even they shift focus to address changing populations and economic trends.

Fort Myers carries the majority of the region's broadcast media, which reach to the Charlotte Harbor and the South Coasts. Much of the Sarasota Bay coast's TV comes from Tampa.

ITunes App: **Sanibel & Captiva Islands Essential Guide** (http://sutromedia .com/apps/Sanibel_FL), by Chelle Koster Walton. Complete with locator maps, images, and interactive capabilities, this app contains 100 evaluative reviews of beaches, attractions, restaurants, accommodations, shopping, and day trips.

Charlotte Harbor Coast

Newspapers: **Boca Beacon** (941-964-2995 or 800-749-2995; www.bocabeacon .com), P.O. Box 313, Boca Grande 33921. Weekly.

Charlotte Sun-Herald (941-206-1000 or 877-818-6204; www.sunnewspaper.net), 23170 Harborview Rd., Charlotte Harbor 33980. Daily.

Englewood Sun-Herald (941-681-3000; www.sunnewspaper.net), 167 W. Dearborn St., Englewood 34223. Daily.

Gasparilla Gazette (941-964-2728; www.gasparillagazette.com), P.O. Box 929, Boca Grande 33921. Weekly.

Punta Gorda/Port Charlotte Florida Weekly (941-621-3422), 1205 Elizabeth St. #G, Punta Gorda 33950. Local and national news and features.

Magazines: **Harbor Style** (941-205-2410), P.O. Box 511656, Punta Gorda 33951. Covers lifestyle in the Charlotte Harbor area.

Island Coast

Newspapers: **Cape Coral Breeze** (239-574-1110; www.breezenewspapers.com), 2510 Del Prado Blvd., Cape Coral 33904. Daily.

Fort Myers Beach Bulletin (239-463-4421; www.breezenewspapers.com), 19260 San Carlos Blvd., Fort Myers Beach 33931. Weekly.

Fort Myers Florida Weekly (239-333-2135), 4300 Ford St., #105, Fort Myers 33916. Local and national news and features.

Island Reporter (239-472-1587; www.breezenewspapers.com), 2340 Periwinkle Way, Sanibel Island 33957. Weekly.

News-Press (239-335-0200; www.news-press.com), 2442 Dr. Martin Luther King Jr. Blvd., Fort Myers 33901. The 10th-largest newspaper in the state in terms of circulation, it publishes editions for Charlotte County and Bonita Springs.

Observer Papers (239-765-0400; www.flguide.com), 17274 San Carlos Blvd., Fort Myers Beach 33931. Publishes weekly editions for Fort Myers Beach and other neighborhoods.

Pine Island Eagle (239-283-2022; www.breezenewspapers.com), 10700 Stringfellow Rd., Suite 60, Bokeelia 33922. Weekly.

Sanibel-Captiva Islander (239-472-5185; www.breezenewspapers.com), 395 Tarpon Bay Rd. #13, Sanibel Island 33957. Weekly; free subscription.

Magazines: **Times of the Islands** (239-472-0205; www.toti.com), P.O. Box 1227, Sanibel Island 33957. Covers the local arts, business, cuisine, nature, and travel scenes. Also publishes *RSW Living* and *Gulf & Main*—same magazines, different covers for mainland distribution.

Television: **WBBH-TV,** Fort Myers, NBC

WFTX-TV, Cape Coral, FOX

WINK-TV, Fort Myers, CBS

WZVN-TV, Fort Myers, ABC

Sarasota Bay Coast

Newspapers: **Bradenton Herald** (941-748-0411; www.bradenton.com), 102 Manatee Ave. W., Bradenton 34205. Daily.

Creative Loafing (941-365-6776; www.sarasota.creativeloafing.com), 1383 Fifth St., Sarasota 34236. Giveaway entertainment weekly with a youthful, irreverent voice.

Longboat Observer (941-383-5509; www.yourobserver.com), 5570 Gulf of Mexico Dr., Longboat Key 34228. Weekly.

Pelican Press (941-349-4949 or 888-577-6770; www.pelicanpressonline.com), 5011 Ocean Blvd., #206, Sarasota 34242. Weekly covering Siesta Key and Sarasota.

Sarasota Herald-Tribune (941-361-4800; www.heraldtribune.com), 1741 Main St., Sarasota 34236. Florida's eighth-largest daily in terms of circulation.

Venice Gondolier (941-207-1000; www.venicegondolier.com), 200 E. Venice Ave., Venice 34285. Published three times weekly.

Magazines: **Sarasota Magazine** (941-487-1100 or 800-881-2394; www.sarasota magazine.com), 330 S. Pineapple Ave., Suite 205, Sarasota 34236. Lifestyle for upscale Sarasotans.

Sarasota Scene (941-365-1119; www.scenesarasota.com), 1343 Main St., Suite 201, Sarasota 34236. Weekly covering the Sarasota-Bradenton area.

SRQ (941-365-7702), 337 S. Pineapple Ave., Sarasota 34236. SRQ is Sarasota-Bradenton International Airport's code; this slick magazine covers the dining, political, and shopping scene.

West Coast Woman (941-954-3300; www.westcoastwoman.com), P.O. Box 819, Sarasota 34230. Monthly free publication.

Television: **BLAB-TV,** Sarasota

SNN-TV, Sarasota News Now

WWSB-TV, Sarasota, ABC

South Coast

Newspapers: **The Banner** (239-263-4839; www.mybannerhub.com), 26381 S. Tamiami Trail #116, Bonita Springs 34134. Weekly Wednesday tabloid-sized paper serving Bonita Springs, Estero, and vicinity.

Bonita Daily News (239-213-6064; www.bonitanews.com), 26381 Tamiami Trl. #116, Bonita Springs 34135.

Marco Eagle (239-213-5301; www.marconews.com), 579 Elkcam Circle, Marco Island 34146. Daily tabloid-sized newspaper operated by *Naples Daily News.*

Marco Island Sun Times (239-394-4050; www.marcoislandflorida.com), 1857 Marco Rd. Unit #216, Marco Island 34145. Free distribution paper. Weekly.

Naples Daily News (239-262-3161; www.naplesnews.com), 1100 Immokalee Rd., Naples 34110. Daily; publisher of the two newspapers listed above.

Naples Florida Weekly (239-325-1960), 2025 J&C Blvd. #5, Naples 34109. Local and national news and features.

Magazines: **Gulfshore Business** (239-449-4124 or 800-220-4853; www.gulfshore business.com), 9051 N. Tamiami Trail, Suite 202, Naples 34108. Monthly covering Southwest Florida's business news.

Gulfshore Life (239-449-4111 or 800-220-4853; www.gulfshorelife.com), 3560 Kraft Rd. #301, Naples 34108. Longtime slick lifestyle and news guide to the southwest coast.

Naples Illustrated (239-434-6966; www.naplesillustrated.com), 3066 Tamiami Trail N., Suite 102, Naples 34103. Haute lifestyles glossy.

Television: **WTVK-TV,** Bonita Springs, CW

REAL ESTATE Real estate prices run the gamut from reasonable to ultraexpensive. In parts of Bradenton, Sarasota, and Fort Myers, planned communities cater to young families. Exclusive areas such as Longboat Key, Casey Key, Manasota Key, Sanibel Island, Captiva Island, and Naples are known for their pricey waterfront homes and golfing developments. The most reasonable real estate, naturally, lies inland, away from the water. Florida's $25,000 homestead exemption gives residents a tax break on primary home purchases.

Real estate publications can be found on the newsstands, or check local newspapers. Otherwise, contact the agencies listed below.

Florida Association of Realtors (407-438-1400; www.floridarealtors.org), 7025 Augusta National Dr., Orlando 32822.

Naples Area Board of Realtors (239-597-1666; www.naplesarea.com), 1455 Pine Ridge Rd., Naples 34109.

Realtors Association of Greater Fort Myers and Fort Myers Beach (239-936-3537; www.swflrealtors.com), 2840 Winkler Ave., Fort Myers 33916.

Sanibel & Captiva Islands Association of Realtors (239-472-9353; www .sanibelrealtors.com), 2353 Periwinkle Way #201, Sanibel Island 33957.

Sarasota Association of Realtors (941-923-2315; www.sarasotarealtors.com), 3590 Tuttle Ave. S., Sarasota 34239.

REGIONAL READING Books about the region are available in bookstores and through online outlets.

Biography & Reminiscence: Brown, Loren G. *Totch: A Life in the Everglades.* Gainesville, FL: University Press of Florida, 1993. A folksy, firsthand adventure tour of Ten Thousand Islands through the words of a former native.

Lindbergh, Anne Morrow. *Gift from the Sea.* New York: Pantheon/Village Books, 1955. A small book packed with sea-inspired wisdom from Charles Lindbergh's wife, who died in 2001. Strong evidence points to Captiva as the book's inspiration.

Newton, James. *Uncommon Friends.* New York: Harcourt, Brace, Jovanovich, 1987. Local man's memories of his friendships with Fort Myers's illustrious winters: Thomas Edison, Henry Ford, Harvey Firestone, and Charles Lindbergh.

Orlean, Susan. *The Orchid Thief: A True Story of Beauty and Obsession.* New York: Random House, 1998. Set in Fakahatchee Strand Preserve State Park,

JAMES NEWTON'S AUTOBIOGRAPHY, *UNCOMMON FRIENDS,* INSPIRED THIS DOWNTOWN FORT MYERS SCULPTURE, WHICH PORTRAYS CAMPING TRIPS THAT HENRY FORD, HARVEY FIRESTONE, AND THOMAS EDISON SHARED DURING THEIR VISITS TO THE AREA.

Naples, and other local venues, Orlean tells a bizarre nonfiction tale about the elusive ghost orchid and the people who sought it.

St. Claire, Dana. *Cracker: The Cracker Culture in Florida History.* Daytona Beach, FL: The Museum of Arts and Sciences, 1998.

Weeks, David C. *Ringling: The Florida Years, 1911–1936.* Gainesville, FL: University Press of Florida, 1993.

Cookbooks: White, Randy Wayne. *Randy Wayne White's Gulf Coast Cookbook: With Memories and Photos of Sanibel Island.* Guilford, CT: The Lyons Press, 2006. Southwest Florida's most popular murder-mystery novelist combines local history with cuisine.

Fiction: Hiaasen, Carl. *Nature Girl.* New York: Alfred A. Knopf, 2006. Florida's favorite mystery man sets his 13th novel in Everglades City.

Hudler, Ad. *All This Belongs to Me.* New York: Ballantine Publishing, 2006. Set in Fort Myers, its plot revolves around the Edison Estates.

MacDonald, John D. Many of his Travis McGee and other mysteries take place in a Sarasota Bay coast setting, where he had a home.

Matthiessen, Peter. *Bone by Bone.* New York: Random House, 1999. The parents of this award-winning author lived on Sanibel Island. This is the final book in a historical trilogy about the posse killing of a murderer who hid out in the frontier of Ten Thousand Islands.

————. *Killing Mr. Watson.* New York: Random House, 1990. First book in the trilogy.

————. *Lost Man's River.* New York: Random House, 1997. Second book in the trilogy.

Smith, Patrick D. *A Land Remembered.* Sarasota, FL: Pineapple Press, 1984. This definitive historical novel about Florida's Cracker and cow-hunting eras features many scenes set in the Fort Myers and Everglades areas.

White, Randy Wayne. *Sanibel Flats.* New York: St. Martin's Press, 1990. Mystery by a local fishing guide/journalist in a local setting. Several books in his Doc Ford series take place mostly along the Gulf Coast.

History: Anholt, Betty. *Sanibel's Story: Voices & Images from Calusa to Incorporation.* Virginia Beach, VA: Donning, 1998. Written by a longtime island resident and historian.

Boca Grande Historical Society. *Boca Grande: Lives of an Island.* 2006. A human history with black-and-white photographs.

Buck, Pat Ringling et al. *A History of Visual Art in Sarasota.* University Press of Florida, 2003. Written by a Ringling heir with illustrations.

Hill, Yvonne and Marguerite Jordan. *Sanibel Island.* Charleston, SC: Arcadia Publishing, 2008. One in the Images of America series, it concentrates on the island's African-American heritage through historic photographs.

Natural History: Douglas, Marjory Stoneman. *The Everglades: River of Grass.* St. Simons, GA: Mockingbird Books, 1947. The book that focused the nation's attention on the developing plight of the pristine Everglades.

Toops, Connie. *The Florida Everglades.* Stillwater, MN: Voyageur Press, 1998. Written by a former national park ranger.

Pictorial: Butcher, Clyde. *Clyde Butcher: Portfolio I.* Fort Myers, FL: Shade Tree Press, 1994. The master of natural landscape photography collects his haunting, black-and-white, large-format images in a coffee-table edition.

Travel: MacPerry, I. *Indian Mounds You Can Visit.* St. Petersburg, FL: Great Outdoors Publishing, 1993. Covers the entire west coast of Florida, arranged by county.

Walton, Chelle Koster. *Adventure Guide to Tampa Bay and Florida's West Coast.* 3rd ed. Edison, NJ: Hunter Publishing, 2004. Covers Tampa to the western Everglades.

Check It Out: Out-of-print books you can find in local libraries when you're visiting. Bickel, Karl A. *The Mangrove Coast: The Story of the West Coast of Florida.* 4th ed. New York: Coward-McCann, 1989. Vintage regional history of the area from Tampa Bay to Ten Thousand Islands, from the time of Ponce de León to 1885, spiced with romantic embellishments.

Beater, Jack. *Pirates & Buried Treasure.* St. Petersburg, FL: Great Outdoors Publishing, 1959. Somewhat factual, ever-colorful account of José Gaspar and his cohorts, by the area's foremost legendaire.

Board, Prudy Taylor, and Esther B. Colcord. *Historic Fort Myers.* Virginia Beach, VA: Donning, 1992. Largely photographic treatment, written by two of the area's leading historians.

————. *Pages from the Past*. Virginia Beach, VA: Donning, 1990. Largely photographic treatment of Fort Myers's history.

Briggs, Mildred. *Pioneers of Bonita Springs (Facts and Folklore)*. Bonita Springs, 1976. Pirates, Indian healers, outlaws, and more.

Campbell, George R. *The Nature of Things on Sanibel*. Fort Myers, FL: Press Printing, 1978. Factual yet entertaining background on native fauna and flora.

Dormer, Elinore M. *The Sea Shell Islands: A History of Sanibel and Captiva*. Tallahassee, FL: Rose Printing, 1987. The definitive work on island and regional history.

Fritz, Florence. *Unknown Florida*. Coral Gables, FL: University of Miami Press, 1963. Focuses on the southernmost Gulf Coast.

Gonzales, Thomas A. *The Caloosahatchee: History of the Caloosahatchee River and the City of Fort Myers, Florida*. Fort Myers Beach, FL: Island Press, 1982. Memories of a native son, descendant of the city's first settler.

Grismer, Karl H. *The Story of Fort Myers*. Fort Myers Beach, FL Island Press, 1982.

————. *The Story of Sarasota*. Tampa, FL: The Florida G Press, 1946.

Hann, John H., ed. *Missions to the Calusa*. Gainesville, FL: University of Florida Press, 1991.

Jordan, Elaine Blohm. *Pine Island, The Forgotten Island*. Pine Island, FL: n.p., 1982.

————. *Tales of Pine Island*. Ellijay, GA: Jordan Ink Publishing, 1985.

Marth, Del. *Yesterday's Sarasota*. Miami, FL: E. A. Seemann Publishing, 1977. Primarily pictorial history.

Matthews, Janet Snyder. *Edge of Wilderness: A Settlement History of Manatee River and Sarasota Bay*. Sarasota, FL: Coastal Press, 1983.

————. *Journey to Centennial Sarasota*. Sarasota, FL: Pine Level Press, 1989.

————. *Venice: Journey to Horse and Chaise*. Sarasota, FL: Pine Level Press, 1989.

Matthews, Kenneth, and Robert McDevitt. *The Unlikely Legacy*. Sarasota, FL: Aaron Publishers, 1980. The story of John Ringling, the circus, and Sarasota.

Peeples, Vernon. *Punta Gorda and the Charlotte Harbor Area*. Virginia Beach, VA: Donning, 1986. Pictorial history authored by a local politician.

Ripple, Jeff. *Southwest Florida's Wetland Wilderness: Big Cypress Swamp and the Ten Thousand Islands*. Gainesville, FL: University Press of Florida, 1992. This book celebrates the natural history of one of the most diverse, endangered, and beautiful ecosystems in the world. Stunning black-and-white photography by Clyde Butcher.

Romans, Bernard. *A Concise Natural History of East and West Florida*. Gainesville, FL: University of Florida Press, 1962. A facsimile reproduction of the 1775 edition.

Schell, Rolfe F. *De Soto Didn't Land at Tampa*. Fort Myers Beach, FL: Island Press, 1966.

————. *History of Fort Myers Beach*. Fort Myers Beach, FL: Island Press, 1980.

Gables, FL: University of Miami Press, 1966.

Widmer, Randolph J. *The Evolution of the Calusa*. Tuscaloosa, AL: University of
Alabama Press, 1988. Very technical discussion of the "nonagricultural chiefdom
on the Southwest Florida Coast."

Zeiss, Betsy. *The Other Side of the River: Historical Cape Coral*. Cape Coral FL:
n.p., 1986.

ROAD SERVICE Information on the **AAA Auto Club** can be found at www.aaa
.com. Each of the following offices provides 24-hour emergency road service.
941-798-2211; 6210 Manatee Ave. W., Bradenton

941-929-2299; 3844 Bee Ridge Rd., Sarasota

941-362-2500; 258 Ringling Shopping Center, Sarasota

239-939-6500; 2516 Colonial Blvd., Fort Myers

239-594-5006; 5410 Airport Pulling Rd. N., Naples

SERVICES FOR THE PHYSICALLY IMPAIRED Regulations concerning dis-
abled access vary, depending on locale. In general, most restaurants, parks, attractions, and resorts provide physically impaired visitors with special ramps, bathroom
stalls, and hotel rooms. Some beaches, particularly in the Naples area, provide fat-
wheeled beach chairs for the physically challenged.

TOURIST INFORMATION **Visit Florida** (888-7FLA-USA; www.visitflorida
.com), 661 E. Jefferson St., Suite 300, Tallahassee 32301.

Charlotte Harbor Coast

Boca Grande Area Chamber of Commerce (941-964-0568; www.bocagrande
chamber.com), 5800 Gasparilla Rd., Suite A1, Boca Grande 33921. Information
center located in Courtyard Plaza at the island's north end.

Charlotte County Chamber of Commerce (941-627-2222; www.charlotte
countychamber.org), 2702 Tamiami Trail, Port Charlotte 33952; and (941-639-
2222), 311 W. Retta Esplanade, Punta Gorda 33950.

Charlotte Harbor Visitor & Convention Bureau (941-743-1900 or 800-652-
6090; www.charlotteharbortravel.com), 18501 Murdock Circle, Suite 502, Port
Charlotte 33948.

Englewood–Cape Haze Area Chamber of Commerce (941-474-5511 or 800-
603-7198; www.englewoodchamber.com), 1160 McCall Rd. S., Englewood 34223.

Punta Gorda Chamber of Commerce (941-639-3720; www.puntagordachamber
.com), 252 W. Marion Ave., Punta Gorda 33950. Information center at Marion
Ave. and Sullivan St.

Island Coast

Cape Coral Chamber of Commerce (239-549-6900 or 800-226-9609; www
.capecoralchamber.com), P.O. Box 100747, Cape Coral 33910. Information center
at 2051 Cape Coral Pkwy. E.

Estero Chamber of Commerce (239-948-7990; www.esterochamber.org), P.O.
Box 588, Estero 33928.

Greater Fort Myers Beach Chamber of Commerce (239-454-7500 or 800-782-9283; www.fmbchamber.com), 17200 San Carlos Blvd., Fort Myers Beach 33931.

Greater Fort Myers Chamber of Commerce (239-332-3624 or 800-366-3622; www.fortmyers.org), 2310 Edwards Dr., Fort Myers 33902. Welcome center located downtown.

Greater Pine Island Chamber of Commerce (239-283-0888; www.pineisland chamber.org), P.O. Box 525, Matlacha 33993. Information center located before the bridge to Matlacha at 3640 Pine Island Rd.

Lee County Visitor & Convention Bureau (239-338-3500 or 800-237-6444; www.fortmyers-sanibel.com), University Park, 12800 University Drive #550, Fort Myers 33907.

North Fort Myers Chamber of Commerce (239-997-9111; www.northfort myerschamber.org), 2787 N. Tamiami Trail #10, North Fort Myers 33903.

Sanibel-Captiva Islands Chamber of Commerce (239-472-1080; www.sanibel -captiva.org), 1159 Causeway Rd., Sanibel Island 33957. Information center located shortly after the causeway approach to Sanibel.

Southwest Florida Hispanic Chamber of Commerce (239-418-1441; www .hispanicchamberflorida.org), 10051 McGregor Blvd., Suite 204, Fort Myers 33919.

Sarasota Bay Coast

Anna Maria Island Chamber of Commerce (941-778-1541; www.amichamber .org), 5313 Gulf Dr., Holmes Beach 34217.

Bradenton Area Convention & Visitors Bureau (941-729-9177 or 800-4-MANATEE; www.flagulfislands.com), P.O. Box 1000, Bradenton 34206.

Downtown Partnership of Sarasota (941-366-5621; www.downtownsarasota .com), 1945 Fruitville Rd., Sarasota 34236.

Longboat Key Chamber of Commerce (941-387-9519; www.longboatkey chamber.com), Whitney Beach Plaza, 6854 Gulf of Mexico Dr., Longboat Key 34228.

Manatee Chamber of Commerce (941-748-3411; www.manateechamber.com), 222 Tenth St. W., Bradenton 34205.

Sarasota Convention & Visitors Bureau (941-957-1877 or 800-522-9799; www .sarasotafl.org), 701 N. Tamiami Trail, Sarasota 34236. Besides information, it has a history museum that visitors are free to browse.

Siesta Key Chamber of Commerce (941-349-3800 or 866-831-7778; www.siesta keychamber.com), 5118 Ocean Blvd., Siesta Key 34242.

Venice Area Chamber of Commerce (941-488-2236; www.venicechamber .com), 597 S. Tamiami Trail, Venice 34285.

South Coast

Bonita Springs Area Chamber of Commerce (239-992-2943 or 800-226-2943; www.bonitaspringschamber.com), 25071 Chamber of Commerce Dr., Bonita Springs 34135.

Everglades Area Chamber of Commerce (239-695-3172 or 800-914-6355; www.evergladeschamber.net), P.O. Box 130, Everglades City 34139. Welcome center corner of US 41 and County Route 29 (CR 29).

Greater Naples Marco Everglades Convention & Visitors Bureau (239-252-2384 or 800-688-3600; www.paradisecoast.com), 2800 N. Horseshoe Blvd. #218, Naples 34104.

Marco Island Area Chamber of Commerce (239-394-7549 or 800-788-MARCO; www.marcoislandchamber.org), 1102 N. Collier Blvd., Marco Island 34145.

Naples Chamber of Commerce (239-262-6141; www.napleschamber.org), 2390 Tamiami Trail N., Naples 34103.

✳ If Time Is Short

Not enough time to do it all on this trip to southwest Florida? Here are some highlights I suggest to weekenders and short-term vacationers who wonder how they can best spend their precious time. Beach time, of course, is a high priority for those with only a few days to spend in the sun. I list must-see beaches as well as other attractions, adventures, restaurants, and lodgings you should not miss.

Sarasota Bay Coast

✪ **Siesta Key County Beach** (941-861-2150; Midnight Pass Rd. at Beach Way Dr., Siesta Key), despite its weekend and high-season crowds, is the area's ultimate beach. Its sands are white and fluffy beyond belief. Have dinner at **Ophelia's on the Bay** (941-349-2212; www.opheliasonthebay.net; 9105 Midnight Pass Rd., Siesta Key), ingenious fare with a calming view.

✪ **Downtown Sarasota** is a happening place. Take in a play and circle the galleries of the Theatre and Arts District. Don't miss the shops of **Palm Avenue** and the galleries of ✪ **Towles Court Artist Colony** (www.towlescourt.com; 1943 Morrill St., Sarasota).

✪ **The John and Mable Ringling Museum of Art,** the **Ringling Estate,** and its various circus and Gilded Age attractions (941-355-5101; www.ringling.org; 5401 Bay Shore Rd., Sarasota) crown in glory Sarasota's famed cultural scene. ✪ **Longboat Key** provides a drive on the coast's wealthy side. Depending on your budget, dine in high style at **The Colony Dining Room** (941-383-5558; www.colonybeachresort.com; 1620 Gulf of Mexico Dr., Longboat Key) or in the spirit of maritime fun at ✪ **Mar-Vista Dockside Restaurant & Pub** (941-383-2391; www.groupersandwich.com; 760 Broadway St., Longboat Key).

Stop at ✪ **Mote Marine Aquarium** (941-388-4441 or 800-691-MOTE; www.mote.org; 1600 Ken Thompson Pkwy., Sarasota) to check out the interactive immersion theater and other fishy stuff.

Charlotte Harbor Coast

The best of Charlotte Harbor lies in its hidden-from-the-spotlight barrier islands. **Manasota Key** and **Englewood Beach** boast sunny beaches flecked with shark teeth. For a unique and nature-intensive lodging experience, book at ✪ **Manasota Beach Club** (941-474-2614; www.manasotabeachclub.com; 7660 Manasota Key Rd., Englewood), a long-standing beach resort with accommodations from rustic to lavish.

On Gasparilla Island, **Boca Grande** supplies a full day of beaching, shopping, and dining. Have lunch or dinner at ✪ **PJ's Seagrille** (239-964-0806; www.pjseagrille.com; 312 Park Ave., Boca Grande) and savor something from the sea, inventive and well-crafted. For a different flavor of island life, take a room at the old, gracious **Gasparilla Inn** (239-964-4500 or 800-996-1913; www.gasparillainn.com; 500 Palm Ave., Boca Grande), as the Vanderbilts and Du Ponts have since 1912.

Explore the extensive aquatic preserves of Charlotte Harbor aboard a catamaran or kayak with ✪ **Grande Tours** (239-697-8825; www.grandetours.com; 12575 Placida Rd., Placida). For an island wilderness adventure that returns you to the days of Florida cow-hunting, ride the bouncy swamp buggy through a modern-day cattle and alligator ranch at ✪ **Babcock Wilderness Adventures** (941-637-0551 or 800-500-5583; www.babcockwilderness.com; 800 FL 31, Punta Gorda).

Island Coast

Fort Myers's finest attraction, the ✪ **Edison & Ford Winter Estates** (239-334-7419; www.efwefla.org; 2350 McGregor Blvd., Fort Myers), peeks into the times and genius of America's greatest inventors, who lived side by side in winter months long past. Dine Victorian in the two historic homes that make up ✪ **The Veranda** (239-332-2065; www.verandarestaurant.com; 2122 Second St., Fort Myers), which specializes in Southern charm and fine cuisine.

Much of what's special about the Island Coast has to do with what's wild. More than half of Sanibel Island is devoted to the ✪ **J. N. "Ding" Darling National Wildlife Refuge** (239-472-1100; www.fws.gov/dingdarling; 1 Wildlife Dr., off Sanibel-Captiva Rd., Sanibel Island), home to alligators, roseate spoonbills, manatees, river otters, and bobcats. The best way to see it is by tram or kayak tour from **Tarpon Bay Explorers** (239-472-8900; www.tarponbayexplorers.com; 900 Tarpon Bay Rd., Sanibel Island).

Sanibel's beaches are renowned for their bountiful shells and minimal impact on nature's birthright beauty. Most natural and secluded is ✪ **Bowman's Beach** (Bowman's Beach Rd. off Sanibel-Captiva Rd.). To find the utmost in remote beaches, rent a boat or hop a charter to unbridged **Cayo Costa Island** and **North Captiva Island,** where state parks preserve slices of Old Florida.

For lively beaching, follow CR 865 through Estero Island's **Fort Myers Beach** and down along lovely, undeveloped Lovers Key en route to ✪ **Bonita Beach.** On the way you'll pass bustling resort scenes and quiet island vistas.

South Coast

To explore the highbrow face of Naples and its environs, stop for afternoon tea at the ✪ **Ritz-Carlton Naples** (239-598-3300 or 800-241-3333; www.ritzcarlton.com; 280 Vanderbilt Beach Rd., Naples) and take in a concert and art stroll at the **Philharmonic Center of the Arts** (239-597-1900 or 800-597-1900; www.thephil.org; 5833 Pelican Bay Blvd., Naples) and the ✪ **Naples Museum of Art** next door (239-597-1900; www.thephil.org; 5833 Pelican Bay Blvd., Naples). Downtown's ✪ **Fifth Avenue South** has evolved into a fashionable shopping and sidewalk-dining district. Try **Bistro 821** (239-261-5821; www.bistro821.com; 821 Fifth Ave. S., Naples) for an example of the finest in Naples's cutting-edge chic.

To really have experienced Naples, you must do sunset at the ✪ **Naples Fishing Pier** (12th Ave. S.). It's a nightly ritual for fishermen, strollers, lovers, and pelicans. By day the pier is the center of activity along a beach that stretches for miles.

My favorite part of Marco Island is ✪ **Goodland.** A little fishing village "on pause," it serves fresh seafood and country fun in its restaurants and introduces the unruly flavor of Ten Thousand Islands and the Florida Everglades.

✪ **Everglades City** is headquarters for tours that explore this labyrinthine land down under. ✪ **Everglades National Park** (239-695-2591 or 866-628-2591; www.nps.gov/ever; Everglades Ranger Station, Everglades City) has a base here, conducts boat tours, and rents kayaks for launching into the 98-mile **Wilderness Trail.**

✴ Chelle's High Fives

Here, I give a "high five" to my top picks in a number of offbeat categories. These are the crème de la crème of Southwest Florida, whether you're looking for the best martini or the swankiest jewelry. Within the chapters, look for starred entries to indicate the High Fivers.

BEACHY KEEN RESORTS

1. Palm Island Resort, Cape Haze
2. Manasota Beach Club, Manasota Key
3. Colony Beach and Tennis Resort, Longboat Key
4. Marco Island Marriott Beach Resort, Golf Club & Spa, Marco Island
5. LaPlaya Beach & Golf Resort, Vanderbilt Beach

FAMILY-LOVING RESORTS

1. Sundial Beach Resort, Sanibel Island
2. Colony Beach and Tennis Resort, Longboat Key
3. Sanibel Harbour Resort & Spa, Fort Myers
4. Palm Island Resort, Cape Haze
5. South Seas Island Resort, Captiva Island

KIDS LOVE THE SHELL-SHAPED SLIDE AT SUNDIAL BEACH RESORT'S POOL.

CITY-SMART HOTELS

1. The Ritz-Carlton Sarasota
2. Bellasera Hotel, Naples
3. Trianon Bonita Bay, Bonita Springs
4. Hotel Indigo, Sarasota
5. Courtyard by Marriott Bradenton Sarasota Riverfront

INNS AND B&B'S

1. Harrington House B&B, Sarasota
2. Collier Inn & Cottages, Useppa Island
3. Gasparilla Inn, Boca Grande
4. The Cypress, Sarasota
5. Island Inn, Sanibel Island

COTTAGE BY THE SEA

1. Rolling Waves Cottages, Longboat Key
2. Cabbage Key Inn, Cabbage Key
3. Jensen's Twin Palm Cottages & Marina, Captiva Island
4. Gulf Breeze Cottages and Motel, Sanibel Island
5. Manasota Beach Club, Manasota Key

SPLURGE ACCOMMODATIONS

1. The Ritz-Carlton Naples
2. Sanibel Harbour Resort & Spa, Fort Myers
3. Naples Grande Resort & Club
4. Marco Beach Ocean Resort, Marco Island
5. Hyatt Regency Coconut Point Resort & Spa, Bonita Springs

MARTINI MECCAS

1. Blu Sushi, Fort Myers
2. Red's Fresh Seafood House & Tavern, Bokeelia
3. Monkey Room, Colony Beach and Tennis Resort, Longboat Key
4. Cà d'Zan Lounge, The Ritz-Carlton Sarasota
5. Blue Water Bistro, Estero

TABLES WITH A WATER VIEW

1. Sale e Pepe, Marco Island
2. Old Salty Dog, Lido Key
3. Mar-Vista Dockside Restaurant & Pub, Longboat Key
4. The Crow's Nest, Venice
5. The Dock at Crayton Cove, Naples

SEAFOOD NOSHING

1. PJ's Seagrille, Boca Grande
2. Captain Brian's Seafood Market Restaurant, Sarasota
3. Star Fish Company, Cortez
4. Captain Eddie's Seafood Restaurant, Nokomis
5. Casey Key Fish House, Casey Key

KEY LIME PIE-IN-THE-SKY

1. Ophelia's on the Bay, Siesta Key
2. Gramma Dot's, Sanibel Island
3. Havana Café, Chokoloskee
4. Randy's Paradise Shrimp, Bonita Springs
5. Casey Key Fish House, Osprey

ROMANTIC RESTAURANTS

1. Beach Bistro, Holmes Beach
2. Sale e Pepe, Marco Island
3. The Veranda, Fort Myers
4. Café L'Europe, Sarasota
5. Portofino Waterfront Dining, Port Charlotte

CREATIVE CUISINE

1. Derek's Culinary Casual, Sarasota
2. The Perfect Caper, Punta Gorda
3. Chops City Grill, Bonita Springs
4. Michael's on East, Sarasota
5. Handsome Harry's Third Street Bistro, Naples

ETHNIC EATS

1. Bha! Bha!, Naples
2. Selva Grill, Sarasota
3. Blu Sushi, Fort Myers
4. Alvarez Mexican Food, Palmetto
5. Siam Hut, Cape Coral

OLD FLORIDA FUNK

1. Cabbage Key Inn, Cabbage Key
2. Little Bar Restaurant, Goodland
3. New Pass Grill & Bait Shop, Lido Key
4. Capri Fish House, Isles of Capri
5. Snook Haven, Venice

BREAKFAST

1. Breakfast Plus, Marco Island
2. Crave, Fort Myers
3. The Broken Egg, Siesta Key
4. Skillets Café, Naples
5. Gulf Drive Café, Bradenton Beach

DELI/FOOD MARKETS

1. Morton's Market, Sarasota
2. Sarasota Olive Oil Company
3. Wynn's, Naples
4. Sandy Butler Gourmet Market, Fort Myers Beach
5. Mario's Italian Meat Market & Deli, Fort Myers

ARCHITECTURAL GEMS

1. Cà d'Zan, Ringling Estates, Sarasota
2. Gamble Plantation Mansion, Bradenton
3. Sarasota Opera House
4. Gasparilla Inn, Boca Grande
5. Van Wezel Performing Arts Hall, Sarasota

HISTORY ALIVE

1. Historic Spanish Point, Osprey
2. Edison & Ford Winter Estates, Fort Myers
3. De Soto National Memorial, Bradenton
4. Koreshan State Historic Site, Estero
5. Collier County Museum, Naples

KID COOL

1. G.WIZ, Sarasota
2. Imaginarium, Fort Myers
3. Sun-n-Fun Lagoon, Naples
4. Greenwell's Bat-A-Ball and Family Fun Park, Cape Coral
5. Sun Splash Family Waterpark, Cape Coral

QUIRKY MUSEUMS

1. Gasparilla Island Maritime Museum, Boca Grande
2. Ringling Circus Museum & Tibbals Learning Center, Sarasota
3. Sarasota Classic Car Museum, Sarasota
4. Anna Maria Island Historical Museum
5. Bailey-Matthews Shell Museum, Sanibel Island

ON STAGE

1. Van Wezel Performing Arts Hall, Sarasota
2. Asolo Center for the Performing Arts, Sarasota
3. Philharmonic Center for the Arts, Naples
4. Barbara B. Mann Performing Arts Hall, Fort Myers
5. Circus Sarasota

NIGHT PROWLING

1. Beach Club, Siesta Key
2. The Gator Club, Sarasota
3. Crow's Nest Lounge, 'Tween Waters Inn, Captiva Island
4. Famous Fish, Marco Island
5. McCabe's Irish Pub, Naples

BOATING ADVENTURES

1. Florida Sailing & Cruising School, North Fort Myers
2. Offshore Sailing School, Captiva Island
3. Grande Tours, Placida
4. Captiva Cruises, Captiva Island
5. King Fisher Cruise Lines, Punta Gorda

NATURE PRESERVED

1. Everglades National Park
2. J. N. "Ding" Darling National Wildlife Refuge, Sanibel Island
3. Rookery Bay National Estuarine Research Reserve, Naples
4. Corkscrew Swamp Sanctuary, Naples
5. Collier-Seminole State Park, Naples

ECO-ATTRACTIONS

1. Mote Marine Aquarium, Sarasota
2. Babcock Wilderness Adventures, Punta Gorda
3. Rookery Bay Environmental Learning Center, Naples
4. Manatee Park, Fort Myers
5. Conservancy Nature Center, Naples

BIKEWAYS

1. W. J. Janes Memorial Scenic Drive, Fakahatchee Strand Preserve State Park, Naples
2. Sanibel Island
3. Longboat Key
4. Cape Haze Pioneer Trail, Cape Haze
5. Historical Manatee Riverwalk, Bradenton

PADDLE HAPPY

1. Wilderness Waterway, Everglades National Park
2. Great Calusa Blueway, Greater Fort Myers
3. Paradise Coast Blueway, Greater Naples
4. Tarpon Bay/J. N. "Ding" Darling National Wildlife Refuge, Sanibel Island
5. Matlacha Aquatic Preserve, Pine Island

TAKE A HIKE

1. Fakahatchee Strand Preserve State Park, Naples
2. Big Cypress National Preserve, Everglades City
3. Collier-Seminole State Park, Naples
4. Oscar Scherer State Park, Osprey
5. J. N. "Ding" Darling National Wildlife Refuge, Sanibel Island

SHELL-SHOCKED BEACHES

1. Bowman's Beach, Sanibel Island
2. Cayo Costa State Park/Johnson Shoals
3. Bonita Beach
4. Key Island, Naples
5. Venice Beach

SECLUDED BEACHES

1. Cayo Costa State Park, Boca Grande
2. Key Island, Naples
3. Stump Pass Beach State Park, Englewood Beach
4. Don Pedro Island State Park, Boca Grande
5. Palmer Point Beach, Siesta Key

PLAYFUL BEACHES

1. Siesta Key County Beach, Siesta Key
2. Lynn Hall Memorial Park, Fort Myers Beach
3. Manatee County Park, Holmes Beach
4. Coquina Beach, Bradenton Beach
5. Lowdermilk Park, Naples

REEL FISHY

1. Boca Grande Pass, Boca Grande
2. Nokomis Beach's North Jetty, Casey Key
3. Venice Fishing Pier
4. Naples Fishing Pier
5. Fort Myers Beach Pier

NAPLES MUSEUM OF ART UPHOLDS THE TOWN'S REPUTATION FOR FINE CULTURE.

SHOPPING ARENAS

1. St. Armands Circle, Sarasota
2. Fifth Avenue South, Naples
3. Downtown Sarasota
4. The Village at Venetian Bay, Naples
5. Olde Englewood Village

ART APPRECIATION

1. The John and Mable Ringling Museum of Art, Sarasota
2. Patty & Jay Baker Naples Museum of Art
3. Towles Court Artist Colony, Sarasota
4. Village of the Arts, Bradenton
5. The von Liebig Art Center, Naples

BLING!

1. Port Royal Jewelers, Naples
2. Sarasota Estate & Jewelry
3. Al Morgan, Punta Gorda
4. Congress Jewelers, Sanibel Island
5. Wm. Phelps, Custom Jeweler, Naples

FESTIVALS

1. Edison Festival of Light, February, Fort Myers
2. Ringling Medieval Fair, February, Sarasota
3. Everglades Seafood Festival, February, Everglades City
4. Mang Mania Tropical Fruit Fair, July, Pine Island/Cape Coral
5. Shark's Tooth & Seafood Festival, April, Venice

HOMEY HOMETOWNS

1. Goodland
2. Punta Gorda
3. Englewood
4. Everglades City
5. Matlacha

INDEX